WOMEN AND LITERATURE IN BRITAIN 1700–1800

This collection of new essays brings together feminist critics, cultural historians, and historians of publishing to provide a unique and up-to-date introduction to eighteenth-century women's writing and its contexts. It was during this period that women began to contribute in significantly large numbers to a rapidly expanding print culture. Fourteen contributors here document the range and diversity of that contribution. They analyse the social, legal, and ideological constructions of women which women writers had to negotiate, and explore women's writing across a wide spectrum of genres – from fiction to broadside ballads, meditative poetry to confessional memoirs – as well as women's involvement as printers, sellers, and purchasers of printed texts. A chronology of women and literature in the period and guide to further reading are also included.

An invaluable overview of women and literary culture in the period, *Women and Literature in Britain, 1700–1800* is also an important contribution to our understanding of women's roles in the emergent public sphere of print.

WOMEN AND LITERATURE IN BRITAIN
1700–1800

EDITED BY
VIVIEN JONES
University of Leeds

CAMBRIDGE
UNIVERSITY PRESS

PUBLISHED BY THE PRESS SYNDICATE OF THE UNIVERSITY OF CAMBRIDGE
The Pitt Building, Trumpington Street, Cambridge, United Kingdom

CAMBRIDGE UNIVERSITY PRESS
The Edinburgh Building, Cambridge CB2 2RU, UK http://www.cup.cam.ac.uk
40 West 20th Street, New York, NY 10011–4211, USA http://www.cup.org
10 Stamford Road, Oakleigh, Melbourne 3166, Australia

First published 2000

Printed in the United Kingdom at the University Press, Cambridge

Typeset in Monotype Baskerville 11/12¼ pt. [SE]

A catalogue record for this book is available from the British Library

Library of Congress cataloguing in publication data

Women and literature in Britain, 1700–1800 / edited by Vivien Jones.
p. cm.
Includes index.
ISBN 0 521 58347 0 (hardback)   ISBN 0 521 58680 1 (paperback)
1. English literature – Women authors – History and criticism.
2. Women and literature – Great Britain – History – 18th century.
3. English literature – 18th century – History and criticism.
4. Great Britain – Intellectual life – 18th century.   5. Women
intellectuals – Great Britain.   I. Jones, Vivien, 1952– .
PR113.W655 1999
820.9′9287′09033–dc21   99-22555 CIP

ISBN 0 521 58347 0 hardback
ISBN 0 521 58680 1 paperback

Contents

Illustrations

Contributors

ROS BALLASTER is a Fellow in English Literature at Mansfield College, Oxford University. She is the author of *Seductive Forms: Women's Amatory Fiction from 1684 to 1740* (1992) and edited Delarivier Manley's *New Atalantis* in 1992 and Jane Austen's *Sense and Sensibility* in 1995 for Penguin Classics. She is currently working on a book on constructions of the Orient in Restoration and early eighteenth-century culture.

CLARE BRANT is a Lecturer at King's College London. She is the author of a forthcoming book, *Eighteenth-Century Letters and British Culture*, which argues for the variety and significance of epistolary writing, and of numerous articles on eighteenth-century literature and gender. She is the co-editor, with Diane Purkiss, of *Women, Texts and Histories 1575–1760* (1992), and the co-editor, with Yun Lee Too, of *Rethinking Sexual Harassment* (1994).

MARGARET ANNE DOODY is Andrew W. Mellon Professor of Humanities and Professor of English at Vanderbilt University, in Nashville, Tennessee, where she is currently Director of the Program in Comparative Literature. The Canadian-born writer is the author of two published novels and several critical books, including *The Daring Muse: Augustan Poetry Reconsidered* (1985) and *Frances Burney: the Life in the Works* (1988). She has published a number of articles on women writers of the eighteenth and early nineteenth centuries. Her most recent critical book is *The True Story of the Novel* (1998).

DIANNE DUGAW is a professor of English at the University of Oregon. She is the author of *Warrior Women and Popular Balladry, 1650–1850* (1989) and editor of *The Anglo-American Ballad: a Folklore Casebook* (1995). She has published numerous articles on topics in literary history, folklore, music, and gender studies and has recently completed a study of eighteenth-century popular culture and the work of John Gay.

JAN FERGUS is a professor of English at Lehigh University. She is finishing a book on the eighteenth-century reading public entitled *Readers and Fictions*, and has published articles on that topic as well as essays and two books on Jane Austen.

ISOBEL GRUNDY taught for many years at Queen Mary College, London University. Since 1990 she has been Henry Marshall Tory Professor at the University of Alberta, Canada. She has published on women writers of the long eighteenth century, on Samuel Johnson, and on Lady Mary Wortley Montagu (most recently a new biography, 1999). She is Director of the Chawton House Library in Hampshire, a Fellow of the Royal Society of Canada, and a Co-investigator on the Orlando Project, which is writing in both printed and electronic form the first history of women's writing in the British Isles.

HARRIET GUEST is a senior lecturer in the Centre for Eighteenth-Century Studies at the University of York. She is the author of *A Form of Sound Words: the Religious Poetry of Christopher Smart* (1989), and has published numerous essays on eighteenth-century literature and culture, the most recent of which is '"These Neuter Somethings": Gender Difference and Commercial Culture in Mid-Eighteenth Century-England' in Sharpe and Zwicker (eds.), *Refiguring Revolutions* (1998). She is currently completing a book on representations of femininity, learning, and patriotism between 1750 and 1810.

VIVIEN JONES is a senior lecturer in the School of English, University of Leeds. She has published widely on gender and writing in the eighteenth century and is the editor of *Women in the Eighteenth Century: Constructions of Femininity* (1990), *The Young Lady's Pocket Library, or Parental Monitor* (1995), and of Jane Austen's *Pride and Prejudice* for Penguin Classics (1996). She is currently writing a book on the cultural significance of the seduction narrative from 1740 to 1800.

PAULA MCDOWELL is associate professor of English at the University of Maryland, College Park. Her book, *The Women of Grub Street: Press, Politics, and Gender in the London Literary Marketplace 1678–1730* (1998) was published in the Oxford Paperback Series by Clarendon Press. She is currently at work on a book entitled *'The Tongue Can No Man Tame': Popular Oral Culture in Working London 1670–1730*, as well as on a facsimile edition of the nearly eighty works of London printer-author Elinor James.

FELICITY A. NUSSBAUM, Professor of English at the University of California, Los Angeles, is the author most recently of *Torrid Zones: Maternity, Sexuality, and Empire in Eighteenth-Century English Narratives* (1995), and *The Autobiographical Subject: Gender and Ideology in Eighteenth-Century England* (1989), co-recipient of the American Association for Eighteenth-Century Studies' Louis Gottschalk Prize. Her current work centres on the affiliations among race, gender, and monstrosity.

RUTH PERRY is Professor of Literature at the Massachusetts Institute of Technology. She is the author of *Women, Letters, and the Novel* (1980) and *The Celebrated Mary Astell: an Early English Feminist* (1986), the editor of George Ballard's 1752 *Memoirs of Several Ladies of Great Britain* (1985), and co-editor of a volume of essays on nurturing creativity, *Mothering the Mind* (1984), as well as numerous articles on eighteenth-century literature and the influence of gender on the production of art. She is currently completing a history of kinship and the family in relation to the novel in England 1750–1810. She is the daughter of an anthropologist.

GILLIAN SKINNER is the author of *Sensibility and Economics in the Novel: the Price of a Tear* (1999) and of articles on eighteenth-century fiction, and has taught widely in higher education. In 1994 she was a Visiting Associate Professor at California State University, Hayward, and she is currently a Tutor and Scholar-in-Residence at St Chad's College, University of Durham.

ANGELA J. SMALLWOOD lectures in eighteenth-century English literature at the University of Nottingham and held a British Academy Research Readership 1991–93 in order to work on women playwrights. As well as contributing to the ongoing CD-ROM publication, *Annotated Bibliography for English Studies*, on Fielding, Smollett, and eighteenth-century drama and theatre, she has published *Fielding and the Woman Question: the Novels of Henry Fielding and Feminist Debate 1700–1750* (1989) and is currently working on a book-length study of women writers and the eighteenth-century theatre.

KATHRYN SUTHERLAND is Reader in Bibliography and Textual Criticism and Professorial Fellow of St Anne's College, Oxford. She has published widely on fictional and non-fictional writings of the Scottish Enlightenment and Romantic periods, particularly the works of Adam Smith, Hannah More, Jane Austen, and Walter Scott.

Acknowledgements

Above all, I want to thank the contributors to this volume for their enthusiasm, co-operation, and scholarship. I want, too, to thank Josie Dixon of Cambridge University Press for her attentive and helpful reading at various stages, as well as for her patience. I am grateful to Helen Berry, Michael Brennan, David Fairer, and Jan Thaddeus for help with references, and, as always, to Anna, Luke, and Rick Jones, to Angela Keane, and to John Whale for their support.

VIVIEN JONES

Chronology

The Chronology begins in 1688, the date of the 'Glorious Revolution', often taken as the symbolic beginning of the eighteenth century. Individual writers' dates are not included here, but the dates of women writers, where available, can be found in the Index.

Contexts	Writers and texts
1688	'Glorious Revolution': Dutch Protestant William of Orange invited to England; Catholic James II escapes to France	Jane Barker, *Poetical Recreations*; Aphra Behn, *Oroonoko*; Elinor James, *Mrs James's Advice to the Citizens of London* (and many other political pamphlets before her death 1715); George Savile, Marquis of Halifax, *Lady's New Years Gift: or, Advice to a Daughter*
1689	Accession of William III, and Mary II (daughter of Charles II); Revolution Settlement; war with France (ends 1697)	
1690	Battle of the Boyne	John Locke, *Essay Concerning Human Understanding* and *Two Treatises of Government*
1691	Society for Reformation of Manners founded	
1692		John Dunton, *Athenian Mercury*
1693		John Dunton, *Ladies' Mercury*
1694	Bank of England established; death of Mary II	Mary Astell, *A Serious Proposal to the Ladies*
1695	Lapse of Licensing Act ends pre-publication censorship, and limitation of printing	*Truth Vindicated by the Faithful Testimony and Writings Of . . . Elizabeth Bathurst* (published by Quaker printer Tace Sowle); Catharine Trotter, *Agnes de Castro*
1696		[Judith Drake], *Essay in Defence of the Female Sex*; Elizabeth Singer Rowe, *Poems on Several Occasions*

Year	Historical events	Literary and cultural events
1697		Mary Astell, *A Serious Proposal to the Ladies*, part II
1698		Catharine Trotter, *Fatal Friendship*; John Vanbrugh, *Provok'd Wife*
1699		
1700		Mary Astell, *Reflections upon Marriage*; William Congreve, *Way of the World*; John Dryden, *Fables*
1701	Act of Settlement ensures Protestant succession; Jethro Tull's seed drill	Mary, Lady Chudleigh, *Ladies Defence*; Catharine Trotter, *Unhappy Penitent*; Susannah Centlivre, *Stolen Heiress*
1702	Death of William III; accession of Queen Anne (daughter of Charles II); war (of Spanish Succession) declared with France and Spain	
1703	Newton elected President of Royal Society	Sarah Fyge Egerton, *Poems on Several Occasions*; Isaac Newton, *Optics*; Mary Astell, *The Christian Religion . . . by a Daughter of the Church of England*; Delarivier Manley, *Secret History of Queen Zarah*
1704	Battle of Blenheim	
1705		George Farquhar, *Recruiting Officer*; George Farquhar, *Beaux' Stratagem*; Fénélon, *Treatise on Education of Daughters* (trans.)
1706		
1707	Act of Union unites Scotland and England	
1708	United East India Company created out of merger of 'Old' and 'New' East India Companies	
1709	First Copyright Act; Abraham Darby founds ironworks at Coalbrookdale, Shropshire	Joseph Addison and Richard Steele, *The Tatler* (runs until 1711); Susannah Centlivre, *Busy Body*; Elizabeth Elstob (trans.), *English-Saxon Homily*; Delarivier Manley, *New Atalantis* and (probably) *The Female Tatler* (runs until 1710)

	Contexts	Writers and texts
1710	Queen Anne dismisses Whig government; Tories under Harley take power	Mary, Lady Chudleigh, *Essays upon Several Subjects*; Delarivier Manley collaborates with Swift on Tory *Examiner* (runs until 1711)
1711		Joseph Addison and Richard Steele, *The Spectator* (runs until 1712; briefly revived 1714); Earl of Shaftesbury, *Characteristics*
1712	Last conviction for witchcraft in England; Handel settles in England	Jane Barker, *Love Intrigues*; Anne Finch, Countess of Winchilsea, *Miscellany Poems*
1713	War of Spanish Succession ended by Treaty of Utrecht	Bernard Mandeville, *Fable of the Bees*; Delarivier Manley, *History of Rivella*; Alexander Pope, *Rape of the Lock* (5 canto version)
1714	Death of Queen Anne; accession of Hanoverian George I; Tory government dismissed	Jane Barker, *Exilius*; Daniel Defoe, *Family Instructor*; Elizabeth Elstob, *Rudiments of Grammar*
1715	First Jacobite Rebellion; death of Louis XIV	
1716	Lady Mary Wortley Montagu travels to Turkey; St Paul's Cathedral completed	Lady Mary Wortley Montagu, three pirated 'Town Eclogues' published in *Court Poems*
1717		
1718		Susannah Centlivre, *A Bold Stroke for a Wife*
1719		Daniel Defoe, *Robinson Crusoe*; Eliza Haywood, *Love in Excess*
1720	South Sea Company crashes in 'South Sea Bubble'	
1721	Start of Walpole's ministry; first smallpox inoculations introduced from Turkey by Lady Mary Wortley Montagu)	Penelope Aubin, *Strange Adventures of the Count de Vineuil* (and 6 further novels before death 1728)
1722	Guy's Hospital founded	Eliza Haywood, *British Recluse* (and c. 40 further prose fictions in 1720s); Daniel Defoe, *Moll Flanders*; Richard Steele, *Conscious Lovers*

Year	Events	Literature
1723	Statute passed permitting parishes to open workhouses independently	Jane Barker, *Patchwork Screen for the Ladies*
1724		Mary Davys, *Reform'd Coquet*; Daniel Defoe, *Roxana*; Eliza Haywood, *Poems on Several Occasions*; [Bernard Mandeville], *Modest Defence of Public Stews*
1725		
1726	Voltaire in England	Jane Barker, *Lining of the Patch-Work Screen*; Daniel Defoe, *Considerations upon Streetwalkers*; Jonathan Swift, *Gulliver's Travels*
1727	Death of George I; accession of son, George II	
1728		Mary Davys, *Accomplish'd Rake*; Ephraim Chambers, *Cyclopaedia*; John Gay, *Beggar's Opera*; Elizabeth Singer Rowe, *Friendship in Death and Letters Moral and Entertaining* (completed 1732)
1729	'Yorke and Talbot' judgement supports slave owners' claims	
1730	Methodist Society founded; Francis Charteris receives royal pardon having been convicted for rape of a serving-maid	Stephen Duck, *Thresher's Labour*; Henry Fielding, *Tom Thumb*; James Thomson, *Seasons*
1731		*Gentleman's Magazine* begins publication
1732	Vauxhall Gardens opens; Covent Garden Opera House founded	Elizabeth Boyd, *Happy Unfortunate*; William Hogarth, *A Harlot's Progress*
1733	John Kay invents fly-shuttle	William Hogarth, *A Rake's Progress*; Lady Mary Wortley Montagu, *Verses Address'd to the Imitator of Horace*
1734	(Approx. date) technique of delivering live babies by means of forceps becomes public knowledge, contributing to rise of man-midwife	
1735	Abraham Darby perfects use of coke to smelt iron	[Sarah Chapone], *Hardships of the English Laws in Relation to Wives*; Alexander Pope, 'Epistle to a Lady. Of the Characters of Women'

Contexts	Writers and texts
1736 Repeal of English laws against witchcraft; gin riots	
1737 Theatre Licensing Act regulates plays; death of Queen Caroline	Lady Mary Wortley Montagu, *Nonsense of Common-Sense*
1738	
1739 Foundling Hospital established	Mary Collier, *Woman's Labour*; David Hume, *Treatise of Human Nature*; 'Sophia', *Woman Not Inferior to Man*
1740 War of Austrian Succession begins (ends 1748)	Eliza Haywood, *Female Spectator*; Samuel Richardson, *Pamela*; Wetenhall Wilkes, *Letter of Genteel and Moral Advice to a Young Lady*
1741 First performance of Handel's *Messiah*	Henry Fielding, *Shamela*; David Hume, *Essays, Moral and Philosophical*; Samuel Richardson, *Pamela* (part II); Wetenhall Wilkes, *Essay on the Pleasures and Advantages of Female Literature*
1742 Prime Minister Walpole resigns	Henry Fielding, *Joseph Andrews*
1743	Alexander Pope, *Dunciad* (four books)
1744	Edward Moore, *Fables for the Female Sex*
1745 Second Jacobite Rebellion	William Hogarth, *Marriage à la Mode*
1746 Battle of Culloden	Eliza Haywood, *The Parrot*
1747	David Garrick, *Miss in her Teens*; Lady Mary Wortley Montagu, *Six Town Eclogues*; Samuel Richardson, *Clarissa* (completed 1748)
1748 Discovery of ruins of Pompeii	Mary Leapor, *Poems upon Several Occasions* (post. published; vol. II 1751); Teresia Constantia Phillips, *Apology for the Conduct of Mrs T. C. Phillips*; Laetitia Pilkington, *Memoirs* (completed 1754)
1749 British Lying-in Hospital founded	*Monthly Review* begins publication; Henry Fielding, *Tom Jones*; Sarah Fielding, *The Governess*

Year		
1750		Samuel Johnson, *The Rambler* (runs until 1752); Mary Jones, *Miscellanies in Prose and Verse*; Charlotte Lennox, *Life of Harriot Stuart*; first version of *Female Soldier* (life of Hannah Snell)
1751	Law passed forbidding sale of spirits by small shopkeepers	Henry Fielding, *Amelia*; Thomas Gray, *Elegy in a Country Churchyard*; Eliza Haywood, *History of Miss Betsy Thoughtless*; Frances Anne, Lady Vane, 'Memoirs of a Lady of Quality' included in Smollett's *Peregrine Pickle*
1752	Gregorian calendar adopted	Charlotte Lennox, *Female Quixote*; William Smellie, *Treatise on Midwifery*
1753	'Hardwicke's' Marriage Act regularises conditions for legal marriage; British Museum founded	Jane Collier, *Essay on the Art of Ingeniously Tormenting*; Sarah Fielding, *David Simple*; Eliza Haywood, *History of Jemmy and Jenny Jessamy*; William Hogarth, *Analysis of Beauty*; Samuel Richardson, *Sir Charles Grandison* (completed 1754)
1754	Society for the Encouragement of Arts, Manufactures, and Commerce	John Duncombe, *Feminiad*
1755	Lisbon earthquake	Frances Brooke, *Old Maid*; Charlotte Charke, *Narrative of the Life of Mrs Charlotte Charke*; [George Colman and Bonnell Thornton, eds.], *Poems by Eminent Ladies*; Samuel Johnson, *Dictionary*; Mary Masters, *Familiar Letters and Poems*
1756	Seven Years War begins	*Critical Review* begins publication
1757		John Brown, *Estimate of the Manners and Principles of the Times*; Edmund Burke, *Philosophical Enquiry into . . . the Sublime and the Beautiful*; Thomas Gray, *Odes*
1758	Magdalen House for Penitent Prostitutes founded in London	Elizabeth Carter, *All the Works of Epictetus*; Charlotte Lennox, *Henrietta*

	Contexts	Writers and texts
1759	British Museum opened	Sarah Fielding, *Countess of Dellwyn*; Oliver Goldsmith, *Enquiry into the Present State of Polite Learning*; Adam Smith, *Theory of Moral Sentiments*; Laurence Sterne, *Tristram Shandy* (completed 1767); Voltaire, *Candide*
1760	Death of George II; accession of grandson, George III	Sarah Fielding, *Ophelia*; James Macpherson, *Fragments of Ancient Poetry* (first of *Poems of Ossian*); Elizabeth Montagu, *Dialogues of the Dead*; Elizabeth Nihell, *Art of Midwifery*
1761	Resignation of Pitt (the Elder); Bridgewater Canal	Sarah Pennington, *An Unfortunate Mother's Advice to her Absent Daughters*; J.-J. Rousseau, *La Nouvelle Héloïse*
1762	Bute's ministry	Elizabeth Carter, *Poems on Several Occasions*; Catherine Jemmat, *Memoirs*; J.-J. Rousseau, *Emile* and *Contrat Social*; Sarah Scott, *Millenium Hall*; Frances Sheridan, *Memoirs of Miss Sidney Bidulph*
1763	Treaty of Paris ends Seven Years War	Frances Brooke, *Julia Mandeville*; Catharine Macaulay; *History of England* (completed 1783); Lady Mary Wortley Montagu, *Embassy Letters* (written 1716); Frances Sheridan, *The Discovery*
1764		Phebe Gibbes, *Life and Adventures of Mr Francis Clive*; Horace Walpole, *Castle of Otranto*
1765		William Blackstone, *Commentaries on the Laws of England* (completed 1769); Alison Cockburn, 'Flowers of the Forest'
1766		James Fordyce, *Sermons to Young Women*; Oliver Goldsmith, *Vicar of Wakefield*; Catherine Jemmat, *Miscellanies in Prose and Verse*; Sarah Scott, *History of Sir George Ellison*

Year	Events	Publications
1767	Royal Crescent, Bath; Rousseau in England	Adam Ferguson, *Essay on Civil Society* Laurence Sterne, *Sentimental Journey* Elizabeth Montagu, *Essay on the Writings and Genius of Shakespeare*
1768	Cook's first voyage	
1769	Royal Academy founded; Watt patents steam engine; Wilkes expelled from Commons, re-elected three times; Cook in Tahiti	
1770	Cook arrives in 'Botany Bay'	*Lady's Magazine* begins publication; Oliver Goldsmith, *Deserted Village*
1771	Richard Arkwright opens first spinning mill; first edition of *Encyclopaedia Britannica*	Elizabeth Griffith, *History of Lady Barton*; Henry Mackenzie, *Man of Feeling*; Ann Skinn, *Old Maid*
1772	Lord Mansfield's judgement in James Somerset case extends right of habeas corpus to slaves; Cook's second voyage; Pantheon (pleasure-dome) opened in Oxford Street, London	
1773	Boston Tea Party	Anna Laetitia Barbauld, *Poems*; Hester Chapone, *Letters on the Improvement of the Mind*; Oliver Goldsmith, *She Stoops to Conquer*; William Russell (trans.), *Essay on the Character, Manners, and Genius of Women in Different Ages*; Phillis Wheatley, *Poems on Various Subjects*
1774	House of Lords settles copyright law, eliminating perpetual copyright; Humane Society formed; Omai (brought by Cook from Raiatea) in London; Joseph Priestley discovers oxygen	Earl of Chesterfield, *Letters to his Son*; Goethe, *Sorrows of Young Werther*; John Gregory, *Father's Legacy to his Daughters*; Sarah Scott, *Female Advocate*
1775	American War of Independence begins	Hester Chapone, *Miscellanies in Prose and Verse*; R. B. Sheridan, *The Rivals*
1776	American Declaration of Independence; Cook's third voyage	Mary Deverell, *Sermons on Various Subjects*; Edward Gibbon, *Decline and Fall* (completed 1788); Elizabeth Griffith, *Juliana Harley*; Adam Smith, *Wealth of Nations*
1777		R. B. Sheridan, *School for Scandal*
1778	British defeated at Saratoga	Frances Burney, *Evelina*; Phebe Gibbes, *Friendship in a Nunnery*; Mary Hamilton, *Munster Village*; Hannah More, *Percy*; Clara Reeve, *Old English Baron*

Contexts		Writers and texts
1779	Samuel Crompton's spinning mule; machine riots; first iron bridge built at Coalbrookdale	William Alexander, *History of Women*; Hannah Cowley, *Who's the Dupe?*; Phebe Gibbes, *Hartly House, Calcutta*; Samuel Johnson, *Lives of the Poets* (completed 1781); Hannah More, *Fatal Falsehood*
1780	Gordon Riots (anti-Catholic); Yorkshire petition for parliamentary reform	Hannah Cowley, *Belle's Stratagem*; Sophia Lee, *Chapter of Accidents*; Anna Seward, *Elegy on Captain Cook*
1781		J.-J. Rousseau, *Confessions*
1782		Frances Burney, *Cecilia*
1783	American independence conceded; Pitt becomes Prime Minister	Jane Cave, *Poems on Various Subjects*
1784	Partial control of East India Company by parliament established; first hydrogen balloon ascent in England by Lunardi	Anna Seward, *Louisa, A Poetical Novel*; Charlotte Smith, *Elegiac Sonnets*
1785		Agnes Maria Bennett, *Anna; or, Memoirs of a Welch Heiress*; Clara Reeve, *Progress of Romance*; Ann Yearsley, *Poems on Several Occasions*
1786		Robert Burns, *Poems, Chiefly in the Scottish Dialect*; Hannah Cowley, *School for Greybeards*; Hester Thrale Piozzi, *Anecdotes of the Late Samuel Johnson*; Sarah Trimmer, *Fabulous Histories: Designed for the Instruction of Children*; Helen Maria Williams, *Poems, in Two Volumes*
1787	American constitution signed	Elizabeth Steele, *Memoirs of Miss Sophia Baddeley*; Sarah Trimmer, *The Oeconomy of Charity*; Mary Wollstonecraft, *Thoughts on the Education of Daughters*; Ann Yearsley, *Poems on Various Subjects*
1788	Botany Bay prison colony founded	*Analytical Review* and *The Times* begin publication; Elizabeth Gooch, *Appeal to the Public*; Charlotte Smith, *Emmeline*; Mary Wollstonecraft, *Mary*

1789	Fall of the Bastille: start of French Revolution; first steam-powered cotton factory founded in Manchester; George III's first spell of madness; Regency Bill; mutiny on the Bounty	William Blake, *Songs of Innocence*; Hannah More, *Slavery: a Poem*; Mary Robinson, *Julia St Lawrence*
1790	Parliament retains Test and Corporation Acts (anti-Dissenters)	Edmund Burke, *Reflections on the Revolution in France*; Catharine Macaulay, *Letters on Education*; Helen Maria Williams, *Letters from France* (first of eight volumes 1790–6) and *Julia*; Mary Wollstonecraft, *Vindication of the Rights of Men*
1791	Parliament rejects bill to abolish slave trade; Joseph Priestley's house burned by loyalist mob	James Boswell, *Life of Johnson*; Elizabeth Inchbald, *A Simple Story*; Tom Paine, *Rights of Man*; Ann Radcliffe, *Romance of the Forest*; Mary Robinson, *Poems*
1792	London Corresponding Society, sympathetic to revolutionary principles, founded; Association for the Preservation of Liberty and Property founded	Anna Laetitia Barbauld, *Poems*; Elizabeth Gooch, *Memoirs*; *Poetical Works of Janet Little, the Scotch Milkmaid*; Hannah More, *Village Politics*; Clara Reeve, *Plans of Education*; Charlotte Smith, *Desmond*; Mary Wollstonecraft, *Vindication of the Rights of Woman*
1793	Execution of Louis XVI of France and Marie Antoinette; revolutionary 'Terror' in Paris; Britain declares war on France	William Godwin, *Enquiry Concerning Political Justice*; Laetitia Matilda Hawkins, *Letters on the Female Mind*; Mary Hays, *Letters and Essays, Moral and Miscellaneous*; Charlotte Smith, *Old Manor House*; Jane West, *Advantages of Education*; William Wordsworth, *Descriptive Sketches* and *Evening Walk*
1794	Suspension of habeas corpus; prominent radicals tried for treason and acquitted by juries; record food prices after failure of harvest; Robespierre executed in France	William Godwin, *Caleb Williams*; Ann Radcliffe, *Mysteries of Udolpho*; Charlotte Smith, *Banished Man*; Mary Wollstonecraft, *Historical and Moral View of . . . French Revolution*

	Contexts	Writers and texts
1795	Further rises in food prices; Pitt's 'Two Acts' ban meetings of over 50 people	Maria Edgeworth, *Letters for Literary Ladies*; Eliza Fenwick, *Secresy*; Hannah More, *Cheap Repository Tracts* (completed 1798); Margaret Stephen, *Domestic Midwife*; Ann Yearsley, *Royal Captives*
1796	Jenner develops smallpox vaccination	Jane Austen begins *Pride and Prejudice* (published 1813); Frances Burney, *Camilla*; Elizabeth Hamilton, *Letters of a Hindoo Rajah*; Mary Hays, *Memoirs of Emma Courtney*; Elizabeth Inchbald, *Nature and Art*; M. G. Lewis, *The Monk*; Mary Robinson, *Angelina*; Regina Maria Roche, *Children of the Abbey*; Anna Seward, *Llangollen Vale, With Other Poems*; Mary Wollstonecraft, *Letters Written in . . . Sweden, Norway and Denmark*
1797	Surgeons' Court of Assistants turns down request to institute professional midwifery qualification; Napoleon becomes commander of French army	Jane Austen begins *Sense and Sensibility* (published 1811); Martha Mears (midwife), *Pupil of Nature*; Ann Radcliffe, *The Italian*
1798	Irish Rebellion; habeas corpus suspended	Jane Austen, *Northanger Abbey* (post. publ. 1818); Jeremy Bentham, *Political Economy*; S. T. Coleridge and William Wordsworth *Lyrical Ballads*; Maria and R. L. Edgeworth, *Practical Education*; William Godwin, *Memoir of Mary Wollstonecraft*; Mary Hays, *Appeal to the Men of Great Britain in behalf of Women*; Elizabeth Inchbald, *Lovers' Vows*; Thomas Malthus, *Essay on . . . Population*; Richard Polwhele, *The Unsex'd Females*; Regina Maria Roche, *Clermont*; Priscilla Wakefield, *Reflections on the Present Condition of the Female Sex*; Mary Wollstonecraft, *Wrongs of Woman* (post. publ.)

| 1799 | Royal Institution founded; London Corresponding Society banned; Napoleon becomes Consul in France | Mary Hays, *Victim of Prejudice*; Hannah More, *Strictures on the Modern System of Female Education*; Mary Ann Radcliffe, *Female Advocate*; Mary Robinson, *Letter to the Women of England*; Anna Seward, *Original Sonnets* |
| 1800 | Food riots; first iron-frame printing-press; copyright law extended to Ireland | Maria Edgeworth, *Castle Rackrent*; Elizabeth Hamilton, *Memoirs of Modern Philosophers*; Mary Robinson, *Lyrical Tales* |

Introduction

Vivien Jones

> There never was perhaps an age wherein the fair sex made so con-
> spicuous a figure with regard to literary accomplishments as in our
> own. We may all remember the time, when a woman who could
> *spell* was looked on as an extraordinary phenomenon, and a *reading*
> and *writing* wife was considered as a miracle; but the case at present
> is quite otherwise . . . The men *retreat*, and the women *advance*. The
> men prate and dress; the women read and write: it is no wonder,
> therefore, that they should get the upper hand of us; nor would we
> be at all surprised, if, in the next age, women should give lectures
> in the classics, and men employ themselves in knotting and needle-
> work.
>
>

Critical Review, 1762[1]
>

If we are to believe this anxious (and almost certainly male) reviewer, the
relationship of women and literature was changing so radically by the
mid eighteenth century that it promised to undermine men's and
women's established social roles, and to alter the very basis of accepted
gender positions. Anxiety makes for exaggeration, but in registering the
newness of women's 'conspicuous . . . figure with regard to literary
accomplishments', the review is simply repeating what was becoming a
commonplace of the time. It's a commonplace which has been rediscovered and confirmed by twentieth-century feminist literary scholarship:
though women were active as writers and readers in earlier periods, it
was during the eighteenth century that they began to contribute in
significantly large numbers to an increasingly powerful print culture.
One of the functions of this volume of essays by scholars and critics who
are experts in the field of eighteenth-century women's writing is to
define and document that contribution, to add to our constantly growing
understanding of just how wide-ranging and diverse women's roles
within print culture actually were. Appropriately enough, the texts discussed are equally diverse. They extend well beyond the conventionally

'literary' to include popular forms, such as ballads or satirical broad-
sheets, as well as archival sources: private writings in letters and diaries;
the commercial records of booksellers and publishers; and legal documents – wills and trial reports, for example. Thus the volume as a whole
gives a sense not only of the wealth of material which has survived to us
from this increasingly literate culture but also, in the particular empha-
ses of individual essays, of the way in which a focus on texts from
different levels and areas of print culture might suggest very different
conclusions about women's positions within it, and very different interpretations of what 'women and literature' could, or might, mean.

To the reviewer quoted above, at least, it meant fundamental change.
In that note of self-conscious anxiety, qualified as it is by a grudging pride
in progress, we glimpse something of the urgency and ambivalence with
which contemporary audiences responded to women's 'conspicuous-
ness' in print. The perception that numbers of educated and literary
women were increasing – and with far-reaching effects – becomes at least
as significant as the documentary accuracy of the claim itself; indeed, the
two cannot be understood in isolation from each other. As an integral
part of the important task of documentation and retrieval, then, the
essays which follow also address the wider cultural impact of the conjunction between women and literature. They explore the social, economic, and ideological contexts in which women's writing, and reading,
took place; and they analyse the meanings attributed to, and generated
by, this comparatively new phenomenon. In this introductory essay, I
shall be highlighting some of the contexts, key terms, and issues which
recur – whether implicitly or explicitly – across the volume: both those
which shaped women's literary identities in the eighteenth century; and
those more immediately associated with current critical debate, with the
preoccupations which modern literary and cultural historians bring to
bear on the text(s) of the past. And I shall keep returning to this anxious
reviewer, and to his suggestion that women's 'literary accomplishments'
disturb the very basis of sexual difference and of social organisation, in
an attempt to understand just what was at stake as women made themselves increasingly conspicuous within literary culture.

THE MEANINGS OF LITERACY

Any such understanding must start with the fundamental question of
female literacy, of the differences masked by describing eighteenth-
century society as 'increasingly literate'. The review suggests a process

of recent and rapid improvement – from a situation in which most 'wives' could barely write, much less spell, to one in which women are beginning to establish themselves as contributors at even the most elite level of literary culture. The implication, in other words, is that both basic literacy and a more sophisticated literariness are for women fairly recent developments. Historians' attempts to measure female literacy present a slightly different picture in which, not surprisingly perhaps, rapid growth in basic literacy precedes by at least a generation or so any noticeable increase in the numbers of women writing and publishing. According to now generally accepted (but still very approximate) figures, only 10 per cent of women could sign their names in 1640 (33 per cent of men) compared with 30 per cent in 1700 (50 per cent of men) and 40 (60) per cent in 1760. Broadly speaking, then, the most rapid increase in literacy – for both men and women – appears to have taken place in the seventeenth century, continued more slowly during the first half of the eighteenth, and actually stagnated in the second half of the century – the period during which publication levels really took off. The rather precarious basis of such measurements is the ability to sign, rather than simply make a mark, on legal documents (including, for example, marriage registers). This therefore excludes the not uncommon cases of those who could read but not write, as well as those people – including large numbers of women – who remain statistically invisible because they had little occasion to sign any such documents (women were required to sign marriage registers only after the 1753 Marriage Act).

The largest increase, predictably, was among the 'middling' sort: tradespeople, civil servants, and the lower end of the professional classes; but there are wide variations between regions, age groups, and different occupations: levels in London and in urban centres tend to be higher than elsewhere; younger people were more likely to be literate than their parents' generation; shopkeepers, for example, tended to be more literate than needleworkers, who were more literate than domestic servants.[2] It's something of a shock to realise that, as far as women are concerned, illiteracy was still the condition of the majority even at the mid century, but it's also true that, through reading aloud in households or coffee-houses, for example, or through the reciting of ballads and broadsides by street-hawkers, or the reproduction of popular texts like Richardson's *Pamela* (1740) in visual or dramatised forms, print culture profoundly affected the lives of many who could not actually read. An awareness of literacy's uneven distribution and of the coexistence of very different levels of literary competence is important: a reminder that, if we are to do justice to the full variety of women's experiences of eighteenth-century print culture, 'literature' must be used flexibly to cover not simply the productions of a cultural elite (which would include the majority of novels), but also those popular and more ephemeral genres, or those writings which never reached publication, which have often been overlooked in traditional literary histories.[3]

Some of these productions remain as elusive and difficult to quantify as literacy itself but, on the whole, it is much easier to measure the number of women's publications than it is to assess how many of them could read or write, and it is clear that the numbers of publications in all genres – and particularly by middling women – rose steeply in the last third of the century. However, as the bookseller James Lackington claimed in 1792: 'the sale of books in general has increased prodigiously within the last twenty years. According to the best estimation I have been able to make, I suppose that more than four times the number of books are sold now than were sold twenty years since.'[4] Increased numbers of publications by women, in other words, are simply part of a more general explosion in the market for printed texts. Yet it is women's writing that is repeatedly singled out for comment, a disproportionate reaction which raises questions not just about literacy levels, but about what literacy, and literariness, meant.

Above all, both for society in general, and for the individuals concerned, the ability to read and write is a measure of progress and status. Literacy carries the potential to transcend boundaries: of class, most obviously; but also, for example, the gendered boundary between public and private; and even gender itself. One of the first reasons for teaching people to read was so that they could read the Bible for themselves; and within an Enlightenment Protestant tradition, the dissemination of rational ideas through education and the community of print is a touchstone of civilisation, a means of defence and control over the 'primitive', defined in terms of superstition, brute violence, and mere sensual gratification. In principle at least, this educative project extends to marginalised groups: sometimes to the labouring classes and colonial subjects; much more commonly to women of the upper and middling classes. Women occupy a peculiarly contradictory position within this Enlightenment discourse of improvement. In practice, the education they received was likely to be a carefully restricted version of the curriculum offered to their brothers; at the same time, however, educated women are frequently celebrated as a touchstone of civilisation. Thus in 1711, Joseph Addison cites women as one of the most important constituents of the intended audience for *The Spectator*, a new periodical dedi-

cated to 'recover[ing]' society out of its 'desperate state of Vice and
Folly' through the 'constant and assiduous Culture' of the mind:

> But there are none to whom this Paper will be more useful than to the female
> World. I have often thought there has not been sufficient Pains taken in finding
> out proper Employments and Diversions for the Fair ones. Their Amusements
> seem contrived for them, rather as they are Women, than as they are reason-
> able Creatures.[5]

Later in the century, Scottish Enlightenment historians used the education and status of women as a way of measuring the progress of society
from its origins in 'savage life', where 'men are dull, phlegmatic, and
almost destitute of susceptibility' and 'women have hardly any mental
qualifications', to the situation in 'civilized countries', where women
'have a thousand arts' to 'maintain a balance of power against the men'.[6]
And in John Duncombe's *The Feminiad: a Poem* (1754), in praise of women
writers, 'The freeborn sons of *Britain's* polished isle' distinguish themselves from 'eastern tyrants' by the liberty they allow to women for
mental, as well as physical, beautification:

> Our *British* nymphs with happier omens rove,
> At Freedom's call, thro' Wisdom's sacred grove,
> And, as with lavish hand each sister Grace
> Shapes the fair form and regulates the face,
> Each sister Muse, in blissful union join'd,
> Adorns, improves, and beautifies the mind.[7]

In all of these texts, there is a manifest, and characteristic, tension
between an enlightened commitment to equality, and a discourse of
difference and hierarchy; between a progressivist belief in access to education and literature, and a tendency to restrict the terms on which such
access might be enjoyed. In the last two examples, the progress of British
women is demonstrated only at the expense of other cultures whose
'dullness' or 'tyranny' justifies colonial expansion.[8] And in all three,
claims to acknowledge women as 'reasonable creatures' are compromised by the language of indulgent gallantry which re-categorises them
as 'the Fair ones' (*Spectator*, 46) and their writings as 'vary'd charms'
(*Feminiad*, p. 171). Objectified and contained as ornaments of progress,
women's active and equal participation in literary culture was less
readily accepted.

PUBLIC SPHERES

Nevertheless, once they have been admitted, through literacy, to the possibility of personal and social improvement, women can never again be

wholly excluded. And for women who have access to books, in a culture which increasingly defines and communicates with itself through the medium of print, firm distinctions between public and private worlds become difficult to maintain. For example, *The Spectator*, like other periodicals, encouraged readers to take an active part by writing letters to the editors, but the ability simply to read (or just to hear and discuss) the daily *Spectator* papers was sufficient qualification for membership of this influential imagined community of polite and enlightened individuals – for women as much as for men. Indeed, in the same essay in which he encourages female participation, Addison describes the way in which the *Spectator*'s polite culture of improvement functions equally well in masculine or feminine spaces: 'in Clubs and Assemblies, at Tea-Tables and in Coffee-Houses' (44). Though the gatherings themselves might remain dominantly gendered (clubs and coffee-houses were almost exclusively male), the vision is of a community of interests, generated by shared reading, which begins to break down binary divisions. Recent criticism, following on from the work of Jürgen Habermas, has identified this 'public sphere' of polite culture, created in large part through the medium of print, as a key site in the formation of opinion and thus as a focus for social and political power.[9] Feminist critics continue to debate the precise nature and extent of women's inevitably limited participation in the Habermasian public sphere, and have pointed out that, in naming the gendered categories they appear to resist, publications like *The Spectator* also perpetuate the separate spheres of private and public.[10] But current research is increasingly unwilling to assume the absolute efficacy of the public/private distinction, and is uncovering all kinds of ways in which women contributed to the complex network of communications through which public opinion is formed.[11]

The women readers addressed by *The Spectator* and similar publications are from the leisured classes. At other levels of society, literacy and numeracy meant progress, control, and public participation of a more practical kind. The author of *An Essay in Defence of the Female Sex* (1696), for example, very much an Enlightenment text, urges women's right to learn the business of trade on the grounds that:

they might supply the places of abundance of lusty Men now employ'd in sedentary Business; which would be a mighty profit to the Nation by sending those Men to Employments, where hands and Strength are more requir'd . . . Beside that it might prevent the ruine of many Families, which is often occasion'd by the Death of Merchants in full Business, and leaving their Accounts perplex'd, and embroil'd to a Widdow and Orphans.[12]

Written from within a Dissenting tradition, and for the trading and professional class, and long before Adam Smith's account of the division of labour, this makes active female participation in the economy central to the survival and 'profit' of both nation and family. Education here is in the first instance a means to greater financial security and economic efficiency, and thence to social improvement.

Education has also given this woman the means to speak on behalf of her class, and sex, and to imagine an expanded public sphere, unrestricted by the barriers of religious affiliation or gender – a vision which would not be realised in legal terms until 1828, when Dissenters were permitted to take public office, but which certainly became increasingly operative during the eighteenth century at the level of financial and intellectual connections. Refusing any kind of established hierarchy, and particularly the 'Arbitrary, Tyrannical Authority' which 'the Divines' hold over definitions of 'learning', this writer capitalises on the fact that Dissenters (as well as Catholics and all women) were excluded by law from the classical education offered at the universities of Oxford and Cambridge, and she favours a cosmopolitan education in European languages (pp. 212–13). Even more iconoclastically, she makes a case for the civilising value of girls' reading-matter:

For Girles after they can Read and Write (if they be of any Fashion) are taught such things as take not up their whole time, and not being suffer'd to run about at liberty as Boys, are furnish'd among other toys with Books, such as *Romances, Novels, Plays* and *Poems*; which though they read carelessly only for Diversion, yet unawares to them, give 'em very early a considerable Command both of Words and Sense. (p. 213)[13]

And she proceeds to 'turn their own Artillery' of words against men in a series of satirical portraits of male types. Underlying this witty defence of undervalued genres is the even more radical suggestion that reading of any kind, even reading thought of as primarily for 'Diversion' and pleasure, is a source of improvement. Indeed, the pleasures of the text are a strategic part of the *Essay*'s own very serious project, as the writer teases men out of their 'Rustick Freedom' and away from the 'grave, serious Trifles' of their 'Publick Affairs' (pp. 217, 216).

Written at the very beginning of our period, the *Essay in Defence* makes education and social improvement its subject and gaily reverses the accepted categories dictated by 'custom'. Seizing the democratising potential of print, this female writer enters the public sphere of publication in order to advocate wider dissemination of the 'private', social, and linguistic skills associated with women and the feminine. Education provides an alternative form of enfranchisement, and the uses women make of this opportunity – as the *Critical*'s reviewer recognised – are clearly very difficult to police. It's little wonder, then, that women's increasingly vociferous participation produced anxious responses. The reversals imagined in the *Essay* advocate precisely that feminisation of culture feared by the later reviewer. As both texts recognise, the question of women and literature is a question of power. The proliferation of women's writing challenges the gendered control of knowledge, and in doing so it raises questions of sexual difference which go to the very heart of social and cultural identities.

I want now to return in more detail to the review with which I began, and to its representation of sexual difference. Through its focus not simply on women, but on the mobile, culturally defined, categories of femininity and masculinity, the language of the review makes the issue of women and literature inseparable from other contemporary preoccupations. Most notably, it evokes what was seen as the other great democratising threat in the eighteenth century: the commercial expansion which led to 'the birth of a consumer society'.[14]

FEMININITIES AND COMMERCE

The review plays on familiar eighteenth-century assumptions about sexual difference. Most obviously, a belief in difference itself, in the roles of the sexes as naturally and inescapably complementary, is evident in the dance-like symmetry of the sentence structure: 'The men *retreat*, and the women *advance*. The men prate and dress; the women read and write.' Women's progress in the previously masculine arena of reading and writing is matched by men's regression into a feminised superficiality. Men's discourse is now an uncontrolled and purposeless 'prating' rather than rational discussion; it is men rather than women who 'dress' as the slaves of fashion; and at the present rate, the next age will see the completion of this reversal of roles, with women the elite educators and men reduced to decorative, non-literary, pastimes. The reviewer's hyperbolic reversals register the perceived seriousness of the present crisis. They work because traditional associations – of women with subjection to material and, implicitly, trivial concerns, and of men with reason, knowledge, and control – can be taken for granted; and they make it only too clear that complementarity is in fact subject to a hierarchical value system in which 'feminine' attributes are disempowered. But it is difficult to tell who exactly is the butt of these schematic imaginings: the women who are getting 'the upper hand'; or the feminised men who let them do so. Like the *Spectator* earlier in the century, the *Critical* attracted a mixed readership and the review plays to that audience. It flatters the literate women who might identify with the progress described, even as it reminds them of the oddity of their achievement (so recently considered a 'miracle'); it thus appeals to male readers' confidence in their right to pronounce upon the roles appropriate to both sexes, but as a precarious defence against a modern form of masculinity defined precisely by its surrender of proper cultural authority, where authority is identified unambiguously with education and literary achievement.

The reviewer's ambivalent allegiances are symptomatic: the neatly complementary gender roles which he invokes are becoming inescapably blurred in the face of women's (masculine and progressive) literary sophistication and men's (feminine and culturally enervating) preoccupation with sociability and fashion. They are perhaps particularly difficult to hold on to given the topic of the review: a collection of poems by Elizabeth Carter, member of the 'Bluestocking' circle of learned women, and best known in 1762 for her translation of works by the Greek Stoic philosopher, Epictetus. The work of a scholar in that most male of preserves, the classics, cannot be dismissed, as so many publications by women were, as merely 'pretty', nor easily condescended to as bearing 'every mark of a female production'.[15] Nevertheless, the reviewer uses the opportunity of Carter's publication in a different genre to generalise about women's writing. Having commented on 'the fertility of her genius, the warmth of her imagination, and the harmony of her numbers', the review goes on:

It has often been remarked, with what degree of truth we will not pretend to determine, that the female muse is seldom altogether so chaste as could be wished, and that most of our lady-writers are rather deficient in point of morality. To the honour of Mrs Carter it may be said, that there is scarce a line in this volume which doth not breathe the purest sentiments, and tend in some measure to the advancement of religion and virtue, which is, in our opinion, their strongest recommendation. (p. 181)

'Fertility'; 'warmth'; 'harmony'; 'chaste'; 'purest': the vocabulary of critical approval works hard to reassert gender difference. In spite (or perhaps because) of her classical learning, Carter's poems can be safely endorsed as the properly didactic productions of a virtuous feminine sensibility, and explicitly defined in opposition to those 'lady-writers . . . deficient in point of morality'. As is often the case, the focus on femininities here is indicative of there being other things at stake: most obviously masculine authority, but also the cultural authority of certain kinds of literature, both of which are threatened by the opportunities to 'prate and dress' offered by a leisured consumer culture, a culture which, implicitly, also sanctions the productions of a 'wanton' female muse.[16] Opposed femininities, defined either by the 'purest sentiments' or by moral 'deficiency', are thus used to help forge a precarious distinction between polite culture and the world of fashion and consumerism.

Two concepts central to an understanding of women and literature come together here: the figure of the virtuous, usually domestic, female; and the feminised and feminising figure of material consumption. The review's ready attribution of Carter's poetry to the 'modest muse' lends support to a familiar critical account of eighteenth-century women and women's writing, whereby the period during which women became increasingly 'conspicuous' as writers was also the period during which 'the pressure towards respectability', the pressure to make their writing (and their behaviour more generally) conform to codes of feminine modesty, was increasingly acutely felt. The argument is an important one, and several of the essays here offer evidence of ways in which women's writing in various genres shows the effects of such constraint.[17] But, as this volume also makes clear, it would be wrong to think of the discourse of feminine respectability in isolation from other cultural discourses. Even conduct books, the advice manuals which are often cited interchangeably in support of the dominance of the 'proper lady', differ from each other in all kinds of significant ways. Powerful though it is – for middle-class women at least – the ideal of modest respectability is strategically and variously invoked in response to particular circumstances, and the demand that women be inconspicuous operates particularly, as in this review, in reaction to what was increasingly seen as conspicuous consumption.[18]

The review's gendered reversals echo a common mid-century response to a commercially driven culture, a response most famously formulated in John Brown's *Estimate of the Manners and Principles of the Times* (1757) where both the practice and the effects of commerce are associated with excess, with lack of control – and therefore with the feminine: 'the Character of the Manners of our Times . . . will probably appear to be that of a "*vain, luxurious,* and *selfish* EFFEMINACY"'.[19] It's easy to see how this dangerously feminine taste for material pleasures also implicates women themselves. Indeed, throughout the period, women's propensity for consumption is represented both as the excuse for commercial expansion and as a symptom of its irresponsibility, a contradiction most famously, and most subtly, realised in Pope's barbed celebration in *The Rape of the Lock* (1714) of Belinda at her dressing-table, surrounded by the chaos of commodities through which she creates herself:

> The Tortoise here and Elephant unite,
> Transform'd to *Combs*, the speckled and the white.
> Here Files of Pins extend their shining Rows,
> Puffs, Powders, Patches, Bibles, Billet-doux.[20]

Here, myths of origin (not to mention actual exotic animals) become personal adornments, as Belinda's combs reunite the elephant and tortoise which in Hindu iconography support the world; and the absolute triumph of style is signalled in the multiplicity of bibles – designed, presumably, to suit different outfits and occasions. This is very different from the rational female reader evoked by the almost exactly contemporary *Spectator*. Her full meaning depended precisely on her *not* being the image-conscious consumer represented in Belinda – just as Elizabeth Carter's decorous femininity is evaluated by the *Critical* in terms of its difference from the effeminacy of the male fashion victim and from the moral deficiency of those other lady writers. The strategic use of gender by these self-styled guardians of cultural value persists, even if the terms used to define virtuous femininity have shifted slightly over the intervening fifty years.

Again, however, a focus on texts produced outside of polite culture suggests other readings of the conjunction between commerce, consumerism, and the feminine. In Defoe's *Moll Flanders* (1722), for example (produced out of a social context very similar to the *Essay in Defence*), the heroine is born in Newgate into the world of urban criminality, and forced at times to live as a thief and prostitute, but in the end she makes her fortune, and achieves respectability in the secular paradise of the New World, where convicts can become justices of the peace and 'many a Newgate-bird becomes a great man'.[21] Moll's capital is her body, together with a certain amount of education gleaned alongside the daughters of the household where she is given refuge from destitution. She performs the roles of prostitute or lady as required in order to survive, and her career draws attention to opposed forms of femininity as, precisely, contingent performances. Her early aspiration to the ambiguous status of the independent 'gentlewoman', her ability throughout (given the right clothes) to pass herself off as a member of the gentry, and her ultimate achievement of financial and social success, expose the way in which feminine identities endorsed by the moralised discourse of politeness are actually dependent on economic circumstances. Economic circumstances determine the ability to display the accessories, the consumer items, which distinguish a particular social or gender identity – whether those are the right clothes, as in Moll's case, or the habit of reading the right kinds of publications.

In a recent essay, Ann Bermingham reminds us of some of the changes in taste which consumer culture brought to 'social, domestic, and economic life' in the course of the eighteenth century. She lists, for example, 'a new concern with personal appearance (mirrors, gloves, buttons, ribbons, and other fashion apparel), a taste for amusement (novels, musical instruments, amateur art supplies, plays, concerts, and opera), an interest in science (telescopes, air pumps, orreries), and a desire for privacy (window curtains)'.[22] 'Literature', or more broadly 'the arts', is categorised here as just another example of the rage to consume – a provocative, but salutary, reminder that the rapid growth in publications is a symptom of the consumer revolution, and that their contents too are susceptible to commodification. The new genre of reviewing, for example, underlines this commodity status: it helps the book-buying audience make choices by describing new publications; it also makes the subject-matter of those publications into a form of shared cultural capital, available for discussion by the eighteenth century's chattering classes. Modern critics, including the contributors to this volume, remain divided about whether the effects of this consumer revolution were on balance good or bad (for women). Once again, conclusions differ with a focus on different social contexts, cultural practices, and genres. Thus, for example, economic changes appear to have left rural women with fewer opportunities than were available to women in an urban commercial environment; and the writings of highly educated female reformers were more openly hostile to forms of popular consumption than was, say, writing for the theatre.[23] In very general terms, however, it is undoubtedly true that women writers were obvious beneficiaries of the explosion in a consumer taste for 'literature'. As Margaret Doody argues in her essay here, 'If we often sigh over the "commodification of culture", we should recognise that such commodification gave women a chance they had lacked otherwise.'[24]

Bermingham draws on theories of consumption developed by cultural and feminist critics in the 1980s. It is surely no coincidence that this intensely consumerist moment in the twentieth century gave birth to a rethinking which identified consumption, as well as production, as a meaningful and active part of the socio-economic process, and the desire for things as a central factor in the creation of self – a mechanism clearly operative in Pope's image of Belinda. The significance of this for feminism lies in its re-evaluation of an area negatively identified with femininity, superficiality, and passivity; an identification clearly present in eighteenth-century anxieties about the feminisation of culture, but also in modern forms of economic and social theory whose assumptions about the relative value of production and consumption ultimately derive from eighteenth-century traditions of political economy. Instead, recent theories of consumption put this 'feminine' (and often women's) activity at the heart of cultural identity. Equally significantly, they argue that, far from being a state of passive subjection to meanings dictated by the producer, consumption is creative and unpredictable, a site of agency, interpretation, and therefore, potentially, of resistance. And this would be true whether the object concerned were a fashion item or the words of a text.

FORMS OF RESISTANCE

In popular usage, individual words are frequently appropriated to produce unexpected or resistant meanings ('gay', or the rehabilitated 'queer' would be obvious modern examples). The *Critical Review* praised Elizabeth Carter's poetry for its 'purest sentiments', where 'pure' is part of the vocabulary used to define proper femininity. But throughout the eighteenth century, 'pure' and its derivatives were also used colloquially to express approval – the equivalent of a term like 'cool' or 'wicked' in current slang; a 'pure' was also a slang term for a prostitute.[25] In David Garrick's short play *Miss in her Teens* (1747), the two linguistic registers are brought wittily and tellingly together, to interestingly ambiguous effect. Told by her maid, Tag, that the man she really loves has returned from the war, the play's heroine, Biddy, plans to get rid of her now inconvenient suitors, Fribble and Dash:

BIDDY Let me see – what shall I do with my two gallants? I must at least part with 'em decently. Suppose I set 'em together by the ears? The luckiest thought in the world! For if they won't quarrel (as I believe they won't) I can break with 'em for cowards and very justly dismiss 'em my service.

And if they will fight and one of 'em should be killed, the other will
certainly be hanged or run away, and so I shall very handsomely get rid
of both. I am glad I have settled it so purely.

Enter Tag.

Well, Tag, are they safe?

TAG   I think so. The door's double-locked and I have the key in my pocket.

BIDDY   That's pure.[26]

The contradictorily gendered meanings of 'pure' are highlighted in this
juxtaposition of the colloquial exclamation with the more mixed register of 'I am glad I have settled it so purely' – both spoken by the virgi-
nal but very far from helpless heroine. *Miss in her Teens* is an afterpiece: a
short play performed after the main entertainment and to a more
heterogeneous audience. Intended for popular consumption, the appropriately mixed register in Garrick's presentation of Biddy draws attention to the narrow linguistic and class basis on which the ideal of the
unambiguously 'pure' woman rests. This linguistic self-consciousness
could be seen to rebound negatively on Biddy and thus on women in
general – a punning, and rather predictable pointer to the tainted purity
even of misses in their teens. But a more subversive audience response
is equally possible – indeed, given the right actress, more likely. The
play's witty use of colloquial meanings turns the repressive language of
conduct-book discourse into a comment on the furthering of Biddy's
own desires, and to laugh with the heroine is to resist any easy reduction
of femininity to predetermined categories.

At a more explicit level of resistance, women writers appropriated and
redirected current discourses in order to make what in our terms would
be described as feminist arguments on behalf of women. As we have
already seen, in the *Essay in Defence of the Female Sex* contemporary arguments about civic and religious inequalities provide a vocabulary
through which the writer can also attack the 'unreasonable Authority
[men] so much affect over us'.[27] Just over a hundred years later, at the
very end of our period, Mary Robinson used the terminology of
Enlightenment reason to pose 'this plain and rational question, – is not
woman a human being, gifted with all the feelings that inhabit the bosom
of man?'.[28] Though the term was unavailable in the eighteenth century,
we have no hesitation in describing such demands as 'feminist'. In doing
so, we register that desire to forge continuities with the women and the
texts of the past which makes us interested in 'women and literature' –
in any period – in the first place. But the discontinuities and the strange-
nesses of the past are also exciting and instructive. Modern feminisms

have their origins in Enlightenment modes of thought, but modern feminists would be unwilling to endorse Mary Robinson's use of the singular term 'woman', wanting instead to stress 'the differences among women or, perhaps more exactly, the differences *within women*'.[29] The differences among and within eighteenth-century women, and the importance of these differences in understanding the literature they read and produced are clearly demonstrated in the essays which follow.

This is a particularly exciting moment in critical discussions about women and literature in the eighteenth century. Not least, of course, as Isobel Grundy's essay at the beginning of part two demonstrates, because of the wealth of texts by women recently rediscovered and available in print, on microfilm, or in electronic form. But also because, in the area of eighteenth-century studies, this theoretical attention to differences 'among' and 'within', the concern to understand the diverse particularities of women's lives and of the circumstances in which literature is produced, has resulted in an increasingly productive interdisciplinarity between literary critics, social and cultural historians, and historians of publishing – an interdisciplinarity evident both within and across the essays in this volume. Attention to diversity and particularity has also involved a growing emphasis on female agency: both as a theoretical possibility, and as a historical actuality supported by the growing literary and documentary evidence of women's active involvement at all levels of (print) culture. And it has begun to dislodge some of the familiar narratives about women and literature in this period: asking us to adjust our assumptions about the hegemony of fiction, for example, or to rethink the gendered division between public and private spheres.

In making their distinctive contribution to these debates, the essays in this volume engage with earlier critical and scholarly work which has significantly shaped our understanding of women's writing in the eighteenth century; and they approach the question of women and literature in many different, and complementary, ways. The essays by Kathryn Sutherland, Harriet Guest, and Felicity A. Nussbaum, in the opening section on femininities, analyse shifting constructions of femininity in both literary and non-literary texts, and the ways in which these discourses of gender interact throughout the century with other cultural preoccupations – commercial and colonial expansion; national identity; Dissent and republicanism; and emergent discourses of racial difference. In the second section, on women, family, and the law, Gillian Skinner

and Ruth Perry read literary texts in conjunction with historical sources
to yield important evidence of changes in kinship structures, economic
processes, and legal arrangements, many of which worked to disadvantage women. And the essays by Paula McDowell and Jan Fergus in the
final section of part one use the archival records of printers and booksellers to open up a new understanding of women's practical involvement in print culture, and to rethink what eighteenth-century women
actually read. In part two, the essays by Ros Ballaster, Margaret Anne
Doody, and Angela J. Smallwood on women's writing in the major
genres are complemented by Clare Brant's demonstration of the way in
which many texts by women resist any easy generic categorisation, and
by Dianne Dugaw's exploration of women's involvement and representation in popular cultural forms.

Because of the energy and variety of feminist analysis and investigation over the last quarter of the twentieth century, the map of eighteenth-
century literature has changed beyond recognition – and it continues to
change, as the focus of attention moves beyond polite and middle-class
culture to consider the wider impact of print. So, in the end, perhaps one
of the most exciting things to emerge from this volume is the sense of
how much still remains to be discovered and thought about eighteenth-
century women, and literature.

NOTES

1 Review of Elizabeth Carter's *Poems on Several Occasions*, *Critical Review*, 13
   (1762), 180–1.
2 See: David Cressy, 'Literacy in Context: Meaning and Measurement in
   Early Modern England' in John Brewer and Roy Porter (eds.), *Consumption
   and the World of Goods* (London and New York: Routledge, 1993), pp. 305–19
   (pp. 305, 317); Peter Earle, 'The Female Labour Market in London in the
   Late Seventeenth and Early Eighteenth Centuries', *Economic History Review*,
   2nd ser., 42:3 (1989), 328–53 (p. 343). For a valuable summary of recent
   findings on literacy levels, see J. Paul Hunter, *Before Novels: the Cultural Contexts
   of Eighteenth-Century English Fiction* (New York and London: W. W. Norton,
   1990), pp. 69–85. See also Jan Fergus, ch. 7 of this volume, and 'Guide to
   Further Reading'.
3 For discussion of these kinds of texts, see particularly essays by Paula
   McDowell, Dianne Dugaw, and Clare Brant, chs. 6, 12, and 13 of this
   volume.
4 James Lackington, *Memoirs of the First Forty-Five Years of the Life of James
   Lackington* (London: printed for the author, 1792), p. 386. For numbers of
   novels published, see Cheryl Turner, *Living by the Pen: Women Writers in the*

Eighteenth Century (London and New York: Routledge, 1992), pp. 35–7; on poetry, see Roger Lonsdale's remarks in his 'Introduction' to *Eighteenth-Century Women Poets: an Oxford Anthology* (Oxford University Press, 1989), p. xxi; on drama, see Angela J. Smallwood, ch. 11 below, p. 239; on other genres, see Judith Philips Stanton, 'Statistical profile of women writing in English from 1660 to 1800' in Frederick M. Keener and Susan E. Lorsch (eds.), *Eighteenth-Century Women and the Arts* (New York: Greenwood Press, 1988), pp. 247–54. See also 'Chronology'.

5 *The Spectator*, no. 10 (12 March 1711), ed. Donald F. Bond, 5 vols. (Oxford: Clarendon Press, 1965), 1, 44, 46.

6 William Alexander, *The History of Women, from the Earliest Antiquity, to the Present Time*, 2 vols. (London: Strahan & Cadell, 1779), 1, 170–1.

7 John Duncombe, *The Feminiad: a Poem* (1754), extract rpt. in Vivien Jones (ed.), *Women in the Eighteenth Century: Constructions of Femininity* (London and New York: Routledge, 1990), p. 171.

8 For discussion of conjunctions between discourses of femininity, colonialism, and racial difference, see Felicity A. Nussbaum, ch. 3 of this volume.

9 Jürgen Habermas, *The Structural Transformation of the Public Sphere: an Inquiry into a Category of Bourgeois Society*, trans. Thomas Burger (Cambridge: Polity Press, 1989). See also Michael G. Ketcham, *Transparent Designs: Reading, Performance, and Form in the* Spectator *Papers* (Athens: University of Georgia Press, 1985). *The Spectator* was originally issued in print runs of three or four thousand copies, but the readership has been estimated to be far higher.

10 See, for example, Kathryn Shevelow, *Women and Print Culture: the Construction of Femininity in the Early Periodical* (London and New York: Routledge, 1989).

11 See 'Guide to Further Reading', and for further discussion of the public/private distinction in this volume, see particularly essays by Harriet Guest, Gillian Skinner, Paula McDowell, and Clare Brant, chs. 2, 4, 6, and 13.

12 *An Essay in Defence of the Female Sex* is thought to be by a female physician, Judith Drake. Extract rpt. in Jones, *Women in the Eighteenth Century*, pp. 207–17 (p. 209). For discussion of the Dissenting tradition in women's writing, see Harriet Guest, ch. 2 of this volume.

13 For discussion of contemporary views on the corrupting effects of girls' reading, see Jan Fergus, ch. 7 below, pp. 172–3.

14 See Neil McKendrick, John Brewer, and J. H. Plumb, *The Birth of a Consumer Society: the Commercialization of Eighteenth-century England* (London: Europa, 1982).

15 *Monthly Review*, 77 (1787); 54 (1776), quoted in Cheryl Turner, *Living by the Pen*, pp. 53, 58.

16 In *The Feminiad*, women writers are approved or otherwise, depending on whether they follow a 'modest' or a 'wanton' muse. See Dunton, *The Feminiad*, p. 173.

17 'pressure towards respectability': see Janet Todd, *The Sign of Angellica: Women, Writing and Fiction, 1660–1800* (London: Virago, 1989), p. 128. See also, for

example: Jane Spencer, *The Rise of the Woman Novelist: From Aphra Behn to Jane Austen* (Oxford: Basil Blackwell, 1986); Catherine Gallagher, *Nobody's Story: the Vanishing Acts of Women Writers in the Marketplace 1670–1820* (Oxford: Clarendon Press, 1994). For discussion of ways in which women's fiction and drama manifested, but also challenged, these constraints, see Ros Ballaster and Angela J. Smallwood in chs. 9 and 11 of this volume; for the suggestion that a tendency to 'retreat' might have extended beyond simply women's writing, see Margaret Anne Doody in ch. 10, pp. 229–30.

18 Nancy Armstrong, for example, tends to homogenise advice literature. See *Desire and Domestic Fiction: a Political History of the Novel* (New York and Oxford: Oxford University Press, 1987), and for further discussion of this important book, see Kathryn Sutherland, Ruth Perry, and Ros Ballaster in chs. 1, 5, and 9, below, pp. 25–6, 114, 200–1.

19 John Brown, *An Estimate of the Manners and Principles of the Times* (London: Davis & Reymers, 1757), p. 29.

20 Alexander Pope, *The Rape of the Lock: an heroi-comical poem in five canto's*, I, lines 135–8, *The Poems of Alexander Pope. A one-volume edition of the Twickenham text*, ed. John Butt (London: Methuen, 1963), p. 222.

21 Daniel Defoe, *The Fortunes and Misfortunes of the Famous Moll Flanders* (1722), ed. G. A. Starr, World's Classics (Oxford University Press, 1981), p. 86.

22 Ann Bermingham, 'Introduction' in Ann Bermingham and John Brewer (eds.), *The Consumption of Culture 1600–1800: Image, Object, Text* (London and New York: Routledge, 1995), p. 6. Bermingham cites the historian Lorna Weatherill's important work on patterns of consumption. See Lorna Weatherill, *Consumer Behaviour and Material Culture in Britain, 1660–1760* (London: Routledge, 1988), and 'Guide to Further Reading'.

23 Contrast, for example, Ruth Perry on changing patterns of rural work with Paula McDowell and Dianne Dugaw on women as urban print-workers and hawkers; and Kathryn Sutherland and Harriet Guest on anti-consumption discourses in women's writing with Angela J. Smallwood's analysis of writing for the theatre, actresses, and fashion: see chs. 5, 6, and 12; 1, 2, and 11 of this volume. See also Clare Brant on women writers as users and victims of fashion, ch. 13, pp. 290–2.

24 Below, p. 217.

25 See entries for 'pure', etc. in *OED* and Eric Partridge (ed.), abr. Jacqueline Simpson, *The Penguin Dictionary of Historical Slang* (London: Penguin Books, 1972).

26 David Garrick, *Miss in her Teens*, II.i, in *The Plays of David Garrick*, ed. Harry William Pedicord and Frederick Louis Bergmann, 4 vols. (Carbondale: Southern Illinois University Press, 1980–2), I, 86–7. I want to thank Tim Skelly and students of The Workshop Theatre, University of Leeds, for drawing this text to my attention.

27 *Essay in Defence*, p. 210.

28 'Anne Frances Randall' [Mary Robinson], *A Letter to the Women of England, on the Injustice of Mental Subordination* (1799), extract rpt. in Jones, *Women in the*

Eighteenth Century, p. 238. Though the term 'feminism' was first used at the end of the nineteenth century, and is therefore, strictly speaking, anachronistic in the context of eighteenth-century writing, it can be valuable in suggesting the common ground between modern feminists and those eighteenth-century writers who also sought to identify, and so to change, the forms of oppression and disadvantage experienced by women. Its use does not, of course, imply that their strategies or preoccupations were identical with those of modern feminists.

29 Teresa de Lauretis, 'The Technology of Gender' in *Technologies of Gender: Essays on Theory, Film, and Fiction* (Basingstoke and London: Macmillan, 1987), p. 2. See also, for example, Linda J. Nicholson (ed.), *Feminism/Postmodernism* (New York and London: Routledge, 1990).

PART I

Constructing Women in the Eighteenth Century

Eighteenth-century femininities

CHAPTER I

Writings on education and conduct: arguments for female improvement

Kathryn Sutherland

Religion therefore has been the basis of my plan.
Hester Chapone, *Letters on the Improvement of the Mind*[1]

Within the emergent class society of eighteenth-century Britain, to belong to the middle and to be female was to be in a position of agency and influence in the formation of social relations. To be female and to belong to the middle argues an ability to balance the extremes of either end of the social order and to stand for 'right regulation', a phrase which contemporary women writers invoke like a mantra to justify their own pronouncements. This linking of gender and rank is sustained in the attempts of various women activists to enlarge social and intellectual opportunities for their sex. By the later decades of the century, the middle-class woman has emerged as her sex's genuine representative with the power to censor by her criticism the excessive femininity of the luxury-identified aristocrat and to redeem by the example of her conduct and instruction the undifferentiated existence of her labouring counterpart. To both she exhibits the emulative quality of 'true value'. 'True value', so constructed, resides in such female embodiments as wife, mother, domestic economist, and educator. Its recognition depends on the prescriptive force of a set of mental and emotional qualities culturally defined as 'feminine': sympathy, decorous accomplishment, chastity. This narrowed definition of 'the feminine' exists in explicit opposition to that wider cultural 'feminisation' (of men and women) which was the assumed consequence of deregulated desire within an unhampered commercial economy.[2]

In *Desire and Domestic Fiction: a Political History of the Novel*, Nancy Armstrong argues what has proved in the ten years since its publication an influential thesis. According to Armstrong, the growing fashion for conduct books in Britain in the course of the eighteenth century provided a transitional aristocratic-to-bourgeois culture with a new language in which to conceptualise and articulate its changing institutional relations. In such books, a set of 'rules for sexual exchange', derived from a 'grammar' of female subjectivity, are invoked in order to establish the desired domestic relations and practices of an apparently non-political, private sphere. And through those domestic relations and practices, the necessary economic relations of the modern commercial polity are encoded and reproduced. Consequently, the public focus in the conduct book on the private and the insignificant – its devising of a special kind of educational programme for those who are not to be educated (women) – performs massive ideological work across the gender divide. Through the prescription and management of female value, the conduct book implies larger social structures. The conduct book is about the creation of coherent identity, and the middle-class female as its representative. Armstrong puts it like this: 'In fact, it is accurate to say that such writing as the conduct books helped to generate the belief that there was such a thing as a middle class with clearly established affiliations before it actually existed. If there is any truth in this, then it is also reasonable to claim that the modern individual was first and foremost a female.' In the course of the eighteenth century, the conduct book absorbed aspects of socially and generically diverse earlier forms – devotional writings, the marriage manual, works on household economy and recipe books – to create a composite character-kit, incorporating practical advice on the duties of womanhood, on reading, dress, and desirable accomplishments, with moral instruction on less palatable issues, like the regulation of the affections and the control of moods, and with categories of virtuous identity, as daughter, wife, mother, widow. In confounding assumptions of 'natural' gender difference with definitions of 'proper' or 'suitable' behaviour, the conduct book sought to conceptualise and interpret female behaviour as predictor of social behaviour more generally. It constructs female identity in imagined contention with anti-social, deviant or extreme, forms which its powerful example then exorcises: the irresponsible, the overrefined, the ungoverned, the under- or over-educated. And the genre's relation to the emerging novel of manners, from Haywood and Richardson to Burney and Austen, is well established.[3]

A MIDDLE-CLASS IDEAL

Coherent identity is a limiting and impossible fiction. It is nevertheless a useful fiction, a provisional space which enables society and individual

to act. Thus, for example, the conduct book's construction of the domestic, middle-class female brings into uncomplicated being the fiction of
the rational economic male; more problematically, it constitutes woman
herself as the tractable occupant of a complementary space. Both the
general contours and the details of the convention are sufficiently fixed
by mid century for Jane Collier to invoke them by implication in her
*Essay on the Art of Ingeniously Tormenting; with Proper Rules for the Exercise of
that Pleasant Art* (1753). The first section of this two-part *Essay* is addressed,
'to those, who may be said to have an exterior power from visible authority', such as masters, parents, and husbands; the second offers advice 'to
those, who have an interior power, arising from the affection of the
person on whom they are to work' – chief among these are wives.[4]
Collier's manual holds a mirror to the rules of acceptable conduct, an
inversion of values which satirises bad behaviour and yet manages to
suggest the limitations and frustrations in the approved model. For
example, from advice to a wife:

Carefully study your husband's temper, and find out what he likes, in order
never to do any one thing that will please him.

   If he expresses his approbation of the domestic qualities of a wife; such as
family oeconomy, and that old-fashioned female employment, the needle;
neglect your family as much as ever his temper will bear; and always have your
white gloves on your hands. Tell him, that every woman of spirit ought to hate
and despise a man who could insist on his wife's being a family drudge; and
declare, that you will not submit to be a cook and a semstress to any man. But
if he loves company, and chearful parties of pleasure, and would willingly have
you always with him, nose him with your great love of needle-work and house-
wifery. Or should he be a man of genius, and should employ his leisure hours
in writing, be sure to shew a tasteless indifference to every thing he shews you
of his own. The same indifference, also, may you put on, if he should be a man
who loves reading, and is of so communicative a disposition, as to take delight
in reading to you any of our best and most entertaining authors. If, for instance,
he desires you to hear one of Shakespeare's plays, you may give him perpetual
interruptions, by sometimes going out of the room, sometimes ringing the bell
to give orders for what cannot be wanted till the next day; at other times taking
notice (if your children are in the room), that Molly's cap is awry, or that Jackey
looks pale; and then begin questioning the child, whether he has done any thing
to make himself sick. If you have needle-work in your hands, you may be so
busy in cutting out, and measuring one part with another, that it will plainly
appear to your husband, that you mind not one word he reads. (pp. 123–5)

The unobtrusive arrangement of the household and care of children,
needlework, a taste for canonical literature, an even temper, a ready
accommodation of her husband's moods, and an intelligent interest in

and praise of his pastimes – these are the approved female qualities to be deduced from Collier's disruptive model.

Just how standard they are can be discovered from a comparison with Hester Mulso Chapone's hugely influential *Letters on the Improvement of the Mind, Addressed to a Young Lady* (1773). Addressed by an aunt to her niece, 'in your fifteenth year' (I, 3), this two-volume manual concerns itself with the virtues and skills necessary to the female of middle rank on the brink of adulthood. Chapone's *Letters* was reprinted at least sixteen times in separate editions in the last twenty-five years of the eighteenth century and frequently bound, as was the custom, well into the nineteenth century with other conduct manuals, to form small 'Lady's Libraries' of improving texts. Its premises, and its detailed curriculum, provide the ideological heart of Austen's *Mansfield Park* (1814).

According to Chapone, discretion, the basis for lasting domestic happiness, is only acquired through a programme of 'regulation' and 'government' (letters 4 and 5 entitled 'On the Regulation of the Heart and Affections', and letter 6 'On the Government of the Temper'), which presumes a system of internal and external controls, of self and social checks. Letter 6 opens with the following advice:

The principal virtues or vices of a woman must be of a private and domestic kind. Within the circle of her own family and dependants lies her sphere of action – the scene of almost all those tasks and trials, which must determine her character, and her fate, here, and hereafter. Reflect, for a moment, how much the happiness of her husband, children, and servants, must depend on her temper, and you will see that the greatest good, or evil, which she ever may have in her power to do, may arise from her correcting or indulging its infirmities. (II, 5–6)

Letter 7, 'On Economy', describes economy as that '*art*' and '*virtue*' which 'ought to have the precedence of all other accomplishments' (II, 48), and as most evident when 'nobody's attention is called to any of the little affairs of it' (II, 69). Letter 8, 'On Politeness and Accomplishments', declares that 'the chief of these is a competent share of reading, well chosen and properly regulated', but that '[t]he danger of pedantry and presumption in a woman – of her exciting envy in one sex and jealousy in the other – of her exchanging the graces of imagination for the severity and preciseness of a scholar, would be, I own, sufficient to frighten me from the ambition of seeing my girl remarkable for learning' (II, 115, 121).

Chapone does not quarrel with the exclusively domestic horizons set for women's lives, but rather makes it clear that, together with certain natural capacities (for imagination rather than 'preciseness' (II, 121); and for 'passive' rather than 'active courage' (I, 124–5)), these will confine their education within certain bounds. However, the curriculum she proposes for the fifteen-year-old girl is neither unrigorous nor merely auxiliar, comprising as it does: a systematic study of the Bible; training in accounting and other aspects of household management; translations of the classics and a range of modern literature in French and English, only avoiding sentimental novels; botany, geology, astronomy; geography and chronology (the study of tables of significant times and dates); and, 'the principal study', history – ancient and modern, but particularly the history of Britain and its empire:

I know of nothing equally proper to entertain and improve at the same time, or that is so likely to form and strengthen your judgment, and, by giving you a liberal and comprehensive view of human nature, in some measure to supply the defect of that experience, which is usually attained too late to be of much service to us. (II, 125)

We should not underestimate the positive force of Chapone's recommendations for a sustained programme of study for women and of the conviction that lies behind it: that Christian belief is a matter of reason and is itself the chief instructor of our rational faculties. The conventional emphasis on Christian piety and the social conservatism need to be adjusted in the light of Chapone's equal insistence on the importance of inculcating critical faculties in women, to equip them to reach independent judgements in private life.

It is difficult for the modern reader to enter sympathetically the ideological boundaries of the conduct manual. The problem is twofold: writers whom we would now wish to distinguish on grounds of gender, known political sympathies, or opportunities, often share a common discursive construction (and containment) of femininity; and, alternatively, proposals for female education are subject to inflections of gender, rank (class), and religion that we now find uncomfortable to rearticulate.

For example, as the friend of Elizabeth Carter – the Greek scholar and translator of Epictetus – and member of the 'Bluestocking' group of intellectual women surrounding the society hostess Elizabeth Montagu (to whom Chapone dedicated her *Letters*), Hester Chapone has impeccable credentials as a promoter of women's education. By tracing them we discover her place in a tradition of female intellectual enquiry sustained by personal contact from Mary Astell at the beginning of the century to Hannah More at its close. Montagu, to whom Chapone looks for patronage, was the sister of Sarah Scott, author of the utopian study of female separatism *Millenium Hall* (1762), and their mother was Elizabeth Drake who may have been educated by the famous Bathsua Makin. One-time tutor to Princess Elizabeth, daughter of Charles I, Makin was author of *An Essay to Revive the Antient Education of Gentlewomen* (1673), one of the first systematic programmes for the education of young women, combining conventional instruction in domestic accomplishments with a more ambitious curriculum previously offered only to boys. Montagu, herself a published author on suitable female topics (*Dialogues of the Dead* (1760) and *An Essay on the Writings and Genius of Shakespear* (1769)), is the vital link between the generations of intellectual women in the eighteenth century – Carter, Mary Pendarves Delany, Frances Boscawen, and Catherine Talbot, among the earlier generation; and later, Frances Burney, Hannah More, and Anna Laetitia Aikin (Barbauld). Moreover, through the woman who became her mother-in-law, Sarah Chapone, Hester Mulso Chapone could trace a connection with an even earlier female intellectual tradition. It was while running a girls' boarding school in Gloucestershire in the 1730s that Sarah Chapone discovered the whereabouts of Elizabeth Elstob, the impoverished Anglo-Saxon scholar and champion of women's learning, and arranged for her employment as governess in the family of Montagu's friend, Margaret, Duchess of Portland. Elstob, who died in 1756, had been in her youth a member of the feminist circle surrounding the philosopher and polemicist Mary Astell.[5]

Against this dense network of female authorities empowering Chapone, now place what seems to be a direct literary source for the *Letters on the Improvement of the Mind*, and that is *A Letter, of Genteel and Moral Advice to a Young Lady*, written by the Revd Wetenhall Wilkes for his niece. Here Wilkes lays out his method for educating a young woman 'past the trifling amusements of childhood' and 'entering upon the stage of trial'. His suggested curriculum anticipates in detail, in topics for study and in its methods and general philosophy of female education, that proposed in Chapone's *Letters* thirty years later.

As in his related *Essay on the Pleasures and Advantages of Female Literature* (1741), Wilkes states his commitment to an ungendered capacity for ratiocination. He nevertheless assumes without question a set of natural distinctions between men and women which are reproduced within existing social and domestic institutions (education among them). In particular, he endorses women's retired affectivity as the responsive refinement of men's pro-active encounters within a wider sphere of operation:

If it were but universally considered, that women were created to refine the joys, to soften the cares of humanity, by the most agreeable participation; that they have as great a share in the rational world as men have; and that they have as much reason to aspire to the highest virtues and accomplishments, as the wisest and the gravest philosophers – How many blessings and ornaments might we expect from the fair sex, who are formed by their natural tempers to goodness and tenderness, and so adapted by the brightness and clearness of their minds, to admire and imitate every thing that is polite, virtuous, and divine![6]

This leaves women's rational education in an equivocal position, mortgaged to a strictly privatised function and committed to a social reinforcement that deprives it of all but the narrowest employment. Ironically, this is in contrast to the public parade of the badly educated woman whose knowledge is all in 'Dancing, Dress, or in the various Ceremonies of Visiting' (*Essay*, pp. 16–17).

In distinguishing the educated from the uneducated woman, intellectual expansion, mental space, becomes by general acceptance the corollary of physical restriction. It can be argued that the appropriation of the language of reason by the ideology of domestic containment offers women some scope for self-development and social influence (and we see something of how this works out in the complexly interiorised yet socially confined heroines of Jane Austen's novels). On the other hand, exclusion has its benefits: the stoutly misogynist discourse which denies compatibility between women and reason is diametrically opposed to the evidence for any counter-argument, and the parallel, alternative status of that counter-argument is thus left intact. The intertextual authority of Wilkes's curriculum and method may not overshadow Chapone's extensive female intellectual credentials, but it requires that we adjust any simple gendered assumptions of influence. It also highlights the compromise implicit in women educationalists' mid century plans to promote female seriousness.

FEMALE EDUCATIONALISTS

In the course of the eighteenth century, women educationalists are largely agreed with Mary Astell that women's 'Incapacity, if there be any, is acquired not natural.'[7] But their critique of social institutions tends to lack Astell's providential assurance of divine support and the alternative rational conviction of a revisionist rhetoric of rights. Royalist and High Church, Astell was the author of *A Serious Proposal to the Ladies* (in two parts, 1694 and 1697), and of *The Christian Religion, as profess'd by a Daughter of the Church of England* (1705). Her *Reflections Upon Marriage* (1700; third edition 1706) is an important contribution to debates on political and domestic rights in the turbulent decades of the later seventeenth century. Marriage, the union between man and woman, is an ancient image for political association, and during this period the metaphor gained new currency within the debate over the relation between monarch and people. In the contemporary natural rights theories of Hobbes, Pufendorf, and Locke, argument turned on the conditions under which man rationally gives up his natural freedom within the social order: civil society, they maintain, is a voluntary relinquishing of original freedom for servitude to the state. In the long preface which she added to the third edition of her *Reflections*, Astell offers one of the earliest critiques of the contract analogy when she issues her famous challenge to Locke: 'If *all Men are born free*, how is it that all Women are born slaves?' and she continues: 'why is Slavery so much condemn'd and strove against in one Case, and so highly applauded; and held so necessary and so sacred in another?'[8] How in this climate of political enquiry can women's subjection be presumed to predate social institutions?

The basis of the disagreement is complex – Astell does not seriously argue that women are born slaves. What she does is use the anomalous exclusion of women from contemporary radical arguments for natural rights to reveal the fundamental flaw in those arguments themselves – that reason underlies contractual social relations, between the individual and the state or within marriage. Against natural law, she sets a providentialist commitment to divinely ordained hierarchy, within the public and the private spheres, where government and marriage both bear witness to a necessity for regulation. That regulation is divinely ordained, that wives should in consequence obey their husbands – these are not amenable to rationalisation, in the form of contract logic, even without its implied contradictions (conditional servitude for men/unconditional servitude for women); nor can the fact of abuse within marriage (as within government) be proof of right:

That the Custom of the World has put Women, generally speaking, into a State of Subjection, is not deny'd; but the Right can no more be prov'd from the Fact, than the Predominancy of Vice can justifie it. A certain great Man has endeavour'd to prove by Reasons not contemptible, that in the Original State of things the Woman was the Superior, and that her Subjection to the Man is an Effect of the Fall, and the Punishment of her Sin . . . However this be, 'tis certainly no Arrogance in a Woman to conclude, that she was made for the Service of GOD, and that this is her End. Because GOD made all Things for Himself, and a Rational Mind is too noble a Being to be Made for the Sake and Service of any Creature. The Service she at any time becomes oblig'd to pay to a Man, is only a Business by the Bye. Just as it may be any Man's Business and Duty to keep Hogs; he was not Made for this, but if he hires himself out to such an Employment, he ought conscientiously to perform it. (p. 72)

The High Anglican orthodoxy and resignation with which the Tory Astell challenges the consensualism of the turn-of-the-century constitutional debates (Whig arguments for the right to resist tyranny and the means to secure individual rights) can seem perverse to the modern, usually secular, reader. But in affirming that government, private and public, is an aspect of divine will and not a device of human wisdom to meet the needs of moral and rational beings, she is able to distinguish women's potential (and rights) from the social constraints within which custom (and fact) arbitrarily place it: she constructs a space outside society in which female reason can operate.

Astell's suggestion for women's colleges, communities where women might live and learn together, the poorer members supported by the assets of their wealthier sisters, is a piece of reasoned and gendered idealism. It forms the basis of her two-part treatise *A Serious Proposal* (1694–7), in which she offers a programme of 'useful *knowledge*' to combat 'those pitiful diversions, those revellings and amusements' that commonly constitute women's employment (pp. 20–1). A response to the perceived perils of her commercial age, the *Serious Proposal* is less a detailed curriculum, in the manner of Chapone later, than a disquisition against material attachment which takes as given certain male assumptions about women's relationship to goods within the consumer society, assumptions that will determine the moral parameters of conduct literature through the eighteenth century. *A Serious Proposal*, then, declares at the outset the basis in commercial culture, in society as it is, of women's mental trivialisation.

One such assumption is explored at some length when Astell expounds her belief that a constant exposure to external objects – what she calls 'the little Toys and Vanities of the world' – renders people querulous, inconstant, and incapable of steady concentration; given the 'mistakes of our Education', women are particularly vulnerable to such trivialising contact (pp. 31, 10). In the context of her political and religious allegiances and a long literary tradition urging withdrawal from the world, the remedy Astell suggests – retirement from the corrupting influences of fashionable life – is unremarkably conservative; it is only extreme in the determination with which it pursues its logical end: female mutuality, and material and spiritual self-sufficiency in isolation. For what Astell proposes threatens to unfix the gendered positions with regard to experience in a commercial society, the very positions that conduct literature, in its revised account of women's appropriate mental and physical space, will seek to preserve. She writes:

And first, as to the inconveniences of living in the World; no very small one is that strong *Idea* and warm perception it gives us of its Vanities; since these are ever at hand, constantly thronging about us, they must necessarily push aside all other Objects, and the Mind being prepossess'd and gratefully entertain'd with those pleasing Perceptions which external Objects occasion, takes up with them as its only Good, is not at leisure to taste those delights which arise from a Reflection on its self, nor to receive the *Ideas* which such a Reflection conveys, and consequently forms all its Notions by such *Ideas* only as sensation has furnish'd it with, being unacquainted with those more excellent ones which arise from its own operations and a serious reflection on them, and which are necessary to correct the mistakes, and supply the defects of the other. From whence arises a very partial knowledge of things, nay, almost a perfect ignorance in things of the greatest moment. (pp. 29–30)

Astell appears to distinguish between two kinds of mental operation: at the lower level (above which fashion-identified women tend not to rise), the mind is controlled ('prepossess'd') by the thoughts and desires which external objects create; beyond that, and reserved for those women who retire from the world, is a mental space unoccupied by externalities and filled instead with a nobler store of reflections because they are self-reflections. What is so radical in all this is the clear suggestion that, refusing her socially constructed place in a world of objects, woman will gain access to her truer self; in particular, that the restraint of appetite is an act of self-regard, in which 'pre-possession' (the control exercised over mind by the object world) gives place to self-possession. The quality which for Astell distinguishes retirement is reflection, by which concept and word she encompasses the complexities of an act which is at the same time a withdrawal of female value from the market place and an engagement to trade on different terms.

It is not until the 1790s and the writings of Catharine Macaulay, Hannah More, Mary Ann Radcliffe, Priscilla Wakefield, and Mary Wollstonecraft that a focus on the general moral peril consequent on women's marginalisation again lends the discourses of both rights and providence a powerful purchase on issues of gendered education. Not until an urgent national political argument can again be mounted (100 years after the Glorious Revolution) for a professional female space can women's education be freed from the taint of mere accomplishments, those accessories of the naturally inferior which are in permanent competition in the conduct manuals for women's attention and time. The crisis years of the 1790s saw a revival of a debate current in the crisis years of the 1690s – the constitutional debate over natural rights, on the one hand, and providential order, on the other. In both periods the debate has a particular female, even a feminist, dimension, but more especially in the 1790s because of the enhanced moral status of the domestic sphere (and after a century of women's conduct manuals) in combating public excess of all kinds.

Among radical writers Catharine Macaulay, republican historian and political polemicist, issues the most profound challenge to the socially accommodated curricula for women's education. Written at the end of her career, under her second married name of Macaulay Graham, her *Letters on Education. With Observations on Religious and Metaphysical Subjects* (1790) proposes the abolition of the system of difference on which the conduct manual rests: by refusing to treat female education as a distinct topic (these are *Letters on Education*); by insisting on programmes for the equal, unsegregated education of boys and girls; by promoting energetic physical exercise for girls; by denying the formative influence of nature over social training. Macaulay uses the implied dialogic and familial style of the conduct book (uncles and aunts advising nieces, fathers and mothers advising daughters) to instruct her silent female addressee (Hortensia) in a 'speculative theory of education' that owes much to the arguments of Enlightenment masculinist rationalism – to Rousseau, but also to the Scottish philosophers – with their distinction between natural and civilised behaviour.

Against Rousseau's emphasis on a natural female inferiority, she sets the Scottish Lord Monboddo's sociological insistence that '[i]t is the capital and distinguishing characteristic of our species . . . that we can make ourselves as it were over again' and that 'man, in a state of society, is as artificial a being as his representation on the canvas of the painter.'[9] She accepts the challenge of universal, inevitable artificiality, *contra* Rousseau, as an opportunity to diminish rather than enhance gender difference. In the place of Rousseau's soft and alluring feminine seductress, as represented by Sophie in book 5 of *Emile, or On Education* (1762), she offers an androgynous ideal of womanhood – 'a careless, modest

beauty, grave, manly, noble, full of strength and majesty' – whose reasoned chastity will have power to reform sexual relations and establish
them on a more equal basis (pp. 205–6, 221).

If Macaulay's celebration of female chastity appears to reinscribe the
terms of the conduct manual, it is important to notice how she raises the
arguments and scope of the genre to a higher level. '[T]he education of
individuals is for ever going on, and consists of all the impressions
received through the organs of sense, from the hour of birth to the hour
of death' (p. 274). *Letters on Education* is a tract in the Enlightenment style,
a comparative historical analysis of social and individual government
which situates schooling (a Rousseau-derived syllabus) among a set of
diverse institutions for civil refinement. Of particular significance in
tracing a subsequent, 1790s tradition in female educational writing is the
moral revision implied in her suggestions for religious study and for the
extension of an understanding of God's benevolence beyond the
human-scale. The recommendation that a serious engagement with the
Christian scriptures be postponed until the age of twenty-one (p. 137)
represents both an adjustment to the conventional curriculum of the
conduct book (in which teenage girls are encouraged to set a study of the
scriptures before other educational pursuits) and a Rousseau-derived
attempt to place religious instruction on a more rational footing, as integral to responsible adulthood rather than merely regulatory of adoles-
cent female desire. Taken with the unorthodox interest in unsettling the
divisions between the human and animal kingdoms – the repeated
advice, for example, that children be allowed to keep animals (p. 125) –
the effect is to extend the moral framework of social and individual
enquiry in ways that challenge traditional hierarchical assumptions –
about gender-prescribed codes, but also about human sovereignty and
the power of reason – and that chime with the revisionary perceptions
of other contemporary women writers. For Macaulay, Wollstonecraft,
Maria Edgeworth, and Anna Laetitia Barbauld the implications are
liberal and democratic as well as feminist; for others, conservative activists in the Sunday School movement and lower-class education, like
Sarah Trimmer and Hannah More, the expansion of sympathy to the
unequal or the non-human is more narrowly contained but no less
female-empowering for that. In either case, moral tales about children
and animals are a noticeable feature of female educational tracts in the
last years of the century; in either case, they represent a widening of the
ground on which experience stands.[10]

There is a confidence and expansiveness to Macaulay's argument which stems from her refusal to confine her discursive range within the general economy of female experience. Yet the restriction that gendered experience implies also serves a necessary oppositional function as her subject unfolds. There may be 'No characteristic Difference in Sex', as the title of letter 22 asserts, but 'the defects of female education have ever been a fruitful topic of declamation for the moralist' and 'By the intrigues of women, and their rage for personal power and importance, the whole world has been filled with violence and injury' (pp. 208, 213). Macaulay's vindication of female equality of opportunity implies also a tirade against contemporary European female behaviour, and exposes the persistent anti-female undertow beneath the educational treatise and conduct manual for women in their various forms. What the enlightened female is exhorted to root out and oppose, in herself and in society, is excessive femininity, with its essential taint of moral and commercial corruption.

In the 1790s' writings of Wollstonecraft, More, Wakefield, and Mary Ann Radcliffe, a common enquiry into the conditions for female improvement is linked to a wider political debate concerning the nature and membership of the state, patriotism, and social ethics. By giving a new priority to the economic construction of the feminine role within commercial culture, these writers reassess the conditions for moral refinement by which the conduct manual has attempted to distinguish (and marginalise) female behaviour from public behaviour. Adapting for female use aspects of a traditionally masculinist discourse of civic humanism, they are concerned to justify a more inclusive view of society and to confront those problems which seem to them to have been disregarded in the narrowing public focus of a newer scientific (and male) economic tradition – in particular, the problems of women workers and the poor. In the process, the 1790s sees the conduct manual in the hands of women writers temporarily recast as a more capacious and polemical form.

Priscilla Wakefield's *Reflections on the Present Condition of the Female Sex; with suggestions for its improvement* (1798) appears to issue a challenge to the Scottish commercial historians like Lord Kames, Adam Ferguson, John Millar, and particularly Adam Smith. Wakefield mimics their dominant discourse when she states that 'the progress of civilization [has] raised the importance of the female character', with the result that 'it has become a branch of philosophy, not a little interesting, to ascertain the offices which the different ranks of women are required to fulfil'. But she sees the logical extension of this interest to be the provision of useful employments and (quoting Adam Smith) opportunities for 'productive labour' for all members of society, female as well as male: '[S]ince the female sex is included in the idea of the species, and as women possess the same qualities as men, though perhaps in a different degree, their sex cannot free them from the claim of the public for their proportion of usefulness.'[11]

A Quaker educationalist and philanthropist, Wakefield proposes no large-scale constitutional reform; her concern is to improve women's opportunities within society as it is. But within these limits she is sharply critical of a system which denies to half the population the connection which it elsewhere inscribes as axiomatic, between usefulness and virtue. Her purpose, echoed throughout women's writings in the 1790s, is to enlarge society's recognition of woman beyond the conventional conduct-book ideal of protected wife to include the real circumstances of the widow, the spinster, the impoverished gentlewoman, and the factory hand. Fuelling her concern, as it does the concern of Wollstonecraft, Charlotte Smith, Radcliffe, and many other middle-class women writers, is the exigency of her own economic circumstances. The betrayed dependency of the inadequately educated middle-class female assumes large symbolic significance in fictional and polemical literature of the 1790s and is a direct outcome of a mounting concern that society cannot honour its commitment to the virtuous domestic icon of its own ideological construction:

There is scarcely a more helpless object in the wide circle of misery which the vicissitudes of civilized society display, than a woman genteelly educated, whether single or married, who is deprived, by any unfortunate accident, of the protection and support of male relations; unacquainted with any resource to supply an independent maintenance, she is reduced to the depths of wretchedness, and not infrequently, if she be young and handsome, is driven by despair to those paths which lead to infamy. (p. 66)

Wakefield's definition of female value represents a less mediated engagement with the productive base of commercial society than the conduct manual's conception of woman's role. She argues from a sexually undifferentiated moral code for women's equality of right to engage in economic production, making it clear that women's assumed capacity for the reproduction of value, identified here with virtuous consumption, is dependent on access to material means. Ostensibly addressed to the masculine power-base of society, Wakefield's *Reflections*, like Astell's a century before, are shaped by that sense of purpose which is only discovered in the exclusive act of female self-regard. Wakefield asks women to take it upon themselves to adjust the economic mechanism in their own favour: to establish links between female education and employment and to institute a form of economic protection. Only thus will women avoid the perils of their 'natural' professions, notably prostitution. She pleads for ladies in the upper ranks to employ and patronise female teachers, seamstresses, and hairdressers, and to boycott those shops and products where male labour has supplanted that of women. Her social model is rigidly hierarchical, and as she constructs it from the highest to the lowest ranks, she expounds the necessity for a female labour chain linking the philanthropic services of the nobility and gentry with the educational and commercial opportunities of those in the middle and with those employed in factories, shops, and domestic service. Her reasoned deployment of the gendered terminology of the dominant commercial discourse reveals the arbitrariness of its sexual alignments at the same time as it demands their more rigorous enforcement to curb the transgression of those 'effeminate' traders (p. 153). Consequently, the independence which informs her female economic model is both an attempt to recode male–female relations across the social and moral structure and a reaffirmation of essential sexual difference as female subordination.

In some respects the most interesting of the women writers in the economic moralist tradition is Mary Ann Radcliffe, in her *Female Advocate* (1799). Less detailed in its prescriptions though no less perceptive in its economic survey than Wakefield's book, the power of its analysis lies in its skilful parade and wilful misuse of the accommodated female learning prescribed by the conduct manuals. Its two-part argument – 'The Fatal Consequences of Men Traders Engrossing Women's Occupations' and a continuation demonstrating that 'the Frailty of Female Virtue more frequently originates from embarrass'd Circumstances, than from a depravity of Disposition' – follows the customary shape of women's writings in this mode in apportioning to economic conditions and the failures of education a subsequent moral disposition. For remedy Radcliffe does not propose a violent reordering but a modest adjustment of the status quo, appealing to the dictates of Christianity and sexual appropriateness and even masculine self-interest. But the effect of hearing her measured and rational discourse as a parenthesis within the larger body of male rational discourse is nevertheless deeply ironic. Despite Radcliffe's accomplished mimicry and her clever deployment of the ammunition of patriarchy (she quotes copiously, for example, from *Paradise Lost* and biblical authority in a blatant misappropriation of conduct-book learning), there is no real continuum between male and female reasoning; rather the result is a neat reversal of conventional gender assumptions in the exposure of the selfish and private motivation of male activity and the larger political virtue inherent in its female redress. Radcliffe's argument trades upon the complementarity of the languages of morality and economics as a challenge to society to make available in reality the conditions for virtue that it would enforce ideologically:

No: it was never intended that women should be left destitute in the world, without the common necessaries of life, which they so frequently experience, even without any lawful or reputable means of acquiring them, through the vile practice of men filling such situations as seem calculated, not only to give bread to poor females, but thereby to enable them to tread the paths of virtue, and render them useful members, in some lawful employment, as well as ornaments to their professions and sex. This lovely appearance, alas! is but too often thrown aside, and, frequently, *not* from vicious inclinations, but the absolute necessity of bartering their virtue for bread.

Then, is it not highly worthy the attention of men, men who profess moral virtue and the strictest sense of *honour*, to consider in what mode to redress these grievances! for women were ultimately designed for something better, though they have so long fared otherways.[12]

Like Wakefield and Radcliffe, the Tory Hannah More uses the generic scope of the conduct manual to mount a more ambitious public campaign; but, unlike theirs, hers draws polemical strength from a strict reinforcement of an orthodox female construction: woman in the home and not the workplace. For More, in a brilliant re-routing of Edmund Burke's anti-revolutionary defence of 'the little platoon we belong to in society' as the basis of 'public affections', it is woman's place at the heart of the well-managed family that in the war years of the 1790s makes her an instrument of community stability. Women, too, she implies, can be dutiful citizens. In her conduct books for the middle ranks More calls on her sex '[i]n this moment of alarm and peril' to exercise 'a patriotism at once firm and feminine for the general good!'

For, on the use which women of the superior class may be disposed to make of that power delegated to them by the courtesy of custom, by the honest gallantry of the heart, by the imperious controul of virtuous affections, by the habits of civilized states, by the usages of polished society . . . will depend, in no low degree, the well-being of those states, and the virtue and happiness, nay perhaps the very existence of that society.[13]

This is the national context, a country at war and a way of life to be defended, which More stridently colonises as domestic, female space in the opening pages of *Strictures on the Modern System of Female Education* (1799), a work whose contents pages indicate the degree to which a prov- identialist agenda locates national safety in the reformation of female manners as distinct from the redistribution of economic opportunity: 'On the education of women. The prevailing system tends to establish the errors it ought to correct. Dangers arising from an excessive cultiva- tion of the fine arts'; 'On the moral and religious use of history and geography'; 'On dissipation and the modern habits of fashionable life'; 'On the duty and efficacy of prayer'. A title-page epigraph from Lord Halifax, compiler of the much-reprinted *The Lady's New Years Gift: Or, Advice to a Daughter* (1688), a manual preparing a beloved twelve-year-old child for the inequalities of marriage, announces at once the vindication in custom of More's philosophy.

Just as emphatically as Wakefield, More appeals to gender solidarity; but she reformulates feminist argument for rather different ends. For More, the assertion that social arrangements are as they are by virtue of divine authority serves to constitute the female position not as the weak point in the structure but as the anchor. The correlation of female to divine is a constant in her understanding of social arrangements and is jeopardised only when women deny their ordained duties as women; male deviation from providential ordering, vicious and criminal though it may be, does not imply the same deep disruption. Hence the real obstacle to social improvement is not male institutions but the unre- formed or fashionable woman. More's conservative acceptance of the map of social experience is underpinned by a consciousness that Christianity itself inaugurates female authority. In her writings the bib- lical imperatives of the conduct-book tradition of female morality resur- face as hugely empowering injunctions. It is as if in exposing and emphasising the genre's gendered categorisation of attributes she liter- alises their transforming potential.[14]

Mary Wollstonecraft's *Vindication of the Rights of Woman* (1792), after Macaulay's *Letters on Education* the earliest of these polemical refashion- ings of the conduct book and the best known, is in some ways the least satisfactory. Wollstonecraft's first book-length publication, *Thoughts on the Education of Daughters* (1787), had been a conventional conduct book, in which the arguments and topics of a hundred-year tradition of such manuals by men and women weigh heavy. Here she rehearsed assidu- ously the guidelines laid down by Wilkes and Chapone for the education of women to maximise their potential as rational beings and to minimise their dependence on the life of the senses and of 'present indulgence'. Printed, like *Thoughts on . . . Daughters* for the liberal and Dissenting bookseller Joseph Johnson, the later *Vindication* seemed to some of its first readers a work in the same vein. It was described by an early reviewer (for Johnson's own *Analytical Review*, for which Wollstonecraft had been writing since 1788) as 'in reality . . . an elaborate *treatise on female education*'.[15] Wollstonecraft contextualises her argument thus, 'I may be accused of arrogance; still I must declare what I firmly believe, that all the writers who have written on the subject of female education and manners from Rousseau to Dr Gregory, have contributed to render women more artificial, weak characters, than they would otherwise have been; and, consequently, more useless members of society.'[16] According to one critic, its sustained educational emphasis may explain why the *Vindication* was 'ignored rather than virulently attacked by most of those opposed to the political assumptions Wollstonecraft held'.[17] An argument addressing the shortcomings in contemporary systems for female education would strike a familiar, even hackneyed, note in 1792 and might accommodate, diffuse, or simply disguise many of the *Vindication*'s more unsettling pronouncements.

For Wollstonecraft, the blame for a degraded femininity lies with consumer society, and with its instrument, education; but, like More, she can yet be discovered forging her ideal of womanhood out of the conditions of women's essential difference. Unlike More, however – but like her heroine Catharine Macaulay – Wollstonecraft writes within the doctrine of rights, not providence, and it is the calculated reassertion of the sovereignty of nature that, paradoxically, makes good women's claim to education and reason after the betrayal of socially instituted forms:

Women are, in common with men, rendered weak and luxurious by the relaxing pleasures which wealth procures; but added to this they are made slaves to their persons, and must render them alluring that man may lend them his reason to guide their tottering steps aright. Or should they be ambitious, they must govern their tyrants by sinister tricks, for without rights there cannot be any incumbent duties. The laws respecting woman . . . make an absurd unit of a man and his wife; and then, by the easy transition of only considering him as responsible, she is reduced to a mere cypher.

The being who discharges the duties of its station is independent; and, speaking of women at large, their first duty is to themselves as rational creatures, and the next, in point of importance, as citizens, is that, which includes so many, of a mother. The rank in life which dispenses with their fulfilling this duty, necessarily degrades them by making them mere dolls. Or, should they turn to something more important than merely fitting drapery upon a smooth block, their minds are only occupied by some soft platonic attachment; or, the actual management of an intrigue may keep their thoughts in motion; for when they neglect domestic duties, they have it not in their power to take the field and march and counter-march like soldiers, or wrangle in the senate to keep their faculties from rusting.[18]

Appealing first to that self-interest which Adam Smith inscribes at the centre of the commercial model of society, Wollstonecraft requires women to identify reason as their prime characteristic and to use it to reject their commercially constructed roles as dependent 'cyphers'. Reason she here distinguishes from the stereotype of subversive cunning that Jane Collier animates in her satirical *Essay on the Art of Ingeniously Tormenting*. Indeed, despite assumptions to the contrary, Wollstonecraft's reason ('their first duty is to themselves as rational creatures') is something akin to Astell's rationalist independence in its grounding in a capacity for self-reflection or self-possession. Wollstonecraft next argues that women's second duty is to be mothers; but she is concerned with those conditions under which motherhood can be said to be subject to reason and therefore a function of citizenship rather than of any innate and merely subsidiary disposition. Bold in its demand for the re-estimation of women's social function, the reasoning is yet compromised by that ambiguity about the basis of sexual difference, which leaves the *Vindication*'s larger argument for female rights poised in its attack upon women's social imprisonment somewhere between the sustained economic critiques of Wakefield and Radcliffe and the public reclamation of domestic virtue as practised by More.[19]

Paradoxically, for More, female authority is necessitated by the burden imposed on the domestic economy as the site of constructed appetites and compulsions whose power outstrips any attempt at public rationalisation. As queen of the conduct book, and in her rerouting of the instructive manual to the lower classes through her influential Cheap Repository Tracts, she exhorts late eighteenth-century society to practise responsible consumption and self-vigilance. In the crisis years of the 1790s and early 1800s hers is a conscious feminisation and providential redescription of citizen virtues, justified by the conflation of political and moral aims in the war-oriented discourse of the times and founded on woman's traditional capacity for moral personification.

For female polemicists and moral commentators, from Astell to Chapone and on to Wollstonecraft and More, the production and contesting of social value is bound intimately to issues of female education and improvement as it is prescribed in the conduct book; they write in consciously interpretative or revisionary dialogue with the genre. Theirs, finally, is a holistic and an ethical enquiry which is ultimately distinguished in its wider social and spiritual contextualisation from the ever narrowing agenda of the official (male) economic discourse that its arguments shadow.

NOTES

1 Hester Chapone, *Letters on the Improvement of the Mind, Addressed to a Young Lady*, 2nd edn, 2 vols. (London: H. Hughs for J. Walter, 1773), II, 226.
2 For further discussion of gender and commerce, see 'Introduction', pp. 8–13, and 'Guide to Further Reading'.
3 Nancy Armstrong, *Desire and Domestic Fiction: a Political History of the Novel* (New York and Oxford: Oxford University Press, 1987), pp. 60, 66. Armstrong's study is indebted to Mary Poovey's earlier important work on fiction and conduct literature: see Mary Poovey, *The Proper Lady and the Woman Writer: Ideology as Style in the Works of Mary Wollstonecraft, Mary Shelley, and Jane Austen* (Chicago and London: University of Chicago Press, 1984). For a recent essay arguing for contentious or resistant contemporary readings of conduct literature, see Vivien Jones, 'The Seductions of Conduct: Pleasure and Conduct Literature' in Roy Porter and Marie Mulvey Roberts (eds.), *Pleasure in the Eighteenth Century* (Basingstoke and London: Macmillan, 1996), pp. 108–32.
4 [Jane Collier], *An Essay on the Art of Ingeniously Tormenting; with Proper Rules for the Exercise of that Pleasant Art* (London: A. Millar, 1753), p. 19; rpt. from the 1757 edn, with an introduction by Judith Hawley (Bristol: Thoemmes Press, 1994), same pagination.
5 Elstob's significant engagement with the issue of women's education was largely in the form of intertextual commentary in her Anglo-Saxon publications. See Kathryn Sutherland, 'Editing for a New Century: Elizabeth Elstob's Anglo-Saxon Manifesto and Aelfric's St Gregory Homily' in D. G. Scragg and Paul E. Szarmach (eds.), *The Editing of Old English* (Cambridge: Boydell & Brewer, 1994), pp. 213–37.
6 Wetenhall Wilkes, *A Letter, of Genteel and Moral Advice to a Young Lady: Being a System of Rules and Informations; digested into a new and familiar method, to qualify the fair sex to be useful, and happy in every scene of life* (1740), 8th edn (London: L. Hawe, C. Clarke, R. Collins, 1766), pp. 5–6. See also Wilkes, *An Essay on the Pleasures and Advantages of Female Literature* (London: T. Cooper & R. Caswell, 1741). This volume shares long sections of argument verbatim with the *Letter*.
7 [Mary Astell], *A Serious Proposal to the Ladies, for the Advancement of their true and greatest Interest* (1694), ed. Patricia Springborg (London: Pickering and Chatto, 1997), p. 10.
8 [Mary Astell], *Reflections Upon Marriage. To which is added a Preface, in Answer to Some Objections*, 3rd edn (1706) in Bridget Hill (ed.), *The First English Feminist* (Aldershot, Hants: Gower Publishing, 1986), p. 76.
9 Catharine Macaulay Graham, *Letters on Education. With Observations on Religious and Metaphysical Subjects* (London: C. Dilly, 1790), p. 10.

10 See: Sarah Trimmer, *Fabulous Histories: Designed for the Instruction of Children, Respecting their Treatment of Animals* (1786); Mary Wollstonecraft, *Original Stories from Real Life* (1788); and Maria Edgeworth, *The Parent's Assistant* (1795). There is also a growing market in the period for children's textbooks on travel, natural history, and elementary science, written by women. For example: Priscilla Wakefield, *An Introduction to Botany in a Series of Familiar Letters* (1796), and *The Juvenile Travellers* (1801); and Jane Marcet, *Conversations on Chemistry: in which the Elements of that Science are Familiarly Explained and Illustrated by Experiments* (1806). For further discussion of Anna Laetitia Barbauld, see ch. 2; on women's sympathy with animals, see also ch. 10, pp. 230–2.

11 Priscilla Wakefield, *Reflections on the Present Condition of the Female Sex; with suggestions for its improvement* (London: J. Johnson, 1798), pp. 8, 1–2.

12 Mary Ann Radcliffe, *The Female Advocate; or An Attempt to Recover the Rights of Women from Male Usurpation* (London: Vernor & Hood, 1799), pp. 26–7. On women and work, see also chs. 5 and 6, below.

13 Edmund Burke, *Reflections on the Revolution in France* (1790), ed. Conor Cruise O'Brien (Harmondsworth: Penguin Books, 1982), p. 135; Hannah More, *Strictures on the Modern System of Female Education. With a View of the Principles and Conduct Prevalent Among Women of Rank and Fortune*, 2 vols. (London: Cadell & Davies, 1799), I, 4–6.

14 This coincidence of Christian teaching and feminism in the writings of conservative and moderate women intellectuals is widespread. See, for example, the expanded and much revised version of a handbook originally published in 1787 by Sarah Trimmer, *The Oeconomy of Charity; or An Address to Ladies; adapted to the present state of charitable institutions in England: with a particular view to the cultivation of religious principles, among the lower orders of people*, 2 vols. (London: Longman; Robinson; and J. Johnson, 1801), I, xii, where charity 'proves the importance of the Female Sex in society'.

15 See the *Analytical Review*, 12 (1792), 249; 13 (1792), 530.

16 Mary Wollstonecraft, *Vindication of the Rights of Woman* (1792), ed. Carol H. Poston (New York: Norton, 1988), p. 22; ed. Miriam Brody Kramnick (Harmondsworth: Penguin Books, 1978), p. 103. John Gregory's conduct book, *A Father's Legacy to his Daughters* (1774) went through numerous editions.

17 See R. M. Janes, 'On the Reception of Mary Wollstonecraft's *A Vindication of the Rights of Woman*', *Journal of the History of Ideas*, 39 (1978), 293–302 (p. 294), which also quotes from the contemporary reviews in the *Analytical Review*. (Janes's essay is reprinted in Wollstonecraft, *Rights of Woman*, ed. Poston, pp. 297–307.)

18 Wollstonecraft, *Rights of Woman*, ed. Poston, p. 145; ed. Kramnick, pp. 257–8.

19 For further discussion of this ambiguity in Wollstonecraft, see ch. 4, pp. 104–5.

CHAPTER 2

Eighteenth-century femininity: 'a supposed sexual character'

Harriet Guest

Femininity is a term freighted with a critical history. It was used particularly in feminist literary criticism of the 1970s and early 1980s to refer
to the cultural construction of gender difference – so, for example, the
title of Mary Poovey's influential book *The Proper Lady and the Woman
Writer: Ideology as Style in the Works of Mary Wollstonecraft, Mary Shelley, and
Jane Austen* (1984) contrasted, first, the proper lady, whose femininity was
understood to be constructed by the expectations or impositions of men,
of culture, of ideology, with, secondly, the female – women's subjective
experience of gendered identity. Poovey's title went on immediately to
complicate that opposition: she explained in her preface that 'The
phrase "ideology as style" suggests the lived experience of cultural
values, and it reminds us that all imaginative activity is part of that experience.'[1] Immediately, she suggests, the feminine and female must be
bound up in one another, perhaps not inextricably, but certainly to an
extent that indicates that the experience of being female must itself be
acculturated, cannot take place in some cultural vacuum of pure subjectivity. The title of Vivien Jones's invaluable anthology, *Women in the
Eighteenth Century: Constructions of Femininity* (1990), suggests a more ambiguous relation of contrast and/or identity between the categories of
women and femininity, as her introduction confirms. She explains there
that the anthology does not claim

to provide a documentary account of women's 'real experience' in the period.
Apart from the obvious impossibility of ever fully knowing 'women' in any
period, its subject is written culture, and its concern . . . is with representation,
with 'women' as a culturally defined category which women had to negotiate
and to suffer.[2]

Here that distance between the proper lady and the woman writer is to
some extent reintroduced by the distinction between 'women' represented and categorised, and women who are the active agents of

suffering and negotiation. But that rather slippery distinction is useful to Jones's argument that constructions of femininity need to be thought of with the gendering of discourses which may not be directly concerned with the representation of men and women. It creates an elusive distinction which makes it possible to think about the processes of feminisation perceived to be involved in the increasing cultural dominance of middle-class and commercial values in the century, while recognising that the languages of femininity appropriate to women might follow divergent trajectories, shaped by but distinguishable from those processes of feminisation.

The idea of femininity, then, begins to emerge as enormously complex. Gender difference seems a fundamental category of eighteenth-century forms of thought, shaping and shaped by the complex network of discursive differentiations and convergences that makes up the cultural texture of the period. Perhaps when we first begin to look at eighteenth-century representations of women we are struck by their similarities, by the continuities between the ideas of femininity they express. Both Mary Astell, writing in the 1690s and 1700s, and Mary Wollstonecraft, writing in the 1790s, seem to find it necessary to the authority of their own feminine voice to reject and deny a form of femininity that is constituted in the mutability of fashion, in the desire for and identification with short-term material or physical gratifications. But whereas Astell opposes that rejected femininity to an ideal of religious retirement, Wollstonecraft contrasts it with the independence that results from gainful employment. In the early century, virtuous femininity is often identified in privacy, and in freedom from all but pious desires and ambitions, but by the end of the century virtue is identified more closely with industriousness, which can involve the demand that middle-class women should participate in or at least mimic the forms of productive labour. Through careful consideration of the historical and cultural discourses of the feminine in which particular representations of femininity are embedded, the discursive logic of both the similarities, and the differences, between the two writers begins to come into focus.

The best way to examine this complex discursive logic is through analyses of particular examples. In this essay, I have chosen to focus on some of the issues raised by the work of Anna Laetitia Barbauld across the last four decades of the century, in order to illuminate the usefulness of the category of the feminine as a way of thinking about women's writing and its reception.

FEMININITY, POLITICS, DOMESTICITY

In her *Vindication of the Rights of Woman* of 1792, Mary Wollstonecraft wrote of the 'false system of female manners' which, she argued, 'robs the whole sex of its dignity, and classes the brown and fair with the smiling flowers that only adorn the land'. She remarked that the evaluation of women as merely ornamental 'has ever been the language of men, and the fear of departing from a supposed sexual character, has made even women of superiour sense adopt the same sentiments'. In a footnote, she identifies the woman of 'superiour sense' as Anna Laetitia Barbauld, and quotes in full Barbauld's poem 'To a Lady, with some painted flowers', emphasising and underscoring what she finds most offensive in its 'ignoble comparison' between women and flowers:

> *Flowers, the sole luxury which nature knew,*
> In Eden's pure and guiltless garden grew.
> *To loftier forms are rougher tasks assign'd;*
> *The sheltering oak resists the stormy wind,*
> *The tougher yew repels invading foes,*
> *And the tall pine for future navies grows;*
> *But this soft family, to cares unknown,*
> *Were born for pleasure and delight* ALONE.
> Gay without toil, and lovely without art,
> *They spring to* CHEER *the sense, and* GLAD *the heart.*
> Nor blush, my fair, to own you copy these;
> *Your* BEST, *your* SWEETEST *empire is* – TO PLEASE.[3]

What seems to add fuel to Wollstonecraft's indignation is her admiration for Barbauld as an educationalist and a poet. Barbauld was the daughter of a schoolmaster who taught from 1758 at the Dissenting academy at Warrington, in the north-west of England, originally established to educate Protestants excluded because of their religion from Anglican grammar schools and universities. With her husband she ran a school for boys, and later taught small numbers of male and female pupils independently. Her various publications for children were widely admired for the educational theory they implied.[4]

Wollstonecraft accuses Barbauld of adopting a masquerade of femininity, a disguise that conforms to the 'supposed sexual character' that the language of men creates. To the political opponents of both women, however, Barbauld's pamphlets of the early 1790s defending the revolution in France and its basis in universal natural right seemed to mark precisely her departure from that sexual character, and to characterise her as one of the '*Unsex'd Females*' closest to Wollstonecraft. Horace Walpole, for example, depicted the 'Amazonian allies' of those who attacked Burke's *Reflections on the Revolution in France* as 'headed by Kate Macaulay and the virago Barbauld, whom Mr Burke calls our *Poissardes* [fishwives]'.[5] He told Hannah More that he would never read Barbauld's poetry because 'I cannot forgive the heart of a woman . . . that curses our clergy and feels for negroes.'[6] Walpole alludes to Barbauld's published contributions to the campaigns in 1790 for the repeal of the Corporation and Test Acts which excluded Dissenters from public office, and in 1791 for the bill for abolishing the slave trade. Her support for these causes is characterised by Walpole as unfeminine, inappropriate to the 'heart of a woman', and her response to the *Reflections* associates her and the radical historian Catharine Macaulay, for both Walpole and Burke, with the 'Thracian orgies' of 'the vilest of women' in revolutionary France.[7]

It was not only Barbauld's political activities of the early 1790s which were seen to transgress the 'false system' on which feminine identity depended. The lines Wollstonecraft found so objectionable appeared in Barbauld's *Poems* (1792), but first appeared in the very successful collection of her verse published in 1773. The *Monthly Review* praised the *Poems* of 1773, but thought that she should have 'taken her views of human life from among her female companions, & not altogether under the direction of men, either living or dead'. In contrast to Wollstonecraft's later strictures, this reviewer implied that it was 'the direction of men' that had caused Barbauld to neglect the appropriate sexual character, and to forget that 'There is a sex in minds as well as in bodies.' He is disappointed with Barbauld's work because 'We hoped the *Woman* was going to appear; & that while we admired the genius & learning of her graver compositions, we should be affected by the sensibility & passion of the softer pieces.'[8] The reviewer of the *Poems* of 1773 was disappointed by the absence of feminine sensibility and passion; by Barbauld's failure to display something very close to the 'sexual character' that Wollstonecraft deplored in her poetry. For all these various responses to Barbauld's work it is the gendered character of her writing that is at issue: her willingness or failure to appear properly feminine is the central focus of their criticism.

The character of femininity is central to much of Barbauld's writing, and perhaps most contentiously in 'The Rights of Woman', which she may have written in response to Wollstonecraft's criticisms in 1792, though the poem was first published in the posthumous collected *Works* of 1825. The poem echoes the lines Wollstonecraft found so ignoble in revisiting the theme of woman's 'sweetest empire'. It begins in what are, in the context of Walpole's remarks about 'Amazonian allies', strikingly aggressive and militaristic terms:

> Yes, injured Woman! rise, assert thy right!
> Woman, too long degraded, scorned, opprest;
> O born to rule in partial Law's despite,
> Resume thy native empire o'er the breast!
>
> Go forth arrayed in panoply divine;
> That angel pureness which admits no stain;
> Go, bid proud Man his boasted rule resign,
> And kiss the golden sceptre of thy reign.
>
> Go, gird thyself with grace; collect thy store
> Of bright artillery glancing from afar;
> Soft melting tones thy thundering cannon's roar,
> Blushes and fears thy magazine of war.[9]

The lines employ courtly conventions of gallantry of the kind, for example, that Pope had mocked in his portrayal of 'the fierce Virago' Thalestris, in *The Rape of the Lock* (1714), who scatters metaphorical death 'from both her Eyes'.[10] But those conventions have a more ambivalent resonance coming from the pen of 'the virago Barbauld'; an ambivalence that might be traced here to that notion of women 'born to rule in partial Law's despite'. Women might claim 'native empire o'er the breast' either because both they and the emotions of the breast are ignored by the law, treated by it only with contempt or despite, or because they act in defiant opposition to the law, in despite of it. The second possibility, that what women do is somehow a defiant claim to native rights that should be universal, but that the partiality of the law denies to all but a few, seems to animate the militaristic language of the following stanzas with an energy incongruous with conventions of gallantry.

In the earlier poem that Wollstonecraft so disliked there was a clear contrast between the 'sweetest empire' of feminine softness and leisure, and the 'rougher tasks' of national defence against 'invading foes', and perhaps of imperial expansion by 'future navies'.[11] In this later poem that division is blurred. Barbauld writes in the fourth stanza: 'Thy rights are empire: urge no meaner claim', but the boldness of this imperative is qualified when the rights of women are compared with the 'sacred mysteries' of ancient Greece, which 'Shunning discussion, are revered the most'. The poem goes on to suggest that women may command men as their 'imperial foe', but then discusses the sense in which relations between imperial conqueror and slave, idol and worshipper, must always be mutually contaminating, must always imply the interchangeability of those positions, in terms familiar from discussions of idolatry and empire in a range of eighteenth-century texts, including some of Barbauld's own.[12] The language of idolatry, and the reference to pagan mysteries, work to suggest that the dominance of women can only be that of illusion, of frail fiction. The poem concludes with the notion that when women find themselves, as a result of achieving dominance, both 'Subduing and subdued', they will abandon their claim to rights:

> Then, then, abandon each ambitious thought,
> Conquest or rule thy heart shall feebly move,
> In Nature's school, by her soft maxims taught,
> That separate rights are lost in mutual love. (lines 29–32)

Women are rather ambiguously predicted or conjured to abandon the inequality and struggle implicit in the notion of 'separate rights' in favour of the promised equality of 'mutual love'. The final lines suggest that domestic bliss offers a haven from the condition in which women have been 'too long degraded, scorned, opprest' (line 2).

Barbauld's 'Rights of Woman' is, I think, a troubling text because its use of the language of rights seems to pull it in a different direction to its conclusion, and to emphasise a kind of violence in the language at odds with the praise of mutual love. For G. J. Barker-Benfield, the poem is best understood as a 'rejection of politics . . . repudiating the case Wollstonecraft made against such cultural segregation' in favour of the claims of feminine sensibility. He argues that: 'Barbauld directly restates the "SWEETEST empire" that Wollstonecraft had just challenged.'[13] But he does not discuss the relation between this rejection of political involvement for women and Barbauld's own political activities in the 1790s. The editors of the admirable 1994 edition of Barbauld's *Poems* argue that though 'Revolutionary rhetoric and ideals inform much' of Barbauld's poetry, here the use of that rhetoric is 'ironic as she opposes what she sees as Wollstonecraft's declared war with the male sex'. Later they note that the poem 'need not be read as representing [Barbauld's] considered judgement on women's rights; rather, it is an outburst of anger at Wollstonecraft'.[14] These remarks indicate the difficulty of assessing the relation between Barbauld's opinions on politics and on domesticity, suggesting that if we take her views on mutual love seriously, then we must perceive her political language as ironic, or indeed as a rejected system of value. They seem to be based in the assumption that the final lines of the poem must be understood to indicate that the idea of femininity – perhaps of feminism – that might articulate the language of natural right is incompatible with the more sentimental femininity that abandons ambition for 'mutual love'.

The 'Rights of Woman' does not, however, represent a departure from Barbauld's earlier views on the value of women's contribution to domesticity. From her earliest publications of poems and essays Barbauld had articulated the public language of politics in, for example, the unambiguous classical republicanism of her poem *Corsica*, written in 1769, alongside poems to women which praised a characteristically 'soft' and domestic femininity. In an early essay of 1773, for example, Barbauld alludes to women as 'that part of the species who are formed to shine in families and sweeten society'.[15] When, in the 1770s, it was suggested that Barbauld should establish a college for young ladies, she refused. She argued that though she had 'stepped out of the bounds of female reserve in becoming an author . . . My situation has been peculiar, and would be no rule to others.' She thought that a regular course of instruction could not improve the situation of women while they were 'subject to a regulation like that of the ancient Spartans', under which 'thefts of knowledge in our sex are only connived at while carefully concealed, and if displayed, punished with disgrace'. Middle-class women, she suggested, would be best occupied in learning to become 'good wives or agreeable companions'.[16] But this notion of women's domestic duty may not imply the kind of choice between different kinds of femininity, between sensibility and politics, that Barker-Benfield's discussion suggests. Mary Hays, the friend and advocate for the views of Wollstonecraft, notes with approval in 1793 that her friend, the radical George Dyer, includes Barbauld among the list of 'respectable names' of those women who, as a result of their experience of oppression, feel 'a generous indignation; which when turned against the exclusive claims of the other sex, is favourable to female pretensions; when turned against the tyranny of government, . . . is commonly favourable to the rights of both sexes'.[17] For Hays and Dyer, and indeed for those hostile to Barbauld's politics, her views on feminine domesticity do not seem at odds with her role as a political pamphleteer and campaigner.

PUBLIC AND PRIVATE VIRTUES

Throughout her career, Barbauld seems to have been strongly committed to the belief that men and women should occupy different social stations, and cultivate the gendered characteristics appropriate to them. In an early poem, 'To Dr Aikin on his Complaining that she neglected him, October 20th 1768', she reassures her brother of her constant affection through an account of their personal histories.[18] At first, gender difference was not a factor in their relationship:

> The first warm impulse which our breasts did move,
> 'Twas sympathy, before we knew to love.
> As hand in hand with innocence we stray'd
> Embosom'd deep in Kibworth's tufted shade;
> Where both encircled in one household band,
> And both obedient to one mild command,
> Life's first fair dawn with transport we beheld (lines 19–25)

She and her brother were 'like two scions on one stem' (line 27), and it seems a measure of the unity, the at-one-ness that these lines repeatedly emphasise, that the 'first . . . impulse' between them should be sympathy, which depends on similarity, rather than love, which implies a greater degree of individual distinction. The poem goes on to argue that in continuation of that shared impulse they are now 'By stronger ties endear'd' (line 33) although gender difference does separate them:

> Our path divides – to thee fair fate assign'd
> The nobler labours of a manly mind:
> While mine, more humble works, and lower cares,
> Less shining toils, and meaner praises shares. (lines 49–52)

A gendered division of labour allocates professional ambition exclusively to the 'manly mind', and briefly the poet chafes against this division:

> Yet sure in different moulds they were not cast
> Nor stampt with separate sentiments and taste.
> But hush my heart! nor strive to soar too high,
> Nor for the tree of knowledge vainly sigh;
> Check the fond love of science and of fame,
> A bright, but ah! a too devouring flame.
> Content remain within thy bounded sphere,
> For fancy blooms, the virtues flourish there. (lines 54–61)

Barbauld encourages herself to accept the constraints of gender, and achieve contentment 'within thy bounded sphere'. But this is not necessarily an act of self-effacement or self-abasement. The assertion that their minds were not cast in 'different moulds' remains unchallenged, and she goes on to prophesy that her brother's future success in the medical profession will result from his capacity to display sentiments

usually characterised as feminine. She advises that he should: 'Join to
the sage advice, the tender sigh; / And to the healing hand the pitying
eye', arguing that 'cordial looks' and 'words of balm' will work 'when
drugs would fail' (lines 78–9, 81–2). The reference to the 'tree of knowledge' may also suggest that his professional labours involve a kind of
fall from the prelapsarian innocence of their undifferentiated childhood, and that the 'virtues flourish' in the 'bounded sphere' appropriate to feminine works because they are not understood to involve
specialised ambitions.

The poem suggests that though Barbauld and her brother pursue
paths divided by gender difference, their common upbringing and similarities of mind have forged 'stronger ties' between them. This is
repeated in the concluding discussion of their writing: 'both our breasts
at once the Muses fir'd, / With equal love, but not alike inspir'd' (lines
90–2). Their writings are also differentiated by the gendering of genres,
but their love of the liberal arts is equal. This emphasis on a primary
and undifferentiated equality may imply that gender difference, or at
least the inequality it implies, is largely an effect of the ability of the
brother to choose a professional specialism, a choice that is represented
as a decree of fate which determines that brother and sister shall no
longer pursue the 'same studies' (line 49). Barbauld herself, though she
had to 'Check the fond love of science and of fame' (line 58), participated in the culture of middle-class liberal Whiggery and religious
Dissent. Clearly, she valued professionalism, and was modest about
claiming professional status for her own 'humble works' as a teacher and
a writer of educational books as well as poetry and political pamphlets.
She seems in this poem to accept the divergence between masculine professionalism and the 'bounded sphere' of femininity, but to see that
divergence as secondary or supplementary to a primary equality of
inspiration and capacity.

Barbauld wrote a number of poems to and about women, who are
usually named only in her autograph copies. Most of these are short
'Characters', which praise the women as exemplary figures for demonstrating the qualities and performing the duties appropriate to their
'bounded sphere': she praises them for rearing their children, caring for
the elderly or sick, for piety, and of course for 'that most useful science,
how to please'.[19] In an early 'character' poem, the subject's domestic
virtues are described in an extended comparison with those of 'The
mighty mothers of immortal Rome'. Barbauld writes of the Roman
Matrons that:

> Obscure, in sober dignity retir'd
> They more deserved, than sought to be admir'd:
> The household virtues o'er their honour'd head
> Their simple grace, and modest lustre shed;
> Chaste their attire, their feet unus'd to roam[,]
> They lov'd the sacred threshold of their home,[20]

Barbauld's account alludes to the women of pre-imperial Rome, who represented for many enlightenment theorists an ideal model of familial domesticity. In, for example, William Russell's *Essay on the Character, Manners, and Genius of Women in different ages*, these matrons are credited with all the simplicity and virtue that Roman women were so conspicuously perceived to lack as a symptom or cause of the decline and corruption of imperial Rome. He explains that 'In the infancy of the city, and even till the conquest of Carthage', Roman women lived

shut up in their houses, where a simple and rustic virtue paid everything to instinct, and nothing to elegance; so nearly allied to barbarism, as only to know what it was to be wives and mothers; chaste, without apprehending that they could be otherwise; tender and affectionate, before they had learned the meaning of the words; occupied in duties, and ignorant that there were other pleasures, they spent their lives in retirement, in nursing their children, and in rearing to the republic a race of labourers and of soldiers.[21]

Russell's account is much more concerned than are Barbauld's lines to emphasise that the progress of civilisation is an affair of swings and roundabouts; for it is important to his thesis that: 'in all countries, in proportion as the love of virtue diminishes, we find the value of talents to increase' (I, 59). His account of the virtues of domesticity remains ambivalent about the relation between the admirable simplicity and contemptible barbarism that the lives of Roman women demonstrate. But what he does find praiseworthy is that: 'To these austere manners the Roman women joined an enthusiastic love of their country, which discovered itself upon many great occasions' (I, 53). It is this capacity for patriotism that Barbauld turns to in the second half of her 'Character':

> Yet, true to glory, fan'd the generous flame,
> Bade lovers, brothers, sons aspire to fame;
> In the young bosom cherish'd virtue's seed,
> The secret springs of many a godlike deed!
> So the fair stream in some sequester'd glade,
> With lowly state glides silent through the shade,
> Yet by the smiling meads her urn is blest;

With freshest flowers her rising banks are drest;
And groves of laurel, by her sweetness fed,
High o'er the forest lift their verdant head[.] (lines 11–20)

That 'Yet' of course is teasing – do the 'mighty mothers' contribute to
the laurels of Rome despite or because of their domestic confinement?
The poem sustains a degree of ambiguity about the relation between
their 'household virtues' and the virtues they nurture in the young
bosom.

This 'Character' might seem to describe a fairly innocuous idea of the
influence of domestic women – the kind of idea that enforces the
confinement of domesticity by insisting on its ability to wield secret and
indirect power. Russell's emphasis on the notion that the domesticity of
Roman matrons depended on their ignorance, that it involved the display
of instinctive or negative virtues, might seem to point in this direction.
But the ideal of the Roman matron had a rather different resonance in
a Whiggish and Dissenting context. James Fordyce, the fashionable pres-
byterian preacher Wollstonecraft condemned for using 'artful flattery
and sexual compliments' to cajole his female reader into becoming 'a
house slave',[22] rejected the example of the Roman matron in terms that
may illuminate the way Barbauld's *Poems* of 1773 were reviewed:

The virtues of a Roman Matron, in the better times of that republic, appear on
some accounts to have been greatly respectable. They are such as might be
looked for, from her education amongst a people where ideas of prowess, patriotism, and glory, ran high; where, in effect, these things were regarded as the
summit of human excellence and felicity. But . . . it is manifest to me, that whatever force or grandeur the female mind might in other views derive from them,
such advantage was overbalanced by the loss or the diminution of that gentleness and softness, which ever were, and ever will be, the sovereign charm of the
female character.[23]

A confirmation of Fordyce's fears that women will gain force, grandeur,
and indeed virtue at the expense of the more compliant and impression-
able characteristics of femininity might be seen in the decision of the
radical Whig Catharine Macaulay to use an engraving of herself as a
Roman matron as the frontispiece to the third volume of her *History of
England* (1767). Macaulay's work was widely perceived, by both its admir-
ers and its detractors, to display a masculine or at least defeminised
strength of mind, and a degree of political conviction apparently incompatible with 'gentleness and softness'. She was, Wollstonecraft commented, 'an example of intellectual acquirements supposed to be
incompatible with the weakness of her sex'.[24]

In Barbauld's own writing, the notion that women must limit their

Figure 1 Engraving of Catharine Macaulay as a Roman matron, by G. B. Cipriani after J. Basire. Frontispiece to vol. III of her *History of England* (1767).

ambitions to a more bounded sphere than that available to middle-class men is not understood to preclude the notion that women have public identities and responsibilities. In 1792, Barbauld published a pamphlet of *Remarks on Mr. Gilbert Wakefield's Enquiry into the expediency and propriety of Public or Social Worship*. She argued that:

Public worship is a civic meeting. The temple is the only place where human beings, of every rank and sex and age, meet together for one common purpose, and join together in one common act. Other meetings are either political, or formed for the purposes of splendour and amusement; from both which, in this country, the bulk of inhabitants are of necessity excluded.

Figure 2 Anna Laetitia Barbauld as a Roman matron. Modern cameo cast from the mould produced by Wedgwood in 1775 (no eighteenth-century cameos are known to survive). Reproduced by permission of the Trustees of the Wedgwood Museum, Barlaston, Staffordshire, England.

The argument of the essay is intriguing, because though it is here conducted in terms of the notion that the public, civic business of collective religion can be distinguished from a political assembly, the argument is thoroughly and unambiguously politicised. Barbauld writes that this is 'the only place where man meets man not only as an equal but a brother; and where, by contemplating his duties, he may become sensible of his rights'. She alludes here to the revolutionary principles of liberty, equality and fraternity, and to the slogan of the movement for the abolition of the slave trade: 'Am I not a man and a brother', and confirms those references in characterising this as 'The age which has demolished dungeons, rejected torture, and given so fair a prospect of abolishing the iniquity of the slave-trade.' She explains rather cautiously that the worshipper 'learns philosophy without its pride, and a spirit of liberty without its turbulence'. But in the next sentence she expands on the nature of that philosophy and liberty in terms that also explain the need for caution: 'Every time Social Worship is celebrated, it includes a virtual declaration of the rights of man.'[25]

In the pamphlets she published in the 1790s Barbauld repeatedly emphasises the inclusiveness of her conceptions of the civic, public, and national, but she very rarely explicitly mentions gender as a factor in these arguments. The pamphlet on public worship is unusually direct in its statement that the congregation assembled for this 'virtual declaration of the rights of man' acquires the civic character that lends weight to this declaration because it includes 'human beings, of every rank and sex and age'. But in other pamphlets of the 1790s, she seems at least to imply the presence of women in her conception of the public. So, for example, in the second of her *Civic Sermons to the People* (1792), she represents the relation between the family and state in terms of the analogy of the stream that she had sketched in her earlier 'Character' poem. She explains that the 'first society is called a Family', and argues that 'It is the root of every other society. It is the beginning of order, and kind affections, and mutual helpfulness and provident regulations. If this spring be pure, what proceeds from it will be pure: if it be polluted, the broader waters will be discoloured.' She emphasises that the citizens she addresses must 'Love your Country' not only because of its associations with 'early pleasures, and tender recollections' but because of their voluntary contributions to it: 'because it includes every other object of love, because it unites all separate energies into one energy; all separate wills into one will; and having united and declared them, calls it Law'. The idea of the nation, she argues, is bound into everyday life, however private or 'obscure': 'Love then this Country; unite its idea with your domestic comforts . . . remember that each of you, however inconsiderable, is benefited by your Country; so your Country, however extensive, is benefited by every one of the least of you.' The argument emphasises that what seems most private, domestic and feminine is bound up with what is most public and perhaps masculine, and that every citizen, however weak and defenceless they may seem, has a right to a say in how government is conducted, 'for the plain reason, that all have an equal desire to be happy, and an equal right to be so'.[26]

The theme that Barbauld's essays of the 1790s repeatedly return to is that of the constitution of the public as a religious, civic, and national body, and she is always concerned to emphasise the continuity between the rights of private individuals and of the public in terms that implicitly include women. Barbauld's pamphlets of the 1790s are radical in their insistence that every individual participates in the national political identity, though their lives may be as private as those of the matrons of ancient Rome, and in their implication or assumption that the rights claimed for men are also those of women.

DISCOURSES OF FEMININITY

Barbauld's writing and its reception raise some important questions about the nature of femininity, and how we go about identifying gendered language in eighteenth-century texts. In order to understand how Barbauld's writing could suggest to her contemporaries that she was, on the one hand, a dangerously radical virago, and on the other, a timid creature, complicit in robbing 'the whole sex of its dignity' because of her 'fear of departing from a supposed sexual character' acceptable to men, we need to consider the historical specificity of her writing – the differences between the 1770s and the 1790s, her politics and the implications of the political discourses articulated in her writing, and the changing cultural status and meaning of the 'bounded sphere' she regards as appropriate to women. When Barbauld first published her poetry and essays in the 1760s and 1770s, her writing seemed clearly 'very different from that of other "Daughters of the Nine"' [Muses] in its 'justness of thought & vigour of imagination'. The reviewer commented that 'A woman is as perfect in her kind as a man: she appears inferior only when she quits her station, & aims at excellence out of her province.' Barbauld appeared to be differentiated from the ideal woman writer, imperfect in her femininity, not because 'softer pieces' were absent from her collection, or because she could write with masculine justness and vigour on Corsican republicanism, but because in some sense both the 'graver compositions' *and* the 'softer pieces' were 'out of her province': they avoided 'the subject of Love' and the 'particular distress of some female situations'. Denise Riley remarks that the historical category of the feminine is understood as 'Intimate, particular, familial, pre-rational, extra-civic, soaked in its sexual being'.[27] The absence of the last quality, that saturation in sexuality, in Barbauld's early writing, seems to change the context and orientation, as it were, of the others, so that though she praises the familial, particular, and domestic virtues of women, those qualities seem here to be perceived to extend out of their restrictively feminine province, and perhaps to carry the implications of equality that her poem to her brother articulated, and that her 'Character' poem identified as the source of a distinctively whiggish notion of civic and classically republican virtue.

In *Equivocal Beings: Politics, Gender, and Sentimentality in the 1790s*, Claudia Johnson argues that: 'While the practice of male sentimentality . . . requires the hyperfeminization of women in order to sustain the possibility of sexual differentiation, Wollstonecraft seems to advocate a converse asymmetry, whereby men's hypermasculinity is required to guarantee and ensure the possibility of female rationality.'[28] In these terms it might be argued that, in the early poem to her brother, Barbauld represents a kind of feminised and sentimentalised masculinity as necessary to her brother's success as a doctor: his bedside manner requires him to display qualities of tenderness and perceptive insight, and in order to 'sustain the possibility of sexual differentiation', Barbauld should emphasise the limitations of her own bounded sphere, and represent herself as 'hyper-feminised' or, to combine Riley's terms with Wollstonecraft's, soaked in her 'sexual character'. The poem does contrast her contentment to his ambition, but it seems more concerned to emphasise their similarity, their shared sentiments and primary equality of mind.

In the 1770s, Barbauld's poetry could seem to venture beyond the proper province of femininity because it failed in Johnson's terms to hyperfeminise women, to emphasise the 'particular distress' of the sentimental victim/heroine. It was also, however, perceived – and celebrated – as the exemplary product of one of the learned women whose achievements confirmed the cultural superiority of the British nation, and it could, in this context, seem to demonstrate a femininity whose

exceptional ventures were licensed by the demands of international cultural competition.[29] I have suggested that in the 1790s Barbauld argues
for a relation between the individual and the state that does not distinguish between the civic identities of enfranchised and disenfranchised
men, or men and women, and that emphasises the continuity between
private domestic ties and love of country. But by this time the gendered
distinctions and in particular the definition of feminine domesticity that
Barbauld had employed in the poetry she had first published in 1773 had
taken on a new significance. In the poem 'To a Lady, with some painted
flowers', the reference to 'Eden's pure and guiltless garden' might again
point to a notion of primary equality, but if it does, that seems obscured
by the contrast between the feminised empire of pleasing and the masculine empire of 'rougher tasks'.

In Wollstonecraft's *Vindication of the Rights of Woman* of 1792, the idea
of prelapsarian innocence, which seems important to the positive value
of femininity in Barbauld's poetry, has become a negative quality associated with the 'supposed sexual character' she rejects. She writes, for
example, of the 'deplorable state' of women:

in order to preserve their innocence, as ignorance is courteously termed, truth
is hidden from them, and they are made to assume an artificial character before
their faculties have acquired any strength. Taught from their infancy that
beauty is woman's sceptre, the mind shapes itself to the body, and, roaming
round its gilt cage, only seeks to adorn its prison. Men have various employments and pursuits which engage their attention, and give a character to the
opening mind; but women, confined to one, and having their thoughts constantly directed to the most insignificant part of themselves, seldom extend their
views beyond the triumph of the hour.[30]

Innocence here confines women to an 'artificial character' incapable of
extending its interests or ambitions beyond physical needs and desires; it
is the excuse for denying them the 'various employments and pursuits'
of men. In Maria Edgeworth's *Letters for Literary Ladies* (1795), the gentleman who puts the case against the education of women argues, similarly,
that the character of femininity depends on ignorance or innocence:

we mix with the world without restraint, we converse freely with all classes of
people, with men of wit, of science, of learning, with the artist, the mechanic,
the labourer; every scene of life is open to our view . . . we see things as they
are; but women must always see things through a veil, or cease to be women.[31]

For Wollstonecraft, the ignorance of women is specifically the result of
their confinement to the single employment or pursuit of marriage, and
she argues that:

If marriage be the cement of society, mankind should all be educated after the same model, or the intercourse of the sexes will never deserve the name of fellowship, nor will women ever fulfil the peculiar duties of their sex, till they become enlightened citizens, till they become free by being enabled to earn their own subsistence, independent of men; in the same manner, I mean . . . as one man is independent of another.[32]

Wollstonecraft's argument identifies citizenship with economic independence as a result of employment, and suggests that these identities are the forms of knowledge or experience necessary to produce women capable of fulfilling 'the peculiar duties of their sex', as opposed to the artificial feminine character that is enslaved and made redundant by its ignorance.

Barbauld's writing does not suggest, however, that she understood citizenship to be identical with earned financial independence, or that she perceived innocence necessarily as a condition of ignorance. In Maria Edgeworth's *Letters for Literary Ladies*, the second correspondent, who defends women's right to learning, argues that the domestic confinement of women is the most favourable condition for knowledge. He argues that for men:

In many professions the understanding is but partially cultivated; and general literature must be neglected by those who are occupied in earning bread or amassing riches for their family . . . The other sex have no such constraint upon their understandings; neither the necessity of earning their bread, nor the ambition to shine in public affairs, hurry or prejudice their minds: in domestic life they have leisure to be wise.

He suggests that domestic life puts women in a position to cultivate the kind of comprehensive and disinterested views that characterise liberal independence of mind, and that men, devoted to the specialised pursuit of their division of labour, cannot acquire. He argues that when men recognise that:

they can meet with conversation suited to their taste at home, they will not be driven to clubs for companions; they will invite the men of wit and science of their acquaintance to their own houses, instead of appointing some place of meeting from which ladies are to be excluded. This mixture of the talents and knowledge of both sexes must be advantageous to the interests of society, by increasing domestic happiness. – Private *virtues* are public benefits: if each bee were content in his cell, there could be no grumbling hive; and if each cell were complete, the whole fabric must be perfect.[33]

He suggests that domestic space will become the site where women and men can converse without 'constraint upon their understandings', and where they will 'see things as they are' undistorted by the occupational interests that 'hurry or prejudice their minds'. He concludes rather vaguely that when domesticity has become the site for a kind of ideal and disinterested public exchange, society will be reformed, for 'if each cell were complete, the whole fabric must be perfect'.

George Dyer's accounts of women involved in radical politics may suggest, in terms that are to some extent comparable to those of Edgeworth's correspondent, that women may be capable of more disinterested and liberal views because of their exclusion. His ode 'On Liberty' of 1792 is, he explains in the preface to his *Poems*, intended to praise patriotic virtue that transcends mere political differences. He writes that 'Some may smile to see . . . a duke and an impugner of dukes, a doctor of divinity and a quaker, in the same company. The author has only to say, that his respect is meant to be addressed to public spirit, and not to titles, or mere opposers of titles.' In a stanza which initially imagines Liberty inviting Tom Paine to 'rouse the languid hearts / Of Albion's sons' so that 'Britons kindle into rapture', the poet praises a collection of women whom Liberty has warmed 'With more than manly fire'. The women whom he names were all more or less closely – and notoriously – associated with radical politics, but the publications by them that he lists are not always what most obviously earns them that reputation. Dyer's lines seem to emphasise that he praises their feminine capacity for poetic sentiment as much as, or rather than, their political publications. Addressing Liberty, the 'sweet enthusiast', he claims to 'hear thee warble in Laetitia's song; / Or see thee weep in Charlotte's melting page',

and from Macaulay learn to scourge a venal age.

The feminine warbling and weeping of Barbauld and Charlotte Smith (in her *Elegiac Sonnets*) seem to the poet to indicate as clearly as had Macaulay's attacks on political corruption in her *History of England* (1763–83) that 'the most sensible females, when they turn their attention to political subjects, are more uniformly on the side of liberty than the other sex'.[34] Defending retrospectively his decision to name the women he admired for their commitment to liberty, Dyer later explained that 'the perfecting of the female understanding promotes at once the truest morals, and the best interests of society; a sentiment, that I hold with all the coldness of dispassionate inquiry, and with all the firmness of a settled belief'.[35] Dyer's comments indicate that Barbauld's political reputation as an advocate of liberty and the rights of man – the reputation that identified her as a virago – was tied to the notion that her work promoted 'the best interests of society', and was based in the more feminine qualities of her poetry, and not only in her more polemical publications.

Barbauld and Wollstonecraft had much in common in the early 1790s. Both writers employed arguments about natural rights which, I have suggested, they both perceived to involve the advancement of the rights of women; and both argued that those rights could best be exercised within the context of classically republican ideals: within a context which saw the assumption of full civic or public identity as the expression of the political rights of the individual. In Barbauld's work, for example, it is only when private individuals come together in public worship as a national or civic body that their private and 'separate rights' are forgotten in 'mutual love', in a shared sense of themselves as members of a political community. Where Barbauld and Wollstonecraft seem to diverge most sharply is on the question of femininity. In Wollstonecraft's *Vindication* of 1792 the ideal towards which women should it seems aspire is that of the professional man 'who has his eye steadily fixed on some future advantage' – an ideal which seems to involve jettisoning most of what the *Vindication* itself represented as the characteristics necessary to femininity. For Barbauld, in contrast, the feminine ideal seems much closer to the figure of the Roman matron, or the 'ideal of "republican motherhood"' which Jane Rendall has argued seemed in the late eighteenth century 'to offer a way of uniting public and private responsibilities for women'.[36] Barbauld seems to believe that women can best contribute to public life by adhering to the 'bounded sphere' of what is feminine and private; a sphere in which she suggests the 'virtues flourish' because the separate rights and professional specialisms that define middle-class masculinity are excluded. Her essays suggest that she regards this feminine space as continuous with a more extensive and comprehensive notion of the civic or national public, and indeed, as the basis for the individual's identification with that, because both come into their own when: 'The shops are shut; the artisan is summoned from his loom; and the husbandman from his plough; the whole nation, in the midst of its business, its pleasures, and its pursuits, makes a sudden stop, and wears the semblance, at least, of seriousness and concern.'[37]

Throughout Barbauld's career her notions of femininity, and the femininity of her writing, are contentious. In order to understand how or why they are so disputed we need to consider both the political position they are perceived to speak from – the subject position of the author –

and the circumstances they address; the way, for example, the image of
the Roman matron might have a quite different valence, a different set
of discursive resonances and implications, for different groups. The processes of cultural feminisation might make it possible for the arguments
of Barbauld's political essays of the 1790s to speak for universal natural
rights, because her arguments are based in the rights of private individuals, but that basis might also, I have suggested, make these arguments
distinctively feminine – and perhaps for a brief period these possibilities
are identified here. But her poetry, which is based in a similar valorisa-
tion of private virtue, could seem unambiguously feminine and even
conservative – to Wollstonecraft at least, though not to George Dyer.
Femininity in the eighteenth century is usually contentious, usually available to diverse appropriations, perhaps because it is a cluster of notions
embedded in so many diverse strands of discourse, so evasively applicable to women or to the cultural circumstances they represent.

NOTES

1 Mary Poovey, *The Proper Lady and the Woman Writer: Ideology as Style in the Works
   of Mary Wollstonecraft, Mary Shelley, and Jane Austen* (Chicago University Press,
   1984), p. xiii.
2 Vivien Jones (ed.), *Women in the Eighteenth Century: Constructions of Femininity*
   (London: Routledge, 1990), p. 6.
3 Mary Wollstonecraft, *A Vindication of the Rights of Woman*, ed. Carol H. Poston
   (New York: Norton, 1988), p. 53 and n. 7; ed. Miriam Brody Kramnick
   (Harmondsworth: Penguin Books, 1978), p. 143 and n. 5.
4 For fuller accounts of Barbauld's life see her niece Lucy Aikin's Memoir of
   her, prefixed to *The Works of Anna Laetitia Barbauld*, ed. Lucy Aikin, 2 vols.
   (London: Longman, et al., 1825); Betsy Rodgers, *Georgian Chronicle: Mrs.
   Barbauld and her Family* (London: Methuen, 1958); and the introduction to
   The Poems of Anna Letitia Barbauld, ed. William McCarthy and Elizabeth
   Kraft (Athens: University of Georgia Press, 1994). I have chosen to refer to
   Barbauld by her married name throughout this essay, though she was of
   course known as Aikin before her marriage in 1774.
5 Richard Polwhele, *The Unsex'd Females: a Poem* (London: Cadell & Davies,
   1798), extract rpt. in Jones, *Women in the Eighteenth Century*, pp. 186–91. Horace
   Walpole to Charlotte Berry, 'Strawberry Hill, Dec. 20, 1790, very late at
   night', in Lady Theresa Lewis (ed.), *Extracts from the Journals and Correspondence
   of Miss Berry, from the year 1783 to 1852*, 3 vols. (London: Longmans, 1865), I,
   268.
6 Horace Walpole, letter 2561, to Miss Hannah More, Berkeley Square, 29
   September 1791, in Peter Cunningham (ed.), *The Letters of Horace Walpole,
   Earl of Orford*, 9 vols. (London: Bohn, 1861), IX, 354.

7 Edmund Burke, *Reflections on the Revolution in France*, ed. Conor Cruise O'Brien (Harmondsworth: Penguin Books, 1982), p. 165.

8 The *Epistle to William Wilberforce, Esq. on the Rejection of the Bill for abolishing the Slave Trade* is the only additional poem in the 1792 collection. The review, by William Woodfall, is quoted in Rodgers, *Georgian Chronicle*, pp. 58–60.

9 'The Rights of Woman', *Poems* (1994), no. 90, lines 1–12.

10 Alexander Pope, *The Rape of the Lock: an heroi-comical poem in five canto's*, v, lines 37, 58, in John Butt (ed.), *The Poems of Alexander Pope. A one-volume edition of the Twickenham text* (London: Methuen, 1963), pp. 238, 239.

11 'To a Lady, with some painted Flowers', *Poems* (1994), no. 55, lines 18, 9, 11, 12.

12 'Rights', lines 13, 15, 16, 18. See, for example, Barbauld's *Epistle to Wilberforce*, and for further discussion of discourses of empire, see ch. 3, below.

13 G. J. Barker-Benfield, *The Culture of Sensibility: Sex and Society in Eighteenth-Century Britain* (University of Chicago Press, 1992), pp. 222, 266.

14 *Poems* (1994), pp. xxv, 289.

15 'On Monastic Institutions', in J. and A. L. Aikin, *Miscellaneous Pieces, in prose* (London: J. Johnson, 1773), p. 115.

16 Letter to Elizabeth Montagu, quoted in Aikin's Memoir in *Works*, i, xvii–xix.

17 Mary Hays, *Letters and Essays, Moral, and Miscellaneous* (London: T. Knott, 1793), no. ii, p. 11.

18 *Poems* (1994), no. 7.

19 'Characters: [Sarah Taylor Rigby]', *Poems* (1994), no. 42, line 6.

20 [A Character of Sarah Hallowell Vaughan], *Poems* (1994), no. 14, lines 4, 5–10.

21 William Russell, *Essay on the Character, Manners, and Genius of Women in different ages. Enlarged from the French of M. Thomas*, 2 vols. (London: G. Robinson, 1773), i, 49.

22 Wollstonecraft, *Rights of Woman*, ed. Poston, pp. 94, 95; ed. Kramnick, pp. 193, 195.

23 James Fordyce, *Sermons to Young Women* (1766), 13th edn, 2 vols. (London: T. Cadell, 1809), ii, 183–4.

24 See Bridget Hill, *The Republican Virago: the Life and Times of Catharine Macaulay, Historian* (Oxford: Clarendon Press, 1992), pp. 144–5. Wollstonecraft, *Rights of Woman*, ed. Poston, p. 105; ed. Kramnick, p. 206.

25 *Remarks on Mr. Gilbert Wakefield's Enquiry into the expedience and propriety of Public or Social Worship, Works*, ii, 446, 470, 448.

26 *Civic Sermons to the People. Number II. From mutual Wants spring mutual Happiness* (London: J. Johnson, 1792), pp. 6, 21, 22, 25–6. Cf. Kathryn Sutherland's discussion of domestic and national duty in the work of Hannah More, above, pp. 40–1.

27 Woodfall, in Rodgers, *Georgian Chronicle*, pp. 58–60. Denise Riley, *'Am I that Name?': Feminism and the Category of 'Women' in History* (London: Macmillan, 1988), p. 41.

28 Claudia L. Johnson, *Equivocal Beings: Politics, Gender, and Sentimentality in the*

1790s: Wollstonecraft, Radcliffe, Burney, Austen (University of Chicago Press, 1995), p. 45.

29 See, for example, Mary Scott, *The Female Advocate; a Poem* (1774) (Augustan Reprint Society, no. 224, Los Angeles: William Andrews Clark Memorial Library, 1984).

30 Wollstonecraft, *Rights of Woman*, ed. Poston, p. 44; ed. Kramnick, p. 131.

31 Maria Edgeworth, 'Letter from a Gentleman to his friend, upon the birth of a daughter', *Letters for Literary Ladies, to which is added An Essay on the Noble Science of Self-Justification*, ed. Claire Connolly (London: Everyman, 1993), pp. 2–3. This edition reproduces the 2nd rev. edn of 1798.

32 Wollstonecraft, *Rights of Woman*, ed. Poston, p. 165; ed. Kramnick, p. 283.

33 Edgeworth, 'Answer to the Preceding Letter', *Letters for Literary Ladies*, pp. 27, 36–7.

34 George Dyer, *Poems* (London: J. Johnson, 1792), 'Preface', p. viii; Ode VII, 'On Liberty', stanza 7, and see pp. 36–7nn. Dyer praises Wollstonecraft for her *Vindication* of 1792, Ann Jebb for her political essays of the 1780s, Helen Maria Williams for *Letters from France* (probably those of 1790), and Mary Hays as 'an admirer and imitator of Mrs Charlotte Smith'. The notes also specify Smith's *Elegiac Sonnets* (1784; 6th enlarged edn 1792). Exceptionally, no particular publication by Barbauld is singled out in the notes.

35 George Dyer, *Poems* (London: J. Johnson, 1800), pp. lxvi–lxvii. Dyer noted Russell's translation of Thomas's *Essay on the Character of Women* in support of this belief (p. lxvi, n.). Only the title-page and preface of this edition of Dyer's *Poems* were published.

36 Wollstonecraft, *Rights of Woman*, ed. Poston, p. 60; ed. Kramnick, p. 151; Jane Rendall, *The Origins of Modern Feminism: Women in Britain, France and the United States 1780–1860* (London: Macmillan, 1985), p. 34.

37 [A. L. Barbauld], *Sins of the Government, Sins of the Nation; or, A Discourse for the Fast, appointed on April 19, 1793. By a Volunteer* (London: J. Johnson, 1793), p. 1.

CHAPTER 3

Women and race: 'a difference of complexion'

Felicity A. Nussbaum

The racial history of eighteenth-century England is marked at its beginning by the Royal African Company's relinquishing its monopoly over slavery, and at its conclusion by the growth of the abolition movement. In 1729 the joint opinion known as 'Yorke and Talbot' established that a slave was not guaranteed freedom by baptism nor by setting foot in the mother country, and his owner might legally insist that the slave return to the islands or the colonies. Any Englishman possessed the right to trade in black flesh. At the same time that 15,000 Negroes lived in London and many thousands of slaves were transported to the West Indies and to the American colonies, Lord Mansfield, a Chief Justice of England, finally extended the protection of habeas corpus, the requirement that a defendant appear in person before a court, to the slave James Somerset in 1772, and thus to all black people in England – though he did not extend that privilege to grant them wages or poor law relief. The actual legal status of slaves in Britain remained ambiguous since chattel slavery persisted until the official abolition of colonial slavery in 1834. As Folarin Shyllon observes, 'Although the opinion was overruled in the Somerset case by the Mansfield decree, the 1729 opinion issued at Lincoln's Inn Hall remained the slave owners' Bill of Rights and the slave hunters' charter, and made every black man, woman, or child unsafe and under imminent threat of removal by force into slavery, until Emancipation in 1834.'[1]

DISCOURSES OF RACE

Though 'race' has been described as 'one of the central conceptual inventions of modernity', David Goldberg usefully identifies the 'liberal paradox' that forms when 'modernity commits itself to idealised principles of liberty, equality and fraternity . . . [but] there is a multiplication of racial identities and the sets of exclusions that prompt and rationalise, enable and sustain' inequalities.[2] Debate persists as to whether the early versions of racism that foster these exclusions were significantly different from the scientific biological racism of later periods. Ann Laura Stoler succinctly summarises the problem: 'Some argue that racism was systematically embraced by the seventeenth century, others hold that it had not yet emerged in its consolidated, pure somatic form.' Since racial discourses of the early modern period eventually became 'the organizing grammar of an imperial order in which modernity, the civilising mission and the "measure of man" were framed',[3] were these discourses already the conceptual frameworks that dominated the eighteenth century? George L. Mosse, for example, argues that 'It was in the eighteenth century that the structure of racial thought was consolidated and determined for the next one and three-quarter centuries.'[4] Race is, of course, neither simply a biological essence nor a discursive practice. It is instead, as Michael Omi and Howard Winant have argued, *'an unstable and "decentered" complex of social meanings constantly being transformed by political struggle* . . . The crucial task . . . is to suggest how the widely disparate circumstances of individual and group racial identities, and of the racial institutions and social practices with which these identities are intertwined, are formed and transformed over time. This takes place . . . through *political contestation over racial meanings.'*[5]

   In the mid eighteenth century there was available both an essentialist racism ('race' as a series of exclusions based upon biological and behavioural traits) and the language of cultural nominalism (the recognition that classifications are simply convenient labels), which Henry Louis Gates, Jr has called 'a conceptual grammar of antiracism'.[6] I argue here that various manifestations of 'race' in language and culture coexist in the mid eighteenth century rather than solidifying into the more 'consolidated, pure somatic form' of later racial science, and that strategic confusions persist regarding the meanings assigned to skin colourings, physiognomies, nations, and their relation to interior value. Examining these contradictions at their historical formation helps us to loosen pigmentation from its ascribed racialised meanings. My claim is not of course that modern racism originates in the eighteenth century, but instead that unfamiliar hybrids of racial attitudes require us to rethink racism's genealogy and its representation in literary texts. Complexion, the topic on which I will focus, is both an aesthetic standard of beauty and value in the emerging empire, and a crux of race, gender, and class negotiation.

In an analogy common enough to eighteenth-century England, David Hume drew a comparison between a Negro and a parrot in a notoriously racist and deeply influential footnote in the 1753–4 edition of his essay, 'Of National Characters'. Hume singles out a Jamaican man of learning as an exceptional being akin to a speaking parrot; he claims that the educated Negro, like a parrot who imitates a few words, is a freakish example of an anomalous species:

Not to mention our colonies, there are NEGROE slaves dispersed all over EUROPE, of whom none ever discovered any symptoms of ingenuity; though low people, without education, will start up amongst us, and distinguish them-selves in every profession. In JAMAICA, indeed, they talk of one negroe as a man of parts and learning; but it is likely he is admired for slender accomplishments, like a parrot, who speaks a few words plainly.[7]

Similarly, in an earlier reference to parrots in Richard Steele's *Tatler* no. 245, a Black-moor servant boy first asserts his spiritual worth but then acknowledges that his value is more exactly a commercial one: 'I am as good as my Lady her self as I am a Christian, and many other Things: But for all this, the Parrot who came over with me from our Country is as much esteemed by her as I am. Besides this, the Shock-Dog has a Collar that cost almost as much as mine.'[8] In both of these examples, Hume's footnote and Steele's *Tatler*, the parrot possesses an equivalency to an African who is valued no more than a lapdog's collar, and the lines between man, commodity, and beast are blurred. The principles of dis-crimination are calibrated along a colour line (the lighter shades are superior to black) and along a hierarchy of creatures (human is superior to animal); and the lower ranges of each are assumed to be parallel. The status of the Negro as man, property, or exotic bird seems perilously uncertain, especially when we try to reconcile Hume's assertions that learned Negroes are analogous to talking parrots with the antislavery stand that he adopted elsewhere. For Hume, his claim that Negroes resemble beasts is apparently not sufficient rationale for claiming their persons as property.

Novelist and essayist Eliza Haywood also alludes to the relationship between skin colour and cognitive ability in *The Parrot* (1746), a gossipy but politically astute periodical.[9] The 'parrot', a well-travelled East Indian linguist, chats about 'whatever either the public Prints, or such private Conversation as I am let into, can furnish' (no. 1). In Haywood's rendering, however, the parrot becomes a subversive (though somewhat camouflaged) agent of both antiracism and of antislavery in an account that satirises facile connections drawn between colour and ability:

The Colour [green] I brought into the World with me, and shall never change, it seems, is an Exception against me; – some People will have it that a *Negro* might as well set up for a *Beauty*, as a *green Parrot* for a *good Speaker*, – Preposterous Assertion! As if the *Complection* of the *Body* had any Influence over the *Faculties* of the *Mind*; yet meerly on this score they resolve, right or wrong, to condemn all I say before hand.

But pray how comes it that *green* is a Colour so much disrelished in *England* at present? – Time was when it was otherwise. – Can any Arguments, drawn·from Reason, be given why *red, yellow,* or even *blue,* much less a *motley* Mixture of various Tinctures, should have the Preference? . . . I should have been wholly silent on the Occasion, if it had not reminded me how predominant this Humour is in Mankind, in relation to Things of more Consequence than the *Parrot.*

There is a Nation in the World, I won't say the English, because I have always heard it was unmannerly to expose People's Faults before their Faces; – but there is a certain Nation, who notwithstanding their Reputation and good Sense in some Things, have rendered themselves pretty remarkable for their *liking* and *disliking* to an Excess: (2 August 1746, B3–B4)

Haywood impersonates a parrot, a foreigner, who critiques England for its prejudice against parrots of colour. While in Hume's essay skin colour as a racial indicator hardens into black versus white, Haywood's periodical paper transforms the parrot into an antiracist figure whose rational capacity cannot be determined by his colour. On the other hand, the passage satirically suggests, it would be as preposterous to contend that a Negro with his dark complexion is beautiful as to assume that a parrot may be eloquent. In comically delineating the problems with greenishness, a colour against which there was some political prejudice at the time, Haywood refuses (in a point I shall return to later) to consent to the privileges of 'whiteness', or to assume that a white complexion signals rational capacities; yet at the same time *The Parrot* also elides the categories that carry real social meaning in regard to race. It's not easy being green, but even in the eighteenth century, the only beings held captive because their complexion tended towards a verdant hue were parrots.

Haywood's *Parrot* is also a response to the defeat of the Highland chieftains at Culloden, a battle that firmly established the Protestant succession, brought the end of divine right rule, and shaped Great Britain's self-definition on the brink of new wars fought in behalf of an emerging empire.[10] The years between the Battle of Culloden in 1745 and Lord Mansfield's judgement in 1772 are especially critical to the formation of a racialised national character that is linked to Protestantism even while 'race' is still a very supple category loosely applied to various populations without a necessary connection to physical traits. By the end of the Seven Years' War in 1763, Britain's stature as a free, Protestant, and commercial nation was clear, but the religions and customs of the geographical territories newly appended to England, and to England's arch-rival in the colonial endeavour, Catholic France, presented challenges to these ideas.[11] The Seven Years' War evoked a fresh national self-consciousness that was intricately connected to gender, class status, and the emerging conceptual frameworks of 'race'.[12] The measure against which an increasingly imperial England judged others was an ideal of whiteness which superceded all other differences and which came to be associated with the ruling classes.

Writing at mid century before antislavery debates began to cohere into a recognisable discourse of abolition, both Eliza Haywood and David Hume are situated in the wake of Linnaeus' first edition of *Systema Naturae* (1735) in which man is treated as being a species continuous with animals. In the much-revised tenth edition (1758), the evasive problem of complexion hovers over the text in which the primate mammals are divided into six categories of *homo sapiens:*

1. HOMO
   Sapiens. Diurnal; varying by education and situation
2. Four-footed, mute, hairy. *Wild Man.*
3. Copper-coloured, choleric, erect. *American.*
   Hair black, straight, thick; *nostrils* wide, *face* harsh; *beard* scanty; *obstinate,* content, free. *Paints* himself with fine red lines. *Regulated* by customs.
4. Fair, sanguine, brawny. *European.*
   Hair yellow; brown, flowing; *eyes* blue; *gentle,* acute, inventive. *Covered* with close vestments. *Governed* by laws.
5. Sooty, melancholy, rigid. *Asiatic.*
   Hair black; *eyes* dark; *severe* haughty, covetous. *Covered* with loose garments. *Governed* by opinions.
6. Black, phlegmatic, relaxed. *African.*
   Hair black, frizzled; *skin* silky; *Nose* flat; *lips* tumid; *crafty,* indolent, negligent. *Anoints* himself with grease. *Governed* by caprice.[13]

This version translated from the Latin in 1802 elaborates on earlier categorisations to extend the number of possible categories for discrimination beyond geographic region and skin colour to facial features, hair texture, and social organisation.

In Linnaeus' categorical distinctions the concept of 'complexion' in the mid eighteenth century combines both visible and invisible characteristics that reflect aspects of character. Residual elements of medieval and Renaissance concepts of complexion surface in Linnaeus' scheme. This framework had incorporated the entire body rather than simply the face and divided temperament into sanguine, phlegmatic, choleric, and melancholic examples.[14] Something shared by all humans, complexion, like character and 'blood', is an unstable racial identifier that may be interpreted variously as reflecting an intrinsic quality indicative of moral calibre; as restricting the range of human abilities; or, paradoxically, as a chance variation of nature with only incidental meaning.

Linnaeus' categories in *Systema Naturae* are widely cited, but their significance is much debated. Mary Pratt, for example, finds that this 'explicitly comparative' scheme serves to '"naturalise" the myth of European superiority', while Winthrop Jordan believes that there are only 'hints of ranking' and that the categories are less hierarchical than the more discriminating groupings in the Chain of Being.[15] What seems salient to me about these divisions is that the culturally weighted groupings by which race is made visible are explicitly named: skin colour, humour, and physique are primary indicators of each distinct geographic region as well as eye colour, hair texture, lip size, the absence or presence of a beard, or bodily ornamentation. It falls to interpreters then and now to interpret variously the extent to which visible features of the body and face, of biology and physiognomy, disclose faculties of the mind. 'Race' and the differences of complexion that shaded its meanings justified hierarchies even as benevolent slaveowners asserted the irrelevance of pigmentation as an index to interior qualities.

WOMEN OF COLOUR

'Blackness' in the eighteenth century was used to characterise persons from the East or West Indies, the Americas, Africa, the South Pacific, or even on occasion Ireland; it was also applied to labouring classes, especially coalminers and chimneysweepers. An elusiveness about complexion is endemic to the most compelling representations of race in the literature of the period including characters such as Crusoe's Friday, Imoinda who first appears in Aphra Behn's *Oroonoko* (1688), and Yarico in the Inkle and Yarico fables,[16] and this pervasiveness suggests, I think, that the eighteenth century is uniquely characterised by colour-shifting fictive figures. These popular characters of uncertain colour are most often women, a fact recalling Alexander Pope's line from *Epistle to A Lady* that women embodied 'Matter too soft a lasting mark to bear'.[17] Aphra Behn's Imoinda in *Oroonoko*, for example, turns from black African to blanched European in the story's dramatic version by Thomas Southerne and other eighteenth-century dramatists. Imoinda like her lover Oroonoko is characterised by Roman features incidentally located on an ebony-coloured body that frustrated white men's desire (including that of Trefry) because of her virtue: 'the beautiful *Black Venus*, to our young *Mars*; as charming in her Person as he, and of delicate Vertues'. In Southerne's popular play *Oroonoko* (1695) based on the novel and performed throughout the eighteenth century, Imoinda is white, the daughter of a white European visitor to Oroonoko's adoptive father, though Southerne was also attacked by contemporaries for failing to portray her with 'an *Indian* Air, / . . . and Indian Hue'.[18]

Instead of transmutating from African to Indian or white, Yarico, who is victimised by the Englishman Inkle, becomes African in the multiple forms her story takes throughout the century. The Yarico of Richard Ligon's *True and Exact History of the Island of Barbados* (1657) is 'of excellent shape and colour, for it was a pure bright bay', a naked reddish-brown shade usually describing horses. This colour reference is dropped from Steele's version in *The Spectator*[19] where a clothed Indian Yarico whom Inkle sells to a Barbarian Merchant is charmed by his European complexion. In *Yarico to Inkle An Epistle*, Yarico does not mention her colour, but her naked beauty transforms his pale complexion into 'native Bloom' as she tells of succumbing to his seduction. Within the poetic lines of the Countess of Hereford's *The Story of Inkle and Yarrico* (1738), the Negro Yarico inexplicably evolves into an Indian.[20] Her classical naked beauty, figured as only incidentally black, enraptures Inkle:

> A *Negro* Virgin chanc'd to pass that way;
> He view'd her naked beauties with surprise,
> Her well proportion'd limbs and sprightly eyes!
> With his complexion and gay dress amaz'd,
> The artless Nymph upon the Stranger gaz'd.[21]

At first labelled Negro but distinguished from the cannibals who eat Inkle's shipmates on the barbarous coast, Yarico turns seamlessly into an Indian maiden, apparently to merit his love and become his companion. But when another English ship reaches the shore, Inkle falls into melancholy because he has not gained a fortune. Yarico, a 'doating Virgin', becomes insufficiently distinct from '*A thousand doating maids at home*' to deserve his loyalty, and he abandons her. In George Colman's play (1787)

Yarico, 'a good comely copper' but 'quite dark' and 'Black', is a blend of Indian and Negro while her maid is African.

An equally pliable heroine is the Sable Venus who appears in a poem and engraving in Bryan Edwards's *History . . . of the . . . West Indies* (1794). The barebreasted muscular black woman with cropped curly hair is guided by winged fish who carry her from Angola to the West Indies on an open-shell chariot where she is celebrated as a colour-shifting goddess in sharp contrast to the historical fact that such a voyage was most frequently taken in the bowels of a slave ship. The poem is a variant on the Inkle and Yarico story, though the offspring resulting from the interracial union between the sable Venus and Neptune, disguised as a (white) sea captain, is revered rather than sold, murdered, or orphaned: 'Blest offspring of the warm embrace! / Fond ruler of the crisped race!'.[22] While the Sable Venus does not literally change skin colour within the poem, the naked African woman is understood to be quintessentially white but dyed black in a reversal of the familiar biblical trope of washing an Ethiop white. The goddess of love, 'a beauty clad in sable dye', is in essence a classical white goddess who playfully switches colour and takes on a dark complexion to tease and test her lover:

> Then, playful Goddess! Cease to change,
> Nor in new beauties vainly range;
> Tho' whatsoe'er thy view,
> Try ev'ry form thou canst put on,
> I'll follow thee thro' ev'ry one;
> So staunch am I, so true.

The narrator's wanton appreciation for women of various origins is perversely justified as his loyalty to the white goddess of love whose black skin is merely a disguise rather than as his promiscuous sowing of European seed upon African slave women.

Each of these women, including Imoinda, Yarico, and the Sable Venus, is represented as a kind of female noble savage, a beautiful oddity not dissimilar from Hume's Jamaican man, learned in spite of his complexion. In the case of the women, however, colour does not permeate to the core, and they may be imagined as beauties whose colour is impermanent. Proclaimed to be beautiful by some universal standard, each is sexually compromised and at some level akin to a savage, condemned by her copper, black, or saffron complexion to an irresolvable status in relation to her inherent qualities. These and other cultural fables of colour-shifting attempt to reconcile incommensurable ideas. These women and their varying complexions signal that 'Differences *within* categories . . . are underplayed in order to establish it *between* them',[23] and thus to establish the institutional racism upon which the concept of whiteness relies and according to which all women of colour possess an essential similarity.

Women of colour as they are represented in eighteenth-century England are seldom granted personhood or subjectivity, and a seemingly insurmountable difficulty in analysing women and race in eighteenth-century England is the scant testimony from the women themselves. The only extant writing by black women writers is from those who lived principally in America – Belinda's short 'Petition of an African Slave, to the Legislature of Massachusetts' (1782) and the collected poems of Phillis Wheatley[24] – and the earliest complete slave narrative written by a woman is *The History of Mary Prince, A West Indian Slave* (1831). Crucial to addressing issues of women and race in the period raised by this gap is to intuit, interrogate, and theorise this silence.[25] Yet indigenous women, as Jennifer Morgan has recognised, 'bore an enormous symbolic burden as writers from Walter Ralegh to Edward Long employed them to mark metaphorically the symbiotic boundaries of European national identities and white supremacy'.[26] Real and imagined African and Amerindian women on the edge of the known world come to stand for female transgression and as the embodiment of cultural confusions about the geography of race. As we have seen, in the eighteenth century biological markers are not yet firmly fixed to nation or physiognomy. The easy slippage from one colour to another, from one place of origin to another, may testify to an Enlightenment wish on the one hand to claim the inherent 'whiteness' of all humankind and the inadequacy of pigmentation and physiognomic traits to reveal character, and on the other, to seek the philosophical basis for a racism that would justify a slave trade, an empire, and a race-blind libertinism. Such tales imagine miscegenation but avoid grappling with its material consequences. In doing so, they reflect and perpetrate profound cultural quandaries about colour, complexion, and national origin, and the relationship of those categories to a gendered ideal of virtue culturally located in the figure of the white, middle-class Englishwoman.

WOMEN WRITING RACE: SARAH SCOTT'S *HISTORY OF SIR GEORGE ELLISON*

Englishwomen in the later eighteenth century such as Hannah More, Charlotte Smith, Mary Wollstonecraft, and Ann Yearsley contributed

significantly to the Abolition movement. They recognised powerful similarities between a tyranny based on colour and one based on sex: both
race and gender constructed barriers to rights and privileges for those
who were marginal to the emerging norms. Yet slavery and gendered
oppression were also uneasily and improbably equated, erasing crucial
differences between them.[27] In order to demonstrate the way that external indicators of 'race' fail to form a seamless unity with assumptions
about interior worth, I want to turn briefly to the example of one pivotal
text, Sarah Scott's *The History of Sir George Ellison* (1766), later revised and
condensed as *The Man of Sensibility* (1774). Written just after the Seven
Years' War, before abolition discourse begins to cohere, this ameliorist
novel, committed to gradual social and moral improvement, reflects
both the view that complexion is ephemeral and arbitrary, and that complexion explicitly indicates inherent traits. These intermixed conceptions both display and challenge what is at stake as the nation defines the
parameters of the racial and gendered complexion of British identity *vis
à vis* its colonial others.

Sir George Ellison, a novel that has aroused considerable critical interest in recent years, recounts the eponymous sentimental hero's gaining
a fortune through his marriage to a Jamaican plantation owner, his strategies for improving the institution of slavery, and his return as a widower
to England where he remarries and develops elaborate reformative programmes for abused women, the poor, prisoners, and the disabled.
Sarah Robinson Scott, sister of the 'Queen of the Bluestockings'
Elizabeth Montagu, was born into wealth, privilege, and education.
Scott engaged in philanthropic endeavours with her dear friend Lady
Barbara Montagu to assuage the conditions of the less fortunate. Scott's
manuscript letters to her sister suggest that the figure of the generous Sir
George – who also appears in her earlier feminotopia, *A Description of
Millenium Hall* (1762), a sympathetically portrayed merchant in 'sugars
and spices' – resonated in her mind with that of her philanthropic sister
Elizabeth Montagu. In a passage that has not been previously noted,
Scott draws parallels between the West Indian slaves that the fictional
Ellison owned, and the restless coalminers who worked in the pits con-
trolled by the Montagus. 'Having on some occasions a sort of enthusias-
tic warmth in my nature', Scott writes,

I can fancy that I see you among the Colliers what I made Sir George Ellison
among his Blacks; your Subjects are little inferior either in untowardness or
gloominess of complexion . . . However, I am persuaded you will find less ingratitude among colliers than among their superiors, it is the refinements of life that

give the pride of petulance which are the great sources of ingratitude, we see little of it in untaught nature; savages are won by the smallest benefits, they give their very souls in return; unaccustomed to refine away obligations, and too humble to be pained by the weight of a favour, they love their benefactor in proportion as they feel the benefit; the sensations of pleasure and affection rise together.[28]

Here Scott describes a difference of complexion, an 'untowardness or gloominess of complexion', as analogous to class distinctions, and thus something unlikely to respond to change. In her response Elizabeth Montagu judges the colliers, 'these barbarous & savage people',[29] to be as unruly and difficult to manage as slaves, yet also in an exchange of sentiment for beneficence, to be grateful to those who pay their wages. In a circle of logic that returns to the similarities between blacks and colliers, the coalworkers' lack of insolence supposedly derives from their kinship with noble savages who also naively love those who afford them creature comforts. For Montagu, even as she is empowered to a position of authority rarely achieved by an eighteenth-century woman in controlling the coal mines, to believe otherwise would destroy her economic privilege. Montagu exemplifies the way that eighteenth-century racial discourse serves, as Michel Foucault has suggested in another context, as a '"defense" of the nobility against encroachments on its privilege and sources of wealth'.[30] In the economy of philanthropy operating here, the smallest amount of payment needs to be proffered for the most substantial return in labour. Scott justifies Montagu's racist views because of her philanthropy. Racial discourse is evacuated of its assumptions of inferiority in its objects who are regarded as sweetly simple, not inhuman. For Scott, Montagu and Ellison are interchangeable privileged patriarchs who deservedly determine the fate of those who labour in their behalf.

Interested in the family's investment in Northumberland coalmines as early as the 1760s, Montagu became principally responsible for them after her husband's death in May 1775. On occasion she considered giving the colliers a feast as a perquisite:

I used to give my colliery people a feast when I came hither, but as the good souls (men and women) are very apt to get drunk, and, when drunk, very joyful, and sing, and dance, and hollow, and whoop, I dare not, on this occasion, trust their discretion to behave with proper gravity; so I content myself with killing a fat beast once a week, and sending to each family, once, a piece of meat. It will take time to get round to all my black friends. I had fifty-nine boys and girls to sup in the courtyard last night on rice pudding and boil'd beef; to-morrow night I shall have as many. It is very pleasant to see how the poor things cram themselves, and the expense is not great. We buy rice cheap, and skimmed milk and coarse beef serve the occasion. Some have more children than their labour will cloathe, and on such I shall bestow some apparel. Some benefits of this sort, and a general kind behaviour, gives to the coal-owner, as well as to them, a good deal of advantage. Our pitmen are afraid of being turned off, and that fear keeps an order and regularity amongst them that is very uncommon.[31]

The parallel to Ellison's treatment of his slaves is remarkable, and 'blackness' is here figured as a sign of labour independent of actual skin colour.

In the midst of news of the horror wrought by the French Revolution, Elizabeth Montagu celebrates in May 1792 what her sister Sarah Scott calls a 'sable Gala', an occasion when Montagu invited the London chimneysweeps to dine in her garden each May Day. The mode for discussing their 'blackness' is clearly that of a benevolent superior providing entertainment for lesser beings, though the exact nature of that inferiority is not exactly conveyed:

In the hearts of your black Guests too [the gala night] wou'd reign unmixed with ennui, or envy, or any of the malevolent & baleful passions, a happiness perhaps seldom to be found in so large a company of superior orders. One shares too in that festival the pleasure the young ones of sable receive from the sight the more for thinking it a lesson of benevolence for their hearts which may have lasting good effects, after the sport is over.[32]

As patron of the sweeps, Montagu annually diverted them from the tedium of their task in this 'fête chrétienne'. The lowly sweeps share a certain common nature with the 'black' colliers whom Montagu had characterised as savage and barbaric. Montagu's racialised language in which the colliers are untaught savages, their coal-dusted skin earning them the appellation 'blacks', is applied to the labouring classes in order to justify profit-taking, and it also elides the difference between chattel slavery and paid labour. Both Ellison and Montagu use their property to display their virtue, and gender is erased. Social rank becomes the obfuscating mask for maintaining difference without cruelty, or insisting on an inferiority here specified as 'blackness' and 'savageness', but within humanity. The 'blackness' of slaves and coalminers makes them synonymous, and class serves as a supplement to race.

According to the first edition of Samuel Johnson's *Dictionary of the English Language* (1755), race simply connotes lineage: 'a family ascending', 'a family descending', a 'generation', or 'a particular breed'.[33] In *Sir George Ellison* 'race' is a word applied with equal weight to the female sex ('a race somewhat superior to monkeys') or to webs of spiders ('Mr Ellison felt a little compunction at the thought of destroying so numerous a race').[34] Though the nuances of usage in these passages from so subtle and satirical a mind as Sarah Scott's suggest connections between gender and race in the first instance and between the animal world and race in the other, 'race' and 'complexion', like race and slavery, were not synonymous. Recent interpretations of the racial politics of *Sir George Ellison* vary in ascertaining whether Scott is making an early veiled appeal for abolition or whether she is simply engaged in amelioration. In fact, Sarah Scott when writing to her sister equivocates on taking a stand: 'I am not Politician enough to fancy I can form any proper judgement on the subject of their [West Indians'] grievances, so I hear all sides in silence, & am not at all the wiser for what either say, tho' I have friends who are very warm on each, but their warmth is not likely to make them more instructive.'[35] Some have claimed that the novel is an abolitionist one, one that encourages the education and subsequent manumission of slaves, but only by understating Sir George Ellison's economic collusion and ignoring the way that the hero's charitable impulses rely upon the spoils of slavery for funding.[36]

In the novel Ellison marries a wealthy widow in Jamaica who possesses 'a considerable plantation, cultivated by a numerous race of slaves' (p. 10). The sentimental manliness of Scott's hero pointedly contrasts to the first Mrs Ellison, whose racist attitudes about complexion seem linked to a femininity gone askew. Sir George strongly contests her views even as he displays various traditionally defined feminine characteristics. By depicting this unhappy first marriage Scott strongly resists the idea that women are inherently more sentimental than men or kinder to slaves; in fact, the opposite would seem to pertain when applied to an Englishman abroad and a Jamaican-born woman. Mrs Ellison exemplifies the special inhumanity of the trope of a plantation owner's wife who is capable of perhaps greater cruelty than her husband. Thus Ellison's economic motives seem less vicious, and Englishwomen at home, such as the second Mrs Ellison, appear in their domestic context to be appropriately sentimental without the gross sensuality of nativeborn women or the cruelty of Englishwomen abroad whose moral principles, like their complexions, have baked in the tropical sun.[37]

Sir George and the first Mrs Ellison debate as to whether slaves are fellow creatures and worthy of the same sentiment that the wife lavishes on her lapdog, an excessive and misplaced feeling. The controversy occasions Mrs Ellison's insulting her husband for possessing 'less spirit than a sucking babe' and for 'tamely forgiving' the slaves. George's masculinity is at issue in the discussion because he dares to engage in amelioration, though his brand of sentimentality seems thoroughly admirable in

Scott's terms. In a sense, too, Sir George's first marriage demonstrates the dangers of intermarriage. It may not be too much of a strain to say that in marrying a (white) Jamaican woman rather than a native Englishwoman, Ellison treats his stint in Jamaica as a rite of passage that truly meritorious Englishmen must endure in order to earn racial and class privilege. Eighteenth-century Jamaica represents a site of persistent violence and turbulence, curiously embodied in a woman who exemplifies the worst aspects of the islands. Mrs Ellison is the antithesis of the proper English lady: manly, emotionally controlling, weepy, a bad mother, a racist. In contrast to her, Sir George opines that the subordination of slaves 'makes me hate the country' (p. 15), and he determines to educate the progeny of their union in England against his wife's wishes: 'as she has conceived a dislike to England, which even her son's being there could not conquer' (p. 29). Their nasty Jamaican-born child is a parody of imperial arrogance in acting as lord over the world, 'a little fury, bursting with pride, passion, insolence, and obstinacy' (p. 29). When Ellison wants to move with his son to England to improve his temperament, Mrs Ellison abruptly and conveniently dies of a tropical fever just as the novel shifts its venue from periphery to metropole. Upon his return to British soil, Ellison at first sublimates his desire for the beautiful Miss Allin. The novel contrasts the idealised delicate white femininity of Miss Allin, whose complexion is 'extremely fine, clear as alabaster, and heightened with a gentle blooming red in her cheeks' (p. 54), with the brash saccharine temperament of the first Mrs Ellison, an Englishwoman spoiled by the Jamaican sun.[38] In England slavery's meaning quickly dissipates into a metaphor for gender relations since Ellison is assured of 'the happiness of his Negroes' (p. 138) by his Jamaican steward. And once his son's naturally violent temper is mitigated by an English education, Ellison grants him 'a proper sum of ready money to purchase new slaves' (p. 138) without acknowledging any contradiction between his attitudes towards complexion and slavery.

George Ellison's sympathetic disposition towards human equality, like Montagu's, stresses that 'complexion' should not be the basis for cruel and inhumane treatment, though Ellison unselfconsciously defends the profit motive. Because of their colour the slaves are paradoxically both legitimate property and human beings. Ellison's sentimental attempts to alleviate their misery echo antislavery arguments. Yet the 'difference of complexion' seems crucial to sorting out the conflicting attitudes that Ellison reveals, and in three specific passages 'complexion' figures centrally:

The thing which had chiefly hurt him during his abode in Jamaica, was the cruelty exercised on one part of mankind; as if the difference of complexion excluded them from the human race, or indeed as if their not being human could be an excuse for making them wretched. (p. 10)

Mr Ellison's house contained also many children of inferior rank; his servants had intermarried, the blacks with blacks, the white servants with those of their own colour; for though he promoted their marrying, he did not wish an union between those of different complexions, the connection appearing indelicate and almost unnatural. (p. 139)

Indeed, my dear . . . I must call them so [fellow creatures], till you can prove to me, that the distinguishing marks of humanity lie in the complexion or turn of features. When you and I are laid in the grave, our lowest black slave will be as great as we are; in the next world perhaps much greater; the present difference is merely adventitious, not natural. But we will not at present pursue this subject. (p. 13)

These three examples incorporate the incongruity between – to use modern terminology – a conceptual grammar of antiracism and a racist essentialism. There is something of a gap, for example, between Ellison's stand against sexual intermixture as unnatural and his argument that 'the present difference [of complexion] is merely adventitious, not natural'. In particular, in the first passage Ellison objects to a difference in complexion as the justification for cruelty, and yet complexion is a racialised marker that determines the right to inclusion or exclusion from the human race. Ellison entertains both the possibility that complexion is an indication of the limits of the human, and that it is not. In the first quotation affinities are to be honoured among different complexions because of a common humanity, while in the second passage differences supersede affinities when intermarriage is threatened. Finally, in the third passage the question of the significance of blood affinities and variations in pigmentation is deferred until the afterlife where moral barometers may determine that black is sometimes superior to white.

Ellison's years in Jamaica, while harmful to his health, allow him to formulate a benevolent and gentle masculinity in contrast to his first wife's unfeminine meanness on the one hand, and to a rebellious but restrainable slave population on the other. Certainly race is used to differentiate between women while reasserting male privilege; but Scott also manages to create an appealing man who manoeuvres between a nationally hybrid woman and an Englishwoman, thus re-establishing his economic and social power through sentiment rather than violence or rapacity. Scott evidences cultural anxieties about race even as she renegotiates the social valences of complexion's palette, if not its economic investments. In *Sir George Ellison* Sarah Scott speculates about the extent to which feminised, sentimental men may be aligned with a set of increasingly institutionalised power relations that constitute 'whiteness'. The New World enables Ellison's exploration of this alternative version of manliness while still protecting his vested interests, and he returns to England to solidify and more fully articulate his new-found amalgamation and an original sort of manly character more appropriate to England than its colonies.[39] In short, the mechanism for the construction of race operates from Ellison's empowerment as an Englishman, a coloniser, a man of relative privilege, and a man of feeling.

COMPLEXION AND DIFFERENCE

No single analysis of race, gender, or class is sufficient to explain the ways in which these categories are mutually constitutive in eighteenth-century texts written by women or about women. Rather they are exemplary of the confusions that were operating within the lexicon of the cultural construction of race and of a racism bound to colour. 'Complexion' in this period serves to isolate and exclude the human from the subhuman, the beautiful from the ugly, and the metropole from the periphery, as the concept of difference fluctuates between being an indelible indicator of intrinsic character or something random and accidental. Complexion is a site where categories are negotiated, not simply as racialised skin on which gender is imposed, as a sexualised bodily feature on which race is played out, or as a class indicator that erases race and gender. Crucial to formulating a national aesthetic, complexion in its myriad and unpredictable manifestations is also a somatic sign of the national character and makes of whiteness an inalienable right as Britain claims an imperial identity. When pigmentation and bodily features become the intractable differences that carry economic and social meanings, they evolve into *the* difference of complexion that exemplifies the 'race' of national character on which the political systems that undergird inequalities are based. Aphra Behn, Eliza Haywood, Sarah Scott, and Elizabeth Montagu, like the abolitionist women who succeed them in the later eighteenth and early nineteenth centuries, variously negotiate their investments in the racialised language of complexion as they contribute to arguments on race, class, and gender.

In sum, inconsistencies are *characteristic* of racial discourse and related cultural practices in mid eighteenth-century England rather than the exception. The brilliant Jamaican man, the desirable Sable Venus, and the faithful Indian Yarico present enigmas because intelligence, beauty, virtue, and high rank are incompatible with bestiality and inferiority; and the shifting colours of the women indicate the slippery shades of Otherness. Yet they all share a difference of complexion that distinguishes them from whiteness and Englishness. In our readings of race in the Enlightenment, we have unravelled racial concepts in writings by and about women to show that a politics of complexion is driven by cultural understandings of aesthetic and economic values, and to reveal critical negotiations of racial meanings and gender hierarchies. At the same time, to ignore the categories of colour that have real effects leads to a diffuse and ineffectual racial politics. In the course of the nineteenth century, scientific racism was to elide differences into an increasingly rigidified binary of black and white, but in the eighteenth century the relation between pigmentation and the faculties of the mind, between bodily features and character, between 'blood' and social privilege, remained unstable. To explore the literary genealogy of these attitudes about race and gender is to take a step towards articulating alternative ways of conceptualising colouring – and a step towards dismantling the current differences of complexion upon which the exclusions of institutionalised racism continue to be based.

NOTES

I am grateful to the UCLA graduate students in my seminar, 'Race and Gender in the Eighteenth Century', whose discussions have contributed to this chapter, and to Roxann Wheeler.

1 Folarin Shyllon, *Black People in Britain, 1555–1833* (London: Oxford University Press, 1977), pp. 4–27 (p. 5). I am indebted to this important book.

2 David Theo Goldberg, *Racist Culture: Philosophy and the Politics of Meaning* (Oxford: Blackwell, 1993). See also: George L. Mosse, *Toward the Final Solution: a History of European Racism* (Madison: University of Wisconsin Press, 1978); Benedict Anderson, *Imagined Communities* (London: Verso, 1991).

3 Ann Laura Stoler, *Race and the Education of Desire: Foucault's 'History of Sexuality' and the Colonial Order of Things* (Durham, NC and London: Duke University Press, 1995), p. 27.

4 Mosse, *Toward the Final Solution*, p. xvi.

5 Michael Omi and Howard Winant, *Racial Formation in the United States: from the 1960s to the 1980s* (London: Routledge & Kegan Paul, 1986), pp. 68–9.

6 Henry Louis Gates, Jr, 'Critical Remarks' in David Theo Goldberg (ed.), *Anatomy of Racism* (Minneapolis: University of Minnesota Press, 1990), p. 323.

7 David Hume, *Essays Moral, Political, and Literary*, ed. Eugene F. Miller, rev. edn (Indianapolis: Liberty Fund, 1987), p. 208.

8 Richard Steele, *The Tatler* (Thursday, 2 November 1710), ed. Donald F. Bond, 3 vols. (Oxford: Clarendon Press, 1987), III, 256.

9 *The Parrot. With a Compendium of the Times*. By the Authoress of The Female Spectator (London: T. Gardner, 1746). *The Parrot* appeared in nine numbers from 2 August until 4 October 1746.

10 Though Haywood attacked Robert Walpole in *The Adventures of Eovaai* (1736) and she evidenced Tory sympathies, her political views cannot be characterised simply.

11 See Linda Colley, *Britons: Forging the Nation, 1707–1837* (New Haven: Yale University Press, 1992), esp. p. 103.

12 On the emergence of 'race' in the later eighteenth century, see Nicholas Hudson, 'From "Nation" to "Race": the Origin of Racial Classification in Eighteenth-Century Thought', *Eighteenth-Century Studies*, 29:3 (1996), 247–64.

13 Charles Linné [Linnaeus], *A General System of Nature, through the Three Grand Kingdoms of Animals, Vegetables, and Minerals, Systematically Divided . . .*, trans. William Turton, M.D., 7 vols. (London: Lackington, Allen, & Company, 1802) I, 9. This first English translation of the multi-volumed treatise is inexact and incomplete.

14 Lynn Thorndike, 'De Complexionibus', *Isis*, 49, pt. 4 no. 158 (December 1958), 398–408.

15 Mary Louise Pratt, *Imperial Eyes: Travel Writing and Transculturation* (London: Routledge, 1992), p. 32; Winthrop Jordan, *White Over Black: American Attitudes Toward the Negro 1550–1812* (Chapel Hill: University of North Carolina Press, 1968), p. 221.

16 Wylie Sypher, *Guinea's Captive Kings: British Anti-Slavery Literature of the 18th Century* (Chapel Hill: University of North Carolina Press, 1942), pp. 105ff.

17 Alexander Pope, *Moral Essays*, 'Epistle II. To a Lady', line 3, *The Poems of Alexander Pope. A one-volume edition of the Twickenham text*, ed. John Butt (London: Methuen, 1963), p. 560. Daniel Defoe's Friday in *Robinson Crusoe*, variously represented as Carib, African, and white, is the most significant male character of the eighteenth century who persistently changes colour.

18 Aphra Behn, *Oroonoko: or, the Royal Slave. A True History*, *The Works of Aphra Behn*, ed. Janet Todd, 7 vols. (London: William Pickering, 1992–6), *Volume III. The Fair Jilt and Other Short Stories* (1995), p. 63. Thomas Southerne, *Oroonoko*, ed. Maximillian E. Novak and David Stuart Rodes (Lincoln: University of Nebraska Press, 1976), 'Introduction', p. xxxvii n.73, and II.ii.

19 [Richard Steele], *The Spectator*, no. 11 (13 March 1711), ed. Donald F. Bond, 5 vols. (Oxford: Clarendon Press, 1965), I, 49–51. Wylie Sypher observes that the anonymous 'Story of Inkle and Yarico' in *London Magazine* (May 1734) 'begins the confusion between the Indian Yarico and the Negress Yarico'

because Yarico is African there. Sypher emphasises the mythological qualities of 'the Negro who is not a Negro' (*Guinea's Captive Kings*, p. 131).

20 For various versions of the story, see Lawrence Marsden Price, *Inkle and Yarico Album* (Berkeley: University of California Press, 1937) and Peter Hulme, *Colonial Encounters: Europe and the Native Caribbean 1492–1797* (London and New York: Routledge, 1986).

21 Price, *Inkle and Yarico Album*, p. 6.

22 Bryan Edwards, *The History, Civil and Commercial, of the British Colonies in the West Indies: In Two Volumes* (London: John Stockdale, 1794), II, 32. *The Sable Venus; an Ode* is allegedly written in Jamaica in 1765.

23 Razia Aziz, 'Feminism and the challenge of racism: Deviance or difference?' in Heidi Safia Mirza (ed.), *Black British Feminism: a Reader* (London and New York: Routledge, 1997), p. 72.

24 For a convenient edition of Belinda's petition, see Vincent Carretta (ed.), *Unchained Voices: An Anthology of Black Authors in the English-Speaking World of the 18th Century* (Lexington: University Press of Kentucky, 1996), pp. 142–4. Wheatley's work was published as *Poems on Various Subjects, Religious and Moral* (London: A. Bell, 1773).

25 See, for example: Kim Hall, 'Reading What Isn't There: "Black" Studies in Early Modern England', *Stanford Humanities Review*, 3:1 (Winter 1993), 23–33; Jenny Sharpe, ' "Something Akin to Freedom": the Case of Mary Prince', *differences*, 8:1 (1996), 31–56.

26 Jennifer L. Morgan, ' "Some Could Suckle over Their Shoulder": Male Travelers, Female Bodies, and the Gendering of Racial Ideology, 1500–1700', *William and Mary Quarterly*, 3rd ser., 54:1 (1997), 167–92 (p. 169); and see Felicity A. Nussbaum, *Torrid Zones: Maternity, Sexuality, and Empire in Eighteenth-Century English Narratives* (Baltimore: Johns Hopkins University Press, 1995).

27 Moira Ferguson's *Subject to Others: British Women Writers and Colonial Slavery, 1670–1834* (New York and London: Routledge, 1992) provides a useful introduction to the scope of Englishwomen's involvement, and see Margaret Anne Doody's discussion of Hannah More's *Slavery, A Poem*, below pp. 233–4.

28 Sarah (Robinson) Scott to Elizabeth (Robinson) Montagu 20 July [1766] [Sandleford] [Berks], MO 5333. All subsequent references to the Montagu letters are from the Huntington Library Montagu Collection, and I am grateful for permission to cite these manuscripts.

29 Elizabeth (Robinson) Montagu to Sarah (Robinson) Scott, 17 July 1766 Denton [Hall] [Northumberland], MO 5840.

30 For a fuller discussion, see Stoler, *Race and the Education of Desire*, p. 59. Benedict Anderson, in *Imagined Communities*, also argues that racism begins with seventeenth-century aristocratic sympathies towards divine right rule.

31 Letter from Elizabeth Montagu to Mrs Wm. Robinson, 10 July 1775 in John Doran, *A Lady of the Last Century* (London: Richard Bentley & Sons, 1873), pp. 142–3.

32 Sarah (Robinson) Scott to Elizabeth (Robinson) Montagu, 13 May [1792],
    MO 5485. Upon Montagu's death the chimneysweeps issued an ode of grat-
    itude to her.

33 Johnson cites Milton's line: 'Instead / Of spirits malign, a better *race* to bring
    / Into their vacant room'. Johnson gave no special attention to complexion
    as an indicator of race, though he does include under the second definition,
    'the colour of the external parts of any body', an example from Addison's
    Spectator, no. 262: 'If I write on a black man, I run over all the eminent
    persons of that *complexion*.'

34 Sarah Scott, *The History of Sir George Ellison*, ed. Betty Rizzo (Lexington:
    University of Kentucky Press, 1995), pp. 40, 45. All subsequent references
    will be cited parenthetically in the text.

35 Sarah (Robinson) Scott to Elizabeth (Robinson) Montagu, 9 February
    [1766] [Bath] [Somerset], MO 5321. Elizabeth Montagu, a subscriber to the
    first edition of Olaudah Equiano's *Interesting Narrative of the Life of Olaudah
    Equiano, or Gustavus Vassa, the African, written by himself* (1789), voiced opposi-
    tion to slavery in a letter to Sarah Scott, 16 January [1788] [London], MO
    5796: 'I can with pleasure tell you that there is great reason to hope the slave
    trade will be abolish'd, such horrible accounts of the African Princes . . . &
    our usuage [*sic*] of the poor wretches we purchased, are now publishd, & in
    evry ones hands; that Mr Wilberforces application to Parliament on this
    subject can hardly fail of having a happy effect.'

36 For differing views, see Eve W. Stoddard, 'A Serious Proposal for Slavery
    Reform: Sarah Scott's *Sir George Ellison*', *Eighteenth-Century Studies*, 28:4 (1995),
    379–96; Moira Ferguson, *Subject to Others*, p. 104; and Markman Ellis, *The
    Politics of Sensibility: Race, Gender and Commerce in the Sentimental Novel*
    (Cambridge University Press, 1996), pp. 87–114. Sir George's economic col-
    lusion anticipates that of Sir Thomas Bertram in Antigua, in Jane Austen's
    Mansfield Park (1814).

37 I am indebted to Harriet Guest for discussions about this point.

38 'Whiteness', writes Charles Mills in *The Racial Contract* (Ithaca: Cornell
    University Press, 1997), 'is not really a color at all, but a set of power rela-
    tions' (p. 127), among which, I would add, is social class.

39 Winthrop Jordan comments that it 'was important, if incalculably so, that
    English discovery of black Africans came at a time when the accepted stan-
    dard of ideal beauty was a fair complexion of rose and white', *White Over
    Black*, p. 9.

Women, family, and the law

CHAPTER 4

Women's status as legal and civic subjects: 'A worse condition than slavery itself'?

Gillian Skinner

At least in theory, the legal status of the single woman in the eighteenth century was the same as that of a man. A woman's legal position was crucially affected depending on whether she was single (*feme sole*) or married (*feme covert*). If she was single, she 'enjoyed, for the most part, the same rights and responsibilities as did men. She owned property and chattels, which she could bequeath by will. She made contracts; she sued and was sued.'[1] Yet while the *feme sole* may have had the same legal status as a man, her gender would always make a straightforward equivalence difficult.[2] This is underlined when it is borne in mind that this equivalence applied only in *private* law:

The public law position of all women, *sole* and *covert*, may be easily described: in public law there was no place for them, except on the throne. They sat neither in the Council nor in the House of Commons or the House of Lords (though if they were peeresses and they married commoners, their husbands might sit in the Lords by courtesy). Neither did they serve on juries or vote.[3]

The exclusion from consideration in public law bears an obvious and important relation to women's exclusion from citizenship, discussed in the final part of this chapter, although, as I shall suggest, this is not the same as saying either that women had no political role or that they had no public life.

Once a woman married, everything altered. Where the *feme sole* was viewed in legal theory, with whatever tensions, as an individual before the law, with the ability to be responsible for herself and her actions, and the capacity to own property, the married woman was seen quite differently. Given that marriage was accepted as the desired goal for most if not all women, and that the majority of women did marry, it is to the legal status of the married woman that I shall now turn my attention.

MARRIAGE: 'THE GREATEST AND MOST SERIOUS AFFAIR OF LIFE'

> It has never historically been the case and is not now the case that marriage can be regarded as a private relationship not subject to public definition and public control. Public interests in the control of human sexuality and reproduction and in the socialisation of children were asserted in the early modern period and continue to be asserted today.
>
> Susan Staves, *Married Women's Separate Property in England*[4]

Since the publication of Lawrence Stone's *The Family, Sex and Marriage in England 1500–1800* (1977), the eighteenth century has been seen as the period during which the ideal of the companionate marriage took hold. There have been plenty of cavils and caveats in the twenty-odd years since Stone's book appeared, but there is broad agreement that, whatever the lived reality, the *representation* of marriage certainly moved towards such an ideal in the literature of the period.[5] However, the mutuality and equality imagined as the keystones of the companionate marriage are, unsurprisingly, absent from the contemporary legal interpretation of the state, which emphasised the hierarchical nature of the relationship, famously described by Sir William Blackstone in 1771:

> By marriage the husband and wife are one person in law: that is, the very being or legal existence of the woman is suspended during the marriage, or at least is incorporated and consolidated into that of the husband: under whose wing, protection, and *cover*, she performs every thing; and is therefore called in our law-french a *fem-covert*.[6]

Within this concept of coverture, which applied at common law for all civil and even some criminal suits, a married woman had no separate legal identity. Her existence was, figuratively, 'covered', subsumed into that of her husband. Upon marriage, a woman's property passed into the control of her husband; she was not able to enter into contracts, to sue or be sued. She had no legal rights over her children, nor did she have the right to leave her husband's house without his permission – if she did so, she gave up her right to his support, but could also be legally compelled to return. The law 'regarded a husband as his wife's guardian, and he had the right to control her actions and even chastise her "with a stick no thicker than his thumb"'. As this indicates, the law effectively infantilised married women, treating them as incapable of handling their own affairs.[7]

Yet while the ideological and practical impact of such a legal attitude should not be underestimated, neither should the legal position be taken as straightforwardly indicative of social practice. Amy Louise Erickson has found that, despite coverture, 'In practice, wives at all social levels . . . managed finances on their own behalf and jointly with their husbands':

In legal theory, wives were in a radically different condition to unmarried and widowed women. But coverture was – socially at least – a fiction . . . There is considerable evidence of the continuity of women's property through marriage, even apart from formal marriage settlements.[8]

The legal status of women in the eighteenth century is of crucial importance in understanding developing ideological trends of the period, and tells us something of the practical difficulties women must have had to face; but, as ever, the gap between the ideology and the lived experience remains, and studies such as those of Staves and Erickson simultaneously enlighten us and remind us of how much remains subject to conjecture.[9]

Common law was not the only kind of law affecting the position of married women. Church courts, for example, stood as 'a competing and parallel jurisdiction'.[10] They had jurisdiction over the validity of marriages, heard claims for the restitution of conjugal rights, and could grant annulments and separations. (There was, of course, no divorce as we understand it in this period.[11]) Although gradually losing power, ecclesiastical courts did a lot of matrimonial business into the nineteenth century and, significantly, women as well as men could sue in these courts.

Hardwicke's Marriage Act of 1753, which changed the official definition of what constituted a legal marriage, was one of the factors which contributed to the ecclesiastical courts' loss of power. Before Hardwicke's Act, a marriage did not have to be performed by a clergyman or follow any particular ceremonial procedure. A verbal contract between a man and a woman by itself created a binding marriage that rendered any subsequent marriages bigamous. Although valid in church law, however, contract marriage was not recognised in common law and thus no property rights could be asserted on the basis of a contract marriage. Clandestine marriage, on the other hand, carried full property rights, and this was significant since one of the stated reasons for the suppression of clandestine marriage was to prevent minor heirs and heiresses from being persuaded into secret but legally binding marriages by their social and financial inferiors.[12] A clandestine marriage was one performed by a clergyman, often with numerous irregularities as to the strict

letter of canon law; but it was nevertheless valid, until the Marriage Act
made it a requirement that, for a marriage to be recognised, it must be
performed with banns or a licence, before witnesses and an authorised
clergyman, with parental permission for minors, and must be duly
recorded in an official Marriage Register.

Equity, dealt with in the court of Chancery, was the other kind of law
with particular significance for women. It was equity that made it possible for married women to own property, despite coverture, via the
setting up of trusts, and thus 'afforded the *feme covert* her most effective
legal protection'.[13] Equity offered ways in which the *feme covert* could look
after her interests, allowing her to sue her husband (and, as the corollary,
he to sue her) and treating her, at least with respect to her separate property, as a *feme sole*.[14] It is perhaps not surprising, then, that equity has been
seen by legal historians as responsible for gradual but positive changes
in the position of married women with regard to property. Susan Staves,
however, is cautious about such liberal confidence in the positive
progress of the law. Most importantly, she suggests that the gradual
erosion of rights to dower in favour of jointure cannot be seen as an
unmitigated good. Dower was the common law entitlement of a widow
to a life estate in one-third of all the real property which her husband
had owned during their marriage. A jointure guaranteed a widow a
certain annual income from land. This could be worth considerably
more than the one-third decreed by dower, but it could also be worth
considerably less, and if there was a prenuptial settlement of jointure on
the wife, her right to dower was automatically forfeited. Although dower
rights did not finally disappear in English law until 1925, and were not
even substantially weakened in law until the Dower Act of 1833, during
the eighteenth century dower was in practice replaced by jointure,
causing the disappearance of 'the communally enforced right to a third'
and the acceptance of 'the bargain so private that the courts decline to
inquire into the issue of whether or not an individual jointure or testamentary devise is a fair bargain or a competent maintenance'. Thus here
equity helped erode a common law right of married women. (And it
should also be remembered that only the well-to-do could afford to go
through the equity courts: those lower down the social scale had to wait
for the nineteenth-century Married Women's Property Acts to benefit
from the equity doctrines their social superiors had had access to in the
eighteenth century.)[15]

Dower and jointure provided for widows, but married women were
also able to own property – through trusts, set up before marriage to

keep a wife's property, or part of it, separate from her husband's. However, control of the wife's 'separate estate' then passed to the (almost invariably male) trustees, rather than to the wife herself, and the motives for setting up trusts were complex and not always related to the needs of the woman involved: for example, allowing a wife's father to pass property directly to his grandchildren. Pin money, on the other hand, was something a wife could have control over, despite coverture. This was an amount paid per year by a husband to his wife for her own use, intended to be used for clothes and other personal expenses. The contract to pay pin money was often part of the marriage settlement, but agreements were made in various ways, and pin money provides a particularly interesting example of the ideological debates over marriage and women's property. One problem was that it involved the husband contracting with the wife to pay her money which could be plausibly seen as *necessary* to her maintenance. The making of a contract between husband and wife was not popular within common law, since it seemed to contradict the notion that they were 'one person'. Furthermore, the husband had a duty in common law to support his wife, so agreements to pay pin money could be seen as rendering contractual what had been an obligation. The real purposes of paying pin money seem to have been partial maintenance on the one hand and a kind of 'insurance' on the other – to provide the wife with an income in case her husband were mean or hit hard times, or the couple separated. But neither of these purposes, Staves contends, were 'fully acknowledged in either official discourse or in legal theory', since both undermined the institution of marriage as it was preferred to be understood: 'Indeed, that the law and modern fashion allowed pin money was a subject of satire and a fact almost universally lamented by gentleman moralists.' For Samuel Richardson, for example, pin money 'makes a wife independent, and destroys love, by putting it out of a man's power to lay any obligation upon her, that might engage gratitude, and kindle affection'.[16]

For many commentators, then, pin money was anathema to a loving marriage. Richardson writes in unmistakably sentimental terms, with his emphasis on obligation and gratitude, and the implication that within the sentimental unit, or family, no explicit regulation is required, since the union of feeling hearts ensures that the interests of all members are fundamentally the same. Susan Moller Okin has argued that the developing ideal of the companionate marriage in the eighteenth century was responsible in several ways for 'a new rationale for the subordination of women', not least because

the legitimacy of male rule both within and outside the family is reinforced . . .
on the grounds that the interests of the family are totally united, that family relations, unlike those outside, are based only on love, and that therefore husbands
and fathers can be safely entrusted with power within the household and with
the right of representing their families' interests in the political realm.[17]

Thus the arguments surrounding pin money can be seen as part of
broader ideological debates about the social and political functions of
marriage and the family and the place of women within these institutions.

Fiction was fertile ground in which to produce the ideal of the companionate marriage, dealing as it so often did with the period of courtship and ending with the desired marriage, with scant regard for details
of marriage settlements, every confidence in the happiness of the loving
couple, and little investigation into the practicalities of daily married life.
Yet many eighteenth-century novels are nevertheless importantly conscious of the difficulties and debates within and about marriage.
Richardson's *Pamela, II* (1741), Henry Fielding's *Amelia* (1751), Sarah
Fielding's *The Countess of Dellwyn* (1759), Frances Sheridan's *The Memoirs of
Miss Sidney Bidulph* (1762), and Elizabeth Griffith's *The History of Lady
Barton* (1771), for example, all depict their protagonists' experiences of
marriage and all of them, in varying degrees, consider its social and eco-
nomic consequences alongside the emotional and personal ramifications.
But nowhere are the political and economic bones of eighteenth-century
marriage laid so bare as they are in Eliza Haywood's *The History of Miss
Betsy Thoughtless* (1751).

For most of its generous length, *Betsy Thoughtless* is a courtship novel,
dealing with the experiences of its young, attractive – and thoughtless –
heroine as she acquires suitors, enjoys power over them, and determines
to put off marriage for as long as possible, recognising that with marriage
will come an end to that power. ' "I wonder" ', she muses at one point,

'what can make the generality of women so fond of marrying?—It looks to me
like an infatuation.—Just as if it were not a greater pleasure to be courted, com-
plimented, admired, and addressed by a number, than be confined to one, who
from a slave becomes a master, and, perhaps, uses his authority in a manner dis-
agreeable enough.'[18]

Her behaviour alienates her most attractive and respectable suitor, Mr
Trueworth, who withdraws from the lists when he is deceived by a
jealous rival into believing that Betsy has borne an illegitimate child.
Frustrated by the departure of so desirable a suitor, her guardians and

two brothers put further pressure on Betsy to marry. In her single state she represents a constant source of anxiety; as her guardian Mr Goodman puts it: 'her youth,—her beauty,—the gaiety of her temper, and the little vanities of her sex, are every day exposing her to temptations fatal to reputation' (p. 292). *Betsy Thoughtless* represents marriage as containment: as a single woman, Betsy chooses her own friends, falls into dubious company, and gets into a variety of scrapes; marriage, for her male advisers and relations, is a way of getting Betsy under control. From a legal point of view, of course, this is only too true: the *feme sole*, with her legal existence and agency, becomes the *feme covert*, with all the attendant disabilities.

Accordingly, Betsy is persuaded to marry a long-standing suitor, Mr Munden, and the novel is transformed from one of courtship to one concerned with aspects of eighteenth-century married life rarely depicted in such detail. Pin money provides the arena for the first dispute between the couple, as the scanty allowance Mrs Munden receives from her husband for housekeeping forces her to 'have recourse for a supply to her own little purse' (p. 440). Immediately the unofficial 'insurance' function of pin money is illustrated. When Betsy complains, Mr Munden first expresses his contempt for pin money (' "nothing certainly is more idle, since a woman ought to have nothing apart from her husband" ' (p. 442)), and then, far from offering any rise in housekeeping, suggests that more items should come out of her pin money than is already the case: ' "as for example . . . coffee, – tea, – chocolate, – with all the appendages belonging to them" ' (p. 442).[19] An indignant Betsy is visited by the wife of one of her former guardians, Lady Trusty, who advises her not to allow herself ' "to be either menaced, or cajoled, out of even the smallest part" ' of her rights, while behaving ' "with all the softness it is in your power to assume" ' (p. 445). Lady Trusty's advice strongly recalls Susan Staves's summary of one of the general problems the legal system had with women and property:

it frequently happened that, despite separate property being secured to them, women were unwilling or unable even to hang on to it, being, as contemporaries said, 'kissed or kicked,' 'bullied or coaxed' out of it by husbands who had physical or emotional power that rendered their wives' legal powers nugatory.[20]

Lady Trusty's concern that Betsy not be 'menaced or cajoled' echoes the phrasing quoted by Staves and suggests an awareness that such persuasion or coercion was far from unusual. When a second altercation over housekeeping and pin money occurs, the violence of Mr Munden's reaction, added to his insistence that yet further inroads be made into Betsy's pin money, prompts the narrator to exclaim,

How utterly impossible was it for her now to observe the rules laid down to her by Lady Trusty! – Could she after this submit to put in practice any softening arts she had been advised to win her lordly tyrant into temper? – Could she, I say, have done this, without being guilty of a meanness, which all wives must have condemned her for. (p. 448)

Nevertheless, if Betsy is not prepared to practise 'softening arts', the options available to her at this point are severely limited. She makes it clear to her husband that 'she would never be prevailed upon to recede from any part of what was her due by contract' (p. 448), but what that means in practice is unclear. Theoretically, had Mr Munden failed to pay her pin money in full, she could sue, but in practical terms this was virtually impossible; as Staves writes more generally of the enforcement of pin money contracts, 'if she sued him and he lacked the will or the resources to pay her, she would . . . have had to have been prepared to see him imprisoned for failure to pay. It is hard to imagine that a gentlewoman who had her husband imprisoned for failure to pay her pin money would have been warmly received in polite society'.[21] Disputes between husband and wife were supposed to be kept strictly private and although Betsy confides in Lady Trusty, this confidence becomes the means by which the dispute is both kept relatively private and ultimately resolved. Lady Trusty is determined that a resolution should be found: '"to live in the manner you are likely to do together . . . cannot but be very displeasing in the eye of heaven and must also expose both of you to the censure and contempt of the world, when once it comes to be known and talked of"' (p. 451). Thus she prompts her husband Sir Ralph to speak to Mr Munden and an agreement is reached which includes the addition of a guinea per week to the housekeeping and brings the couple back to a temporary semblance of contentment.

The depiction of pin money in *Betsy Thoughtless* supports both the notion that marriage does not preclude contractual obligations and the corresponding notion that a wife therefore has legally enforceable rights within the relationship, even if the question of enforcement of those rights comes down in the end to the well-intentioned intervention of friends. One of the objections to pin money, it will be remembered, was that a contract to pay such money was destructive of love, but Haywood sets her examination of it in the context of a marriage loveless from the start and implies that pin money provided one of a wife's few sources of security (so long as she has influential friends prepared to support her) against a husband motivated solely by his own self-interest.

Yet while *Betsy Thoughtless* does not shrink from displaying the economic bases of marriage, the novel still plays its part in the construction of the companionate ideal. Betsy is released from her miserable marriage by the death of Mr Munden, and goes on to marry Mr Trueworth, also now fortuitously widowed. When Lady Trusty attempts to make her consider two financially advantageous offers of marriage, Betsy makes clear her adherence to the ideal:

'I shall always pay a just regard to the advice of my friends, and particularly to your ladyship; but as I have been once a sacrifice to their persuasions, I hope you will have the goodness to forgive me, when I say, that if ever I become a wife again, love, an infinity of love, shall be the chief inducement.' (p. 563)

Trueworth duly arrives, having waited the decent period of a year, to spring into Betsy's arms, 'which of themselves opened to receive him' (p. 564). Even in the midst of this conventionally happy ending, the novel does mention the marriage settlement, but it does so merely to underscore Mr Trueworth's merits, the terms of the settlement convincing Sir Ralph 'both of the greatness of his generosity, and the sincerity of his love to the lady he was about to make his wife' (p. 567). We discover that, if widowed, Betsy is to receive a jointure of £800 a year (twice as much as Mr Munden settled on her), but no mention at all is made of pin money and her response to the generous jointure is to accept it '"as a proof of your affection, but heaven forbid I should ever live to receive any other advantage from it"' (p. 568). The ending retreats from the legal and economic analysis of marriage into the conventional treatment of marriage *as* ending, its obvious felicities needing no elaboration.

THE LAW, VISIBILITY, AND VIRTUE

Even where it might theoretically have offered some protection or redress, there were always bars to women having recourse to the law. One such bar was ignorance. This is of course also true of men, but the degree of ignorance about legal possibilities must generally have been greater in women, as the author of *The Hardships of the English Laws in relation to Wives* (1735) laments:

if we reflect how extreamly ignorant all young Women are as to points in Law, and how their Education and Way of Life, shuts them out from the Knowledge of their true Interest in almost all things, we shall find that their Trust and

Confidence in the Man they love, and Inability to make use of the Proper
Means to guard against his Falsehood, leave few in a Condition to make use of
that Precaution.[22]

Clare Brant points out further that 'knowledge did not ensure comprehension since the specialization of legal language kept it baffling'. She
quotes Laetitia Pilkington:

there are so many loop-holes [in the law] that even persons conversant with it
may be deceived: how then should a female be on her guard, against the pro-
fessors of a certain kind of unintelligible jargon, whose skill is to puzzle the
cause, or a science where
      Endless tautologies and doubts perplex
      Too harsh a study for our softer sex![23]

Other constraints on women's use of the law were financial; one who
had much bitter experience remarked how 'the Law went on heavily
without the valuable thing call'd Money'.[24] Many men must also have
found the law a discouragingly expensive process, but once again women
would have been more likely than men to experience this handicap, particularly as frequently they were attempting to use the law to force
payment of maintenance from an unwilling husband, thus precisely
setting out from a position of financial instability.

A further bar to women having recourse to the law, as is implied in the
case of suing for non-payment of pin money, was the problem of the
publicity contingent upon legal proceedings. *Betsy Thoughtless* contains
several examples of reluctance to proceed at law through fear of the consequences of the ensuing publicity. When Betsy leaves Mr Munden, for
example, the lawyer attempting to persuade him to grant her a separate
maintenance urges him to consider how, '"when the affairs of a family
are laid open, and every dispute between the husband and the wife
exposed before a court of judicature, or even in a petition to a lord chan-
cellor, the whole becomes a public talk, and furnishes a matter of ridicule for the unthinking scoffers of the Age"' (p. 534). If a man faced
ridicule in such situations, a woman could face more damaging consequences from the exposure of a legal process. In perhaps her most potentially disastrous adventure, Betsy is courted by a supposed baronet, Sir
Frederick Fineer. Having failed to persuade her into a clandestine marriage (*Betsy Thoughtless* was published shortly before the 1753 Marriage
Act), Sir Frederick resorts to deception and has Betsy lured to his lodgings on the pretext that he has run himself through and is dying as a
result of her obduracy. Once in his room, Betsy is forced to take part in
a marriage ceremony and as soon as this is over, Fineer leaps from his

sick-bed and attempts to rape her, crying, ' "Your resistance is vain . . . you are my wife, and as such I shall enjoy you." ' Betsy is rescued because her screams are heard by Mr Trueworth who, by happy coincidence, is in the house. Shortly after the rescue, Betsy's two brothers confer with Mr Trueworth, 'to consider what was to be done for the chastisement of the villain, as the prosecuting him by law would expose their sister's folly, and prove the most mortal stab that could be given to her reputation' (p. 382). Mr Trueworth agrees, and advises that they must content themselves 'with barely caning' Fineer (p. 383) – but even this proves impracticable since the villain has predictably absconded when they attempt to find him. The law cannot be used to punish the 'villain' of the piece, because the exposure involved in legal proceedings would injure the victim: reputation – that is, Betsy's reputation as a sexually chaste woman – must be preserved at all costs, even if this means allowing the real criminal to get away scot free. As her brother Francis exclaims earlier in the novel: ' "What avails your being virtuous? . . . I hope, – and believe you are so; – but your reputation is of more consequence to your family" ' (p. 335).

The same problem is highlighted in Mary Hays's *The Victim of Prejudice* (1799), in which Sir Peter Osborne, rapist and persecutor of the heroine, tellingly enumerates the legal disabilities of women:

'Who will credit the tale you mean to tell? What testimony or witnesses can you produce that will not make against you? Where are your resources to sustain the vexation and delay of a suit of law, which you wildly threaten? Who would support you against my wealth and influence? How would your delicacy shrink from the idea of becoming, in open court, the sport of ribaldry, the theme of obscene jesters?'[25]

Here, and in the Fineer episode from *Betsy Thoughtless*, the law is seen as of little use in protecting virtue, since the resulting publicity itself damages virtue. This is a problem specifically for women, as Lady Mary Wortley Montagu recognised when she differentiated between the situations of men and women, and commented that a woman's 'virtue must only shine to her own recollection, and loses that name when it is ostentatiously expos'd to the World'.[26] To be 'expos'd to the World' is tantamount to loss of chastity, since no genuinely chaste female could endure such exposure, as Sir Peter's speech cruelly implies: the victim of rape cannot seek justice since the very attempt to do so would result in a repetition of her trauma.

It is significant, then, that research has suggested women *were* at times able to use the law to their advantage, even in the area of reputation.

Anna Clark has shown how 'defamation threatened [working women's] economic independence. Women in charge of small businesses went to court to clear their names not just for their own satisfaction but to protect their livelihoods, a concern recognised in law.'[27] Crucially, however, the women who achieved this were, by definition, from the trading classes. Defamation of a middle- or upper-class woman would threaten not economic independence, but rather her access to necessary economic dependence, given that it would threaten either her prospect of marrying or her security within marriage. Clark's study underlines the crucial link between chastity and property in the period. For if chastity was what Mary Wollstonecraft called a 'sexual virtue',[28] it was also a virtue clearly related to class, since the chastity of a woman mattered principally in relation to the transmission of property:

As Samuel Johnson made clear, 'confusion of progeny constitutes the essence of the crime', and where the inheritance of an estate was concerned a man needed to know that the children born to his wife were his own. It was on women's chastity, Johnson claimed, that 'all the property in the world depends'. Where there was no question of an inheritance, and little or no property was involved, the attitude to pre-marital chastity was far more tolerant.[29]

Given the importance of chastity among the propertied and the morally damaging significance of visibility for middle- and upper-class women, it is only too clear how, as Clare Brant comments, 'reputation helped restrict economic options for non-working-class women'.[30] In their study of the middle class of the late eighteenth and early nineteenth centuries, Leonore Davidoff and Catherine Hall frequently refer to the growing conflict between the desirability of middle-class women contributing their labour to the family enterprise and the importance of conforming to a developing definition of femininity 'which ran directly counter to acting as a visibly independent economic agent'. Thus there arose 'the expectation that within an enterprise women could do preparation of products and services or finance as long as these activities were kept out of sight'.[31] This kind of conflict is already clearly evident in fiction of the second half of the eighteenth century, in which the struggle to find appropriate work for the middle-class woman features with increasing urgency.[32]

The ideological implications of this gradual reduction of women's visibility go beyond simply sexual reputation. In *Family and the Law in Eighteenth-Century Fiction*, John P. Zomchick describes how the law developed to favour the needs of an expanding commercial society: 'Through the interrelation of law and economics, the subject is conceived not only as a carrier of rights but also as an economic agent. In fact . . . rights and economic agency go hand-in-hand, contributing to a new "sense of identity" for human nature.'[33] The problematic relation of women to both rights and economic agency suggests the difficulties that may lie in attempting to conceive them as 'subjects', as autonomous individuals, in this way and points to the close relationship between the legal status of women in the eighteenth century and their civic status.

CITIZENSHIP

While it was possible for a married woman to own property in the eighteenth century, there were severe limitations which frequently prevented this resulting in any noticeable increase in married women's power. These limitations arose from the development of 'a set of special rules to maximise the probabilities that married women's separate property would provide secure maintenance for the women and children upon whom it was settled and minimise the possibilities that women could take property intended for maintenance and use it as capital'.[34] From this unwillingness, even refusal, to see women's property as capital stems women's lack of economic power and agency. And that lack is one of the key factors in women's exclusion from citizenship.

In the early eighteenth century, ideas of citizenship were rooted in property and, more specifically, in the ownership of land. Ownership of land was thought to confer independence and disinterestedness, to allow the individual to remain free from the corrupting influences attendant upon relying on others for employment and income. This civic humanist ideal was, as David Lieberman points out, 'a deeply moralised ideal of citizenship, conceived as the active exercise of civic virtue and participation in the common good'.[35] As well as more homely qualities such as prudence and frugality, civic virtue incorporated valour and patriotism and included the notion of being prepared to fight and die for one's country. The masculine emphasis of such an ideal is not hard to see: citizenship as understood in civic humanist terms is an exclusively male domain.

Women's exclusion from citizenship was thus intimately linked to their relationship with property. They were not wholly excluded from owning property, but when they did so it was assumed that their interest in it would be purely as a means of support. They were not expected to manage it in such a way as to increase revenues or expand their influence; on the contrary, they were assumed to lack the ability to do so,

for such an ability would be out of keeping with contemporary ideals of
femininity, particularly as the sentimental ideology developing from mid
century figured women as creatures of emotion rather than reason.[36]
Staves sees women's assumed lack of rationality as the link between their
exclusion from citizenship and their inferior status as owners of property. The male owner of 'even a moderate-sized estate' was 'entitled to
use the land as a capital resource' and 'entitled to a degree of social pres-
tige and a degree of political power'; the female owner was expected to
live off the income, not to 'meddle with the land', and presumably to pass
it on to more capable male hands in due course.[37]

Land still retained a distinctive ideological importance at the end of
the century, though other forms of property were beginning to gain in
value and significance. Alongside civic humanist ideas, more radical
understandings of citizenship were being developed. The decade following the French Revolution saw intense discussion of such matters in both
France and Britain, but the roots of the challenge to a notion of citizenship based on privilege lay further back, in seventeenth-century philosophy, and specifically in the writings of Hobbes and Locke, both of
whom argued for the natural equality and freedom of human beings. It
was on this philosophical basis that revolutionary writers proceeded,
proclaiming 'the rights of man' as a result of the natural equality into
which all were born.[38] Thus a conception of citizenship developed for
which property was no longer a prerequisite.

As Susan Moller Okin has pointed out, the arguments of Hobbes and
Locke, with their stress on equality, present 'an impossible intellectual
problem to a society still determined to uphold the unequal treatment of
men and women'.[39] For Okin, the newly sentimental family of the eighteenth century, with its emphasis on women's role as domestic and dependent rather than outward-looking and self-sufficient, and on women's
talents as in the areas of sentiment and feeling rather than those of
reason and judgement, bears significant responsibility for the continuing
exclusion of women from definitions of citizenship. Certainly it is to this
construction of women that Mary Wollstonecraft felt compelled to
respond in her *Vindication of the Rights of Woman* (1792).

In the *Vindication*, Wollstonecraft argued that the categorisation of
women as creatures of feeling rather than reason was the product of a
faulty education and environment and had nothing to do with supposedly innate characteristics. Moving from the spiritual equality of men
and women, she wrote that 'if woman be allowed to have an immortal
soul, she must have, as the employment of life, an understanding to

improve', and she dared to suppose 'that society will some time or other be so constituted, that man must necessarily fulfil the duties of a citizen, or be despised, and that while he was employed in any of the departments of civil life, his wife, also an active citizen, should be equally intent to manage her family, educate her children, and assist her neighbours'.[40] This serves to illustrate only too clearly, however, what Carole Pateman has called 'Wollstonecraft's dilemma'.[41] The wife here, clearly designated 'an active citizen', yet expresses her citizenship in different ways from her husband; while he is 'employed in any of the departments of civil life', she is concerned with her family, her children, her neighbours – with, in other words, the traditional duties of woman as mother and nurturer in her immediate community. Wollstonecraft did not ignore other possibilities for women: she argued for the importance of women having a variety of respectable employment opportunities which would mean that they 'would not then marry for a support', and she even went so far as to suggest, briefly, 'that women ought to have representatives, instead of being arbitrarily governed without having any direct share allowed them in the deliberations of government'. Generally speaking, however, she argued for 'the peculiar duties of women' – those of wife and mother – to be taken seriously as the duties of a citizen.[42] And it is here that the dilemma arises because, as Pateman explains,

within the existing patriarchal conception of citizenship, the choice always has to be made between equality and difference, or between equality and womanhood. On the one hand, to demand 'equality' is to strive for equality with men (to call for the 'rights of men and citizens' to be extended to women), which means that women must become (like) men. On the other hand, to insist, like some contemporary feminists, that women's distinctive attributes, capacities and activities be revalued and treated as a contribution to citizenship is to demand the impossible; such 'difference' is precisely what patriarchal citizenship excludes.[43]

Though they were excluded from citizenship, women were nevertheless included in the political order. Indeed, (male) citizenship was defined precisely in terms of its difference from the position of women: women were subordinates who, while they had no place in the public sphere as citizens, had a distinctive political duty to perform in the private sphere, as mothers. In the last decade of the eighteenth century, when the 'rights of man' were asserted, women's contribution to political life was encompassed by the doctrine of republican motherhood: 'a republican mother was excluded from citizenship, but she had a crucial political part to play in bearing and rearing sons who embodied republican virtues. She remained an auxiliary to the commonwealth but an auxiliary who made a fundamental political contribution.'[44]

This firm placing of women as 'auxiliary' to the political order is echoed in Davidoff and Hall's description of women's pronounced marginality in political and civic life: 'They could attend the assizes as spectators, but they could never hope to play any part in the administration of the law or share in its majestic spectacle.' And they conclude that 'the common sense of the nineteenth-century social world' was that 'Men were to be active in the world as citizens and entrepreneurs, women were to be dependent as wives and mothers.'[45]

Davidoff and Hall's formulation agrees with the well-known and much-discussed notion of the development of 'separate spheres' for men and women during the eighteenth century and particularly in the nineteenth. It is important, however, to emphasise in conclusion the extent to which this is an area of debate, especially in eighteenth-century studies. The degree to which the ideology of separate spheres actually coincides with lived experience in the period remains uncertain. Amanda Vickery, for example, in her recent study of the everyday lives of the daughters of 'gentlemen' in northern England, concludes that: 'the household and family were not the limit of an elite woman's horizon. Nor was the house in any simple sense a private, domestic sphere . . . Genteel families were linked to the world in a multiplicity of ways . . . All these social roles were expressed through a variety of encounters which took place in the home.'[46] And Lawrence E. Klein suggests that we need to investigate much more thoroughly how 'private' and 'public' were understood in the eighteenth century itself. He dissects the public sphere, finding different modes of life understood as 'public' in the period, from some of which women were excluded but in some of which they were present and active.[47] It is important to reflect that in allowing 'public' to have multiple significance, it may be that women's exclusion from citizenship (which, during the eighteenth century, was complete) does not necessarily preclude their having a public life.

NOTES

1 Janelle Greenberg, 'The Legal Status of the English Woman in Early Eighteenth-Century Common Law and Equity', *Studies in Eighteenth-Century Culture*, 4 (1975), 172.

2 This lack of equivalence is pertinently illustrated by the difficulties of Samuel Richardson's heroine Clarissa Harlowe. Contradictions emerge when Clarissa, as *feme sole*, is bequeathed her grandfather's estate. Clarissa's independent possession of land destabilises the accepted connection

between property and chastity in women that is confirmed by, for example, settlement of land in the marriage contract. Clarissa's sexual identity – the importance of chastity – overlays her legal identity, so that her independent possession of property implies a potential lack of chastity which, in turn, suggests that she cannot possess the self-control necessary to qualify as an autonomous individual capable of bearing the responsibility of ownership. See: Harriet Guest, 'A Double Lustre: Femininity and Sociable Commerce, *1730–60*', *Eighteenth-Century Studies*, 23 (1990), 488; John P. Zomchick, *Family and the Law in Eighteenth-Century Fiction: the Public Conscience in the Private Sphere* (Cambridge University Press, 1993), p. 60; and further discussion by Ruth Perry in ch. 5 of this volume, pp. 122–9.

3 Greenberg, 'Legal Status', 172.

4 Susan Staves, *Married Women's Separate Property in England, 1660–1833* (Cambridge, MA: Harvard University Press, 1990), pp. 6–7.

5 Lawrence Stone, *The Family, Sex and Marriage in England 1500–1800* (London: Weidenfeld & Nicholson, 1977), esp. part 4, 'The Closed Domesticated Nuclear Family 1640–1800'. See also Randolph Trumbach, *The Rise of the Egalitarian Family: Aristocratic Kinship and Domestic Relations in Eighteenth-Century England* (New York, San Francisco, and London: Academic Press, 1978). Zomchick, for example, writes that 'Despite the criticisms of Stone's thesis, the very fact that he presents a coherent picture of this type [of family] is *prima facie* evidence of its ideological power . . . This is the family that all the protagonists long for' (*Family and the Law*, p. 19). See also 'Guide to Further Reading'.

6 William Blackstone, *Commentaries on the Laws of England* (1771; London: Reeves & Turner, 1896), p. 97.

7 Jane Rendall, *Women in an Industrializing Society: England 1750–1880* (Oxford: Basil Blackwell, 1990), p. 35. See also Greenberg, 'Legal Status', 172–5.

8 Amy Louise Erickson, *Women and Property in Early Modern England* (London: Routledge, 1993), pp. 225, 226.

9 As Staves puts it, problems result from 'historians, fallaciously, inferring social practice and social consequences from their knowledge of legal rules and legal arrangements' (*Separate Property*, p. 204). See also Erickson, *Women and Property*, p. 226.

10 Staves, *Separate Property*, p. 19.

11 Divorce by Act of Parliament became a possibility for the very wealthy in the seventeenth century, but only 131 Acts were passed between 1670 and 1799, almost all instituted by husbands, and only 17 were passed before 1750. For details see Stone, *The Family, Sex and Marriage*, pp. 37–8 and *Road to Divorce: England, 1530–1987* (Oxford University Press, 1990).

12 For more detailed description and discussion of contract and clandestine marriage, see: Eve Tavor Bannet, 'The Marriage Act of 1753: "A Most Cruel Law for the Fair Sex" ', *Eighteenth-Century Studies*, 30 (1997), 233–5; Lawrence Stone, *Uncertain Unions: Marriage in England 1660–1753* (Oxford University Press, 1992), pp. 17–22; Erica Harth, 'The Virtue of Love: Lord Hardwicke's Marriage Act', *Cultural Critique*, 9 (Spring 1988), 123–54.

13 Greenberg, 'Legal Status', 176.

14 For further discussion of the issues arising from this, see Greenberg, 'Legal Status', 177–8; Staves, *Separate Property*, pp. 152–3.

15 Staves, *Separate Property*, p. 129, and see p. 31. For discussion of ways in which legal changes disadvantaged daughters, see ch. 5, below pp. 118–21.

16 Staves, *Separate Property*, pp. 144, 158; Richardson in *The Rambler*, no. 97, *The Yale Edition of the Works of Samuel Johnson: The Rambler*, ed. W. J. Bate and Albrecht Strauss, 3 vols. (New Haven: Yale University Press, 1969), 11, 158; quoted in Staves, *Separate Property*, p. 159.

17 Susan Moller Okin, 'Women and the Making of the Sentimental Family', *Philosophy and Public Affairs*, 11 (1982), 74, quoted Staves, *Separate Property*, p. 226.

18 Eliza Haywood, *The History of Miss Betsy Thoughtless* (1751), ed. Beth Fowkes Tobin, World's Classics (Oxford University Press, 1997), p. 431. Subsequent references appear in the text. For further discussion of *Betsy Thoughtless*, see ch. 9, below pp. 208–10.

19 Mr Munden's choice of commodities is interesting. On women's relation to consumerism, see 'Introduction', pp. 10–13.

20 Staves, *Separate Property*, p. 135.

21 Ibid., p. 142.

22 [Sarah Chapone], *The Hardships of the English Laws in relation to Wives* (London: W. Bowyer for J. Roberts, 1735), p. 33. An extract from *Hardships* can be found in Vivien Jones (ed.), *Women in the Eighteenth Century: Constructions of Femininity* (London and New York: Routledge, 1990), pp. 217–25. The anonymous *Laws Respecting Women as they Regard their Natural Rights* (London: J. Johnson, 1771) is another attempt to dispel women's ignorance, as well as to protest against their inequality before the law.

23 Clare Brant, 'Speaking of Women: Scandal and the Law in the Mid-Eighteenth Century' in Clare Brant and Diane Purkiss (eds.), *Women, Texts and Histories 1575–1760* (London and New York: Routledge, 1992), pp. 258–9.

24 Elizabeth Justice, *Amelia, or, The Distress'd Wife: A HISTORY founded on REAL Circumstances. By a Private GENTLEWOMAN* (1751), quoted in Brant, 'Speaking of Women', p. 260.

25 Mary Hays, *The Victim of Prejudice* (1799), ed. Eleanor Ty (Peterborough, ON: Broadview Press, 1994), p. 119.

26 *The Nonsense of Common-Sense*, Tuesday, 24 January 1738, in Lady Mary Wortley Montagu, *Essays and Poems and Simplicity, a Comedy*, ed. Robert Halsband and Isobel Grundy (Oxford: Clarendon Press, 1977; rpt. 1993), p. 133.

27 Anna Clark, 'Whores and Gossips: Sexual Reputations in London 1770–1825' in Arina Angerman, et al. (eds.), *Current Issues in Women's History* (London and New York: Routledge, 1989), pp. 231–48, summarised by Brant, 'Speaking of Women', p. 247.

28 Mary Wollstonecraft, *Vindication of the Rights of Woman* (1792), ed. Carol H. Poston (New York: Norton, 1988), p. 121; ed. Miriam Brody Kramnick (Harmondsworth: Penguin Books, 1978), p. 227. Wollstonecraft vigorously

argues against the existence of 'sexual virtues' (i.e. virtues appropriate only to one sex); on chastity specifically she writes, 'instead of furnishing the vicious or idle with a pretext for violating some sacred duty, by terming it a sexual one, it would be wiser to show that nature has not made any difference' (p. 140; p. 250).

29 Bridget Hill, *Women, Work and Sexual Politics in Eighteenth-Century England* (Oxford: Basil Blackwell, 1989), p. 180.

30 Brant, 'Speaking of Women', p. 248.

31 Leonore Davidoff and Catherine Hall, *Family Fortunes: Men and Women of the English Middle Class, 1780–1850* (1987; rpt. London: Routledge, 1994), pp. 315, 275. On the competing imperatives for women to be both visibly virtuous, yet retired from view, see also Guest, 'A Double Lustre'.

32 See my *Sensibility and Economics in the Novel, 1740–1800: the Price of a Tear* (London: Macmillan, 1999), esp. the discussions of Sarah Fielding's *The Countess of Dellwyn* (1759), Agnes Maria Bennett's *Anna: or Memoirs of a Welch Heiress* (1785), Mary Hays's *Memoirs of Emma Courtney* (1796), and Mary Wollstonecraft's *The Wrongs of Woman* (1798). For further discussion of the issue of women's employability, see ch. 1 of this volume, pp. 37–40; for discussion of women in printing and publishing businesses, see ch. 6.

33 Zomchick, *Family and the Law*, p. 25.

34 Staves, *Separate Property*, p. 135; see also pp. 141–2, 152–3, 154–7, for further details of these differences.

35 David Lieberman, 'Property, Commerce and the Common Law: Attitudes to Legal Change in the Eighteenth Century' in John Brewer and Susan Staves (eds.), *Early Modern Conceptions of Property* (London and New York: Routledge, 1995), p. 145. Lieberman offers a useful summary of civic humanism as proposed by J. G. A. Pocock. For more detailed discussion of the concept, see Pocock's *The Machiavellian Moment: Florentine Political Thought and the Atlantic Republican Tradition* (Princeton, NJ and London: Princeton University Press, 1975), esp. chs. 3, 14.

36 For further discussion of the discourse of sensibility, see ch. 9, pp. 210–13, and 'Guide to Further Reading'.

37 Staves, *Separate Property*, pp. 226–7.

38 Wollstonecraft's *Vindication of the Rights of Men* (1790) was the first response to Edmund Burke's conservative *Reflections on the Revolution in France* (1790), followed more famously by Thomas Paine's *The Rights of Man* (1791) and her own *Vindication of the Rights of Woman* (1792).

39 Okin, 'Women and the Making of the Sentimental Family', 65.

40 Wollstonecraft, *Rights of Woman*, ed. Poston, pp. 63, 146; ed. Kramnick, pp. 155, 258–9.

41 Carole Pateman, 'Equality, Difference, Subordination: the Politics of Motherhood and Women's Citizenship' in Gisela Bock and Susan James (eds.), *Beyond Equality and Difference: Citizenship, Feminist Politics and Female Subjectivity* (London: Routledge, 1992), p. 20.

42 Wollstonecraft, *Rights of Woman*, ed. Poston, pp. 148, 147, 63; ed. Kramnick, pp. 261, 260, 155.

43 Pateman, 'Equality, Difference, Subordination', p. 20.

44 Ibid., pp. 19–20. For further discussion of citizenship in Wollstonecraft, see ch. 1 of this volume, pp. 41–3; on ideas of republican motherhood, see ch. 2, pp. 54–60.

45 Davidoff and Hall, *Family Fortunes*, pp. 445, 450.

46 Amanda Vickery, *The Gentleman's Daughter: Women's Lives in Georgian England* (New Haven, CN: Yale University Press, 1998), p. 9. For an example of this kind of encounter, see Clare Brant's discussion of Hester Thrale in ch. 13, below p. 295. For public and private as they relate to 'middling', rather than elite, women, see Margaret R. Hunt, *The Middling Sort: Commerce, Gender, and the Family in England, 1680–1780* (Berkeley, Los Angeles, and London: University of California Press, 1996), esp. chs. 3, 5, 8.

47 Lawrence E. Klein, 'Gender and the Public/Private Distinction in the Eighteenth Century: Some Questions About Evidence and Analytic Procedure', *Eighteenth-Century Studies*, 29 (1995), 103–5. For an extensive discussion of the separate spheres debate, see the special issue of *Prose Studies*, 18 (December 1995), especially the introductory essays by Paula R. Backscheider and Timothy Dykstal in which they give, respectively, a more hostile and a more accommodating view of the usefulness of the concept.

CHAPTER 5

Women in families: the great disinheritance

Ruth Perry

We need . . . an analysis of the evolution of sexual exchange along the lines of Marx's discussion in *Capital* of the evolution of money and commodities.

Gayle Rubin, 'Traffic in Women'

From beginning to end, then, landowners' legal history is much to be seen as the effort to overcome the common law rights of daughters.

Eileen Spring, *Law, Land, & Family*[1]

CHANGING FAMILY STRUCTURES

Sometime between the end of the seventeenth century and the middle of the eighteenth century, a momentous shift in the structure of kinship occurred in English society. It is a shift that has gone unrecorded by demographic historians because it did not result in changes visible in the parish records and susceptible of analysis by computer. It may have contributed to the younger age at which people got married in the eighteenth century and to the general rise in nuptuality – and hence to the doubling of the English population – or it may itself have been caused by these demographic phenomena. The shift I am referring to involves a psychological shift in the meaning of family and kinship, a change in the axis of what constituted the primary kin group. While its overall patterning has thus far eluded historians of the family, all of its constitutive parts have been noted and described in the vast literature concerning the family, sex, and marriage in eighteenth-century England.[2] The shift was one of emphasis: the biologically given family into which one was born was gradually becoming secondary to the chosen family constructed by marriage.

This shift in the axis of kinship was tied to the changing fortunes of England, including its position in an international colonial economy, the realignment of the various classes, the evolution of a cash economy, 'proto-industrialization' in manufacturing,[3] the growing importance of land-based capitalism or large-scale agriculture, and the new need for capital accumulation in order to achieve economic success in whatever class or endeavour. These developments were altering the social structures of English society and putting pressure on the traditional kinship system that had been a hallmark of English society since earlier times. This traditional bilateral, cognatic system was relatively symmetrical with respect to gender: lineage had always been traced through both the maternal and paternal lines; daughters inherited as well as sons; and widows had substantial property rights in their deceased husbands' estates. Its tenets stipulated, for example, that daughters inherited property before collateral male relatives. Moreover, according to Amy Louise Erickson, 'ecclesiastical rules of inheritance in intestacy [i.e. dying without a will] followed Roman civil law, in so far as all children, regardless of sex, were entitled to equal portions of their parents' moveable goods. Similarly, the goods of unmarried people dying intestate were equally divided among all their siblings.'[4]

What changed by the middle of the eighteenth century were not only the legal rules governing inheritance, restructured so as to concentrate rather than redistribute wealth in families – usually in the male line – but also a psychological downplaying of this bilateral, cognatic kindred system. It was gradually replaced with a kin system that favoured affinal bonds (bonds of marriage) over consanguineal bonds (bonds of blood), and that privileged the conjugal family over the lineal family psychologically. This shift was overdetermined. But certainly one strand of explanation for it has to do with the increased possibilities for social mobility, and the spread of democratic ideology which supported it. These reduced the absolute determining significance of the family into which one had been born. The importance of who one married, on the other hand, was gaining significance. Thus, the shift that I am describing is one in which a person's blood relations or consanguineal kin became less important, while his or her conjugal relations and affinal kin took on a greater significance in determining his or her place in the world. The developing system involved the revaluing of all kin relations – relations among siblings; inter-generational obligation, whether between parents and children or uncles, aunts, nieces and nephews; the degree of connection felt to maternal and paternal cousins; the strength of bonds with relatives created by marriage such as in-laws or step-siblings. Thus the change affected everyone in families: men and women, boys and girls, young and old.

Women lost more ground in this shift than they gained. For while there was potential in the new system for marrying 'up' – witness Pamela Andrews in Samuel Richardson's *Pamela* (1740) – on the whole it weakened women's position to lose their leverage as daughters and sisters, members of a prior family, and to be reduced to being primarily 'chickens brought up for the tables of other men', as Clarissa's brother, James Harlowe, puts it in Richardson's *Clarissa* (1747–8). As Mr B. explains in *Pamela*, 'A man ennobles the woman he takes, be she *who* she will; and adopts her into his own rank, be it *what* it will.'[5] His formulation implies that every woman is intrinsically orphaned, lacking social identity until she is 'adopted' by a husband and brought into his family.[6]

A full analysis of the meaning of this kinship shift would have to examine changes across all of women's kin positions. I want here to examine the disinheritance of daughters as one major symptom of the loss entailed. Although I will use historical sources to corroborate the changes I am positing, much of my evidence comes from literary sources, for fiction is where the culture most fully explored the social dislocations caused by this shift in kinship priorities.

DISINHERITED DAUGHTERS

Visible signs of the disinheritance of daughters are everywhere in the literature of the period: in portraits of younger sisters victimised by the machinations of step-mothers, cousins, evil servants, self-serving siblings; in images of educated and respectable women who find themselves, through no fault of their own, alone in the world without 'friends' – that is to say, relatives or protectors; in stories of orphans who turn out to be well-born after all and who, by the end of the novel, are miraculously reunited with their missing mothers, fathers, sisters, or brothers; in stories of illegally diverted fortunes set right by indisputable documents long hidden in inherited caskets and then corroborated in the flesh by the minute testimony of ancient, loyal servants; and most dramatically, in tearful tales of daughters long-separated from their fathers but recognised and lovingly claimed in the end because of their uncanny resemblance to their dear departed mothers. These are the literary formulas that bear testimony to some new, tragic displacement of daughters. In all of these familiar plots, daughters are somehow forced out of their families of origin at the beginning of the story but relocated again in time to claim their rightful names and fortunes. Justice is invariably served and in the end they inherit what is due them, so they can marry the men they love as fully endowed equals.

These textual enactments, whatever their particular form, obsessively refer to the dispossession of daughters as the originating problem: this is the social disruption that needs to be resolved, the disquieting circumstance from which all subsequent adventures flow. Many critics have offered explanations for this focus on isolated women. Long ago, Myra Jehlen argued that the embattled heroine of the eighteenth-century novel represented the drama of the suppressed interior self, doomed in the newly alienated materialist public world. My own earlier formulation was that middle-class women, who, unlike the men of their class were expected to eschew productive labour, best illustrated the pleasures and dangers of heightened and privatised consciousness represented by the new culture of novels. Others have claimed that the lone woman best represented the new, individualistic, self-made person; only her inner worth and not her family name or property determine what she will become. '[T]he modern individual was first and foremost a woman', Nancy Armstrong asserted in her political history of the domestic woman – meaning that women were the first members of society to be judged on the basis of their own subjective qualities of mind and heart, rather than on the basis of their inherited class, status, or origins.[7] In her formulation, Armstrong implies that the ties of filiation that bind people to their families and communities were loosened first for women, with the result that women were the first beings conceptualised as atomised, free-standing, isolated individuals in the modern world.[8] While all of these formulations are in some sense true, I now think that this compulsively repeated plot premise – the dispossession of daughters – is a mythic recording of a banal truth: shifts in the social and economic purposes of kinship in the course of the seventeenth century resulted in a reconception of the daughter's place in the family as temporary, partial, and burdensome.

Many novels by women register this sense of protagonists being unfairly de-legitimated; rightful inheritors having to make their way in the world without being recognised as such, sometimes without a name. All of Frances Burney's heroines contend sooner or later with having been disinherited: in *Evelina* (1778), the eponymous heroine is repeatedly embarrassed by her lack of a family name, and the heroines of both *Cecilia* (1782) and *The Wanderer* (1814) illustrate the excruciating difficulties for a woman without name or family. Charlotte Smith's *Emmeline* (1788); Mary Robinson's *The Natural Daughter* (1799); Elizabeth Helme's *Louisa; or the Cottage on the Moor* (1787) – these are other well-known late eighteenth-century novels featuring disinherited daughters who triumph in the end by proving that their births were legitimate after all. Usually the offspring of a love-match made secretly behind the backs of controlling, prideful, or venal parents and then tragically terminated by the death of one or both of the secretly married couple, the infant daughter is cast adrift in the world. But however the plot is managed, the denouement always involves an explanation that absolutely vindicates the heroine's rightful claim to inherit name and (usually) property.

One of the most elaborate versions of this narrative of lost identity, discovery, and validation is Clara Reeve's *The Old English Baron*. Although the plot of re-legitimation is worked out through a male protagonist, the novel was written by a woman who lived through the mid-century changes I am positing. Set in the feudal past and involving mostly male characters, the situations and forms of expressiveness in this novel are transposed from the female-centred sentimental novel of the day: the main characters blanch and blush and weep as often as they engage in manly exercise and swordplay. Its plot, too, like the sentimental novels mentioned above, features a child whose pedigree is lost but who proves his (her) legitimacy and claims his (her) rightful place in the family lineage.[9]

Edmund, the hero, apparently the son of a peasant but with accomplishments and bearing far above his station, discovers by supernatural means that he is the rightful heir to Castle Lovel. With the help of several father figures (an old servant, a priest, the knight Sir Philip Harclay, just returned from the Holy Land and a friend in his youth to Edmund's real father, and, finally, Baron Fitz-Owen, present occupant of the castle) Edmund proves his legitimacy and claims his inheritance. The source of evil in this novel is envy born of rancorous intra-familial competition; but in the end, love and generosity of spirit prevail. In the climactic scene in which Edmund is acknowledged as the rightful heir to the castle by both Baron Fitz-Owen and Sir Philip Harclay, the two men to whom he most owes filial obedience, he throws himself at their feet and embraces their knees, unable to 'utter a word'. When they raise him up, symbolically as well as literally, he faints into the arms of Sir Philip, 'deprived of strength and almost of life' by the emotional strain.[10] A hero with the sensibility of a woman, Edmund occupies a feminised position in this novel: patient and enduring when his class position requires it, and supplicating rather than demanding, grateful rather than triumphant, when he receives undeniable proof of his real social position.

Published in 1777 as *The Champion of Virtue* and reissued in 1778 under the new title, *The Old English Baron* was the most popular of Clara Reeve's novels. It went through ten editions by 1800, and was translated into French and German. Reeve announced her novel as the 'literary offspring' of Walpole's *Castle of Otranto* (1764). Imitating the gothic trappings and atmosphere of *Otranto*, and, superficially, the plot line, Reeve makes very different use of her materials. Although, like Theodore in *Otranto*, her protagonist is a handsome peasant who carries his birthright in his visage and looks just like the noble ancestor's portrait on the wall, Edmund does not want to destroy the present tenants of his noble family's castle, but to be acknowledged by them. Whereas Theodore does generational battle to supplant the incestuous father, Edmund above all desires the father's emotional and legal acceptance. The point in Reeve's novel is not to triumph over Baron Fitz-Owen and his sons, but to be acknowledged by them as legitimate; not to overturn established authority but to be welcomed by it. When Edmund returns to take possession of Castle Lovel, all the doors spring open of their own accord (p. 130).

Indeed, the structural oddity of this novel is that the sequence of supernatural discovery is completed before the novel is halfway over and the entire second half is devoted to working out in painstaking detail the means by which Edmund can claim his place. And he shores up in writing each step along the way, so as to clinch his case quietly and effectively without disrupting or displacing the rest of the noble family into which he is so unexpectedly inserted. Fathers and sons, real and symbolic, are compulsively reintroduced, recombined, and reunited with much shedding of tears. Pledges of obedience are obsessively repeated, furnishing the dramatic events. But these emotionally laden protestations of eternal loyalty, made by servants to masters, sons to fathers and fathers to sons, brothers to brothers and cousins to cousins, are all guaranteed by the legalistic recording of Edmund's discoveries and reversals. This is no romance world in which revelation alone changes rank and property ownership. The changes revealed by dreams and ghostly visitation must be bureaucratically registered to be effective. The murdering interloper must make over his property to Edmund in writing with witnesses. Commissioners are appointed to investigate and document Edmund's alleged discoveries about his birth and the reader retraces with them the steps to visible proof: bloody armour, the aristocratic tokens found with the infant and mother, testimony of servants and adoptive parents. An account of all the extant evidence is drawn up and attested to. After this satisfactory scrutiny they proclaim: 'that there could be no collusion between them, and that the proofs were indisputable' (p. 133). The money that has changed hands in the years that Castle Lovel has been unlawfully held by others must be calculated: the purchase price, the yearly rents, the expenses of Edmund's education – all these are part of the functional solution that gets worked out. In addition to these monetary adjustments, the estates and entourages of all the principals are sorted out and re-assigned at the end of the novel – who will live where with whom – in an attempt to square worldly accounts with moral and social readjustments. Sir Philip and the Baron discuss the best way to establish legally Edmund's legitimacy and they decide to appeal to the king for a parliamentary writ.

Because Edmund's story symbolically enacts the longed-for restitution of the disinherited daughter reclaiming her rightful place in the family, it is only poetic justice that *The Old English Baron* was dedicated to Samuel Richardson's daughter. Within the world of the novel itself, female lineage is portrayed as competing with – and disruptive of – male lineage. For example, the villainous relatives who try to discredit and even kill Edmund are the Baron's maternal nephews, his sister's sons. When Sir Philip Harclay, Edmund's protector, introduces him into society as his adopted son while working out his strategy to regain Edmund's proper patrimony, he gives Edmund the temporary name of Seagrave, a name borrowed from Sir Philip's mother's family. Actual female relatives in the novel, on the other hand, have no functional role beyond cementing the entitlements of the male line. Daughters are deployed by their fathers to ratify alliances by marriage. The endogamous first cousin marriage that completes the integration of Edmund's lineage, and that of the Baron Fitz-Owen, is welcomed on the last page of the novel as 'the band of love that unites all my children to me, and to each other' (p. 152).

The mixture of conventions in this novel, the way it begins as gothic romance and ends with realistic legal consequences, can be read as the narrative of one kind of family dissolving into another. Edmund's champions begin by vowing fealty to him, but by the end of the novel they are calculating damages, witnessing testamentary documents, and appealing to the government for bureaucratic writs. Although bodily evidence is important in the narrative – such as the fact that Edmund is a dead ringer for Sir Arthur Lovel's youthful portrait or that a skeleton tied neck to heels is discovered locked in a trunk just where the evil Sir Walter Lovel confessed to burying it – such bodily evidence coexists with equally important testamentary evidence, such as statements made separately by two witnesses and then corroboratively compared (this happens no less than five times), or written statements prepared and signed for legal filing. Evidence of the senses must be validated by written documentation if it is to have the weight of truth; it is legal language that makes things real. As Edmund says in another context: 'words are all my inheritance' (p. 25).

This preference for written proof, good even at long distance and valuable in any context, more durable than custom or memory, goes with the emphasis in this novel on the equal viability of adoptive families with blood or consanguineal families. All of Edmund's fathers are adoptive fathers – because both his biological parents are dead. The last of his line, Edmund inspires family-like loyalty in others, voluntary bonds of love and obligation that are quite as powerful as those given by birth. Nonetheless, the cross-cousin marriages that tie up the novel with its final bow at the end ratify these chosen and voluntary relationships with a blood bond and naturalise in biology what had been socially constructed. Thus the created family and the biologically given family dissolve back and forth into one another, neither sufficient to the requirements of narrative, together satisfying a need in the readership to see both kinds of family configuration in play. The denied biological relationship starts off the action, asserting itself with the aid of the supernatural and offering as a primal motive, family revenge and restitution. But this motive is soon supplemented by connections based on affinity, loyalty to merit, to character, to intrinsic quality – all of which are made fully equivalent to blood relationships, sooner or later, by legal means. Thus the feudal coexists with the bureaucratic in this oddly mixed tale of birth and merit. Written by a conservative woman who believed both in class and racial determinants of social status, but who, as a woman, knew that gender prejudice hindered the reward of merit in women, this novel simultaneously dramatises the wish-fulfilment fantasy of the wrongfully disinherited child who rises to take his (her) rightful place, while it reinscribes the natural entitlement of class.[11]

The disinheritance illustrated by this novel of the 1770s did not, of course, happen overnight. It had been building slowly for several centuries, with the erosion of provisions for daughters (and wives and widows) in equity, manorial, and ecclesiastical as well as in common law. Amy Louise Erickson has argued that British historians' emphasis on common law, with its primogenitary emphasis, to the exclusion of the other three forms of law, is anachronistic and often results in a misapprehension of Englishwomen's entitlements in earlier centuries. Women's property rights were often better protected under equity, chancery, and ecclesiastical law, she claims, than under common law. Hence, familiarity with just this body of case law misrepresents the entitlements that were being chipped away.[12] Under provisions in ecclesiastical law, for example, a family's land descended to daughters in the event that there were no sons; England had always had large landowners who were women. But in the late seventeenth and early eighteenth centuries, a number of provisions in common law limited women's inheritance of land and a series of statutes in ecclesiastical law reduced women's rights to their husbands' or fathers' moveable goods, limiting their entitlements from as much as two-thirds to one-third or less.[13]

Eileen Spring argues that the proportion of families who by chance will have no heirs at all and only female collateral relatives, combined with those who will have only female heirs, adds up to at least a quarter of all cases. If the earlier provisions of ecclesiastical and common law had been faithfully followed, these are the cases in which inherited property would have passed to women.[14] But over the previous century or so, property owners who were heads of families had tampered with these rules, reducing the number of inheritances going directly to women to less than 8 per cent. This was true even before the invention of the strict settlement in the middle of the seventeenth century. Using data collected by Lawrence and Jeanne Stone, and by Peter Laslett, Spring demonstrates how collateral male relatives – such as the brothers of a woman's father, or even a nephew – were often placed in the inheritance line before the woman, if there were no male offspring in a family. This was done, presumably, to keep the property attached to the family name.

The strict settlement codified these arrangements.[15] A legal document drawn up as part of a marriage contract, the strict settlement designated provisions for the as yet unborn children of the coming union, ensuring that the property jointly owned by the new couple would be entailed on any males born to the line. The full value of the property to be entailed on male offspring could be further enhanced by limiting the monetary share set aside from it for possible female children. Estates were thus protected against future owners who might have a change of heart about dynastic aggrandisement and leave the family property instead to an adored daughter. Women's hereditary rights in property were thus inexorably made secondary to the imperative for accumulation – 'engrossing' was the eighteenth-century word – in large landowning families.

If proportions of family property designated for daughters of noble families declined, thus increasing the size of estates passed from father to son, middle-class daughters were also deployed in the service of their families' fortunes – either to enrich or ennoble them. The novels of the second half of the eighteenth century abound with examples of young women thus used by their families. Indeed, it is difficult to think of a single novel in which no woman is pressured to marry against her will – or not to marry where she wishes to – because of some family exigency that creates an unresolvable dilemma between duty and desire. Even if this standard fictional situation did not reflect a social reality, it conditioned the oppositional terms in which marriage choice and inheritance were commonly considered: daughters were not expected to share equally in the resources of their families of origin, despite the foundation in law for them to do so.

Nor was the disinheritance of daughters confined to the propertied classes. In the rural labouring class or servant class, the position of daughters altered too, so far as we can determine, although this came chronologically a little later. The Parliamentary Enclosure Acts of the second half of the eighteenth century were closing out what was left of the English peasantry by the 1770s.[16] Feudal tenures had been put on a cash rent basis, and few labouring-class people could avoid the cash nexus, whether to sell their labour, their surplus produce, or their cottage manufactures. Such families were increasingly dependent on the money economy for their livelihood, and the sheer lack of possibilities for earning, not to mention the level of wages set for women in this new cash economy, reduced their economic value to their families and probably their psychological value as well. The centuries-old system of service-in-husbandry was falling into disuse, even in the labouring classes, further reducing the options for unmarried daughters. As late as the beginning of the eighteenth-century, 60 per cent of young people of both sexes were still 'life-cycle' servants of this sort, supplying labour and learning skills in some other household as a stage in their own lives.[17] But the discontinuance of this practice – presumably a function of the rise in food prices and other subsistence costs, which made it cheaper to hire seasonal day labour than to board so many servants – bore heavily on the daughters of cottagers, farmers, yeomen, and labouring-class families. It made them more of an economic burden on their families of origin and put a premium on getting married as their only way of leaving the jurisdiction of their parents.

The commercialisation of the English economy, the growing proportion of the population dependent on waged labour for a livelihood, the rise in men's wages for day labour and the decline in women's employment opportunities along with their lower wage rates, together with the disappearance of a land base to support non-waged subsistence – these factors were accompanied by a significant drop in the age of marriage for both men and women, a slight rise in the size of households, and a sudden spurt of proto-industrial cottage industry among cottagers and small landowners in order to make their rent and pay their expenses. This kind of small, rural, manufacture – weaving, spinning, gloving, straw-plaiting, lace-making, leather-working, calico-printing, hand or framework knitting – thrived in many of the still unenclosed villages supported by arable agriculture.[18] These goods were being produced in domestic settings for non-local markets, by a range of family members, to supplement the family income. As E. J. Hobsbawm observed: the *obvious* way of industrial expansion in the eighteenth century was 'not to construct factories, but to extend the so-called domestic system'.[19]

Women's labour within their families was key to this process of proto-industrialisation. They created the subsistence on which this small-time manufacturing depended, tending a few animals such as chickens or cows that added protein to the family's diet, making butter and cheese for home consumption, spinning and weaving the family's linen, growing vegetables for home consumption in a kitchen garden, gathering fuel, cooking, washing, and the like. They also participated in the production itself, whether combing wool, dressing and spinning flax, weaving silk, or seaming and finishing the stocking or other garment produced by framework knitting.[20] When women left domestic manufacture and joined the waged work-force, their economic leverage within their families declined significantly. There was an enormous difference between income that supplemented a basic subsistence and income that was expected to buy all necessities, including housing; and women's wages were usually a third less than men's wages.

While the drive to consolidate large landholdings among aristocrats and the upper gentry promoted the development of strict settlement, dowry-jointure exchanges, and trusts for women, thus reducing wealthy women's independent access to their inherited estates, among the cottager class, enclosure of 'waste' lands undercut labouring women's access to rural subsistence. For different but interrelated reasons, then, women of both the landowning and working classes lost economic power within the family and status in society in the course of the eighteenth century. Only in middle-class families was women's place re-evaluated without being seen as a net loss, and a new ideology evolved to naturalise it.[21]

CLARISSA AND THE CHANGING FAMILY

Samuel Richardson's *Clarissa*, written in the middle of the century by a man who had lived as an adult through all these changes, may be the most complete fictional statement of this process. The structure and progression of events in *Clarissa* enact all these issues with the clarity of dumbshow. Like an economic morality play, the action demonstrates the combined effects of primogeniture and capital accumulation for female offspring in landowning families, of class mobility and 'family aggrandizement' – as Clarissa herself puts it (p. 82) – on the position of middle-class daughters, and even the effects of diminished subsistence economies on labouring-class women. Clarissa's entrapment proceeds inexorably despite her moral perfection, her powerful intelligence, and verbal acuity.

The family, as it is represented at mid century, is hardly a nuclear family. Besides parents and children, the 'Harlowes' consist of Clarissa's parents' siblings, cousins, and servants. As Clarissa remarks, 'never was there a family more united in its different branches than ours. Our uncles consider us as their own children, and declare that it is for our sakes that they live single' (p. 56). In this delicately balanced power structure, her paternal uncles – her father's brothers – have significant authority, certainly more than her maternal aunt – her mother's half-sister. These male relatives, together with her father, line up their interests behind the inheriting son, James Harlowe Jr. Although her uncles have always loved her, they are not willing to sacrifice their relationship to the heir of what promises to be a great estate, for the sake of a younger sister refusing to play her part in the family's aggrandising fortune. Arabella anatomises the peculiarities of what their grandfather has done in his will – the crucial beginning of this novel. 'To leave the acquired part of his estate from the next heirs, his own sons, to a grandchild', she exclaims. That is, to have improved a fortune and added to it, but not to leave it all together in one piece was contrary to the spirit of the age. And then to leave it 'to his *youngest* grandchild! a *daughter* too!' only adds insult to injury (p. 194).

As early as her fourth letter to Anna Howe, Clarissa observes her brother's power in the family hierarchy. When he returns from inspecting his estates in Scotland and Yorkshire (property left him by a generous godmother), Clarissa notes that he thanks his father for waiting to consult him about Lovelace's suit 'in such a manner, I thought, as a superior would do when he commended an inferior for having well performed his duty in his absence' (p. 48). This distortion of inter-generational as well as cross-gender relations is caused by the combined effects of primogeniture and strict settlement, whose result was to entail the family wealth upon the first-born son when he reached his majority and thus to reduce the father's claims to no more than a life tenancy in the estate. Clarissa tries repeatedly to reassert an earlier 'more natural' family dynamic, to return family relations to what they were before being distorted by acquisitiveness and her brother's will to power. '[Y]ou are *only* my brother', she keeps telling him (p. 57).

Clarissa's story illustrates how women could be deprived of their rightful inheritance and psychologically blackmailed, as well as threatened legally if they resisted their dispossession. The novel further shows how the ownership of property is tied to power, even within the family, and how the disinheritance of their rightful access to property could throw women on the mercy of their families and turn them into little more than slaves to their male relatives. Clarissa declares to her mother, 'although I am to be treated by my brother and, through his instigations, by my papa, as a slave in this point, and not as a daughter, yet my mind is not that of a slave' (p. 111). 'It is hard . . . to be forbid to enter into the cause of all,' she pleads, when refused the right to defend herself against her brother, to expose his venal motives for misconstruing her attitude, 'because I must not speak disrespectfully of one who supposes me in the way of his ambition, and treats me like a slave –' (p. 95).

To her brother, Clarissa is a financial liability. Her inheritance from her grandfather, as she explains, 'lopped off one branch of my brother's expectation' (p. 77). The dowry inflation of the early eighteenth century, noted by Habakkuk in his famous article on the growing use of marriage alliances to amass great estates, undoubtedly drove a wedge between inheriting brothers and their portioned sisters: inheritance law and the drive to accumulate larger and larger estates constructed their material interests increasingly at odds with one another.[22] James Harlowe Jr wants to marry Clarissa to Solmes because his promised terms, as her mother explains, 'will very probably prevent your grandfather's estate going out of the family and may be a means to bring a still greater into it' (p. 98). She resists his violent attempt to dispose of her hand, enacted literally by her brother when he grabs, crushes, and violently tosses her hand and arm, making her weep with pain (p. 304). In addition to thus embodying the economic allegory precisely, Richardson's genius in splitting patriarchal authority between Clarissa's father and her brother permits him to criticise the misuse of male power, while preserving and reinscribing it. This doubled attitude is what feminists weigh in their debates about Richardson's treatment of women. He simultaneously represents his heroine as obedient and independent, respectful of her father but scornful of her brother, fully aware of the illegitimacy of male power but never unnaturally – ungenteelly, unfemininely – disrespectful of patriarchal authority.

In traditional societies, the exchange of women accomplished not the accumulation of property and capital, but, according to Lévi-Strauss among others, forestalled violence, created alliances between clans, cemented peace treaties, and the like. Giving one's daughter in marriage was a political pledge of good faith; she became a hostage to one's peaceful intentions. It was precisely because she carried the clan's blood in her veins that a daughter could function as a kind of voucher for good intentions in such exchanges between clans.[23] Examined in this context, the social meaning of the Harlowes' change of heart about Clarissa in the months before she finally flees her father's house recapitulates the changing position of daughters within a family structure undergoing the transition to capitalistic modes of accumulation. When Mrs Harlowe asks Clarissa to maintain her correspondence with Lovelace for the sake of family peace – to pacify him and to prevent him from responding with physical force to James Harlowe Jr's provocative gestures – Clarissa functions as a kind of propitiatory offering, maintaining the balance of power between the two families, ensuring that their individual male representatives will not fight a duel and spill blood. But what begins as a collective tribal offering ends up as the sacrifice of an individual on the altar of Mammon, as the meaning and functioning of the Harlowe family changes before our eyes. Although Clarissa began her correspondence with Lovelace 'with general approbation' (p. 47) and continues it to keep the peace, it becomes an increasingly desperate last resort in her retreat from a family that refuses to recognise her rights within it.

Clarissa can be read as a kind of everywoman, standing for womankind under siege. Her fate records not only the historical trajectory of middle-class women but also, in its trace elements, the dissolution of the subsistence economies and the impoverishment of rural women who depended on these economies during a time in which most of England's remaining common lands were being privatised – that is, enclosed. Rural women had traditionally made in-kind contributions to their family economies, exploiting the resources of the commons and 'waste' lands to gather fuel, raise gardens, and support cows, chickens, and hogs, rather than entering the arena of waged labour. As their potential contributions to the family's livelihood were cut back with the transfer of common lands for grazing and gardening into private hands, their dependence on male wage-earners increased. As I explained earlier, the movement from subsistence economies and household production for use, to a market economy and production for profit, weakened women's claims within the family.

Clarissa's skill in managing the Harlowe establishment – relieving her mother of her 'household cares' – illustrates this contribution of domestic labour even among women of the propertied classes. Early in the process of her subjugation, her brother proposes that she go to Scotland to put his house there in order; but her mother needs her skills at home and Clarissa has no mind to be her brother's housekeeper, where she is sure to be 'treated rather as a servant than as a sister', demonstrating the ambiguous difference between the labours of women of one class and another. As things worsen, 'the keys of everything are taken from [her]' (p. 116) and Clarissa is forbidden to continue her responsibilities in the Harlowe household. Disgraced, her employment is taken from her, signalling an end to her mobility (she is no longer allowed to go to church), her power (her own servant, Hannah, is dismissed), and her usefulness within the household.

Indeed, throughout her struggles with her family while still in her father's house, Clarissa's autonomy is best protected in those places associated with the subsistence economies that had customarily been controlled by women. 'I dare not ask to go to my dairy-house,' she writes to Anna Howe, 'for I am now afraid of being thought to have a wish to enjoy that independence to which [my grandfather's] will has entitled me' (p. 56). The 'dairy-house', originally called 'The Grove' by her grandfather, had been renamed synecdochally for the dairy-house that he erected and fitted up on the premises for Clarissa's use and pastime. This estate he left free and clear to Clarissa for her own use, giving her economic independence from her family. Dairying was one of the most important subsistence economies traditionally managed by women's labour and made possible their customary access to common or 'waste' land for pasturage and fodder. Indeed, when their family allotments permitted them to keep cows, women could pursue the practice professionally – for a healthy profit – as well as to feed their families. Although very labour intensive, there was enough profit margin in keeping cows when pasturage was free for an enterprising woman to earn enough from selling her butter and cheese to make the rent on the family farm.[24] So beneficial were cows understood to be for women's welfare, that it was not uncommon for parish overseers to bestow a cow upon a single, poor woman as a way of maintaining her, like a kind of social security pension. For women with children, a cow or a few cows provided an important dietary supplement of milk and cheese for the family: after the period of the heaviest land enclosures, rural children no longer drank milk as a matter of course and the majority of rural labourers could no longer eat cheese every day.

In the period in which *Clarissa* was being read, dairying was being contested as a system of kin-based production, a locus of women's expertise and skill. Men had begun to show an interest in this relatively lucrative business and to write treatises about the practice of dairying, often decrying women's ignorance about the matter and offering up-to-the-moment scientific advice for better dairy processing. Middlemen, buying up the produce of small-time dairywomen to ship to urban centres or to supply the army, were beginning to transform dairying into a system of capitalised production with transportation and distant markets.[25] The dairy was beginning to be contested as women's space, the 'unchallenged preserve of female authority and labour',[26] and the site of women's economic independence. As more and more common land was enclosed, so that pasturage had to be rented, housewives no longer had the wherewithal to pursue dairying as a profitable hobby and part of their subsistence economy. That dairying was doomed to disappear as a safety net for labouring-class women makes the discussion in *Clarissa* about the heroine's inheritance still more poignant. Anna Howe is convinced that the 'dairy-house' is Clarissa's best possible hope for a satisfactory life. But Clarissa is afraid to claim it as a refuge because she knows her male relatives will litigate if she does. Not only will it then appear to the world that she is claiming contested property not legally hers, but she is not willing to survive on those terms, at the cost of losing her family.

The other important site of Clarissa's independence was the poultry-yard, where she left her letters for Anna Howe. Keeping chickens was the other standard kin-based subsistence economy grounded in access to common or 'waste' lands. Milk and eggs – symbolic female substances – thus carry resonances of gender-specific labours from another era. Clarissa's poultry-yard is also associated with her inherited estate, her 'dairy-house', in so far as her favourite birds – her bantams, pheasants, and pea-hens – come from The Grove and were recommended to her care by her grandfather (p. 66). Evocative of pastoral scenes and wholesome country life, the poultry-yard is on Green Lane, which, as Clarissa writes to Anna Howe, runs past two or three farmhouses. Anna was to send her servant Robert there ('out of livery, if you please') to exchange the letters of these two disobedient daughters, tokens of their defiance and individualism. It is in the empowering poultry-yard, hidden by a high hedge, that Clarissa overhears her brother and sister laughing and talking with Solmes about how to subdue her (p. 225) – information that helps her to better understand what she is up against.

Thus many elements of the historical processes that attenuated the position of daughters within their families of origin are present in some recognisable form in Richardson's *Clarissa*. Eroded by a number of developments associated with capital accumulation and the disruption of customary use relations, women's rights within their families came to be less well defined. I have been arguing that the position of daughters in English society is diagnostically represented by Clarissa in miniature, in her deteriorating relations with the Harlowe family. Clarissa's brother is simply giving voice to a commonplace sentiment when he declares that 'daughters were but encumbrances and drawbacks upon a family' (p. 77).

The weakened position of mothers and maternal relatives was another effect of the capitalisation of the family with concentration of wealth in the male line and the growing sense that although women could be expected to be agents of this process of accumulation they were never its beneficiaries. As the Harlowe family demonstrates its real basis in the accumulation of capital, Clarissa is pushed farther and farther out of the kin network and the claims of the maternal line – her mother and her mother's kin, the relatives in traditional kin formations most responsible for protecting female offspring – are simultaneously weakened. It is no coincidence that Cousin Morden, Clarissa's ultimate defender and trustee of her grandfather's will, is a maternal relative and is sojourning in Italy, a country coded female in most eighteenth-century English fiction. Richardson explains the diminished power of Clarissa's maternal relatives by inventing a financial obligation owed by Mr Hervey, her mother's sister's husband, although the diminished rights of mothers and of maternal relatives over the persons and property of children is a fact of legal history that needs no objective correlative. In Richardson's plot, Clarissa's brutal brother has paid off a mortgage on a part of Mr Hervey's estate and taken the debt upon himself. This is, according to Anna Howe, 'a small favour . . . from kindred to kindred: but such a one, it is plain, as has laid the whole family of the Herveys under obligation to the ungenerous lender' (p. 212). This indebtedness is used to explain Mrs Hervey's uneasy silence in the face of the obvious tyranny of

Clarissa's paternal relations, although it does not account for the passivity of Clarissa's mother.

I have been arguing that *Clarissa* is a novel about the dissolutions of 'family values' – at least with respect to daughters. 'Our family has been strangely discomposed' (p. 41) writes Clarissa to Anna at the outset. 'You are all too rich to be happy', replies her friend. Competitive and individualistic rather than co-operative and communal, members of this family appear to be afraid of one another, their interests at odds rather than collective. The novel is a masterpiece of indirect communication, of intelligence gathered by snooping, spying, overhearing, everyone secretly monitoring everyone else's conversations. Thus, the family of consanguinity is represented as unstable, its ties of affection and obligation all but effaced by material considerations.

Nevertheless, despite being mercilessly persecuted by them, Clarissa remains loyal to her family – it is part of her traditionalism – much to Lovelace's irritation. 'Sordid ties!' he exclaims; 'Mere cradle-prejudices!' (p. 145). She would prefer never to marry at all, but to remain living at home, as she explains to her 'second papa', her uncle Harlowe:

Marriage is a very solemn engagement, enough to make a young creature's heart ache, with the *best* prospects, when she thinks seriously of it!—To be given up to a strange man; to be engrafted into a strange family; to give up her very name . . . to be obliged to prefer this strange man to father, mother—to everybody. (p. 148)

Her pain at being forced out of the family is continually before us, both because of Lovelace's perfidy and because of her incessant longing to be reinstated in *some* family – even *his* family. She leaves with Lovelace originally hoping for the protection of his maternal aunts. Indeed, the only thing he offers her that really tempts her is his family. Every time she is pushed to desperate measures, the one thing that reconciles her to patience is the possibility of kin. 'Father-sick' and 'family-proud' (p. 521) he calls her, playing to this one unabashed desire of hers with all his skill. When he first delays their marriage by holding out the hope that his uncle, Lord M., can be present as a kind of surrogate father, what draws in Clarissa, even more than the marriage itself, is the possibility of the 'paternal wing'. '*Father* had a sweet and venerable sound with it,' she says (p. 599).

Later, when Lovelace creates the impersonated Colonel Tomlinson as a supposed friend and agent of her uncle Harlowe, again holding out the hope of reconciliation with her family, she cries out with an emotion that moves even Lovelace: '[H]ow happy shall I be, when my heart is lightened from the all-sinking weight of a father's curse! When my dear mamma . . . shall once more fold me to her indulgent bosom! When I shall again have uncles and aunts, and a brother and sister' (p. 695). Her later outburst similarly affects him: 'Oh Mr Lovelace . . . what a happiness, if my dear uncle could be prevailed upon to be personally a father on this occasion, to *the poor fatherless girl*.' (p. 709). These scenes move Lovelace to tears for all his sneering about 'mother-spoilt' and 'father-fond' – testifying to their cultural power at the time. For what *Clarissa* enacts – besides the power of language to recreate emotion and reinterpret event – is the dispossession of daughters in the new capitalist dispensation, and the daughter's difficulty in finding a place in the world to belong to once this dispossession had taken effect.

All the orphaned women in eighteenth-century fiction are witness to this cutting loose, this great disinheritance, a function of changing legal, political, and economic systems. Extruded from their consanguineal families and forced to bargain for terms with their potential families by marriage, caught between one system and another, daughters were an early casualty of the effects of capitalism on social relations.

NOTES

1 Gayle Rubin, 'The Traffic in Women: Notes on the "Political Economy" of Sex' in Rayna R. Reiter (ed.), *Toward an Anthropology of Women* (New York: Monthly Review Press, 1875), pp. 157–210 (pp. 204–5); Eileen Spring, *Law, Land, & Family: Aristocratic Inheritance in England, 1300 to 1800* (Chapel Hill and London: University of North Carolina Press, 1993), p. 35.

2 For further discussion, see ch. 4, p. 92; and 'Guide to Further Reading'.

3 The term is described and analysed in an historiographical review of the subject by Rab Houston and K. D. M. Snell, 'Proto-industrialization? Cottage Industry, Social Change, and Industrial Revolution', *The Historical Journal*, 27:2 (1984), 473–92.

4 Amy Louise Erickson, *Women and Property in Early Modern England* (New York and London: Routledge, 1993), p. 28.

5 Samuel Richardson, *Clarissa: or the History of a Young Lady*, ed. Angus Ross, (Harmondsworth: Penguin Books, 1985), p. 77; Samuel Richardson, *Pamela or, Virtue Rewarded*, ed. Peter Sabor, intro. by Margaret A. Doody (Harmondsworth: Penguin Books, 1980), p. 441.

6 I am indebted for this observation to Maaja Stewart, *Domestic Realities and Imperial Fictions* (Athens and London: University of Georgia Press, 1993), p. 163.

7 See: Myra Jehlen, 'Archimedes and the Paradox of Feminist Criticism',

Signs, 6:4 (1981), 575–601; Ruth Perry, *Women, Letters, and the Novel* (New York: AMS Press, 1980), ch. 6, 'Romantic Love and Sexual Fantasy in Epistolary Fiction', pp. 137–67; Nancy Armstrong, *Desire and Domestic Fiction: a Political History of the Novel* (New York and Oxford: Oxford University Press, 1987), p. 8.

8 Susan Staves makes this point in her classic article, 'British Seduced Maidens', where she refers to the trope of the seduced maiden as the sign 'that English society was changing from a society in which persons were defined in terms of their status, including their status in the family, to one in which persons were thought of as individuals.' *Eighteenth-Century Studies*, 14 (1980–1), 109–34 (p. 122).

9 Ann Radcliffe's first novel, the anonymously published *The Castles of Athlin and Dunbayne: a Highland Story* (1789) is another gothic novel about a hero who appears to be born to a peasant family but turns out to be highborn royalty and in the end comes into his rightful inheritance.

10 *The Old English Baron: a Gothic Story*, ed. James Trainer (London: Oxford University Press, 1967), p. 141.

11 In her *Plans of Education* (London: Hookham & Carpenter, 1792), Reeve asserts that the abolition of slavery in the West Indies is quixotic and denies stories of cruelty on the part of English slaveowners. Later in this epistolary fiction, she ascribes racist ideas to the more or less admirable Lord A—, who opposes miscegenation as bound to produce 'a vile mongrel race of people, such as no friend to Britain can ever wish to inhabit it', and suggests as a remedy that all Negroes be banished from Britain (p. 91). At the same time, this text defends women's right to live alone, to improve their (equal) minds, and to support themselves by working (pp. 119–23, 138–9, and passim).

12 Amy Louise Erickson, 'Common law versus common practice: the use of marriage settlements in early modern England', *Economic History Review*, 2nd ser., 43:1 (1990), 21–39.

13 Erickson, *Women and Property in Early Modern England*, pp. 28–9.

14 See Spring, *Law, Land, & Family*, pp. 10–15. She cites E. A. Wrigley's famous calculation that in a stationary population there is a 40 per cent chance that a man will die without leaving a male heir. E. A. Wrigley, 'Fertility Strategy for the Individual and the Group' in Charles Tilly (ed.), *Historical Studies of Changing Fertility* (Princeton University Press, 1978), pp. 150–1.

15 Lloyd Bonfield has argued that the strict settlement was not simply a legal device intended to concentrate landed wealth in the hands of the male heir. Although it often functioned that way, it conceded alienability of the estate to the next generation and at the same time provided for the portions of female offspring and younger sons to be paid from the estate. Lloyd Bonfield, 'Affective Families, Open Elites and Strict Family Settlements in Early Modern England', *Economic History Review*, 2nd ser., 39:3 (1986), 341–54.

16 J. M. Neeson summarises the arguments about the vestigial existence of an

English peasantry in *Commoners: Common Right, Enclosure and Social Change in England, 1700–1820* (Cambridge University Press, 1993), pp. 8–9.

17 'Life-cycle servants' is Peter Laslett's phrase in *The World We Have Lost: Further Explored* (London: Methuen, 1983), pp. 16. Ann Kussmaul estimates that half the youth of England had the experience of service-in-husbandry. *Servants in Husbandry in Early Modern England* (Cambridge University Press, 1981), pp. 1–2.

18 Houston and Snell, 'Proto-industrialization?', 473–92.

19 E. J. Hobsbawm, *The Age of Revolution 1789–1848* (1964), p. 55, quoted in Eric Richards, 'Women in the British Economy Since About 1700: an Interpretation', *History*, 59 (1974), 345.

20 Maxine Berg, 'Women's Work, Mechanisation and the Early Phases of Industrialisation in England' in Patrick Joyce (ed.), *The Historical Meanings of Work* (Cambridge University Press, 1987), pp. 64–98.

21 See Armstrong, *Desire and Domestic Fiction*, ch. 2, 'The Rise of the Domestic Woman', pp. 59–95.

22 H. J. Habakkuk, 'Marriage settlements in the Eighteenth Century', *Transactions of the Royal Historical Society*, 4th ser., 32 (1950), 15–30.

23 See Claude Lévi-Strauss, *The Elementary Structures of Kinship* (Boston: Beacon Press, 1969).

24 For a description of the long hours in a cheese dairy, see Ivy Pinchbeck, *Women Workers and the Industrial Revolution 1750–1850* (1930; rpt. London: Virago Press, 1981), p. 13.

25 Deborah Valenze, *The First Industrial Woman* (New York: Oxford University Press, 1995), ch. 3, 'The Art of Women and the Business of Men: Women's Work and the Dairy Industry', esp. pp. 54–64.

26 Valenze, *The First Industrial Woman*, p. 49.

Women and print

CHAPTER 6

Women and the business of print

Paula McDowell

In 1691, at the age of twenty-five, Tace Sowle succeeded to the London printing business of her father Andrew Sowle, and went on to become the leading Quaker printer of her generation (fl. 1691–1749).[1] Immediately after taking over her family press, she expanded its production, with her name appearing in nearly 300 imprints during the first fifteen years of her career. The Sowle press was the primary channel through which the Society of Friends' works were issued, and Tace Sowle printed the major works of the founders of Quakerism (including George Fox, Margaret Fell Fox, and William Penn, to name only a few). She served as the primary printer of Quaker women's writings, one of the largest categories of women's published writings in this period, and she also oversaw the distribution of Quaker books. For the first half of the eighteenth century, then, Tace Sowle served the largest Non-conformist sect in England not only as the primary printer but also as the primary publisher, warehouser, collecting agent, and adviser on market demands. By the end of its 150-year history, the Sowle press and its successors comprised one of the longest-running printing-houses in the nation, and it was under Tace Sowle's management that the house saw its greatest development.

Tace Sowle's personal talents mark her as an exceptional individual, yet this essay will show that as a woman directly involved in the print trades in this period she was one of many. There was a vast network of women printers and publishers in Britain (especially London), and women participated in the new print culture not only as authors and readers but also as printers, booksellers, hawkers, ballad-singers and others. This essay stresses the *range* of women's activities intersecting with print, arguing that women had more power in early print culture than we have known and of a different kind than we have attended to. Women at all levels of the press helped to shape literary tastes, cultural habits, structures of feeling, and public opinion. What some contemporaries perceived as the problem of the 'women of Grub Street' was much larger than twentieth-century literary critics have understood.

A consideration of women's *diverse* roles as makers of print culture also has implications for our notions of early modern 'authorship'. Authorship is not a solitary activity; rather, writer, reader, printer, and publisher are all part of a 'communications circuit'.[2] This essay suggests the benefits for feminists of a new 'synthetic' model for the study of the literary marketplace, a model linking women print-workers, writers, and consumers. Networks of female involvement merit study, and furthermore, categories within the print trades overlapped. Some women writers also sold books or managed circulating libraries, while some women printers were also authors. The current division of scholarly labour separates those who study texts' ideological content and form (literary critics) from those who study texts' physical production and distribution (publishing historians). But, as three literary and publishing historians working collectively write:

the synthesis of what have until now been separate inquiries – one into women's history in the book trade, and the other into women writers – could prove especially fruitful in increasing our as yet piecemeal information about women working together, and could end the gap between 'book as object' and 'author's text' which is constructed by a literary study which ignores the processes of production.[3]

Women makers of print culture were not only writers and readers, and they were also not only literate elites. While most women writers were of privileged educational background and social rank, women of all classes were affected by print, and in turn, helped to build the nascent literary marketplace. A synthetic model broadens the class spectrum of women we study, and it also opens up women's involvement in a broader variety of texts. To consider 'print culture' from a printer or publisher's point of view is to confront a different textual landscape than literary critics have constructed. It is to gain a new understanding of what were (and were not) the century's dominant forms of printed materials. Whereas today, students of eighteenth-century literature are most likely to study novels, one publishing historian estimates that the proportion of all fiction (new titles and reprints) to total book and pamphlet production for the years 1720–9 was only about 1.1 per cent, rising to 4 per cent by 1770.[4] And while feminist critics have concentrated on women writers of poetry, drama, and especially fiction, a study of women's wider textual involvement suggests that eighteenth-century women as a group were more likely to participate in newspapers and periodicals; religious and political writings such as prayer-books and tracts; schoolbooks, almanacs, and chapbooks; printed visual materials such as engravings, woodcuts, and music; and even the everyday 'stuff' of the print trades, jobbing printing such as posters, tickets, and handbills. To consider women's involvement in these genres is not to avert our gaze to 'marginal' forms. Rather, it is to direct that gaze to some of the most mainstream print genres of this period – and in so doing, to contextualise creative and imaginative genres and, sometimes, to recognise class biases in literary critical traditions of intelligibility and value. As Dianne Dugaw writes in her essay on popular prints elsewhere in this volume, 'Varieties of printed texts set before us categories of class structure.'[5] A full understanding of 'women and the business of print' would include all women and all kinds of printed materials. As (for the most part) professional and academic readers of texts, our reading hierarchies may not be the same as those of the women we study.

This essay begins by outlining women's work in the various sectors of the print trades. It then reviews the evidence for women's involvement, suggesting the special methodological challenges in tracing women. It concludes by suggesting some exciting avenues for research at this point of intersection among scholarly fields (feminist literary criticism and publishing history and media studies). A dramatic rethinking of women's place in early print culture is possible even on the basis of the evidence we already have. New critical paradigms and new directions in archival research will further our understanding of women's founding role in the literary marketplace, the emergence of a political public sphere, and the origins of modern secular feminism in England.

WOMEN IN THE PRINT TRADES

Over the period from 1695 to 1774, the English press underwent some of the most important changes in its history. Before 1695, the guild which oversaw the book trade, the Worshipful Company of Stationers of London, held a royal charter granting its membership sole right to print, publish, or traffic in the printed word. Printing was confined to London and the two university towns, there were strict limits on the number of printers, and texts had to be licensed before they could be printed. During the Civil War period, press controls temporarily collapsed; political upheaval and increased literacy rates had contributed to an unprecedented demand for the printed word. In 1662, the Printing or Licensing Act would revive the principles of government censorship, yet the press would never again be as effectively controlled as it had been prior to the 1640s. In 1695, the Licensing Act was allowed to lapse for good, ending pre-publication censorship and limits on the number of master printers. The situation after 1695 was not that of a 'free press'; government and trade restrictions still limited what could be printed and by whom.[6] Nonetheless, the early eighteenth century was a period of anarchic expansion in the print trades. Whereas before 1695 there were only twenty-four legal printers in all of England, by 1705 there were between sixty-five and seventy printing-houses in London alone.[7] At every level of the press this combination of phenomenal expansion and diminished institutional control was conducive to the participation of women.

The eighteenth-century publishing trades were centralised by modern standards; despite a significant opening-up of provincial markets, London remained the centre of production. As John Feather explains:

The dominance of London publishing was unbroken . . . because it was so strongly entrenched. The provincial trade did indeed undergo revolutionary developments, and was to be of great importance to the London publishers, but it provided a distribution system rather than becoming a rival producer . . . By about 1730, printers were established in most major towns throughout the country. These printers were not engaged in book production, but in newspaper and jobbing work.[8]

The trades were also still family-based. For all but the wealthiest families, home and workshop were the same location, and businesses were passed down through families by intermarriage. In most households, women assisted in the family business as a matter of economic necessity. Tace Sowle's mother, Jane Sowle, worked alongside her father, and Tace's sister Elizabeth was also trained in the family trade.[9] In the upper echelons of the print trades, most women were related to male (or sometimes female) 'freemen' (members) of the Stationers' Company, and this institutional status gave them several rights. The widow of a freeman automatically became a member of the Company herself. If her husband was not in debt, she could retain the family equipment and rights, bind apprentices in her own name, sign contracts, and be granted loans. Theoretically, any woman could obtain the freedom of the Stationers' Company in her own right by apprenticeship or redemption (purchase). In actual fact, however, the number of women who entered the trades by these means was minute. Furthermore, an increasing number of men and women worked outside the regulation and protection of the Stationers' Company altogether. The large number of women who worked as booksellers, for instance, is in part due to the fact that Company membership was not a prerequisite of this aspect of the trade.

Eighteenth-century printing businesses were small by modern standards. A typical establishment might consist of a master printer and his wife (or a widow and a manager), two pressmen per press, a compositor, apprentices, and servants. Two hand presses per printer was the norm. Several widows and daughters of printers carried on family businesses; for instance, Elizabeth Leake, the employer and later mother-in-law of printer-author Samuel Richardson, continued her husband John Leake's business as a printer. Richardson later inherited Elizabeth Leake Senior's 'Printing Presses and Letter Utensils of Trade' by marrying her daughter, also called Elizabeth Leake.[10] While Richardson's exceptional success as a printer made it unnecessary for his own wife to work in the printing-house, even he did not separate home and workplace until very late in his career. Another printer's widow, Hannah Clark, succeeded her husband in 1691 and went on to have a career as a printer that was four times as long as her husband's. While Stationers' Company records date women printers' careers from the time that they were widowed, women like Elizabeth Leake Senior and Hannah Clark must have worked alongside their husbands in order to acquire the skills that enabled them to carry on successfully on their own. When printer Thomas James died in 1710, his wife Elinor continued printing for nine years until her own death in 1719. It is clear from Mrs James's own writings, however, that this woman printer-author viewed herself as a printer *during* her husband's lifetime as well as after his death. In one of her published broadsides, James described herself as 'in the element of Printing above forty years'.[11]

Operating a printing business involved more than manual labour; it also involved training and disciplining apprentices, obtaining financing, and settling accounts. Women printers often juggled these duties with raising children. John Dunton praised one Mrs Green, a printer's wife in Boston, for managing part of Mr Green's business. He also noted that, thanks to Mrs Green's efforts, 'Mr Green enjoys the comfort of his children without knowing any thing of the trouble of them.'[12] Tace Sowle was a skilled compositor, and by her twenties she was also an experienced accountant. When she began negotiating with the Quakers concerning the printing of George Fox's *Works*, she pinned down details such as edition size, font, and paper, and proved unwilling to budge concerning the price: on 11 March 1698, Quaker representatives reported that they had 'treated with Tace Sowle about printing [the second volume] but not having agreed with her'. Later that month they gave in to her demands. She promised to do the job only 'at a price not exceeding one penny per sheet', 'and if she can afford ʸm lower she promiseth she will'.[13] One of the most challenging tasks Sowle faced immediately after taking over her family press was settling her elderly, 'nearly blind' father's accounts. At twenty-five, she attended a meeting of Quaker central organisation, showing this august body of 'antient men Friends' 'several Accounts of Books sent to Barbados and Bristol some Years since and not paid for'.[14]

Given the convenience of having a printing-press in one's own home, it is not surprising that some women printers were also authors. Elinor James wrote, printed, and distributed some seventy broadsides and pamphlets between 1681 and 1716. She may have 'written' these works not with a pen but directly at the printing-press with type. James's papers comment chiefly on national political issues (the Exclusion Crisis, the Revolution of 1688, the East India Companies, the Jacobite invasions, and the South Sea Company, to name only a few). But they also comment on issues relating to the print trades: the disciplining of apprentices, the price of paper, the disadvantages of a free press, and the drinking habits of London journeymen ('for what benefit have you in starving your wives and children, and making yourself sots only fit for hell?').[15] As we shall see, another printer-author, Elizabeth Powell, wrote and printed three newspapers between 1716 and 1720. Like James, Powell used her papers as a forum for public political commentary and complaint. Like James, too, she was arrested for publishing her views.

Printing was not the only aspect of production in which women were employed. Women also worked as engravers, illustrators, and binders, or manufactured printers' supplies such as paper, ink, and type. Bookbinding, in particular, was a 'feminised' area of the print trades. Involving sewing skills most women already had, and so poorly paid that it was an unattractive profession for men, it attracted many women despite a gendered division of labour and thus differential wages for men and women.[16] Several women established reputations as engravers or illustrators. Mid-century printmaker Mary Darly retailed her own prints and those of other engravers, and co-produced an exhibition catalogue with her husband.[17] The century also saw several women typefounders. In the 1770s, Sarah Baskerville carried on her family foundry 'in all its parts, with the same care and accuracy that was formerly observed by Mr Baskerville'.[18] From 1778 to 1809, the two Elizabeth Caslons (mother and daughter-in-law) managed the historic Caslon foundry for thirty-one consecutive years. Contemporary sources acknowledge the role played by the Caslon women in the success and survival of the foundry, praising their skill not only after they were widowed but also, in the case of Elizabeth Caslon Senior, '*during* the life of her husband'.[19]

Outnumbering women producers, however, were women distributors of printed materials. Women worked as booksellers, newspaper and pamphlet-shop owners, and as hawkers of broadsides, ballads and tracts. The terms 'bookseller' and 'publisher' covered a wide variety of functions, including the relatively small number of booksellers who performed services comparable to our modern 'publisher' (financing production, arranging for printing, and overseeing marketing and distribution). There were great variations in power and status among booksellers, who ranged from major publishers to small-time retailers who eked out a living 'haggling over a shop counter'. While some women booksellers did own copyrights and functioned as publishers, most were small-time shopkeepers whose stock included a wide range of non-print items as well as books. While Tace Sowle was a major distributor rather than minor retailer, even her list of stock included 'books on physic, *A Diurnal Speculum, A New Discourse on Trade*'; 'Bibles, Testaments, Concordances, Spelling-Books, Primers, Horn-books; with Writing-Paper, Paper-Books, &c., and Marriage Certificates on Parchment, Stamp'd'.

As chief distributor for the Quakers, Sowle warehoused and shipped several thousands of printed items every year. She shipped works to Quaker meetings and to booksellers in 'Cityes and Great Townes', not only throughout Britain and Ireland but also in continental Europe and 'foreign partes beyond the seas' (the American colonies and the Caribbean).[20] Atypically for a printer, she also retailed books herself. (One of her shops was in Gracechurch Street, next door to the Quaker meeting house.) She employed 'mercury-women', or wholesale pamphlet-sellers, to assist in large-scale distribution, and hawkers to cry smaller topical items in the streets. Quaker missionaries carried her tracts with them on their journeys; as early as 1700, Sowle's books reached political and religious authorities as diverse as the 'Governours of New England and New York' and the 'Czar of Muscovy'.[21] Sowle also spent time marketing Friends' works, binding trade lists into books she printed, and printing the first Quaker bibliography, John Whiting's *A Catalogue of Friends Books* (1708). (This also served as an effective 'sales catalogue' for her press.) Over the course of her fifty-eight-year career as a printer-publisher, Tace Sowle acquired an expert knowledge of

market demands and, as we shall see, made publication recommendations to Quaker central organisation. Even at this time of continuing
censorship, the Quaker elders typically acted on her advice, sometimes
even giving her discretion to print 'what more she sees meet'.[22]

Today literary scholars tend to marginalise so-called 'ephemeral'
forms such as newspapers and pamphlets. These forms of writing are
topical, cheaply produced, and small in scale. They are also often anonymous, and they do not conveniently fit into literary critical paradigms
emphasising authorial subjectivity. Yet newspapers and periodicals were
a major growth area in the eighteenth-century press, and throughout the
period, the pamphlet, not the book, was the dominant form of print
communication.[23] Some of the century's greatest literary works were
first published as pamphlets or in periodicals; Alexander Pope's *The
Dunciad In Three Books* (1728) first appeared as 'an unprepossessing little
pamphlet of fifty-two pages, bearing no author's name'.[24] To understand the importance of pamphlets and newspapers is to begin to
understand the importance of London 'mercury-women', whose cluster
of shops at the Royal Exchange, Temple Bar, and other sites were
among the most important wholesale outlets of the press. Mercury-
women distributed to smaller retailers large quantities of topical items
that needed to move quickly. As one contemporary source explains,
'Those people which go up and down the streets crying News-books,
and selling them by retail, are also called Hawkers and those Women
that sell them wholesale from the Press, are called Mercury Women.'[25]
Tellingly, the only name showing in the imprint of Pope's *Dunciad* was
that of a mercury-woman, Ann Dodd. (Dodd was serving here as a
'trade publisher', a distributor who allowed her name to be printed on
a work for a fee and handled the work's distribution, but who did not
own the copyright.) It would have been Dodd's shop that was the site of
the *Dunciad*'s initial publication: 'On the Day the Book was first vended,
a Crowd of Authors besieg'd the Shop; Entreaties, Advices, Threats of
Law, and Battery, nay Cries of Treason were all employ'd to hinder the
coming out of the *Dunciad*: On the other Side, the Booksellers and
Hawkers made as great Efforts to procure it.'[26] The two Ann Dodds,
Senior and Junior, were among the most important London mercury-
women in Pope's day; also in this rank were Elizabeth Nutt and her
daughters Catherine, Ann, and Sarah. Together, the Dodd and Nutt
women served as the main newspaper suppliers of the nation's largest
city before 1750, distributing leading newspapers and oppositional
papers such as the *Daily Post*, the *London Evening Post*, the *London Journal*,

the *Craftsman*, *Common Sense*, and *Mist's Weekly Journal* as well as a wide variety of pamphlets and tracts.

The least-known, yet furthest-reaching links in the distributive networks of the London press were itinerant hawkers who cried papers and sang ballads in coffee-houses, marketplaces, and streets. Hawkers had regular routes that they travelled daily, first calling on mercury-women or printers' wives to see what materials were ready, then selling the papers they had purchased at a discount. While many hawkers were impromptu employees, some women were locked into this poorly paid, risky line of work for years. Hawker Frances Carver, 'alias Blind Fanny', was arrested in 1718 for singing illegal political ballads. Twenty-five years later, she was committed to Old Bridewell prison for selling unstamped newspapers.[27] Throughout the century, anyone involved in manufacturing or distributing printed materials could be prosecuted as that work's 'publisher', and subjected to the same penalties as the author. Because hawkers often distributed political materials, these women, although frequently illiterate, were more subject than any others to repeated arrest. (Hawkers could also be arrested at any time for 'vagrancy' on the order of a Justice of the Peace.) Despite their precarious situation, though, hawkers' labour was at once commercially indispensable and unique. As itinerants, they could move through public places, following crowds and attracting them with their voices. Their voices were thus an important site for the coalescence of an older oral and newer print culture that characterised this century. Hawkers attracted customers by means of their oral advertising of a pamphlet or song, then sold the printed text as a backup copy.

Hawkers and ballad-singers are also an example of the overlap of production and distribution that characterised the literary marketplace, for these distributors were also 'makers' of texts. Several ballad-singers are known to have 're-written' ballads orally as they cried or sang them. Elizabeth Robartson re-titled 'Honour and Glory, or a Poem On her late Majesty Queen Ann's Birth-day' with the more provocative title, 'the High Church Ballad you may sing it but I dare not'. In so doing, she politicised and commercialised an innately harmless printed text of her own accord with her voice. Discrepancies between ballad-singers' oral versions and the printed texts they marketed sometimes had subversive political implications. Robartson was sent to a 'House of Correction' not for selling the 'Poem On . . . Queen Ann's Birth-day' but rather for advertising it by a 'false Title'.[28] These oral/print discrepancies also have implications for our models of early modern 'authorship'. Who was the author of the subversive meanings Robartson used to market this poem? Hawkers shaped literary and political street culture with their voices, and they also shaped the literary marketplace by convincing printers what to print or reprint. When printer Catherine Clifton was examined by government authorities for her role in producing the seditious ballad 'The Tory's Wholsome Advice', she claimed that 'it was done by a printed Copy which was delivered to her together with a written Copy of the same by one Ann a Ballad Singer whose name she does not know, nor her Habitation, and gave her in Exchange a hundred other printed Ballads'.[29]

While hawkers functioned as makers as well as distributors, and some women printers were also authors, several female authors supplemented their income by marketing books. Poet and novelist Elizabeth Boyd used the profits of her writing to help set herself up in a more dependable line of work than authorship. In the preface to her *The Happy Unfortunate; or the Female Page: a Novel* (1732), Boyd advertised the stock of her pamphlet-shop in St James's where she sold 'Papers, Pens, Ink, Wax, Wafers, Black Lead Pencils, Pocket-Books, Almanacks, Plays, Pamphlets, and all manner of Stationery Goods'. Memoirist Laetitia Pilkington for a time supplemented her income by retailing prints and pamphlets, and even prolific novelist Eliza Haywood had a brief spell as a publisher in Covent Garden 'at the sign of Fame'. Later in the century, Ann Yearsley used the profits of her poetry to set herself up as the proprietor of a circulating library in Bristol. Along with established classics and newer works by women writers, Yearsley retailed 'Perfumery, Essences, Patent Medicines, etc., cheap as in any part of the kingdom'.[30] A synthetic model of literary production reveals points of overlap among women producers, distributors, and consumers of print in ways that a focus on individual authors does not. As publishing historians are now suggesting, 'relationships *within* the print business . . . are often obscured by forms of specialisation . . . the areas of overlap were both more complex and far-reaching than is usually acknowledged'.[31]

LOCATING THE SUBJECT

Why have feminist scholars known so little about these *other* women of print culture until recently, and what are the special challenges we face in learning more about them now? This section will consider the evidence for women's involvement in the print trades, illustrating where women do and do not appear in the records, and 'the need for a critical interpretation of what th[e]se sources offer'.[32] Two chief kinds of book trade evidence are Stationers' Company records and imprints; both are characterised by a misleading gap between what women actually did and how it was recorded. Maureen Bell has described what she calls the 'iceberg effect' of the Stationers' Company records. Women's recorded presence represents only the tip of their actual involvement, and, as far as married women's activity is concerned, 'the existence of the man effectively blocks out any record of activity by the woman'.[33] While Jane Sowle worked in her family printing-house at least as early as the 1680s, her name does not appear in Company records until 1704 when she bound an apprentice in her own name. Even in the case of Tace Sowle, who managed the business for fourteen years before she was married and another twenty-six years after she was widowed, the conventions of the Stationers' Company must be understood. If we did not have Quaker records, we might judge that Tace began managing the Sowle press in 1695 – the date that she was formally recognised by the Company as a master printer. Yet, as we have seen, by 1695 Tace was already a highly experienced printer who was then negotiating with the Quakers concerning the printing of their founders' works. Gaps in the records have been exacerbated by some historians' assumptions: for instance, that women whose names do appear were temporary care-takers of their *husband's* business. As Bell writes, 'the assumption has usually been that the woman was of minor importance, both in the day-to-day running of the business and in the development of the business over time' (p. 13). The amount of work that remains to be done with Stationers' Company records, recognising and reconstructing women's careers, may be suggested by the fact that the standard history of the Company contains only a few passing references to women – despite covering a period of 556 years.[34]

Imprints too tell a partial story, indicating copyright owners and selected retailers but not necessarily who was in charge of a business or shop on a daily basis.[35] Tace Sowle was in charge of her press for fifty-eight years, yet for various reasons, her name appeared in her own imprints only twenty-seven of those years.[36] While on the one hand, the names of women active in the trade did not always appear in imprints, on the other hand, women whose names do appear were not necessar-ily active in the manner we might think. Some women inherited copy-rights or businesses but were never active except as a 'vehicle by which property exchanged hands between men'.[37] Other women inherited businesses but turned them over to a manager. One of the wealthiest women whose name appears in imprints, Catherine Lintot, inherited her father Henry Lintot's copyrights (including his law patent worth £30,000) and within three years had sold her way out of the business. Other women were active in the trade, but not in the manner their imprints might suggest. The names of Abigail Baldwin, Sarah Popping, Rebecca Burleigh, and Elizabeth Morphew are omnipresent in imprints as 'publishers', yet in most instances these women did not own the copyrights of the works they sold and they had never met the authors. As in the case of Dodd and the *Dunciad*, above, these women were serving as 'trade publishers', intermediaries who allowed their name to be printed on topical, satirical, political, or otherwise risky works for a fee and who served as a layer of 'cover' between the author, the copyright-owner, and the law. Dealing in cheap print, and serving as go-betweens, trade publishers were 'inferior to the regular bookseller in caste'.[38] (Again, like bookbinding, this 'inferior' category includes many women.) The 'S[arah] Popping' whose name appears in the imprint of a pamphlet by Pope almost certainly had no direct dealings with Pope; her name also appears in the imprints of works published against him the same year.[39]

The autobiographies of several tradesmen also contain valuable comments on women printers and publishers, but even praise can be interpreted in a number of ways.[40] John Dunton praises printer's widow Ann Snowden for not nagging him to pay his delinquent bills.[41] But is his praise a constative statement, which reports a fact, or a performative statement, which tries to *do* something (that is, bring about the state to which it refers)? If Dunton was reporting a fact, should we read his statement as indicating Snowden's good nature, poor business sense, or wisdom in recognising that Dunton was bankrupt? In reconstructing what women like Snowden, Popping, and Lintot did and did not do, we need to recognise the variety and degrees of women's involvement in the print trades – and beware of over-reading, as of under-reading, the sources we do have.[42]

While women print-workers were systematically excluded from some categories of records, other records show great promise for feminist research. A new angle of vision reveals new questions that can be asked of familiar archival sources (family records, newspapers) as well as of less familiar sources such as State Papers pertaining to press control. Family records such as wills provide information about personal connections and relations, and can even provide insight into women's roles. Wives typically served as their husbands' executors; in so doing, some compiled inventories of their family business. Elinor James's daughter, Jane James, married a printer as her mother had done. When her husband died, she made a detailed inventory of their printing business, from which we can learn that, like her mother, she had a hands-on knowledge of the trade.[43] In contrast, Jane James's father, Thomas James, did not designate her mother Elinor James as his executor, but rather gave this job to his gentlemen friends. While Thomas James did leave Elinor James the family printing-house, he did so only on the harsh condition that she not 'molest my Executors in the Execution of this my Will'. In particular, he instructed his executors not to let his wife touch his splendid personal library of books.[44] Wills reveal unexpected interpersonal relations, and they also reveal connections between women in the trades. Quaker printer Jane Bradford instructed her executor to seek Tace Sowle's advice in putting her grandson out to apprentice.[45] (In her own will, Sowle left thirty pounds to the London Quaker Women's Meeting to use at their discretion for the benefit of the poor.[46])

While family records illuminate personal relations, newspapers allow us to reconstruct women printers' and publishers' careers. Newspaper advertisements typically provide far more detailed publication information than is available in imprints; whereas imprints provide the names of one or two distributors, advertisements list all distributors, allowing students to trace distribution networks and to reconstruct individual women publishers' careers.[47] Women print-workers often used newspapers as a forum for public expression, and newspapers also record some of these women's arrest for expressing their views. The career of printer-author Elizabeth Powell can be reconstructed from newspapers available on microfilm. In July 1715, Powell's husband had been forced into hiding to avoid arrest for treasonous publication. Eight months later, Mrs Powell started what she had intended to be a weekly newspaper: the pointedly titled *Orphan*. In the first and only issue of the *Orphan*, Powell painted a propagandistic picture of her situation, 'an Afflicted Woman struggling for Bread for herself, her Children, and her Distressed Husband, is Banished, stript of his Subsistence, and his Wife and Children left Poor and Bare to shift for themselves' (no. 1, 21 March 1716). Three days later, she was arrested 'for printing an Impudent and scandalous Libel against the Government'.[48] She was later released from prison, probably 'in Commiseration to the extream Poverty of her and her numerous Family'.[49] Two weeks after her release, Powell started a second paper, for which she was also arrested on the very first issue. The motto of the second paper, the *Charitable Mercury and Female Intelligence*, was, 'To speak ill of Grandees, is to run ones self into Danger; but whoever will speak well of 'em must tell Many a Lye' (no. 1, 7 April 1716). Three years later, Powell published a third weekly, the *Orphan Reviv'd: or, Powell's Weekly Journal* (1719–20). While this newspaper was less outspoken, Powell was arrested for a third time in 1720 for reprinting a treasonous pamphlet, *Vox Populi, Vox Dei*. During the period of her imprisonment, she used the public space of the *Orphan Reviv'd* to garner public sympathy. Newspapers allow us to reconstruct this woman printer-author's political and publishing choices – and even, sometimes, her personal character.

As the example of Mrs Powell suggests, female as well as male booktrade workers were prosecuted for distributing illegal printed materials. Accordingly, one of our best sources is State Papers pertaining to press control. Now also available on microfilm, these papers may include arrest, examination, and trial records; the reports of government press spies on women printers and publishers; or petitions written to government officials by women print-workers or by others on their behalf. Women typically petitioned for their own or a family member's release from prison. These documents offer valuable opportunities to study the ways that women understood their publishing activities in relation to their businesses, families, and the state. Petitions also provide insight into gendered constructions of women's work. When Catherine Clifton was taken into custody for printing 'The Tory's Wholsome Advice', her husband Francis Clifton, himself a notorious Jacobite and frequent offender, wrote to the Secretary of State's office apologising for her actions and representing her as having 'inadvertently' printed a seditious text that he would never have condoned.[50] In actual fact, as we have seen, Catherine Clifton quite self-consciously purchased 'The Tory's Wholsome Advice' from 'one Ann a Ballad-Singer', and printed it herself in a matter of hours. Discrepancies such as this one, between what one woman printer did and how her husband represented it to another man, alert us to the need for caution in interpreting these records – and to the exciting possibilities for feminist reassessment of archival materials.

CHANGING THE SUBJECT

New critical paradigms and interdisciplinary collaborations are helping feminists to rediscover archival sources, and in turn, new archival findings are giving rise to new, more inclusive critical models. We now have some broad surveys of women in the book trades, yet we still lack individual case studies of all except a very few women printers and publishers.[51] We need studies of women's specific job duties, trade status, independent economic power, and publishing careers. The eighteenth century was a transitional period in the print trades (and in women's positions), and we also need studies of *changes* in the nature and extent of women's work. We need to know more about the effects on particular groups of women of capitalisation and professionalisation: was the shift from family industry to capitalist industry good or bad for women print-workers, and what was the relation between socio-economic shifts and narrowing notions of ideal feminine behaviour? While in 1700 the labour of women in book-trade households was typically vital to the success of the economic family, by 1800 the economic efficiency of book-trade wives was less crucial to the success of family businesses. Changing economic conditions gave rise to new ideological notions about women's nature and roles, and the idea that a prosperous tradesman 'kept' his wife eventually prevailed. Women print-workers helped to spread new gender ideologies, and they may also have been personally affected by the new ideological conditions they helped create. While most feminist publishing historians see a gradual decline in women's power in the print trades over the century, future studies must place the topic 'women and the business of print' in more specific situations with respect to regional variation, job sector, family background, and social class. New provincial markets, for instance, may have opened up job opportunities for some women print-workers at the same time as changing patterns of trade organisation were closing down opportunities for others.

While we need to explore the possibility of uneven development for women in the print trades, we also need a deeper understanding of the gender-related barriers *all* of these women had to negotiate. Even an eminently successful businesswoman like Sowle still had to navigate barriers of gender; ironically, Sowle's personal name was a potentially disabling reminder of the misogynist adage, 'a woman's best ornament is silence'. (The name 'Tace' stems from the Latin *taceo*, 'to be quiet'.) There may have been personal as well as economic reasons why the first publication recommendation this young woman made to the (all-male) Quaker elders who oversaw publication decisions was that Elizabeth Bathurst's works be reprinted in the form of a collected edition. One of Bathurst's works was a powerful defence of women's speaking, *The Sayings of Women . . . Briefly collected and set together, to shew how the Lord poured out of his Spirit . . . not only on the male, but also on the Female* (1695). Sowle may have been acting here as a woman reader as well as a businesswoman –

recognising the proto-'feminist' potential of her press, seeing another woman's writings into print, and shaping culture through her choice of texts. As usual, the elders listened to her proposal and gave their consent, 'she first Acquainting Charles Bathurst and his wife of it'.[52] Tace Sowle was in one sense dutifully quiet (that is, private) as her name required, yet in another sense, she was as 'public' as any woman in England. Printed texts with her name on them reached three different continents by 1700. We need to understand the relationship between the restrictions women like Sowle faced and the (sometimes astonishing) facts of their real achievements.

We need studies of relationships between women in the print trades, and between women printers, publishers, writers, and readers. Sowle printed more than 100 works by women writers. Some of these women were fellow Quakers (for instance, Bathurst, Anne Docwra, Margaret Fell Fox, Mary Mollineux, and Elizabeth Stirredge). Others were not, such as the leader of the Philadelphian Society, prophet Jane Lead. Sowle was directly responsible for seeing at least one woman's works into print, for as we have seen, it was she who suggested a collection of Bathurst's works. A more inclusive model of women's textual involve-ment will reveal other links between women printers, publishers, writers, and readers – links that may be proto-'feminist' or otherwise ideological as well as economic.

A greater awareness of the 'communications circuit' also helps us to understand women's writings. As the publishing historian John Sutherland has argued: '[T]he material facts of literature's making are neither contextual nor subtextual but, in a primary and inherent sense, textual.'[53] Elinor James's broadsides take on new intelligibility and value when we learn how their material production shaped their textual content. Similarly, Quaker women's autobiographies become less negatively 'formulaic' when we understand the conditions of their production, reproduction, distribution, and use. Recognising women's roles as printers and publishers also helps us to understand contempo-rary *men's* writings – particularly, some gentlemen's concerns regarding women's involvement in the press. An expanding press offered English women large-scale access, for the first time in history, to the closest thing their culture had to a 'mass medium'. Access to print was poten-tially a vehicle of power – whether the woman involved was a printer, hawker, ballad-singer, or author. Women printers and publishers, as well as writers and readers, influenced literature and culture, and it behoves us to consider how our critical models permit recognition of their achievements. As indirect beneficiaries of these women's contributions to the literary marketplace, to the institutionalisation of a critical political press, and to feminism, we need to study these other female 'makers', whose lives, to an even greater extent than those of women writers, were profoundly affected by, even organised around, the new opportunities of print.

NOTES

Special thanks to Kristin Bailey and Sharon Groves for commenting on an earlier version of this essay.

1 Information in this paragraph is derived from my account of Sowle in James K. Bracken and Joel Silver (eds.), *The British Book Trade, 1475–1700*, (Columbia, SC: Bruccoli Clark Layman, 1996), pp. 249–57.

2 This is Robert Darnton's phrase in 'What Is the History of Books?', *Daedalus*, 3 (1982), 65–83.

3 Maureen Bell, George Parfitt, and Simon Shepherd (eds.), *A Biographical Dictionary of English Women Writers 1580–1720* (Boston: G. K. Hall & Co., 1990), p. 293.

4 James Raven, *A Chronological Check-List of Prose Fiction Printed in Britain and Ireland* (New Haven: University of Delaware Press, 1987), p. 10. See also John Feather, 'British Publishing in the Eighteenth Century: a Preliminary Subject Analysis', *The Library*, 6th ser., 8 (1986), 32–46.

5 See ch. 12, p. 265. For further discussion of the variety of women's writing, see also ch. 13.

6 On laws pertaining to the publishing trades and key developments such as the end of perpetual copyright in 1774, see John Feather, 'The English Book Trade and the Law 1695–1799', *Publishing History*, 12 (1982), 51–75.

7 Michael Treadwell, 'London Printers and Printing Houses in 1705', *Publishing History*, 7 (1980), 5–44 (p. 5).

8 John Feather, *A History of British Publishing* (London: Routledge, 1988), pp. 97–8. See also Feather's *The Provincial Book Trade in Eighteenth-Century England* (Cambridge University Press, 1985).

9 Elizabeth Sowle later married William Bradford, one of the family apprentices, and emigrated with him to America, where they became the first Quaker printers in the American colonies.

10 Will of Elizabeth Leake, Guildhall Library, London, MS 9172/Box 118, proved 13 April 1721.

11 *Mrs James's Advice to All Printers in General* (c. 1715), rpt. in John Nichols, *Literary Anecdotes of the Eighteenth Century*, 9 vols. (London: printed for the author, 1812–15), I, 306–7.

12 John Dunton, *The Life and Errors of John Dunton Citizen of London* (1705), 2 vols. (rpt. New York: Burt Franklin, 1969), I, 106.

13 Friends Library, London, Meeting for Sufferings Minutes (hereafter MSM), 25 March 1698.

14 Friends Library, Morning Meeting Minutes (hereafter MMM), 13 April
    1691.

15 *Mrs James's Advice to All Printers in General.*

16 Women were relegated to lower-paid areas such as folding and sewing the
    printed sheets, while men did the binding in leather and other materials. By
    1800 women were paid approximately 10s.6d. per week while men earned
    17s.–18s. (Felicity Hunt, 'Opportunities Lost and Gained: Mechanisation
    and Women's Work in the London Bookbinding and Printing Trades', in
    Angela V. John (ed.), *Unequal Opportunities: Women's Employment in England
    1800–1918* (Oxford: Basil Blackwell, 1986), pp. 71–93 (p. 74).)

17 The catalogue, published with Matthew Darly, was *A Catalogue of Darly's
    Comic Exhibition at No. 39, in the Strand* (n.d.). Mary also published *A Book of
    Caricatures* (1762).

18 Advertisement 6 April 1775, quoted in Talbot Baines Reed, *A History of the
    Old English Letter Foundries* (1887), rev. edn by A. F. Johnson (London: Faber &
    Faber, 1952), p. 284.

19 Nichols, *Literary Anecdotes*, 11, 357, my emphasis. See also: T. C. Hansard,
    Typographia (London: Baldwin, Cradock, & Joy, 1825); C. H. Timperley, *A
    Dictionary of Printers and Printing* (London: H. Johnson, 1839), pp. 744, 834–5;
    and Reed, *A History of the Old English Letter Foundries*, pp. 244–7.

20 Friends Library, MMM, 29 November 1697.

21 Friends Library, MSM, 25 February 1698 and 20 January 1709.

22 Friends Library, MMM, 27 November 1698.

23 Feather, 'British Publishing in the Eighteenth Century', 38.

24 Maynard Mack, *Alexander Pope: a Life* (New Haven, CT and London: Yale
    University Press and W. W. Norton, 1985), p. 457.

25 Blount's *Glossographia*, quoted in D. F. McKenzie, *The London Book Trade in the
    Later Seventeenth Century* (Cambridge: Sandars Lectures, 1976), p. 25.

26 Richard Savage, quoted in Mack, *Alexander Pope*, p. 457.

27 Public Record Office (hereafter PRO), SP 35/11/21, fol. 59, 11 February
    1717/18, and *London Evening Post*, no. 2487, 18 October 1743. For a portrait of
    the ballad-singer Mrs Parker, see below, p. 267.

28 PRO, SP 35/11/21, fol. 59, 11 February 1717/18.

29 PRO, SP 35/21/77, fol. 210, 25 May 1720.

30 Mary Waldron, *Lactilla, Milkwoman of Clifton: the Life and Writings of Ann
    Yearsley, 1753–1806* (Athens, GA: University of Georgia Press, 1996), p. 209.

31 Michael Harris, 'Scratching the Surface: Engravers, Printsellers and the
    London Book Trade in the Mid-Eighteenth Century' in Arnold Hunt, Giles
    Mandelbrote, and Alison Shell (eds.), *The Book Trade and Its Customers:
    Historical Essays for Robin Myers* (Winchester: St Paul's Bibliographies, 1997),
    pp. 95–114 (p. 110, my italics).

32 Maureen Bell, 'Women in the English Book Trade 1557–1700', *Leipziger
    Jahrbuch zur Buchgeschichte*, 6 (1996), 13–45 (p. 16).

33 Bell, 'Women in the English Book Trade 1557–1700', 15. For a summary of
    these records, see Robin Myers, *The Stationers' Company Archive: an Account of
    the Records 1554–1984* (Winchester: St Paul's Bibliographies, 1990).

34 Cyprian Blagden, *The Stationers' Company: a History, 1403–1959* (London: George Allen & Unwin, 1960).

35 The most convenient way to get at imprints now is via the English Short Title Catalogue, an online catalogue listing materials printed in Britain or its colonies from 1483 to 1800 as well as materials printed in English anywhere in the world during those years. Records provide publication details such as copyright owners, selected retailers, format, and sometimes, printers.

36 For the first fifteen years of her career, imprints showed 'T. Sowle', but after she was married, imprints began showing her mother's name. After Jane Sowle died, imprints began showing 'assigns of J. Sowle' (that is, Tace), and after Tace's husband also died Tace continued to use this imprint for another thirteen years. (During these years she was apparently choosing anonymity.) Not until 1736, when she turned seventy, did she return to her initial custom of using her own name in imprints. Taking on a partner, she began using the imprint 'T. Sowle Raylton and Luke Hinde', and did so until her death another ten years later.

37 C. J. Mitchell, 'Women in the Eighteenth-Century Book Trades' in O. M. Brack (ed.), *Writers, Books, and Trade: an Eighteenth-Century English Miscellany for William B. Todd* (New York: AMS Press, 1994), pp. 25–75 (p. 44).

38 Michael Treadwell, 'London Trade Publishers 1675–1750', *The Library*, 6th ser., 4 (1982), 99–134 (p. 102).

39 The Pope pamphlet on which Popping's name appears is *A full and true account of a horrid and barbarous revenge by poison, on the body of Mr Edmund Curll, bookseller* (1716).

40 See Dunton, *Life and Errors*; Nichols, *Literary Anecdotes*; Thomas Gent, *The Life of Mr Thomas Gent, Printer, of York; Written by Himself* (1746; London: Thomas Thorpe, 1832); and James Lackington, *Memoirs of the First Forty-Five Years of the Life of James Lackington* (London: printed for the author, 1792).

41 Dunton, *Life and Errors*, I, 251.

42 The same is true for dictionaries of trade personnel. We need to understand the editorial principles of these compilations and the nature of the records on which they are based. See D. F. McKenzie, *Stationers' Company Apprentices 1701–1800* (Oxford Bibliographical Society Publications, NS 19 (1978)); H. R. Plomer, *A Dictionary of the Printers and Booksellers who were at work in England, Scotland and Ireland from 1668 to 1725* (Bibliographical Society, printed at Oxford University Press, 1922); H. R. Plomer, G. H. Bushnell, and E. R. McC. Dix, *A Dictionary of the Printers and Booksellers who were at work in England Scotland and Ireland from 1726 to 1775* (Bibliographical Society, printed at Oxford University Press, 1932); and Ian Maxted, *The London Book Trades 1775–1800: a Preliminary Checklist of Members* (Kent: William Dawson & Sons, 1977). Cf. Jan Fergus's discussion of the difficulties posed by primary sources, ch. 7 below, pp. 158–9.

43 Will of Thomas Ilive, Guildhall Library, MS 9052/Box 42, proved 5 January 1725; inventory by Jane Ilive included with will.

44 Will of Thomas James, PRO, Prob. 11/515/109, proved 9 May 1710.

45 Will of Jane Bradford, Guildhall Library, MS 9172/Box 109, proved 1 October 1715.

46 Will of Tace Sowle Raylton, PRO, Prob. 11/774/354, proved 2 November 1749.

47 For an example, see Beverly Schneller, 'Using Newspaper Advertisements to Study the Book Trade: a Year in the Life of Mary Cooper' in Brack, *Writers, Books, and Trade*, pp. 123–43.

48 *Flying Post*, no. 3779, 24 March 1716.

49 *Weekly Journal*, 31 March 1716.

50 PRO, SP 35/24/75, fol. 225 [1720].

51 For a list of recent studies, see 'Guide to Further Reading'.

52 Friends Library, MMM, 13 July 1691. The title of the edition, printed by Sowle in 1695 and reprinted at least five times before 1800, was *Truth Vindicated By the Faithful Testimony and Writings Of the Innocent Servant and Hand-Maid of the Lord, Elizabeth Bathurst, Deceased*.

53 John Sutherland, 'Publishing History: a Hole at the Centre of Literary Sociology', *Critical Inquiry*, 14 (1988), 574–89 (p. 584).

CHAPTER 7

Women readers: a case study

Jan Fergus

What is perceived as 'popular culture' is often subject to strong criticism. In our own time, we are accustomed to denunciations of cinema and television. In the eighteenth century, moralists denounced the novel as a similarly dangerous popular entertainment and closely associated the genre with women, much in the way that soap opera today is assigned to a female audience. Modern scholars have tended to echo those eighteenth-century moralists who identified reading novels as a particularly female activity. But this identification is inaccurate, like many of the stories told about popular culture in general and about the eighteenth-century 'rise' of the novel in particular.

The classic story of this 'rise' is Ian Watt's: for him, the novel's development from Defoe to Richardson and Fielding reflects social and intellectual change. Watt locates a philosophic and economic individualism in the novel that he associates with the middle class and traces back to Locke; these features dictate what he sees as the novel's characteristic technique, 'formal realism'. Watt's views have influenced debate on the novel since *The Rise of the Novel* was issued in 1957. Feminist critics have been successful in drawing attention to the works of women novelists, whose contributions to and interventions in the genre are excluded from Watt's story. Cultural critics have further enlarged the field of discussion, pointing out that novels were read against other forms that often were more widely popular, like chapbooks or periodical essays or journalism. Some critics have even reversed Watt's premise, arguing like John Bender that the novel's development does not reflect social change; instead it enables change. But because critics continue to challenge Watt, his account circulates still.[1]

J. Paul Hunter documents ways in which newer evidence qualifies Watt's influential assumptions about class, literacy, and gender within the audience for the eighteenth-century English novel. This evidence undermines the ' "triple rise" thesis . . . that that rise of the middle class led to the rise of the reading public, which in turn led to the rise of the novel'.[2] Hunter points out that the real acceleration in literacy occurred 'early on in the seventeenth century, at least three generations before the novel began in any meaningful sense to emerge', concluding that '"new" readers were a necessary but not sufficient condition for the emergence of the English novel' (pp. 66–7, 68). But who were these new readers? The accepted view has been that they were of a class lower than traditional readers (the gentry and professionals) – a group known in the eighteenth century as the 'middling sort'.[3] Furthermore, some of these new readers were women, whose literacy had increased (though not as markedly as men's): 'In the late eighteenth century, female literacy is typically about two thirds of male literacy; in the 1750s, for example, when male literacy was around 60 per cent, female literacy was about 40 per cent' (Hunter, p. 72).

Although literacy does not necessarily imply reading, still less reading novels, scholars and eighteenth-century critics have persisted in characterising the audience for fiction as female. Their evidence for this identification is largely anecdotal or circular. Richard D. Altick asserted in 1957 that after the publication of Samuel Richardson's *Pamela*, 'as the mounting flood of sentimental novels attests, women played an important part in the history of the English reading audience'; here the evidence for female readership lies simply in the increasing production of sentimental novels.[4] Watt's account of female reading is more subtle, suggesting that women 'certainly' read not merely novels but 'religious literature', yet he also echoes the most severe eighteenth-century critics of women and novels by concluding that 'the dominance of women readers in the public for the novel is connected with the characteristic kind of weakness and unreality to which the form is liable'.[5] Even recent scholars like Hunter, assembling nuanced arguments about the novel's cultural contexts, can assert that 'None dare call the place women occupy in novels dominant, but women quickly begin to dominate the writing as well as the reading of novels.'[6] Evidence for the notion that women 'dominated' the fiction-reading public is taken primarily from the accusations of eighteenth-century reviewers and moralists whose laments are well documented.[7]

In *The Woman Reader, 1837–1914*, Kate Flint has called attention to the persistence of cultural fears about women readers:

The patterns of reasoning which lay behind Renaissance prescriptive remarks concerning women's reading were remarkably close, in outline, to ones which were repeated during the next three centuries, linking together preoccupations with bodily and mental fitness. Whilst too great an acquaintance with light reading might lead her sexually astray, either in imagination or reality, it would also distract her from developing intellectually and spiritually.[8]

These anxieties have accompanied accusations that such dangerous reading is pervasive or increasing among women. But was this so in the eighteenth century?

The historical record, where it can be examined, tells a much more complicated story of women's reading. In this essay, I want to tell something of that more complicated story through an analysis of the archives of two Midlands booksellers: the Clays of Daventry, Rugby, Lutterworth, and Warwick (whose records cover 1746–84 with many gaps); and Timothy Stevens of Cirencester (whose records extend from 1780 through 1806). While their customers' behaviour certainly cannot stand for that of all English provincial readers, it is likely to be reasonably representative. These customers are drawn from a fairly wide geographical area, covering parts of Gloucestershire, Wiltshire, Northamptonshire, Leicestershire, and Warwickshire. Furthermore, the customers are quite numerous: the records show that the Clays served well over 2500 adults and schoolboys who bought printed matter, and Stevens between five hundred and a thousand. And evidence from the later Stevens records is generally consistent with – and thus reinforces – findings from the earlier Clay documents. Altogether, these records provide concrete evidence of the ways in which provincial readers, including women, responded to the new fictional forms issued in the eighteenth century: novels, children's books, and magazines. Their customers' purchases and borrowings indicate that, at least in the provinces, the development of the novel after 1740 was not closely associated with or even caused by an expanded, middle-class audience largely composed of women. In the provinces, the proliferation of the novel between 1740 and 1770 did not seem to accompany an expansion of the reading public for fiction. By about 1770, however, the availability of cheaper, more ephemeral, and more specialised sources of fiction – in children's books or magazines aimed at specific audiences, for instance – did seem to enlarge both the male and female fiction-buying public, which then began to include women of the 'middling sort': tradeswomen and tradesmen's wives, farmers' and yeomen's wives. Throughout, however, novels were not as popular, and the tastes of male and female readers of all classes were not as distinct, as many scholars have supposed – or as many eighteenth-century critics alleged. Cultural historians need to understand, then, why these allegations were so widespread.

READING BOOKSELLERS' RECORDS

From these booksellers' records, we can glean evidence about who purchased and/or borrowed novels, and about who took out magazine subscriptions, but this evidence must be interpreted with great care. The numbers of Clay and Stevens customers are respectably high: over two thousand five hundred for Clay and between five hundred and a thousand for Stevens. Nevertheless, caution is necessary in drawing conclusions from the customers' purchasing. For example, because the Clay records before 1770 are so patchy, covering primarily the years 1746–8, 1758–9, and 1764–6, nothing can be concluded about the popularity of works not issued during those years. Since both Clay and Stevens operated small circulating libraries, these records provide unique information about book borrowing during the period – indeed, the only extant information about borrowing from *any* commercial circulating libraries in eighteenth-century England. Even more caution, however, is needed in interpreting this material. Failure to borrow certain books or genres, for instance, may occur because the small libraries simply did not make them available.

The complex interrelationships among women, fiction, and the market are easiest to observe in the case of magazine subscriptions – the most popular source of prose fiction among provincial women customers.[9] By the mid-1760s, the Clays' magazine audience had reached 180 subscribers – but just 10 were women, despite the appearance of several magazines designed especially for them. Only one of the ten women who took magazines between December 1764 and March 1766 ordered a copy of the *Court Miscellany, or Lady's New Magazine*. By contrast, in the 1770s Wheble's *Lady's Magazine* immediately attracted and sustained a substantial male and female readership: first issued in August 1770, by December of that year it had eleven men and eleven women as subscribers.[10] Both the numbers and the proportion of its female subscribers grew over the next decade, though men continued to maintain subscriptions.[11] The *Lady's* success depended partly on male readers, then. Men's interest in the *Lady's* is underscored by the five Clay customers who were also would-be contributors to the magazine during the 1770s, none of them women: a tapster, a schoolmaster, two schoolboys, and the very minor poet Benjamin West. Only West and the tapster, William Gough (the sole subscriber among the five), ever saw their works in print; the others' contributions were merely acknowledged in the 'Advice to Correspondents' sections.

Attempts to recover women's behaviour from the historical record are often frustrating. The task of measuring women's consumption of fiction in the market is complicated by such instances of intersecting male and female taste, and even more by the problem of registering married women's reading. The Clay magazine subscription records reveal the existence of concealed purchasers – women whose subscriptions were recorded under someone else's name, typically a husband's. A number of subscriptions, for example, go along for years under a man's name, and then suddenly a woman's name appears. A fourth of all women subscribers (28 of 111) were concealed in this way. Twenty-two were married women whose subscriptions appeared under their husbands' names, but six were single women whose brothers or fathers were originally and primarily listed as subscribers. If more Clay records survived, no doubt further instances of concealed subscription would emerge. The reasons for concealed subscription and for women's limited appearance in booksellers' records are clear enough. Married women did not exist legally apart from their husbands and were thus less likely than widows and unmarried women to obtain credit for themselves, and all women were likely to have less disposable income than men. Married women are therefore under-represented in all the accounts I can produce of women readers, probably owing to the exigencies of marriage itself: in all but affluent families, bearing children, raising them, and running households may not have left much time or money for female reading.[12]

The conventional association between women of the middling sort and fiction, then, oversimplifies the story. Although middle-class women were strongly attracted to magazines in the 1770s, they did not show a parallel interest in buying or borrowing other forms of fiction. Before 1770, I can find no evidence of a middle-class female public addicted to fiction in any form, and even after that point, provincial men and women in all but the lower classes showed a fairly comparable interest in fiction. For example, the Warwick shop, in operation between 1770 and 1772, contained the Clays' most ambitious circulating library, but it attracted only 37 borrowers in nineteen months out of more than 300 customers, 20 women and 17 men, for its collection of at least 85 titles, 64 of them works of fiction.[13] Several of these works were newly issued, like Smollett's *Humphry Clinker*, which attracted only four borrowers. Neither sex borrowed novels exclusively, and only one reader, a butcher, John Latimer, borrowed them voraciously.

So far, I have been implying that subscribers or borrowers and readers were identical, and that women who borrowed books or who subscribed to or read magazines could easily be distinguished from men. Obviously, no such easy identification or separation is possible. Buying or borrowing does not (as we know) guarantee reading. Many buyers of magazines could share one subscription, for instance, and some certainly did. Evidence from the Warwick shop, however, indicates that borrowers might have been rather scrupulous in declaring this sort of dissemination. Mrs Parkes, a draper's wife in Warwick, paid for four simultaneous readings of Eliza Haywood's *History of Miss Betsy Thoughtless* (1751) in January 1772. A husband and wife belonging to the gentry, Susannah Maria and Walter Ruding of Kineton, each paid separately for a reading of *The Generous Inconstant* (1771) in October 1771.

The raw numbers for women readers of fiction are evident in figure 3, and they undermine any easy identification between women and fiction: the fiction market for women is not particularly large or broad. The 111 women who took magazines from the Clays represent the widest female market for *any* form of fiction among the Clay or Stevens customers. By contrast, novels attracted twenty-six women buyers and forty-two borrowers among the Clay customers (see also table 1). Because five women belonged to both groups, the actual number of women who spent money to read novels was sixty-three. Eight women among Stevens's customers purchased novels, nine borrowed them, and eight bought plays (a total of twenty customers, since four overlap, one of whom appears in all three categories); a further sixteen were charged with 'reading' in the libraries – no titles were given. (Again, the Stevens records include no magazine subscriptions.) Stevens's groups of fiction readers overlapped slightly more than the Clays' buyers and borrowers did, as the diagrams in figure 3 indicate, and at least half of the twenty women customers for fiction read in the circulating library, along with the sixteen other readers mentioned.

Though these numbers are too small to warrant firm conclusions, there is some indication that, later in the century, women who were interested in one form of prose fiction were likely to be interested in others; at this time, too, more novels were available.[14] In the earlier Clay records, all four different segments of the market – buyers of novels, borrowers of novels, buyers of drama, and subscribers to magazines – remain essentially separate as well as quite small. The greatest proportion of each group does not intersect with any other group. This is especially true of the two largest segments of the market, subscribers and borrowers – those who were obtaining fiction cheaply – at sixpence a copy for a magazine, or two or three pence a volume for borrowed

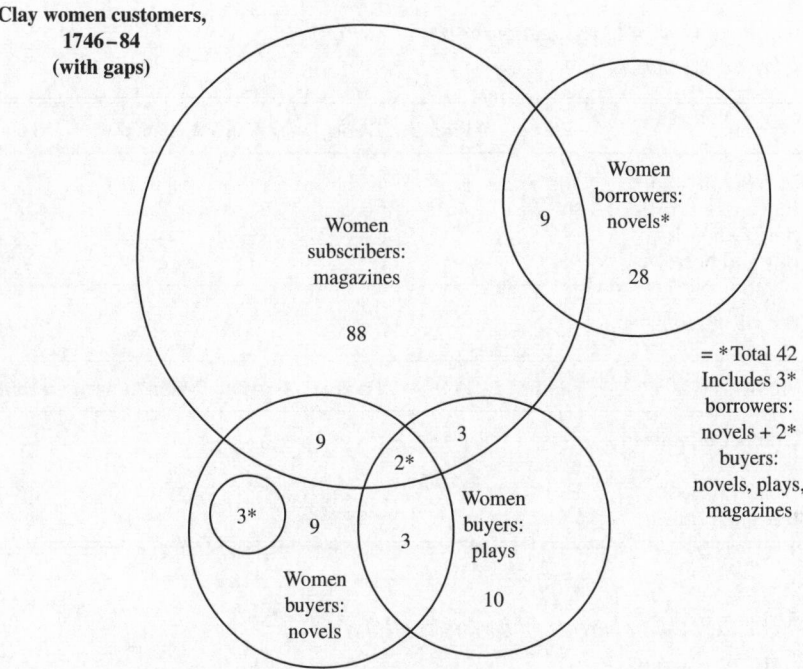

Clay women customers, 1746–84 (with gaps)

Women subscribers: magazines 88

Women borrowers: novels* 9 28

= *Total 42 Includes 3* borrowers: novels + 2* buyers: novels, plays, magazines

Women buyers: novels 3* 9 9 2* 3 3

Women buyers: plays 10

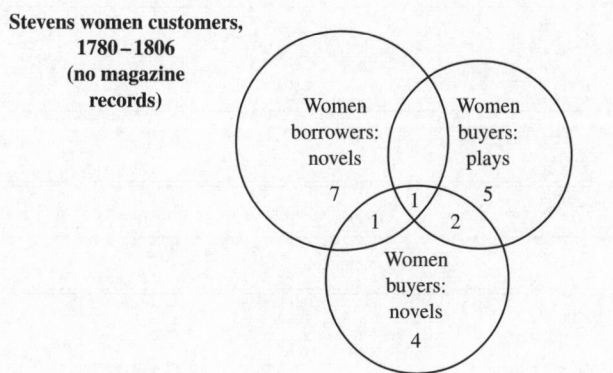

Stevens women customers, 1780–1806 (no magazine records)

Women borrowers: novels 7

Women buyers: plays 5

Women buyers: novels 4

1 1 2

Figure 3 Intersecting markets: magazines, novels, and plays obtained by women

Table 1: *Women buyers and borrowers of novels*
Clay records: novels

Women:	Gentry	Prof.	Trade	Servant	Unknown	Total
Number of women	11	12	9	—	31	63
Buy novels	6	6	6	—	8	26
Borrow novels	7	6	4	—	25	42
Buy and borrow	2	—	1	—	2	5

Stevens records: novels

Women:	Gentry	Prof.	Trade	Servant	Unknown	Total
Number of women	2	4	1	—	8	15
Buy novels	2	1	1	—	4	8
Borrow novels	1	4	—	—	4	9
Buy and borrow	1	1	—	—	—	2

Table 2: *Women buyers and borrowers of plays*
Clay records: plays

Women:	Gentry	Prof.	Trade	Servant	Unknown	Total
Buy plays	3	4	2	2	7	18
Borrow plays	—	—	—	1	2	3
Totals	3	4	2	3	9	21

Stevens records: plays

Women:	Gentry	Prof.	Trade	Servant	Unknown	Total
Buy plays	1	2	2	—	3	8

(No Borrowers)

Table 3: *Women buyers and borrowers of magazines*
Clay records: magazines

Women:	Gentry	Prof.	Trade	Servant	Unknown	Total
Buy magazines	12	28	25	—	46	111

(No Stevens records for magazines)

Table 4: *Women and men as buyers and borrowers of classic novels*
Clay records only

Women:	Gentry	Prof.	Trade	Servant	Unknown	Total
Buy classic novels	2	2	2	—	2	8
Borrow classic novels	1	1	3	—	8	13
Totals	3	3	5	—	10	21

Adult Men:	Gentry	Prof.	Trade	Servant	Unknown	Total
Numbers of men	10	21	6	3	14	51
Buy classic novels	6	8	2	1*	10	27
Borrow classic novels	4	13	4	2	4	27
Buy and borrow						3

*a labourer

Schoolboys:	Rugby School	Daventry Dissenting Academy	Total
Number of boys	39	18	57
Buy classic novels	19	4	23
Borrow classic novels	23	16	39
Buy and borrow	3	2	5

Males:	Total
Total	108
Buy novels	50
Borrow novels	66
Buy and borrow	8

novels. Eighty-eight magazine subscribers obtained no plays and no novels through purchase or lending, though at least four of these did buy other fictional forms like children's books. In other words, about 76 per cent of women who subscribed to magazines (84 of 111) apparently obtained no other fiction from the Clays in any form; these subscribers constituted an even more isolated part of the fictional audience than did Clay borrowers. The separation between women buyers and borrowers of novels is especially strict. The great majority of the Clays' borrowers and subscribers did not seek to obtain other forms that incorporated fiction, not even inexpensive ones like chapbooks or children's books.

If we look at the smaller audiences for more expensive works – plays at 1s.6d. and novels at 2s.6d. (three to five times the cost of a magazine) – we find a greater tendency to obtain other forms of fiction although the majority still did not; these results seem to be true of the larger male audience as well. We also find, consulting figure 3 and tables 1–4, that in both the Clay and Stevens records, the professional classes and the gentry dominate the market for all forms of fiction, though perhaps somewhat less so for magazines. Although plays have often been supposed to rival the novel in popularity among readers, women customers of the Clays and Stevens evidently did not find them as attractive as novels, either to buy or to borrow.

For many students, the most interesting customers for fiction are those who obtained works by the so-called major eighteenth-century novelists: Defoe, Richardson, Fielding, Smollett, Sterne, Goldsmith, and Burney. I use the term 'classic' to describe their novels, but with some discomfort; obviously, these works were not regarded as 'classics' when they were issued, although many reprints and much discussion eventually did elevate some of them to classic status before the century closed. These novelists all retained a provincial audience until at least 1806, when the Stevens records end – which in most cases meant that the novels continued to appeal to new generations of readers. The Clay women customers for classic works are relatively few, as table 4 indicates: a total of twenty-one, thirteen of whom borrowed rather than bought, compared to fifty-one men (twenty-seven of them borrowers). Stevens's female customers for classic fiction are even fewer: just four. Such relatively small populations are best studied in relation to the men who bought and borrowed this form of fiction also. In all, about five times as many men as women bought and borrowed classic fiction from the Clays – a total of at least 108 men, 57 of them schoolboys who were certainly buying and borrowing fiction for themselves, not for wives or daughters at home. Stevens's male customers for novels outnumbered women even more strikingly than the Clays' customers, by a factor of almost ten: twenty-six men bought fifty works by classic novelists and eleven borrowed seventeen (a total of thirty-three male customers, since four overlap), whereas three women bought five and two borrowed two (one woman did both). This disproportion seems to remain when male and female buyers and borrowers of *all* novels are considered. It is important to remember, however, that many of Stevens's customers paid to read by the quarter, not for individual books; we cannot know what they read. Furthermore, the Clay figures are skewed according to the dates of the surviving records: we have records for only *Clarissa*, *Tristram Shandy* (vols. VII and VIII), *Humphry Clinker*, *Evelina*, and *Cecilia* during their first year of issue when purchases were likely to be greatest. None of Fielding's novels came out at a time covered by the records. Partly because the records favour Richardson and Smollett, these were the most popular novelists among the Clay customers. Women greatly preferred Richardson, although none of the five women who borrowed *Sir Charles Grandison* appears to have finished it (they did not withdraw the final volumes). By 1778, when Burney's *Evelina* appeared, individual purchasers of novels were becoming more rare. Predominantly male book clubs tended to replace individuals as buyers of fiction, even among the gentry and professional classes. This replacement helps to account for the fewer purchases of novels among the later Stevens customers.[15] Nonetheless, even if we allow for the suppression or concealment of women readers for various reasons, we must still reject the cliché that women made up the majority of the audience for fiction, as buyers or as borrowers. This notion is simply not borne out by the records of these provincial bookshops and circulating libraries.

CASE STUDIES OF WOMEN CUSTOMERS

All these groups of buyers and borrowers seem, in the end, quite abstract and disembodied without some sense of how individual women behaved. I have therefore analysed in detail the purchasing of two women from each class – the gentry, the professional classes, tradeswomen and farmers' wives, and servants or labourers. I have restricted myself to the more numerous and varied Clay customers and have usually chosen in each class one woman who bought or borrowed a good deal and one who did not. These women are those whom I have been able to document from sources outside the Clay records.

Gentry women do not form the largest group among the Clays' female customers, and in many ways their tastes and habits seem hardest to assess. I suspect that many of them were obtaining books from other sources than the Clays, perhaps from London booksellers or at watering places on visits. One gentlewoman who purchased novels and plays and also borrowed novels was Jane Williamson of Eydon, a daughter of Lucy Knightley Esq., of Fawsley. The Knightleys were an old county family. Jane's husband Richard was a captain in the Northamptonshire militia and bought the manor of Eydon in 1750; it was located nine miles from Daventry. They had ten children baptised between 1753 and 1764; only four survived. Richard Williamson died in 1768; he bought just Le Sage's *The Devil upon Two Sticks* in translation (1708) in the surviving records. Jane Williamson's purchasing did not begin until she became a widow and the lady of the manor of Eydon. She subscribed to Wheble's *Lady's Magazine* at the end of 1771; she borrowed Henry Brooke's *The Fool of Quality* (5 vols., 1765–70) in 1774; in the same year she purchased *The Turkish Spy* (orig. publ. 1687), and five years later the novel *Village Memoirs* (2 vols., 1765; 2nd edn 1775). Above all, she bought plays: so many that she had at least eight volumes bound between 1773 and 1779. The records specify only eight titles, however, all of them classic plays, bought in this order: Steele's *Conscious Lovers*, Centlivre's *Busy Body*, Vanbrugh's *Provok'd Wife*, Steele's *Tender Husband*, Congreve's *Plain Dealer*, Villiers's *Rehearsal*, Southerne's *Oroonoko*, and Otway's *Venice Preserv'd*. Drama was evidently her preferred form of fiction, even though she obtained all forms. Jane Williamson was reasonably well off; documents survive concerning an estate of £6,000 that Mr Lumley had settled on her, and no doubt she had more from her husband's or father's estates.[16]

Not all gentry women were in her position. In Sarah Scott's novel *Millenium Hall* (1762), we learn that for gentlewomen of reduced means, 'retirement in a country town' is the conventional recourse.[17] Two unmarried sisters who almost certainly belonged in this marginal category lived in Rugby, a country town, and borrowed the eight volumes of Samuel Richardson's third edition of *Clarissa* over a three-and-a-half-month period in 1768. Their only purchase in the seven and a half years before 1784 that the Rugby records cover also occurred in 1768: a Ladies' *Diary* for 1769. At some time before April 1768, they had also obtained Gastrell's *Christian Institutes* (1707; 2s.6d.) as well as two copies of the popular *New Week's Preparation for a Worthy Receiving of the Lord's Supper* (orig. publ. 1737; 2s. each), but had not yet paid for them; they did so at some time before August 1770. Mary and Frances Westley apparently did not spend much money on books. A 1710 draft of their father's will left them £200 each (in this draft, William Westley describes himself as a gentleman). The sisters evidently lived on interest; Frances wrote to her connection George Pearson:

I am obliged to you for y^r taking thought about my money, but I cant say I approve of purchasing a Fen Estate I had rather have it out at less interest nigher home wch I hope I shall soon have an opportunity to do.

Low interest on £400, if they inherited that much from their father, would yield so small a yearly income – no more than £20 – that the sisters most likely had more money, perhaps from collateral inheritance. They offered in 1763, for instance, to pay £10 towards the cost of their nephew Littleton Westley's education at Rugby School, and seven years earlier they were able to discharge their nieces' school fees, although they required reimbursement from the girls' guardian. The letters are circumstantial about money and education but have almost nothing to say about books: the only reference occurs when Frances asks Pearson to 'send ye other voll: of [Defoe's] ye tour through great Britain & I will return them together'. The series of letters stops before the sisters borrow *Clarissa* in 1768.[18]

On the whole, professionals were the Clays' and Stevens's best customers for books, and possibly the most dedicated of them all was Catherine Huddesford. In two years and four months covered by one Rugby day book, she bought ten plays, ten novels, and at least twenty-four other works, including poetry, politics, history, voyages, divinity, and the very popular *New Manual of Devotion*. Her husband William was alive during this buying spree; indeed, he was purchasing books too, though less frequently. William died on 23 January 1770; the register for Bourton upon Dunsmore notes that he was 'forty one years Rector of this Parish'. Catherine did not long survive him: she was buried a year and a day later in the same parish although in the meantime she had moved to another Warwickshire parish, Allesley, with her four surviving daughters, the eldest thirty-two and the youngest sixteen, and her son William who had acted as his father's curate for several years before his death. The family was evidently wealthy. When Elizabeth Huddesford, the last of the unmarried daughters, died aged ninety-two on 6 April 1836, her will was sworn 'under £16,000' for the purpose of legacy duty. That sum represents a close approximation of the value of her cash, shares, and furniture. The considerable real estate that Elizabeth also bequeathed was not dutiable, so its value is not included in the £16,000 estimate.[19]

The Huddesfords acquired a library large enough to make it worth Catherine Huddesford's while to get John Clay to value the books after her husband's death.[20] William Huddesford bought a few books from John Clay's Daventry shop in 1746–8, when he resided at Leamington Hastings; he removed to Bourton at some point, nearer to the Rugby shop. When its surviving records begin, in 1768, both William and Catherine are frequent customers although neither ever seems to have borrowed books or subscribed to magazines from the Clays. William belonged to the Rugby Book Society, however, and made a number of his purchases through the club. His wife purchased more than he did. She had three daughters grown up who were living at home and one teenage girl as well. Catherine was evidently acquiring a substantial library, no doubt with family amusement partly in mind. She was particularly attracted to new fiction. All but one of the ten novels that she bought were purchased within a year of publication; five of the ten plays were bought within three months of their first appearance on stage in London.

One of the more interesting professional buyers of fiction was Mistress Ann Harris, later Mrs Fraunces, primarily because her buying was – unlike Catherine Huddesford's – so limited. The daughter of a former bailiff and burgess of Daventry, she bought an inexpensive shilling *Robinson Crusoe* on 31 December 1746, as well as a ninepenny *Crusoe* (a chapbook) five days earlier, along with a ninepenny *Guy Earl of Warwick*. At this time she was thirty-five, which accounts for her being called 'mistress' though she was unmarried. Two years later, on 19 December 1748, she married Joseph Fraunces, an apothecary in Daventry. He died after fourteen years of wedlock, and their only child Elizabeth died six years later at age eighteen. Curiously enough, however, after her marriage Ann Fraunces only once showed any interest in fiction in the more than seven years that the records cover: a query on 23 June 1777 asks whether she read the two volumes of Hugh Kelly's *Memoirs of a Magdalen* (1767) for sixpence; the uncertainty is not resolved in the records. At this time, Ann Fraunces had been a widow for fifteen years. Before the marriage, her husband bought only a 'Philosophical Analysis of Antimony' (1s.) and two gardening books thereafter (18s. and 4s.). After her husband's death, Ann Fraunces bought *Great Importance of a Religious Life* (2s.8d.) and a number of other devotional works, *Every Man His Own Vermin Killer* (1s.6d.), Klopstock's three-volume *Messiah* (9s.), an *Abridgement of the History of the Bible*, and at least one yearly almanack.[21] In 1777, she took the serialised version of Charles Middleton's *New and Complete System of Geography* (1777) – also the year in which she may have read Kelly's novel. Neither Ann Fraunces nor her husband ever subscribed to magazines. They enjoyed at least a middling degree of prosperity, however, as indicated by the sale of Ann Fraunces's household goods after her death. The *Northampton Mercury*'s advertisement for the sale twenty days after she was buried on 4 January 1780, aged sixty-eight, mentions 'Goose Feather Beds, with Moreen and other Hangings; Pier and Dressing Glasses; Mahogany and Walnut-tree Chairs', and so forth; the absence of a library for sale is consistent with the Fraunces's scarce orders for books.

Tradeswomen or farmer's wives who bought or borrowed novels are sparse in the records. So far, only ten have emerged among the Clay customers, along with one possible reader among Stevens's.[22] Sarah Brooke, the widow of an innkeeper in Daventry, shows a taste for fiction coupled with practical works and divinity – a taste evident also in members of the professional classes like Mrs Huddesford and in the gentry as well. The Wheat Sheaf, one of the town's largest inns, had been operated by several generations of Brookes since before 1721. Sarah Brooke gave birth to six children between 1753 and 1759 and managed the inn for at least sixteen years after her husband's death in 1764. The management had passed by 1784 to the husband of her daughter Frances, John Ashworth, whom she was then wishing to sue. During the 1770s, the Wheat Sheaf paid tax on 119 windows, amounting to £12.0s.1d. for each year.[23] It was evidently a large and prosperous establishment.

In 1746–8 and 1758–9, Sarah Brooke does not appear as a Clay customer. Her husband John did buy two books: a rather ominous medical work, *The Distinct Symptoms of the Gravel and Stone* (1759; 1s.6d.), and a two-volume *England's Gazeteer*, perhaps for the convenience of his travelling customers (9s.). After his death, however, Mrs Brooke became a reasonably frequent purchaser of printed matter. The first evidence we have of her interest in fiction is an order for Richardson's *Pamela* in four volumes, bound but not lettered, placed sometime in 1766. At about that time she also bought Robert Dodsley's popular *The Oeconomy of Human Life* (1750; 1s.6d.), Symonds's *Case and Cure of a Deserted Soul* (1639; 1s.), and *Select Remains of the Reverend John Mason* (1736; 1s.6d.).[24] In the next set of records, Mrs Brooke began to obtain fiction in magazines; in June 1770, a few months after the *Court and City Magazine* was first issued, she became a subscriber for five months. A month after she cancelled that subscription, she began to take Wheble's *Lady's Magazine* with the December 1770 issue. It had begun publication in July. Her daughters ordered back issues of this publication, so as to have the complete set; they ordered too a copy of Christopher Anstey's *New Bath Guide* (1766). The eldest daughter, also named Sarah, was about sixteen when she placed this last order; her sister Frances was fifteen, Ann fourteen, and Christian eleven. (The two sons, John and Thomas, do not appear as customers.)[25]

After a four-month break, the Clay records resume in July 1771 with the Miss Brookes, not their mother, listed as subscribers to the *Lady's Magazine*; in only one other instance does a daughter's name supplant a living mother's as a subscriber to a magazine. Mrs Brooke is extraordinary in allowing her young daughters to act, as Fanny Price did in Portsmouth, '*in propria persona* . . . [as] a chuser of books'.[26] The Miss Brookes maintained their subscription to the *Lady's Magazine* at least until August 1780 when the Daventry records end.[27] During the long life of this subscription, the Brookes occasionally obtained fiction in other forms also. The daughters ordered *Robinson Crusoe* as 'a Chap:Bk' in 1771;

in the Clay records, only some thirteen other women appear to order or obtain chapbooks. Mrs Brooke bought Maria Susanna Cooper's two-volume epistolary novel *The Exemplary Mother: Or, Letters between Mrs Villars and her Family* (1769) four years after it had first been published. Mrs Brooke also bought Bishop Soder and Man *On the Sacrament* (2s.), *Lord Chesterfield's Witticisms* (1s.6d.), and Samuel Johnson's ten-shilling abridged *Dictionary*; she was one of only twelve Clay customers who did so. After this time, the sole order for fiction appears in 1774–5, in the daughters' names: two anonymous novels, *Fatal Obedience, or the History of Mr Freeland* (2 vols., 1769) and *True Delicacy, or the History of Lady Frances Tylney and Henry Cecil* (2 vols., 1769).[28]

Interestingly, two of Mrs Brooke's servants attempted to obtain fiction. Her maid ordered *The Wanton Wife of Bath* sometime in 1758, said to be 'a play', but although the title does appear later in the century as a ballad, I can find no such dramatic work apart from John Gay's 1713 comedy, *The Wife of Bath*. In any event, Clay was not able to fill this order: it remains uncrossed-out in the bespoke section. Mrs Brooke's man-servant was one of the two servants in all the Clay records who actually borrowed fiction: he paid to read the seventh volume of *Clarissa* on 18 June 1777.[29]

I have argued elsewhere that servants' purchases from the Clays displayed intellectual curiosity as well as a desire for self-improvement.[30] Male and female servants, with one exception, exhibited very similar tastes: they bought primarily guides, dictionaries, manuals for letter writing, and conduct books. Next they chose religious works; fiction, drama, poetry, and *belles lettres*; almanacs and pocket books; music; jest books; and others. But no woman servant purchased prose fiction – not even the exceptional Mrs Philippa Hayes, the only woman servant who ever borrowed books from the Clays. She was a widow and housekeeper to George Lucy of Charlcote Park, near Stratford-upon-Avon. As house-keeper to a bachelor, she enjoyed some of the privileges of the mistress of a great house, including associating with the surrounding gentry, such as the family of Sir Charles Mordaunt of Walton Hall. She had more disposable income to spend on reading than most servants and perhaps more catholic tastes. Mrs Hayes borrowed Dorothea Mallet Celesia's play *Almida*, Hugh Kelly's *Clementina*, and Richard Cumberland's *West Indian* from Samuel Clay in Warwick in April 1771, all within three months or less of their being first performed in London. Although Mrs Hayes read fiction, she never borrowed any novels from Clay. Apart from the three plays, she withdrew Daniel Defoe's *Tour through the Whole Island of Great Britain* and a *Ladies Pocket Book*. She had actually bought these works, along with Celesia's *Almida*, but returned them and was charged instead for reading them. She purchased in addition *The Memoirs of Charles-Lewis, Baron de Pollnitz* (orig. publ. 1736) on 29 June 1771, and Susannah Carter's *Frugal Housewife* on 14 September; these she evidently chose to keep.[31]

A somewhat more typical servant, Polly Atkins, was left a total of £100 in her employer Edward Sawbridge's will, a legacy she collected some five years after she obtained a copy of William Leybourn's *Panarithmologia: or, the Trader's Sure Guide* for a shilling in 1770. She also ordered one of the most popular plays among the Clay customers, Bickerstaffe's comic opera, *Love in a Village*.[32] This work, first performed in 1762, remained in the repertory throughout the century. No record remains of Polly Atkins's purchases, if any, after her legacy.

CONCLUSIONS: IDENTIFYING FEMALE READERS

Complications emerge in studying the provincial reading public. It is not easy to distinguish between an elite and a popular audience, nor between the tastes of men and women. Class distinctions become slippery the more one knows about individual readers. The Westley sisters' anxieties over money and education suggest that they feel themselves and their relatives to be marginal within their class. In other words, the more that I study these provincial readers, the more I can understand the temptation to lump everyone together as 'middle class', or, more plausibly, to consider professional men and women as members of that class. But it does seem important to try to separate professionals, whose position in society depends to some extent on elite education, from tradesmen and women on the one hand, and from local squires, gentry, and aristocracy on the other. To do this, however, means that the generalisations that we might like to make about gender and class in this world require constant readjustment and qualification, and this rule applies with special force to generalisations about the female reading public. With such reservations, then, I conclude that to some extent, the middle-class provincial female reading public for fiction was created by the market: by a magazine that appealed to women across class lines, the *Lady's*, and that succeeded in attracting readers who would not otherwise have been customers for fictional forms. But these readers did not necessarily go on to consume other fiction. Traditional readers, women of the gentry and the professional classes, were more likely than tradeswomen to read all forms of fiction, from novels to chapbooks. Even so, in the Clay records, the majority of women consumed fiction in one form rather than many, yet a good deal of intersection among the audiences occurred as well, particularly among traditional readers. In the later, smaller, Stevens audience we find more overlapping, perhaps because that audience contained a larger proportion of traditional readers, or perhaps because the trends already visible in the Clay records became more pronounced. That is, we see more reliance on book clubs as a means to obtain new publications, as well as more homogeneity in the audience – the intersection of male and female and of elite and popular taste. Whether these trends were produced by the market, by what was made available to consumers of fiction, or whether they drove the market, is a major question. More thorough analysis of the records is necessary to decide such questions. But what is clear is that in the provinces, the female audience for fiction was not especially large.

More suggestively, the women who did buy fiction, or indeed any printed matter, tended to be widows or single women. While married, Jane Williamson, Ann Fraunces, and Sarah Brooke bought no books at all, and we can't assume that their husbands were buying for them, for their husbands bought very little – nothing to compare with what their wives bought once they were widowed and in control of their households and finances. It may well be that the best way to study the female reading public would be to analyse differences between widows and spinsters and all other women as consumers of print culture.

Finally, if it is true that, as these provincial records suggest, eighteenth-century women were not as early and widely addicted to novels as contemporary moralists asserted, then why did writers of conduct literature and book reviewers so firmly and frequently identify women as the form's consumers? This large cultural question invites thorough treatment, but perhaps a few speculations may be useful here. Margaret Anne Doody has persuasively suggested that a 'feminisation' of the novel is a way to 'limit any damage it may do': 'To pretend that the novel is primarily directed towards females (including those of both middle and upper classes) is reassuring, for women (unlike youthful male aristocrats) are theoretically disabled from bringing concepts into social currency.'[33] This 'reassuring' relegation of potentially damaging novels to women does not preclude anxiety, however. Some contemporary objections to women's reading of novels decried it as a waste of time that took women away from household duties – a reasonably straightforward patriarchal stance. Other objections seem more fraught, however – even hysterical. The isolation of the reader, especially the female reader, was culturally suspect.[34] Women readers were thought to require special care and supervision because, as a *Critical* reviewer put it in 1766, 'a softness of temper renders them . . . susceptible of bad impressions; and if their hearts are not fortified by virtuous principles, they are easily captivated by the follies and vices of the age. Plays and romances warm their imagination, and stimulate their passion.'[35] Implicit here is a fear of female fantasy or sexual stimulation, crystallising in the prevalent male fantasy that women who read novels will reject ordinary men who love them, cherishing instead a romantic daydream.[36] That is, men who worried over female fantasies were fantasising women rejecting them. The uncontrolled imagination here seems to be male.

Possibly the energy with which eighteenth-century moralists expressed increasing anxiety over female novel readers (as well as those in the lower classes) derives in part from a male perception that the written word was now making a broader and more frequent appeal to the imagination, and some of that writing was coming from women. Previous appeals to the female imagination from devotional literature were, after all, largely controlled by men. Suddenly, however, male writers could not control either the reading or writing of women, and perhaps for this reason imagined threatening scenarios, asking what would women readers do? Become sluts? Run away? Fail to find ordinary men – as opposed to men in novels – appealing? Such prognostications appear frequently within anti-novel discourse. Thomas W. Laqueur has argued that three culturally defined threats were seen to arise simultaneously in the 1710s – credit, masturbation, and the novel.[37] Although Laqueur dates the 'rise' of the English novel idiosyncratically (too early or too late by most accounts), he rightly notes that all three threats focus on the uncontrolled imagination or 'fictionality' (p. 121); he concludes that all three (especially masturbation) might best be understood as threats to sociability, 'part of a history of the reconceptualization of private versus public' (p. 127). If men saw women reading novels as engaged in 'solitary vice', we cannot be surprised that these supposed activities were exaggerated as well as denounced with increasing intensity.

NOTES

I wish to thank Ruth Portner as usual for invaluable assistance in researching and writing this essay; thanks are also due to Ruth Perry, Janice Farrar Thaddeus, and my colleagues Patricia Ingham and Scott Gordon. I am also grateful to the National Endowment for the Humanities, which funded the research for the larger project on eighteenth-century readership from which this work on women readers arises.

1 See: Ian Watt, *The Rise of the Novel: Studies in Defoe, Richardson and Fielding* (Berkeley and Los Angeles: University of California Press, 1957; rpt. Harmondsworth: Penguin Books, 1963), ch. 1 passim; Jane Spencer, *The Rise of the Woman Novelist: From Aphra Behn to Jane Austen* (Oxford: Basil Blackwell, 1986); Lennard J. Davis, *Factual Fictions: the Origins of the English Novel* (New York: Columbia University Press, 1983); J. Paul Hunter, *Before Novels: the Cultural Contexts of Eighteenth-Century English Fiction* (New York and London: W. W. Norton & Company, 1990); John Bender, *Imagining the Penitentiary: Fiction and the Architecture of Mind in Eighteenth-Century England* (University of Chicago Press, 1987). For further discussion of the 'rise' of the novel, and women's role within it, see ch. 9 of this volume; for the suggestion that novels were less statistically dominant than has sometimes been thought, see ch. 6, p. 136.

2 Hunter, *Before Novels*, p. 66.

3 For a re-evaluation of what we generally term 'middle-class' behaviour and values in the period, see Margaret R. Hunt, *The Middling Sort: Commerce, Gender, and the Family in England, 1680–1780* (Berkeley, Los Angeles, and London: University of California Press, 1996).

4 Richard D. Altick, *The English Common Reader: a Social History of the Mass Reading Public, 1800–1900* (University of Chicago Press, 1957), p. 45.

5 Watt, *Rise of the Novel*, pp. 151, 299.

6 Hunter, *Before Novels*, p. 272.

7 For classic accounts, see: John Tinnon Taylor, *Early Opposition to the English Novel* (New York: King's Crown Press, 1943); J. M. S. Tompkins, *The Popular Novel in England, 1770–1800* (1932; rpt. London: Methuen, 1969).

8 Kate Flint, *The Woman Reader, 1837–1914* (Oxford: Clarendon Press, 1993), p. 23.

9 Magazine subscribers can be studied only in the Clay day books; unfortunately, Stevens's ledgers record only book purchases.

10 For documentation of these findings and others, see my article, 'Women, Class, and the Growth of Magazine Readership in the Provinces, 1746–1780', *Studies in Eighteenth-Century Culture*, 6 (1986), 41–56. As table 1 (p. 53) there shows, women subscribers formed less than 5 per cent of the market in the earliest records, about 10 per cent in 1770 (23 subscribers), and over 16 per cent in 1779–80 (35 out of 210).

11 In December 1771, the *Lady's Magazine* had thirty-three subscribers, eleven of whom were women; in December 1773, twenty-seven (nine women); December 1774, thirty-four (thirteen women); January 1777, twenty-eight (fourteen women); November 1777, twenty-six (fourteen women); December 1779, twenty-three (fifteen women), and August 1780, eighteen (thirteen women).

12 For discussion of legal and financial restrictions on married women, see ch. 4.

13 Jan Fergus, 'Eighteenth-Century Readers in Provincial England: the Customers of Samuel Clay's Circulating Library and Bookshop in

Warwick, 1770–72', *Papers of the Bibliographical Society of America*, 78 (1984), 171, 173.

14 Some evidence exists that during the politically charged 1790s, novels began to be produced at unprecedented rates (248 from that decade in the British Library, compared to 105 in the 1780s and 58 in the 1770s). See Michael Crump, 'Stranger than Fiction: the Eighteenth-Century True Story' in M. Crump and M. Harris (eds.), *Searching the Eighteenth Century: Papers Presented at the Symposium on the Eighteenth Century Short Title Catalogue in July 1982* (London: British Library, 1983), pp. 59–73. My preliminary survey of the surviving Hookham and Carpenter ledgers (1791–8) indicates that the aristocrats and gentry who patronised these fashionable London booksellers located in New Bond Street behaved as the clichés predict (and as the less privileged customers of the Clays and Stevens did not): in the 1790s, such rich and leisured women tended to buy novels, though not exclusively (Public Record Office C104/75 1–3; hereafter abbreviated as PRO). Similar reading habits are visible in a fifty-three-page list of 'Books Read' for the years 1789–1820 kept by one gentry woman, not a Clay customer: Miss Mary Orlebar of Ecton. At least half of her reading between the ages of fifty-nine and ninety was of novels and plays (Northampton Record Office ZB340/6; hereafter abbreviated as NRO; Warwick County Record Office appears as WCRO).

15 For the increased reliance on the clubs, see Jan Fergus and Ruth Portner, 'Provincial Subscribers to the *Monthly* and *Critical Reviews* and their Book Purchasing' in O. M. Brack, Jr (ed.), *Writers, Books, and Trade: an Eighteenth-Century Miscellany for William B. Todd* (New York: AMS Press, 1994), pp. 157–76.

16 NRO: D3362; Th 84.

17 Sarah Scott, *A Description of Millenium Hall and the Country Adjacent* (1762; rpt. London: Virago, 1986), p. 71. The communal society at Millenium Hall includes 'some young women of near two thousand pounds fortune, the expensive turn of the world now being such that no gentlewoman can live genteelly on the interest of that sum, and they prefer this society to a retirement in a country town' (pp. 70–1).

18 NRO: D2925, 10 December 1768; D2925/2v. WCRO: CR 2405/26; CR 2806/57, 25 February 1758; CR 2806/63, 26 January 1763; CR 2806/69, 15 January 1764.

19 NRO: D2925; WCRO: DR 44/2/1–37; CR 1709/285/2.

20 NRO: D2925/54r.

21 NRO: ML 88; D64, 8 August 1747; D2931, 21 March 1759, ? April 1759; D7719, 9 January 1772, 5 November 1771; ML 699, 23 November 1773; ML 89, 2 November 1774.

22 Stevens charged Elizabeth Selfe, a clothier's wife, four shillings for two quarters' reading on 3 April 1789, but the reading is not specified. The Clay customers include, apart from the three Brookes discussed below: Samuel Clay's wife Mary; John Clay's cousin Elizabeth; Mrs Adams (who inherited her husband's carrier business); Miss Mary Berry, an innkeeper's daughter;

Mrs Fowler, listed as a butcher; Mrs Catherine Hickman, a farmer's wife; and in Warwick, Mrs Allen, a patten-maker, and Mrs Parkes, a draper's wife.

23 NRO: NPL 2161, 2166; 96P/144, 142, 147.

24 NRO: D 2931, 30 May 1759; D 2931, 6 October 1758; ML 692/43v; ML 692, 7 January 1766, 10 March 1766, 14 May 1765.

25 NRO: D 2930/34v, 37r, 38r, 26v.

26 Jane Austen, *Mansfield Park* (1814), III, ch. ix, ed. Kathryn Sutherland (London: Penguin Books, 1987), p. 330.

27 The Miss Brookes switched to the rival Robinson's *Lady's Magazine* with the November 1771 issue, after Robinson and Roberts had sued Wheble to stop publishing his magazine. Wheble did not do so until sometime in 1772.

28 NRO: D 7719/4r; ML 699, 30 September 1773, 2 November 1773, 3 January 1774, 19 April 1773.

29 NRO: D 2931/19r; ML 88.

30 Jan Fergus, 'Provincial Servants' Reading in the Eighteenth Century' in James Raven, Helen Small, and Naomi Tadmor (eds.), *The Practice and Representation of Reading in England* (Cambridge University Press, 1995), pp. 202–25.

31 NRO: D 2929; and see Fergus, 'Provincial Servants' Reading', p. 222.

32 NRO: D 2930, 12 December 1770, 13v.

33 Margaret Anne Doody, *The True Story of the Novel* (New Brunswick, NJ: Rutgers University Press, 1996; London: HarperCollins, 1997), p. 278.

34 See especially Hunter, *Before Novels*, pp. 40–2; Flint, *The Woman Reader*, ch. 1 passim.

35 *Critical Review*, 22 (1766), 18.

36 Taylor, *Early Opposition to the English Novel*, pp. 71–2.

37 Thomas W. Laqueur, 'Credit, Novels, Masturbation' in Susan Leigh Foster (ed.), *Choreographing History* (Bloomington: Indiana University Press, 1995), pp. 119–28.

PART II

Writing Women in the Eighteenth Century

CHAPTER 8

(Re)discovering women's texts

Isobel Grundy

Discovery has a bad name in the late twentieth century. The old idea that Columbus 'discovered' America is now recognised to be Eurocentric. America was there already, full of human societies whose rich experience had not included the knowledge of Europe. Electricity, too, was pulsing through the air and through the human brain before anybody discovered it. Early texts by women have most of them served the purpose for which they were written; but a text which is not now in the hands of readers is in some sense nonexistent.

Still, it is worth pausing over what we mean by (re)discovery and why we need it, before proceeding to what has been done and what needs doing. 'Undiscovered' may mean unknown, or lost, or merely neglected. No one at all seems to have read or even heard of the little autobiographies of Martha Moulsworth and Mary More between the time of their composition in the mid seventeenth century, and that time in the 1980s and 1990s when Robert C. Evans and Barbara Wiedemann, and Margaret Ezell, came on them in the course of research. Neither of these early modern women offered her work to the public. But within a decade of their 'discovery' each has had hundreds of readers. Moulsworth has had the text of her poem published with elaborate apparatus; Mary More occupies a central chapter in a monograph by Ezell which includes the text of her prose account.[1] These works were unknown for so long because, it seems, their authors wrote – although with great artistry and polish – purely for their own satisfaction.

A similar fate can overtake works written for fame or for cash. Sarah Gardner's comedy *The Advertisement* was staged for her benefit in 1777. The cast turned in a disgraceful performance, though the audience was fairly positive. The play was never put on again. Of course the censorship office retained a manuscript copy; but no one had cause to look at it. Gardner's manuscript, *and* her angry narrative of how the play was killed, lay for 180 years in a cupboard or recess in Colyton in Devon, until a Sunday morning when the householder decided to strip some wallpaper. The play is still unpublished and unprinted, but it has been written about; it is available.[2]

Rediscovery has proved necessary for others not half so well hidden as Gardner. After the inimitable Laetitia Pilkington at last received a serious scholarly edition, Margaret Doody marvelled at the way in which, for so long, scholars of Jonathan Swift have managed to make use of Pilkington without attending to her, and have blithely ignored the need to examine or elucidate the various problems and issues raised by her work.[3] Because she wrote about Swift, she has had her footnote in literary history; but in that footnote she has not figured as a writer – neither as biographer, autobiographer, humorist, satirist, or poet – but solely as a member of Swift's entourage, or as an amusingly scandalous little divorcée.

Further up the scale of visibility than Pilkington, Aphra Behn and Frances Burney have never been lost; but they have been unacceptable and therefore unavailable. Behn has been seen (like Pilkington) as sexy and scandalous, Burney as virtuous and boring. They experienced two rather different individual unveiling processes. Behn became available in anthologies for classroom use well before scholarly editors got to grips with her works, while Joyce Hemlow's rigorous and expensive edition of Burney's journals and letters (but only the later ones) helped to create the taste which made paperbacks of her longer novels finally feasible.[4] Now Behn and Burney have scholarly biographies, scholarly editions, and stage productions, besides a whole clutch of different paperback texts and critical analyses.

Behn and Burney have achieved both the markers which measure full accessibility (which in turn equates to full canonical status). One is cheap availability, which means chiefly paperbacks, though it may come more and more to mean other and probably electronic forms. The other is scholarly or research availability, which is harder to measure. Cheap availability depends on the market, on publishing and bookselling practices (which just recently have been acting strongly in favour of early women's writing); research availability depends on the state of knowledge. In one sense any extant writing which is in the public domain (not hidden from it as Moulsworth and More and Gardner have been) needs only to be mentioned (whether in a periodical article or in the English Short Title Catalogue)[5] to become available to scholars. Even if a work survives only in a unique copy, once the catalogue knows or suspects it was written by a woman, any student of women's writing is free to travel to the location of that text, or to order herself a copy, by microfilm if necessary.

But the word 'free' is ironical: this freedom costs a lot. For a generation now, any student wanting to work on Lady Mary Wortley Montagu's letters has had a scholarly text available;[6] work on Elizabeth Montagu's letters still demands an extended visit to the Huntington Library in California. A student of Behn's works or Burney's plays can now order up Janet Todd's or Peter Sabor's edition, and can trust the printed text on issues of transcribing, dating, attribution, and the elucidation of puzzling points. A few years ago such a student would have needed either to travel to the New York Public Library (in the case of Burney) or to round up copies of many obscure seventeenth-century texts (in the case of Behn, since she could not wholly trust Montague Summers's edition). Now Behn and Burney are once again in play; people are reading them, responding to them, arguing over them.

I hope these specific examples will communicate the romantic aspect of rediscovery. The manuscripts in the papered-over cupboard, the printed words lying unrecognised and ignored, conjure up an idea of their authors not unlike Virginia Woolf's image in 'Lives of the Obscure': of the stranded ghost waiting in the darkness for us, the scholarly search-party, to advance with lights 'across the waste of years to the rescue'.[7] But this remains a metaphor or a fantasy. In practice discovery is usually non-heroic. One stage of it is more like noticing something which was there all the time, in full view but nevertheless overlooked. The next stage is more like a work of renovation: scraping off accretions, dismantling, reconstructing, making good.

Rediscovery is not an event; it is a process. And despite the glamour of the individual find, the individual reprint, the really significant point is the rediscovery of women's writing as a whole. The really significant issue just now is the state of that overall historical process.

When I studied English at Oxford, at the end of the 1950s, Jane Austen was the earliest woman we read. We all (of both sexes) had perfect confidence that no criterion of choice had been used but that of selecting the best. The former omission of the Metaphysical poets had been rectified; all was right with the canon. Women's writing was largely undiscovered by it. We supposed this to be some kind of norm, a timeless or ahistorical condition, and not the product of our particular point in history. The same misconception was presumably shared by, for instance, the selectors of titles for Everyman's Library or the Penguin Classics, who at that date had hardly heard of women writers either.

Even (dare one say it?) Woolf herself had not treated her rescued 'obscure' women authors (Laetitia Pilkington and Ann Taylor, later Gilbert) as if they were real writers at all, and she did not mention Ann's sister Jane. Now Jane, it seems to me, has exactly that power of extracting poetry from the commonplace that one might expect Woolf to admire; and one might also expect her to feel some kinship with Ann's writing of an overdue review, 'As to "Miss Edgeworth," I feel in despair, for I cannot seclude myself, and nurse up my mind as I have always found necessary to composition.'[8] Ann Gilbert's life-writings seem to me to offer many of the pleasures of Woolf's own (an engagement with daily life, with experience felt on the pulses), but Woolf treats her as quaint.

Women were absent from university curricula in those days; but not until many years later did I notice that here and there small, emphatic reinforcements of their exclusion were being enacted. In what was to become my own period, the eighteenth century, established scholars apparently thought it an aspect of their duty to make sure that women's stock did not rise. Harold Williams, editing Swift's letters, wrote this footnote on Mary Barber: 'Swift's infatuation with Mrs Barber led him into an unjustified estimate of her gifts.'[9] R. W. Chapman, editing Samuel Johnson's letters, wrote this footnote on Charlotte Lennox's *Shakespear Illustrated*: 'J. contributed a dedication. He was perhaps too busy to pay much attention to the text, which I am assured is full of absurdities. Like some scholars of our own time, but with better excuse, J. was ever lenient to the work of learned ladies, especially if they had the claim of poverty.'[10] Such gestures of abhorrence would not have been used for minor male contemporaries. Swift's protégé William Dunkin, or Johnson's dedications for Charles Burney or proposals for the Revd William Shaw, could pass without ritual exorcism. Johnson's praise of Lennox is so shocking to Chapman that he both flaunts his willingness to pronounce on a book without reading it, and rushes off the point to insult his female contemporaries. Women writers were not only without status themselves; it seems that without careful management they might also damage the status of their great male contemporaries.

The exclusion of women from university syllabuses in English Literature becomes less surprising in the light of these footnotes. The growth of English as an academic subject had coincided with a period (the late nineteenth and early twentieth centuries) which was strong both in current women's writing and in rediscovery of earlier women's writing. But the shapers of the syllabus were backward-looking. English studies had to earn a reputation for rigour and value comparable to that of classical studies. Philology and textual scholarship were at a premium. Texts were prized for their difficulty; but a history of difficulty in *reception*, such as attends many women's texts, looked less attractive. Woolf's obscure memoir-writers, Pilkington and Gilbert, were strictly recreational reading.

This was, nevertheless (a couple of generations before Williams and Chapman and their footnotes), a time when (re)discovery of women writers was gathering steam in the academy as elsewhere. The first decade of the twentieth century produced works like Myra Reynolds's edition of Anne Finch's poems and the biography of Lady Mary Wortley Montagu by 'George Paston'.[11] But these works of scholarship occupied a minority or marginal position: there was no expectation that their subjects would claim a place in the canon, or that it was incumbent on a specialist in Pope, for instance, to have read them.

A similar status was occupied by Joyce Tompkins's monographs of the 1930s. They dealt explicitly with uncanonical eighteenth-century fiction, therefore predominantly with women authors; they were books for specialists or for the curious, not for the general run of students. Mary Lascelles, at the same period, wrote about such novels as a background to the study of Jane Austen, so her work gained wider currency.[12] But much scholarly discovery of women writers has heretofore shared with its subject-matter a propensity to become lost, and has turned out sooner or later to need rediscovery itself.

The twentieth century was not the first period either of intensive rediscovery or of admirable scholarly work associated with it. Women of the late eighteenth century waded with enthusiasm into the task of collecting and preserving earlier women's writing and getting it published. Mary Berry, sorting and cataloguing letters for the Duke of Devonshire in 1815, became 'an enthusiast for [the] character' of Lady Rachel Russell, turned herself into a fair amateur scholar, and published a biography with a selection of Russell's letters in 1819.[13] When memoirs by Lucy Hutchinson and by Ann, Lady Fanshawe, first appeared in print (in 1806 and 1829 respectively, well over a century after their composition),[14] this crowned the searching and conserving efforts of a whole series of writing women, including Catharine Macaulay the historian, Eleanor Butler and Sarah Ponsonby (the 'Ladies of Llangollen'), and Catherine Fanshawe.

We can now more clearly see the historical causes of the attitudes which shaped my student reading. Syllabuses without women authors were constructed in the shadow of the classics; they persisted in the after-glow of English and of European dominance. The absence of women from syllabuses in England was closely related to the premium which other syllabuses (scorned by Oxbridge undergraduates of the 1950s) placed upon Great Books of the World. Devotion to Great Books is of course a political attitude; and today an interest in women's writing as such looks just as political as does a prejudice against it. Such an inter-est tends to be allied with more general interest in multiple and minor-ity viewpoints, in literature as a site of struggle and debate (rather than as a repository of enduring truths), in voices which sound in discord with dominant ideology.

However eagerly one may wish (as I do myself) to champion women's writing chiefly on account of its literary qualities, this is not the best foundation to support the project of rediscovery. True, many early women are a delight to read: they are passionate or cheeky, moving or incisive. They weave verbal fabrics of intriguing and satisfying complex-ity. With some of them gender produces instant rapport: to many women today it seems that these early writers' views, their tone, even their jokes, would be quite at home in this morning's email. The phrases, characters, or arguments of early women writers have become part of the furniture of my own mind, and seem to me well worth house-room in other people's.

We stand to benefit, I believe, from adopting a more inclusive, less exclusive idea of literary quality, or from learning to apply standards of judgement to the past in a manner rather closer to the way we apply them to our contemporaries. Half a dozen novels are short-listed for the Booker Prize each year, and even those who quibble about the selection do so on the basis that other, more worthy novels have been unjustly passed over. It is assumed that half a dozen good novels every year is a reasonable expectation. But it's hard to win assent to the proposition that half a dozen eighteenth-century novels per year might be actually worth reading today. There is a curious reluctance to accept that both talent and achievement might have been thickly sown in the past.

But even if the short-list principle is accepted, it remains hard to draw up the list. The argument from literary quality is doomed to get bogged down in the incompatibility of subjective judgements. When I wrote that Eliza Fenwick's *Secresy* was one of the finest novels of the 1790s, Terry Castle replied that she finds it bad beyond belief.[15] Debate on this kind of topic is not viable in print, but only around a dinner-table or over a drink. The case for rediscovery must be made on other grounds as well. So when one has praised some author's sensibility and range, and noted (as Woolf notes about her imaginary Mary Carmichael) that she takes her fences like a bird,[16] one still needs *further* arguments for rediscovering her. The argument from literary quality needs reinforcement from the argument for the value of knowledge.

If as students we wish to know, and if as teachers we wish our students to know, something about the workings of gender in society, then we need those early women's voices. They alone can teach us something of how it felt to live as a woman in a culture (so different from our own, yet sharing so much with it) in which the inferiority and subordination of women was utterly taken for granted. They can teach us something important, too, about the impulse to literature – the sources of poems, stories, and so on – something of how to read the work of those who broke into literature from the outside, who in taking up the pen were claiming a privilege which in general was denied to them.

As necessarily present-oriented fields of enquiry, feminism and women's studies are liable to, and are not infrequently weakened by, assertions made in ignorance about the past. The remedies for this include the historian's approach: the application to the past of clear and rigorous twentieth-century conceptual thinking. But even the finest historical research can never convey the nuances of the historical subject's experience as can her own voice. Of course such voices are often unavailable. For some periods and some situations (especially as regards the lower ranks of society) there is indeed a scarcity of women's voices. But in many areas historical generalisations are still being made which ignore, or deny, or misrepresent, the evidence which exists, still unrecovered or disregarded, in those women's own writings.

It is sometimes argued that women who wrote were by definition exceptional, and that therefore their accounts are of limited relevance to understanding the norm. While recognising the value of statistical, norm-directed historical enquiry, I would argue that the concept of a norm is slippery at best, misleading at worst. Feminist scholarly interest focuses particularly on how women interacted with their situation, how they came to terms with or resisted the paths mapped out for them by society. If women's writing over-represents resistance rather than under-representing it, that makes it of more and not less value to feminist historians.

To summarise, therefore, early women's writing needs rediscovering because much of it is still forgotten, because it can prove a delight to read, because without it our notions of literature become misleadingly one-sided, and because it offers insights into the historical condition of women (and therefore obliquely into our own situation) which are unavailable from other sources.

In the process of recovery we have come a long way. The later-medieval writers Julian of Norwich and Margery Kempe, for example, are now readily available. The latter, who was first published only in 1940, has now been modernised in two separate, competing paperback texts. The Renaissance has been equally well served.[17] Not only Aemilia Lanyer (who left a single, manageable published volume of poetry) but also the Countess of Pembroke and Lady Mary Wroth, whose works are more voluminous, are available in wonderfully informed scholarly editions[18] and well represented in anthologies for teaching.

It is instructive to look at the problems these Renaissance women present to their editors. Margery Kempe's simple disappearance has nothing on them. Lanyer, with her one-volume output, is the least problematic, yet she suffered the indignity of being reprinted by A. L. Rowse in 1978 under the title *The Poems of Shakespeare's Dark Lady*. Rowse was a seasoned scholar who, starting from scratch, successfully unearthed many of the facts of Lanyer's life. But his conviction that she was the dark lady of Shakespeare's sonnets rested on almost nothing but the desire that it should be so – since from his viewpoint this alone could give his discovery of her some interest. Now that Susanne Woods has rescued Lanyer from Rowse,[19] it is easy to feel superior to him, but more salutary to reflect that all scholars have an investment in the newsworthiness of their results, and are therefore liable to equivalent temptations. The eighteenth-century equivalent is perhaps a woman like Mary Robinson, whose obvious gossip-column value actively competes with her reputation as a writer.[20]

For Wroth the problem has been one of length and accessibility. Josephine Roberts's sequence of scholarly editions (*Poems* 1983; the *Urania*, as published in 1621, 1995) was tragically interrupted at her death; but the unpublished sequel to the *Urania* has now been edited. For Pembroke the issue has been the long and slow unravelling of her authorship from that of her more famous brother, Sir Philip Sidney. Pembroke's literary career presents an exaggerated version of woman performing her traditional role as helpmeet and enabler of man. On her brother's untimely death she set herself the mission of publishing his

completed works and finishing his uncompleted ones. It is now recognised that the 'New Arcadia' is substantially her work and that 107 of the
150 metrical psalms are solely by her – though the critical history of
those works (like the praise accorded the psalms by John Ruskin in 1877)
attached them not to her name but to Sir Philip's.[21] Neither Sarah
Fielding nor Hester Thrale has ever been so overwhelmed as this by the
reputation of her more famous literary brother or friend; but the same
principle has been at work.

It is worth noting here that presumably not all Lanyer's or Wroth's
works have been, or ever will be, rediscovered. Each of them published:
an unusual but not exceptional step for a gentlewoman of that time to
take. But each of them published as a highly accomplished poet (and
fiction-writer, in the case of Wroth), and neither could have reached that
level of skill without a long apprenticeship. Their early works are lost,
unless some library or some cupboard is holding them in trust for the
future.

In Elizabeth Cary, Lady Falkland, several of these problems are com-
pounded. Her *Tragedy of Mariam* (a youthful work, published as by E. C.,
for Elizabeth Cary) was reprinted by the Malone Society as early as 1914
and now exists in no fewer than five fine scholarly editions.[22] An edition
of some of her more mature works, written as Lady Falkland, is in
process, begun by the late Jeremy Maule. But many of the 'innumerable
slight things in verse' mentioned by her biographer-daughter, many
saints' lives and hymns to the Virgin – works which would have altered
today's critical perspective on her, and would not have made it easier –
are almost certainly gone beyond recall. Her *Edward II* has been edited
by Diane Purkiss with *Mariam* under the title *Plays*, although agreement
that Falkland did indeed write it is not yet quite universal. To class this
generic experiment as a play has the merit of linking it with *Mariam*
(which is far and away its author's best-known work). But at the same
time it separates it from other, less-known aspects of Falkland's broader
oeuvre, and it blurs a fine example of the way women writers so often look
like square pegs in the round generic categories which were developed
without reference to their work.[23]

Generic issues surface again in the case of Lady Anne Clifford, a life-
long diarist and family historian. She inherited from her mother a family
history compiled not on any literary motive but for the express, practical purpose of proving inheritance rights. This she worked at and reworked. Clifford is a significant figure: Woolf used her to stand for the

Common Reader, since her early diary, written at Knole, records and comments on her purely literary (that is, purely recreational) reading. That early diary – the two-and-a-half-years'-worth of it which survives – has recently received the benefit of up-to-date editing. (This not only establishes an accurate text and identifies people named in it, but is open, though tentative, on such matters as the likelihood that Lady Anne's first husband had a homosexual relationship which she was not happy about.)[24] But Clifford's early diary, though incomplete and cryptic in style, is at least continuous and survives in a single version. Her later writings (transcribed by herself and others in longer and shorter versions) are far more difficult to deal with, and demand involvement with *Proceedings of the Archaeological Institute at York*, 1846, and a Roxburghe Club edition of 1916. Clifford stands in rather the position that Cary occupied early in this century.

Clearly the more closely a writer approximates to modern concepts of the literary, the more attractive a proposition she is to scholars, and thus the more likely she is to receive help in her transition into availability. Those women who stuck to short poems or the novel (once they had invented it) have a lead in the race for canonicity. Fine work is being done in these fields, and the accepted outline of literary history transformed, by new editions of women's novels or poetry volumes, like Ann Messenger's and Richard Greene's forthcoming edition of Mary Leapor. Leapor opens a particular gateway: she is perhaps the most complex and rewarding of all the women labouring-class poets of the eighteenth century, and the first to achieve a scholarly edition in (just) the twentieth. (Mary Collier's major work, *The Woman's Labour*, has appeared both as an austere Augustan Reprint (1985) and as an elegant little volume with drawings, edited by E. P. Thompson; but her other poems have not yet been reprinted.)[25]

Collier and Leapor were both great subverters of genres, but they did this mainly within the broadly familiar category of Augustan poetry. Much valuable writing by women falls outside any familiar generic boundary. We must be thankful for the Brown Women Writers Project, for making available in print such texts as Anne Askew's *Examinations* and Jane Sharp's *Midwives Book* (as well as for their longer list of electronic texts).[26] Still availability finds it hard to climb out of the rut of expectations. Why, when Bathsua Makin (one of many women writers whose life-story has recently been rewritten almost unrecognisably, so inaccurate was the now-discredited former version) is now well known for *An*

Essay to Revive the Antient Education of Gentlewomen (published 1673, re-issued as an Augustan Reprint in 1980), is Hannah Wolley still so little heard of?

Makin's reputation is thoroughly earned. She complains in a rousing feminist preface that a learned woman is seen as a comet (something flamboyant and abnormal, boding no good). After an early life connected with the court, she published the book which made her reputation at an advanced age, while running her own school. She proposes a solid and demanding academic syllabus for upper-class girls, which will benefit the status of women in general through a trickle-down effect. Wolley works in a related field. She concerns herself with the education of ladies, gentlewomen, and other women in need of learning; but her concern is less with reading and the classics than with training in the managerial and practical arts of running a complex seventeenth-century household. She began publishing with *The Ladies Directory*, 1661, and issued seven more titles, of which several were reprinted in her lifetime. She is claimed by Elaine Hobby as the first woman to earn her living by her pen, a decade before the incomparably more famous Aphra Behn.[27]

It is easy to see how Makin conforms more closely than Wolley to the object of a modern feminist's desire. The former may be read as suggesting that women's sphere lies in the academy, the latter as suggesting that it lies in the home. But to accept these suggestions would be to overlook the differences between late twentieth-century and late seventeenth-century female experience. Wolley reminds us of difference; it may be that we prefer to be reminded of similarities. Also, where Makin offers a single text (her two earlier publications are heavily specialised and little known), Wolley offers a whole *oeuvre*, none of which any serious scholar of her can afford to ignore. This makes serious study of her less common. Furthermore, what might appear to be her most rewarding work (*The Gentlewomans Companion; or, A Guide to the Female Sex*, 1675, which incorporates a defence of women's abilities and status which clearly responds to Makin as well as to ongoing antifeminist debates) turns out to have been wholly spurious, put together by the male hack Dorman Newman. Wolley's actual texts can be read as making a 'feminist' statement, but they do so by indirection. The overall view she offers of women's lives is arguably more various and fuller of opportunities than Makin's view. But her books cannot be as widely read and discussed as they deserve, until they are there for the reading.

It sometimes seems as if the problems cluster more thickly in the early part of the long eighteenth century, when the generic choices made by so many women were distinctively un-modern. During the Georgian period many women became not only writers but primarily novelists, or else poets and playwrights. This makes them a more attractive proposition for editors. So we have Oxford editions of all Frances Burney's novels, as well as Peter Sabor's splendid edition of her plays. Burney, however, is the good news. Though we have *almost* complete availability of Sarah Fielding's works, the editorial standard varies somewhat; and for any such magisterial undertaking as the ongoing Wesleyan edition of Henry Fielding (or the successive complete editions of Henry which preceded it) we shall no doubt look in vain. The early novelists have fared relatively well: the major though not the complete works of Jane Barker are available from Oxford, New York, and in autumn 1999 the major though not the complete works of Mary Davys are due to join them from Kentucky. Editions of works by Eliza Haywood have been burgeoning like flowers in spring, though the extent and versatility of Haywood's *oeuvre* makes it impossible to hope for completeness, except possibly in electronic form.[28] The hankering for a uniform, scholarly edition which seems so natural in the case of Sarah Fielding seems less so for Haywood, who was all her life an opportunist and a chameleon; women writers can perhaps do without the kind of scholarship industry which once made it a viable proposition to gather into a collected edition all the bagatelles flung into the world by Swift.

But let us consider, just for argument, the case of Phebe Gibbes. Her very first novel, *The Life and Adventures of Mr Francis Clive*, 1764, had a Garland facsimile in 1975. Her *Friendship in a Nunnery, or the American Fugitive*, 1778, was quickly followed by two more eighteenth-century editions (with some variation in title) – which suggests that its controversial handling of American political issues brought it attention from the outset, as it has continued to do in the twentieth century. It has not, however, been reprinted. Her *Hartly House, Calcutta*, 1789, had a paperback reprint in the year of its two-hundredth anniversary, published by Pluto Press in London and in Winchester, Maryland: from a Calcutta edition of 1908. Unfortunately the paperback appeared with 'Anonymous' on its cover; Gibbes's authorship (which is firmly established both by Robert Dodsley's correspondence and the Royal Literary Fund archives) was not then known.

Gibbes is creeping into critical notice, but she is not likely to be rediscovered in the foreseeable future except by those with access to a very good research library indeed. Serious work on her will need to engage with her truly villainous handwriting in the RLF archives, to identify the various untraced works which she there illegibly claims to have written. But, meanwhile, of the half-dozen novels which can be confidently attributed to her, only two have modern reprints and those are unsatisfactory. In this situation she is not likely to cross the threshold of a classroom, and that is a pity. She is perhaps an extreme case, both for the interest of her writing and for the difficulty of getting hold of it; but there are many cases which are similar if not quite so acute.

For scholars setting out to make texts available, various issues jostle for priority. In all the modern editions mentioned above, in the novel series by World's Classics (Oxford University Press), Broadview Press, University of Kentucky Press, and other publishers, and in many other scholarly texts, the authors' work is presented to the reader with a full apparatus of information and explanation. An editor of such a work must identify the copy-text to be reproduced, must reproduce it faithfully, note any points at which it is problematic (such as divergences from other contemporary texts), and provide certain kinds of explanation or contextualisation. This last involves notes on words or passages in the text which readers may not understand, and some account of the author's life, of the place of this work in it, and of issues raised in the text. Some information about the current political situation is absolutely essential for readers of Mary Wollstonecraft's two *Vindications*, as information about the educational situation is for Makin or Wolley, or information about the hair-raising materialities and ideologies of childbirth is for Jane Sharp. Many editions contain much more: chronologies, bibliographies, excerpts from contemporary documents which may throw light on the text in question. For any kind of life-writing a good index is vital to the reader's use and pleasure; fiction *à clef* like that of Delarivier Manley and Eliza Haywood requires a key and an index; travel-writing requires maps, as in Christopher Morris's editions of the journeys of Celia Fiennes.[29] A simple facsimile reproduction has something to recommend it in the period flavour it conveys; but the long 's' and unfamiliar formatting may be obstacles to many readers. Augustan Reprints in this style, of short texts with helpful introductions, can be wholeheartedly recommended. The Garland novel reprints of the 1970s, published with minimal introduction and no annotation, were most welcome at the time (and remain so where no better text has followed), but are less than satisfactory.

Now the traditional editorial methods have been joined by a new option: electronic text, which may be consulted on line or printed out by the user. Electronic publication cannot entirely escape the marketplace economics which make conventional publishers look askance at reprints; but it can to some extent circumvent them. It cannot help readers who lack a computer or access to the World-Wide Web; but access of this kind is rapidly growing easier to attain. Electronic publishing of early material cannot escape, either, the need for high-class editorial input. In the early days of the Web there arose the Gutenberg Project and one or two similar endeavours, which have circulated very seriously deficient texts: a late-Victorian reprint of Lady Mary Wortley Montagu's letters, for instance, in which, through no fault of anyone living at the time of reprinting, many date-and-place headings to letters are purely fictional. The leader in the online field for the early period is the Brown Women Writers Project, whose standards of editorial rigour and accuracy are high.

However strongly a scholar may feel the potential appeal of early women writers to an intelligent general readership, the readership they will actually get will be mostly students: readers under advice and instruction. The relation between such readers and pre-Romantic women writers is something of a paradox. On the one hand, the writers exert a fascination which editors of texts need to respond to and even exploit. Early modern women writers have a burning concern with gender roles which is matched only by our own moment in history. Many of their texts question the attitudes of their age, and students of both sexes find them (despite the difficulties they present) more accessible than the work of their male contemporaries.

On the other hand, the fascination they exert must not be allowed to gloss over their difficulty or their difference. Even intelligently feminist students, even with the best of scholarly and pedagogic help, will not find early modern women's texts instantly accessible or readily relevant on account of their gender. The common ground between the dawn of the twenty-first century and the early modern period is tenuous to say the least. Early women's texts share to the full in that jolting and tantalising remoteness from ourselves which seems to me a chief reason for reading early literature. They think differently; they stretch *our* minds. To read them, to listen to them carefully, we need to feel our own ignorance and to address it. Women have known this since the late eighteenth century, when they invented the historical novel, and the early nineteenth century, when they did scholarly work on foremothers' texts.

Editors therefore need not to minimise but to highlight the way their texts are of their time, not ours: enmeshed in problems which look soluble to us, or passionately involved in issues which look dead, or deeply committed to religious views which look alien.

So how successful have we been in bringing these texts back to light, in making relevance perceptible across barriers of difference? Optimists will answer one way, pessimists another. I have hinted now and then in this piece the temptations that exist to quick and dirty publishing, to texts inadequately or misleadingly presented. It is true that male writers mostly appeared in definitive editions at a time when beautiful scholarly books were, relatively, cheap – while for buyers of female writers today it sometimes seems as if the choice lies between sticking with paperback or taking out a bank loan.

The good news can be summed up as the creation from scratch of a level of awareness of, and openness to, the fact that early women may be worth reading and worth studying. Such an awareness is now commonplace at both popular and academic levels. Forty years ago Joyce Hemlow, a young Canadian, was publishing *The History of Fanny Burney*. Robert Halsband, a young American, had just published *The Life of Lady Mary Wortley Montagu*. Each one was opening a fertile furrow.

During the last half-century a sizeable audience for early women's writing has been reared and recruited almost from scratch. Montagu and Burney, Manley and Lennox, are both on syllabuses and in bookshops, clocking up more readers than ever before. Working at this essay in April 1998, I heard Isabella Whitney's 'Wyll and Testament' being read on Radio 4: not in any self-consciously literary or intellectual context, but as the voice of an interesting Londoner.

We cannot read the minds of our foremothers, and we ought not to try. But it is a good guess that Whitney would have enjoyed being on Radio 4 more than being taught in a classroom. These women wrote not for us but for themselves; we need to read them for themselves. It is more appropriate to see rediscovery in terms of treasure-hunting than of rescue. No scholar today, at whatever level, is likely to share Chapman's attitudes, but none of us is exempt from the temptation to take someone else's word for what the inside of a book is like. Rediscovery, the bringing of lost books to new readers, has made huge strides in our lifetimes, and has done so as part of a broadening of the readership for books of other periods, other cultures. The canon has become broader, more flexible, and more accessible, and at the same time harder to cover in its entirety; complacency among its guardians has become a more difficult attitude to sustain. Rediscovery of early women writers has contributed generously to the excitingly various and non-monolithic intellectual life of our time.

NOTES

1 Martha Moulsworth, '*My Name was Martha*': *a Renaissance Woman's Autobiographical Poem*, ed. Robert C. Evans and Barbara Wiedemann (West Cornwall, CT: Locust Hill Press, 1993); Margaret J. M. Ezell, *The Patriarch's Wife: Literary Evidence and the History of the Family* (Chapel Hill and London: University of North Carolina Press, 1987).

2 Larpent MS 387, Huntington Library, San Marino, California; Isobel Grundy, 'Sarah Gardner: "Such Trumpery" or "A Lustre to Her Sex"', *Tulsa Studies in Women's Literature*, 7 (1988), 7–25.

3 Laetitia Pilkington, *Memoirs* (1748–54), ed. A. C. Elias, Jr (Athens and London: University of Georgia Press, 1997); Margaret Anne Doody in *London Review of Books*, 20 January 1988.

4 *The Works of Aphra Behn*, ed. Janet Todd, 7 vols. (London: William Pickering, 1992–6); *The Journals and Letters of Fanny Burney*, ed. Joyce Hemlow, et al., 12 vols. (Oxford: Clarendon Press, 1972–84); *The Early Journals and Letters of Fanny Burney*, ed. Lars Troide, et al. (Oxford: Clarendon Press, 1988–); Frances Burney, *Complete Plays*, ed. Peter Sabor with Geoffrey M. Sill and Stewart J. Cooke, 2 vols. (London: William Pickering, 1995).

5 Formerly titled the Eighteenth-Century Short Title Catalogue, this massive bibliography (available online) has already listed holdings of major libraries in Britain and North America, and aims to extend its coverage to every extant work published in English before 1800.

6 Lady Mary Wortley Montagu, *Complete Letters*, ed. Robert Halsband, 3 vols. (Oxford: Clarendon Press, 1965–7).

7 'Lives of the Obscure ii. Laetitia Pilkington' in *The Essays of Virginia Woolf*, ed. Andrew McNeillie (London: Hogarth Press, 1986–), IV (1994), 119.

8 Ann Taylor Gilbert, *Autobiography and Other Memorials*, ed. Josiah Gilbert (London: H. S. King, 1874), I, 295.

9 *The Correspondence of Jonathan Swift*, ed. Harold Williams, 5 vols. (Oxford: Clarendon Press, 1963–5), IV, 192n. Swift's praise of Barber was in fact quite muted.

10 *The Letters of Samuel Johnson, with Mrs Thrale's Genuine Letters to him*, ed. R. W. Chapman, 3 vols. (Oxford: Clarendon Press, 1952), I, 44.

11 Anne Finch, Countess of Winchilsea, *Poems*, ed. Myra Reynolds (Chicago: University of Illinois Press, 1903); 'George Paston' [Emily Morse Symonds], *Lady Mary Wortley Montagu and Her Times* (London: Methuen, 1907).

12 J. M. S. Tompkins, *The Popular Novel in England 1770–1800* (1932; rpt. London: Methuen, 1961), *The Polite Marriage . . . eighteenth-century essays* (London: Cambridge University Press, 1938); Mary Lascelles, *Jane Austen and her Art* (Oxford University Press, 1939).

13 [Mary Berry], *Some Account of the Life of Rachael Wriothesley Lady Russell . . .* (London: Longman, et al., 1819). Berry edited Lady Russell's love-letters to her husband, which now hold a place in the history of the intimate famil-iar letter. An earlier publication had selected letters of political interest, i.e. those bearing more on the fame of Lord Russell than of his wife.

14 *Memoirs of Lady Fanshawe . . . written by herself,* ed. Sir N. H. Nicholas (London: Colburn, 1829); Lucy Hutchinson, *Memoirs of the Life of Colonel Hutchinson, Governor of Nottingham Castle and Town,* ed. Revd Julius Hutchinson (London: Longman, et al., 1806).

15 Eliza Fenwick, *Secresy, or The Ruin on the Rock* (1795), ed. Isobel Grundy (Peterborough, ON: Broadview Press, 1994; rev. edn 1998); Terry Castle in *London Review of Books,* 23 February 1995.

16 Virginia Woolf, *A Room of One's Own* (1928; London: Penguin Books, n.d.), 92–3.

17 *The Book of Margery Kempe,* ed. Sanford Brown Meech and H. E. Allen (London: Early English Text Society, 1940); *The Book of Margery Kempe,* trans. by B. A. Windeatt (Harmondsworth: Penguin Books, 1985); Tony D. Triggs, *The Book of Margery Kempe: a New Translation* (Tunbridge Wells: Burns & Oates, 1995). For further discussion of women writers in the Medieval and Renaissance periods, see Carol M. Meale (ed.), *Women and Literature in Britain, 1150–1500* (Cambridge University Press, 1993) and Helen Wilcox (ed.), *Women and Literature in Britain, 1500–1700* (Cambridge University Press, 1996).

18 *The Poems of Aemilia Lanyer: Salve Deus Rex Judaeorum,* ed. Susanne Woods (New York: Oxford University Press, 1993); *The Psalms of Sir Philip Sidney & the Countess of Pembroke,* ed. J. C. A. Rathmell (New York University Press, 1963); *The Triumph of Death & other unpublished & uncollected poems by Mary Sidney, Countess of Pembroke (1561–1621),* ed. G. F. Waller, Salzburg Studies in English Literature 65 (University of Salzburg, 1977); *The Poems of Lady Mary Wroth* (Baton Rouge and London: Louisiana State University Press, 1983); *The First Part of the Countesse of Montgomery's Urania by Lady Mary Wroth,* ed. Josephine A. Roberts, Medieval & Renaissance Texts and Studies 140 and Renaissance English Text Society, 7th ser., 17 (Binghamton, NY, 1995); second part, ed. Josephine A. Roberts, Suzanne Gossett, and Janel Mueller (University of Chicago Press, 1999). The Countess of Pembroke's versions of the Psalms and Petrarch's 'Triumph of Death' are now also available in *The Collected Works of Mary Sidney Herbert, Countess of Pembroke. Volume I: Poems, Translations, and Correspondence. Volume II: The Psalmes of David,* ed. Margaret P. Hannay, Noel J. Kinnamon, and Michael G. Brennan (Oxford: Clarendon Press, 1998).

19 A. L. Rowse (ed.), *The Poems of Shakespeare's Dark Lady: Salve Deus Rex Judaeorum* (London: Cape, 1978). He perpetrated a real howler in reading the word 'brave' as 'brown', and thus creating 'evidence' about Lanyer's complexion. See Suzanne Woods, *Aemilia Lanyer: a Renaissance Woman Poet* (New York: Oxford University Press, 1999).

20 On Mary Robinson, see: M. J. Levy's introduction to her *Memoirs* (London: Peter Owen, 1994), and Clare Brant in ch. 13, below pp. 290–2.

21 Rathmell in Pembroke, *Psalms,* pp. xxiv–xxv. Ruskin published a selection as *Broken Pieces of Sir Philip Sidney's Psalter. Laid up in Store for English Homes*: the second volume of his anthology *Bibliotheca Pastorum* (London and Orpington: Ellis & White, and George Allen, 1877).

22 *The Tragedy of Mariam*: with *The Lady Falkland: Her Life by One of Her Daughters,*

ed. Barry Weller and Margaret Ferguson (Berkeley: University of California Press, 1993); in *Renaissance Drama by Women: Texts and Documents*, ed. S. P. Cerasano and Marion Wynne-Davies (London: Routledge, 1996); ed. Stephanie Wright (Keele University Press, 1996); in *Major Women Writers of Seventeenth-Century England*, ed. James Fitzmaurice, et al. (Ann Arbor: University of Michigan Press, 1996); and in *Renaissance Women: the Plays of Elizabeth Cary; the Poems of Aemilia Lanyer*, ed. Diane Purkiss (London: William Pickering, 1994).

23 For further discussion of genre in relation to women's writing, see ch. 9, pp. 198–201 and especially Clare Brant's discussion of miscellaneity, ch. 13, pp. 285–9.

24 Brenda R. Silver (ed.), ' "Anon" and "The Reader": Virginia Woolf's Last Essays', *Twentieth-Century Literature*, 25 (1979), 356–441; Katherine Acheson (ed.), *The Diary of Anne Clifford, 1616–1619: a Critical Edition* (New York: Garland, 1996).

25 *The Works of Mary Leapor*, ed. Richard Greene and Ann Messenger (Oxford University Press, 1999); '*The Thresher's Labour' by Stephen Duck and 'The Woman's Labour' by Mary Collier: Two Eighteenth Century Poems*, ed. E. P. Thompson and Marian Sugden (London: Merlin Press, 1989). On Mary Leapor see also Margaret Anne Doody, ch. 10, below pp. 224–7.

26 *The Examinations of Anne Askew*, ed. Elaine V. Beilin (New York and Oxford: Oxford University Press, 1996); Jane Sharp, *The Midwives Book; or, The Whole Art of Midwifery* (1671), ed. Elaine Hobby (New York and Oxford: Oxford University Press, 1999).

27 Elaine Hobby, 'A Woman's Best Setting Out is Silence: the Writings of Hannah Wolley' in Gerald Maclean (ed.), *Culture and Society in the Stuart Restoration: Literature, Drama, History* (Cambridge University Press, 1995), pp. 179–200.

28 On Jane Barker, see Margaret Anne Doody, ch. 10, below p. 221; on Eliza Haywood, see Ros Ballaster, ch. 9, pp. 203, 208–10.

29 Christopher Morris (ed.), *The Journeys of Celia Fiennes* (London: Cresset Press, 1947), and *The Illustrated Journeys of Celia Fiennes* (London: Macdonald & Co., 1982). Fiennes's travel writings remained unpublished during her lifetime (1662–1741).

CHAPTER 9

Women and the rise of the novel: sexual prescripts

Ros Ballaster

In 1929, Virginia Woolf spoke of the 'technical difficulty' facing the woman writer: 'that the very form of the sentence does not fit her. It is a sentence made by men; it is too loose, too heavy, too pompous for a woman's use.'[1] In 1755, the actress Charlotte Charke, estranged youngest daughter of the actor-manager, Colley Cibber, opens the story of her life (*A Narrative of the Life of Mrs Charlotte Charke*) with an anecdote describing how, at the age of four, she crept downstairs in the early morning and donned her father's wig, beaver-hat, and sword, and her brother's waistcoat, tying her nightshirt up to resemble breeches. She proceeded to march solemnly up and down a deep ditch bordering the garden, bowing at passers-by. The image in each case is that of the fledgling female writer struggling to don masculine clothing in order to take up the mantle of narrator, but finding that it only makes her ridiculous. It invokes not only the inability of a female 'form' to 'fit' into the patterns and styles of the male, but also techniques of disguise, and the self-conscious display of incommensurability. Charke assures us that '[t]he Drollery of my Figure render'd it impossible, assisted by the Fondness of both Father and Mother, to be angry with me';[2] the act of transgression is disguised as comedy. Charke's narrative proves to be an extended piece of public blackmail, designed to force her father's forgiveness for later, less forgivable acts of transgression (leaving her husband, running into debt, passing as a man in order to avoid her creditors); she punctuates her narrative with direct addresses to Colley Cibber indicating that she will cease to cut a public figure and bring disgrace on him if he will take her back under his wing, reincorporate her into the private domestic space of the family. That agenda suggests that we need to treat with some suspicion women's claims to be poor imitators of a pre-given masculine form in the novel, and take issue with the assumption that the narrative 'sentence' is created by men, sentencing women to a marginal or muted position in relation to narrative. Women writers may rather have

strategically submitted to this 'story' of their own secondariness in narrative form in order to comically diffuse the transgressive possibility that
the novel may have extended the possibility of narcissistic self-invention
rather than dutiful daughterly imitation. The majority of women writers
of the eighteenth century chose, indeed, found it profitable, to cooper-
ate with, rather than resist, a version of the history of the novel as pre-
scripted by men.

The hierarchy of male prescript and female imitation is central to the
plots, forms, and history of the eighteenth-century novel. This chapter
explores the critical debate over the origins and rise of the novel in
eighteenth-century England and the crucial part that notions of gender
play in its formation and interpretation; it goes on to outline the ways in
which women writers at different points in the history of the novel self-
consciously chart the 'secondariness' of women in the content of their
fiction only to reveal the primacy of female agency within the form.
Narrative fictions insistently 'plot' the story of the secret empowerment
of women through a language free from the perils of the spoken word
and the attendant visibility (and hence vulnerability) of the body of the
speaker: novelistic discourse itself.

In this respect, the 'story' of the female protagonist is very different
from that of her female author. The female protagonist must seek shelter
from the risks attendant on public exposure of her body and her
attempts to speak her desire and autonomy publicly: countless novels by
women entail a vain or egotistic heroine's learning, often at an extreme
emotional and physical cost, the limits of her freedom, in order to
prepare her to marry an older, worldly, judgemental, and authoritarian
man. By contrast, her author evades the need for a male protector precisely because the novel allows her to enter a form of authoritative discourse without the 'risk' of physical display of her own proper body (the
heroine stands as surrogate).

ENGENDERED TRADITIONS: SCRIPTING THE 'ORIGINS' AND 'RISE' OF THE ENGLISH NOVEL

Theorists of the 'origins' and 'rise' of the novel seem as attracted as its
eighteenth-century authors to the metaphor of inter-familial struggles
for supremacy. The novel emerges as the protagonist of a romance
quest, a child whose original parenthood is obscured and must be traced
back through the painstaking and more or less obtrusive authorial activities of the literary critic in order to make its true lineage apparent.
Accounts of the eighteenth-century novel incline either towards an aris-

tocratic preference for the revelation of the novel's true nobility (deriving from classical or archetypal sources) or towards a more whiggish, democratising impulse which casts the novel as the hero of the illegitimate, the marginal, and the underdog, rising to preeminence through merit alone and transfiguring its humble origins in the ballad, the popular history, the supernatural tale, into a more inclusive aesthetic achievement.[3] Not only must its true parents be found, however, but for the novel to 'rise' it must, like all children, successfully differentiate itself from its forebears, to form a new autonomous identity.

Different ascriptions of origin have important implications for 'gendering' the novel-child, successfully establishing whether it is male or female, and reading its 'signs' properly. Paternal lineage is found in the sources of 'history' and 'news' by Ian Watt, Lennard Davis, and Robert Mayer,[4] maternal in the source of 'romance' and classical fiction by Margaret Anne Doody, Paul Salzman, and myself.[5] Where the former (paternal) origins are stressed, women writers are most often treated as the weaker imitators of a strong male line; where the latter (maternal) origins are stressed, women writers are presented as more powerful in the evolution of the form's characteristics.

The drive to characterise and fix the novel by ascribing it a gender is a powerful factor in its development and the stakes for women as writers of the novel are high. Margaret Doody claims that the novel comes to hegemony as part of a wider shift towards the diminution and destabilisation of the male psyche and the equivalent expansion of the female (p. 279). The novel in other words, from classical times to the present, has comically enacted the radical instability of masculine forces of social and personal control. It is thus, in its very 'secondariness', 'imitativeness', and 'iterativeness', a mode suited to the woman writer. And women novelists were not slow to exploit this association of the novel with femininity.

Note the interesting ambivalence expressed in the preface to Frances Burney's anonymously published first novel, *Evelina* (1778), as an example of this process. The preface opens with a poem to her biological father addressed as the 'author of my being!' but goes on to express an ambiguous relationship to literary, if not biological, fathers, who must be diverged from if that 'being' is to be a full agent in literature:

In books . . . imitation cannot be shunned too sedulously; for the very perfection of a model which is frequently seen, serves but more forcibly to mark the inferiority of a copy.

To avoid what is common, without adopting what is unnatural, must limit the ambition of the vulgar herd of authors; however zealous, therefore, my veneration of the great writers I have mentioned, however I may feel myself enlightened by the knowledge of Johnson, charmed with the eloquence of Rousseau, softened by the pathetic powers of Richardson, and exhilarated by the wit of Fielding, and humour of Smollet; I yet presume not to attempt pursuing the same ground which they have tracked; whence, though they may have cleared the weeds, they have also culled the flowers, and though they have rendered the path plain, they have left it barren.[6]

Burney's rhetoric underscores apparent daughterly deference to powerful, if benevolent, paternal 'originals' with a hint of self-determining aggression and assertion. On the level of narrative form, if not material familial relations, the woman writer finds herself able to assert her difference, to imagine her secondariness as a form of empowerment rather than submission to the paternal 'prescript'. The passage from Burney also demonstrates the tendency in the later half of the eighteenth century towards a language of early modern 'difference', where the securing of identity through hierarchy and inheritance is replaced by claims for opposition – an identity that is 'different but equal'.

If theorists and historians of the novel dispute its 'origins', the majority agree in viewing the novel as a 'syncretic' or 'problem-solving' genre, its preeminence as a literary form assured by its ability to resolve and mediate conflict. Michael McKeon's important *Origins of the English Novel* has put the most cogent case for the novel as a form which succeeds in providing imaginary resolutions to the sexual and social transformations of the eighteenth century, both 'voicing' and managing categorial instabilities of gender and class in particular.[7] More recently, McKeon's argument has expanded from the generic confinement of his discussion of the novel to consider the eighteenth century more broadly as a period in which a socio-cultural system of difference, and the liberal assumption that a system of difference generates equality, are put into place.[8] For McKeon and also for Nancy Armstrong, whose *Desire and Domestic Fiction* is influenced by Foucault's understanding of sexuality as a powerfully regulatory and distinctively modern construct, the sexual conflicts which preoccupy the eighteenth-century novel are often little more than a displaced means of managing class transformation and in particular the shift from aristocratic to bourgeois hegemony in the period (a variant of Ian Watt's more simple claim for the 'rise of the middle class' at this time). The creation of a cultural as well as economic supremacy for the bourgeois man lies in the idealisation of virtues categorised as 'feminine' – sympathy, nurture, civility – and their appropriation for the male civil subject. Here then, it is through the male imitation of a prior female model that virtue comes to be displayed. Gender must be understood, however, as more than a metaphor or 'cover' for male class virtue in that its changing construction impacts materially on the lives and writings of women themselves.[9]

As Frances Burney's preface illustrates, most women novelists of the eighteenth century tended to locate their own writing in relation to a strong line of male predecessors or contemporaries. It is thus difficult to speak of a 'woman's tradition' in the novel of this period; if women read each others' work they did not, for the most part, openly acknowledge influence. Thus, historians of novels written by women in the eighteenth century tend to focus either on shared patterns of style, language, and theme, without claiming positive imitation, or to group novels by women in terms of shared, often generic, responses to male activity in the field. Jane Spencer charts an increasing identification with their own heroines on the part of female writers in the period, and sees the construction of an alternative value system through the idea of 'romance' as enabling the expression of female desire and autonomy.[10] Janet Todd and Catherine Gallagher take different approaches to a similar preoccupation: the ways in which women writers market themselves in the newly expanded and profitable print culture of the eighteenth century. Where Todd investigates women's attempts to fashion 'signs' of themselves that promote and validate their own writing presence, Gallagher stresses the positive effects of an accent on the absence, silence, or what she terms 'nobodiness', of cultural constructions of femininity in the period.[11] Gallagher takes her cue from McKeon and Armstrong, envisioning the fashioning of the 'civil' subject as an ambiguous process for women, in that it asserts masculine identity through the appropriation of virtues of inter-relationship, sympathy, and submission which are classified as feminine. Developing more fully the metaphor of exchange and circulation at the heart of fictional accounts of sexual and social relations, she argues that women succeeded in 'capitalizing' on the 'insignificance or nothingness' attributed to female sexuality. Authorship itself as the endless transaction, exchange, and dispossession of selfhood in the service of the public is figured by women writers as disparate as Aphra Behn and Frances Burney as a feminine practice (analogous with prostitution or marriage). For Spencer, Todd, and Gallagher the central issue, as in this essay, remains one of the attempt to find a means to 'voice' femininity in ways that confer social power on women as writers.

Novels by women in the eighteenth century stage a series of dramas around writing and reading, exploring processes of self-inscription and advocating the exercise of authority in invisible, private economies of writing and knowledge rather than acts of public utterance. In what follows I indicate briefly how the novels of the early, mid, and late century demonstrate the changing and interlinked class and gender ideologies of their specific moment as well as the ways in which the female 'scriptor' is invested with power by contrast with the female reader or protagonist. In each case, however, we see the discourse of the novel claimed as peculiarly appropriate to women as writers, its hetero-glossia, its multiplicity of voices, providing a kind of insurance against their own act of self-assertion in putting their work on public display. The effortless ironic complexity of Jane Austen can, in this context, be seen not only as the remarkable product of a singular individual, but also the culmination of a century of experiment with the act of control through apparent abnegation of narratorial presence.

COUNTER-SCRIPTING: PLOTS AND PROVIDENTIALISM

The earliest endeavours of women in the novel reveal a marked sense of entry into an environment scripted and controlled by powerful, most often illegitimate, masculine forces. Protagonists often seek to restore the providential 'script' of a theologically grounded 'father' while the plots of active and meddling usurping 'sons' proliferate around them. Consider, for example, Aphra Behn's *Oroonoko, or the Royal Slave* (1688) in which the absence of the governor in the English colony of Surinam leaves its various populations at the mercy of what she describes as 'such notorious Villains as *Newgate* never transported'.[12] The female narrator finds herself powerless to protect the suffering Negro prince, Oroonoko, from these upstart English men, but claims her authority and influence in the telling of stories and the telling of his story in particular: 'I hope, the Reputation of my Pen is considerable enough to make his Glorious Name to survive to all Ages, with that of the brave, the beautiful, and the constant *Imoinda*' (p. 119). Here, then, we find one of the earliest attempts to locate female power not in instrumental public speech but in influential novelistic discourse, indeed to transform the latter into a com-pensation for exclusion from the former.

In these early novels the 'domestic' preoccupations of the later novel are not evident and plots of sexual pursuit, whether those of seduction and betrayal, or those of courtship to marriage, seem to require a more allegorical or metaphorical reading than their successors. These are stories in which the canvas of sexual intrigue serves as the ground for explorations of what constitutes political or civil agency, especially for women. In the novels of Tory satirists (sympathisers with the Stuart monarchs and antagonists to the Revolution settlement of 1688), the forces ranged against the sexually innocent are human and the product of a culture of greed and self-interest associated with mercantilism and a court lacking a powerful symbolic patriarchal head. 'Plotting' in the late seventeenth and early eighteenth century continues to carry the resonance of political or treasonable plotting, reviving memories of the plot-narrating activities of Titus Oates and others in the Popish Plot revelations of the late 1670s and the series of political plots apparently uncovered around the subsequent Exclusion Crisis.[13] Thus Aphra Behn's *Love-Letters between a Nobleman and his Sister* (1684–7), Delarivier Manley's *Secret Memoirs and Manners . . . from the New Atalantis* (1709), and Eliza Haywood's *Memoirs of a Certain Island Adjacent to the Kingdom of Utopia* (1725) and *The Secret History of the Present Intrigues of the Court of Caramania* (1727) present Whig (anti-Catholic pro-Parliament) politicians as sycophants and parasites manipulating a vulnerable monarchy, whose activities as dangerous seducers plotting to destroy female sexual innocence are equivalent to their designs upon the English state. Sexual plotting and political intrigue are parallel activities, the one calling up the other in the reader's consciousness.

The majority of Haywood's novels of the 1720s are not scandal fictions but short novellas of seduction and betrayal. In these novels too, the majority of heroines fall prey to the exploitative 'plotting' of dangerous young rakes, although her most popular novel, *Love in Excess* (1719), concerns the constantly frustrated love of D'Elmont and his young ward, Melliora. Those heroines who do not fall prey to the male plotter are those who manage to rival that power of scripting in their own person. Hence, the nameless heroine of *Fantomina* (1725) learns to maintain the interest of the young man who first seduces her by presenting herself to him for seduction in a series of 'masquerade' disguises: a serving maid, a lonely widow, a mysterious masked aristocrat.[14]

By contrast, Penelope Aubin understands the plotting that endangers her heroines as prescribed not by human forces but by a powerful providential God who tests virtue through adversity. Thus, in *The Strange Adventures of the Count de Vinevil and his Family* (1721), the ostensible hero is murdered by Turks seeking to abduct his lovely daughter Ardelisa from their new home in Constantinople. He dies admitting God's justice in punishing him for exposing his child to dangers abroad and leaves Ardelisa subject to a series of abductions, near rapes, and shipwrecks, until she is reunited with her young husband, Longueville, and rewarded for her persistent patience and virtue. Although Aubin presents her fiction as the rendering of providential messages from her God to her reader, she calls attention to the singularity and authority of her voice as a female providentialist. The powerful model of Defoe's *Robinson Crusoe* is both cited and surmounted in the preface to Count de Vinevil:

As for the truth of what this narrative contains, since Robinson Crusoe has been so well received, which is more improbable, I know no reason why this should be thought a fiction. I hope the world is not grown so abandoned to vice as to believe that there is no such ladies to be found, as would prefer death to infamy; or a man that for remorse of conscience would quit a plentiful fortune, retire, and choose to die in a dismal cell . . . Would men trust in Providence and act according to reason and common justice, they need not to fear any thing; but whilst they defy God and wrong others they must be cowards, and their ends such as they deserve, surprising and infamous.[15]

Aubin sets out to make morality and novelistic discourse compatible terms in an environment that sets them at odds. The difficulty of exercising verbal 'wit' without falling prey to the interpretation of immodesty becomes the topic of a novel by a writer with explicit Whig sympathies, Mary Davys. Davys succeeds in appropriating the self-conscious performative articulateness of her Tory predecessors alongside the moralistic plotting of Aubin but within the new framework of a contractual and consensual model of civil subjecthood associated with Whig theorists of the period.[16]

Davys's short novella of 1724, *The Reformed Coquet*,[17] concerns the 'education' of an orphaned heiress, Amoranda, 'a finished Beauty and Coquet' (p. 258), who figures as the prey for a series of rakish and foolish suitors. An elderly tutor, Formator, is recommended to her by her guardian-uncle, Mr Traffick, and seeks to 'reform' the heroine into a more modest and rational frame of mind. Formator acts to prevent her abduction by her two foolish suitors who plan to force her into choosing one as a husband. He suspects the identity of a female friend, Berinthia, and is proved right when on a boating trip she is revealed to be a man in disguise and would have succeeded in raping Amoranda were it not for the intervention of a young man on horseback, Alanthus, with whom Amoranda promptly falls in love. When fire breaks out in the stables, 'Formator' runs into Amoranda's chamber to rescue her but forgets to don his false beard and is revealed to be Alanthus and the pair are happily united.

If disguise is understood in terms of the plot of the novel as primarily a device used by *men*, it is the female author, Davys, who uses it to most impressive formal effect. Her challenge is the same as that of her hero: how to get frivolous young ladies to conform to moral strictures in the face of more fascinating attractions? She opens her dedication, addressed 'To the Ladies of Great Britain' with the comment that '[a]t a time when the Town is so full of Masquerades, Operas, New Plays, Conjurers, Monsters, and feigned Devils; how can I, Ladies, expect you to throw away an hour upon the less agreeable Amusements my *Coquet* can give you?' (p. 252). The novel is scattered with such allusions to romance, and in particular Spenserian romance. When Amoranda encounters Alanthus on horseback and begs him for protection from her would-be rapist, he responds 'I am no Knight-Errant, nor do I ride in quest of Adventures' and rides away (p. 299). When his sister, Lady Betty, encounters Alanthus at Amoranda's house wearing his disguise of Formator, he says 'This, my dear Sister, is the *Fairy-Land* where I have so long lived Incognito; and there, there's the Enchantress, who, by a natural Magic, has kept me all this while in Chains of love' (p. 319). Davys thus codes to her readers that she is offering a moral realist novel in disguise as a playful fantastic romance. Davys's novel is presented to us as just such a 'natural Magic', which unites the new instructional purposes of the novel with the pleasures of an older, less referential form, the romance. Ultimately then, it is the female scriptor, in the shape of a narrator explicitly identified as female, who manages to negotiate a space for female autonomy even while she tells the story of her heroine's submission to male authority. The author's 'vanity' about the 'beauty' of her own images is licensed where that of her heroine must be curbed. As she puts it in her dedication 'To the Ladies of Great Britain': '[b]ut she who has assurance to write has certainly the vanity of expecting to be read: All Authors see a Beauty in their own Compositions, which perhaps nobody else can find; as Mothers think their own Offspring amiable, how deficient soever Nature has been to them. But whatever my Faults may be, my Design is good, and hope you *British* Ladies will accordingly encourage it' (pp. 252–3).

READING THE SCRIPT: THE REWARDS OF VIRTUE

In Davys's novel we can already see the beginnings of a bourgeois critique of aristocratic libertinism (embodied in the rake-figure of Lord Lofty) and the presentation of a more affective and civil lover in the shape of Formator/Alanthus. The rise of the novel, as numerous critics

following in the footsteps of Ian Watt have noted, coincides with the rise
of bourgeois ideology in England and its attendant valuing of the
domestic virtues and private morality; moral worth, no longer assumed
to be a privilege of birth, must now be proved through action and behaviour. Such ethics might be understood to extend new opportunities to
middle-class women as the embodiment of domestic virtue. However, as
the almost sinister manipulativeness of Formator indicates, women novelists were also aware that confining women to domestic and private
moralities could be as oppressive a tyranny as viewing them solely as
sexual playthings and targets for male lust, an attitude associated with
the libertinism of the earlier Restoration culture.

By the mid eighteenth century, the novel by women has become less
preoccupied with figuring women or feminine modes of behaviour as
viable forms of political agency and more with presenting female protagonists as more or less competent readers of male-authored scripts.
Just as their heroines seek to find empowering modes of critique and
interpretation in relation to the language of their lovers, female authors
are engaged in an attempt to 'read' successfully the implications of the
competition between the two leading male novelists of the period,
Samuel Richardson and Henry Fielding, to become the dominant voice
of bourgeois novelistic culture. Samuel Richardson's *Pamela; or, Virtue
Rewarded* (1740) became an exemplary model for 'domestic' fiction: it rendered through the letters and journal of a servant girl an account of her
virtuous resistance to her master, Mr B.'s, sexual pursuit and of the final
'rewarding' of her virtue through honourable marriage to him. *Pamela*
announces its newness and originality by differentiating itself from the
romance. When Mr B. obtains Pamela's letters from her during her
imprisonment on his estate in Lincolnshire, his response as critic is
'"there is such a pretty air of romance, as you tell your story, in *your* plots,
and *my* plots, that I shall be better directed how to wind up the catas-
trophe of the pretty novel"'.[18] At the same time as Mr B. reads her
writing as romance (which he consistently associates with what he sees
as her tendency to falsehood), he also acknowledges that the conflict
between himself and Pamela is one of narrative form and whose version
of a story will finally win. As Nancy Armstrong puts it in *Desire and
Domestic Fiction*, 'this novel is a struggle in which one fiction captures and
translates the other into its terms' (p. 119). The strenuous virtue of the
Christian novelistic heroine then captures the pagan romance lascivious-
ness of her 'master' – class conflict is dramatically resolved through the
'embourgeoisement' of the aristocrat who separates virtue from status.

This exemplary domestic fiction (or fiction of domestication) does not stage a conflict between fiction and reality, but rather between which mode of fiction (romance or novel) is most capable of resolving conflict and containing the dangers of class mobility.

Henry Fielding's *Tom Jones* (1749), *Joseph Andrews* (1742), and *Shamela* (1741) offer a shrewd critique of the ideological concealment in Richardson's apparently seamless resolution of class and sexual conflict in *Pamela*. Both *Joseph Andrews* and *Shamela* criticise the reduction of the idea of 'virtue' in domestic fiction to nothing more nor less than 'chastity' – a passive virtue of resistance rather than an active heroism. In *Shamela*, Fielding conveys this linguistically by the corruption of the term by his anti-heroine to that of 'vartue'. Inset discourses in *Joseph Andrews* on the nature of justice and corruption in the legal system and in *Shamela* exposing the venal interests of the clergy point to Fielding's desire to retain a more expansive and active, overtly classical, model of virtuous behaviour than the model of the chaste Christian heroine can embody. Most important of all, however, and not unconnected to his critique of the limitations of Richardson's version of bourgeois virtue, is Fielding's insistence on the duplicity of the *narrative mode* of Richardson's novel – Pamela's exclusive narrative authority enables her to render an account in her interest. *Shamela* suggests that the first-person personal voice of the artless, honest heroine is simply a cover for a hungry pursuit of self-advancement. *If* Pamela is a metaphor or figure for bourgeois culture, then, her story according to Fielding is nothing more than an ideological cover-up for the greedy mercantilism of the emergent class she represents. Like Richardson, Fielding sets himself against the romance but in the name of classical austerity and honour rather than empirical realism.

Later critics, like 'Hortensius', the male advocate of the novel over the romance in Clara Reeve's 1785 *The Progress of Romance* who tells his female disputants that Richardson is 'a writer all your own',[19] established Richardson as the defender and advancer of women's power. Fielding's satirical treatment of women as objects of male sexual desire or conniving and manipulative villainesses seems to be part and parcel of a tradition of misogyny that Richardson appears to have been challenging. However, the gender divide between Richardson and Fielding is less transparent than it appears. Two 'domestic' fictions by women – Eliza Haywood's *Betsy Thoughtless* (1751), and Charlotte Lennox's *The Female Quixote* (1752) – ostensibly share with Richardson and Fielding the critique of romance, positing the novel as an alternative model of authoritative fiction; yet they also inscribe a counter-critique of the idealisation of domestic virtue and companionate marriage in the Richardsonian novel without subscribing to Fielding's juridical vision of a revivified masculine heroism moulded from classical and Christian models.

The heroine of Lennox's *The Female Quixote* has been brought up in country retirement by her widowed father on a diet of translations of seventeenth-century French romances that had belonged to her mother. Courted by the man her father desires her to marry – her cousin, Mr Glanville – Arabella rejects him, despite her love for him, because he fails to conform to the strict courtship traditions of the French romances she takes to be accounts of historical fact. Arabella engages in a series of Quixotic misunderstandings due to her determination to read her environment and events around her through the filter of romance precedents. When she dives into the Thames in emulation of her heroine Clelia, in Madeleine de Scudéry's romance of the same name,[20] to escape what she takes to be the attack of rapists (some men riding in Richmond Park), she falls seriously ill. She is brought to a recognition of the 'criminal' fictionality of the romance and converted to an enthusiasm for domestic fiction by her doctor who proves also to be a divine. The doctor explicitly points to Richardson, advising her that an 'admirable Writer of our own Time, has found the Way to convey the most solid Instructions, the noblest Sentiments, and the most exalted Piety, in the pleasing Dress of a Novel'.[21] The doctor's complaint is not about the fictionality of romances but about their 'criminality': they 'soften the Heart to Love, and harden it to Murder . . . they teach Women to exact Vengeance, and Men to execute it' (p. 380). It is the combination of Arabella's belief in their truth, which the doctor rightly observes was not the intention of their creators, and the dangerous cruelty that they incite, as opposed to the management of emotion that he claims domestic fiction promotes, that is pernicious. Arabella's concessions to the doctor, her conversion to domestic ideology, and her agreement to marry Glanville, mark however the book's closure and the containment, indeed silencing, of its heroine. As reader of the novel, Arabella's verbal power comes to an end.

It is this 'enclosure' that Haywood explores in *The History of Miss Betsy Thoughtless* by extending the courtship-to-marriage plot into the realm of domestic relations in marriage itself. Haywood's heroine, Betsy, like Davys's Amoranda, is vain, headstrong, flirtatious but at bottom virtuous. Betsy's numerous suitors offer her different models of the language of courtship including the libertine proposals of a rake, Gayland, and the comical naval metaphors of Captain Hysom (his proposal is framed in terms of having 'tacked about,—shifted [his] sails, and stood for the port directly'). While Betsy does not fall victim to these romantic overtures, she has more difficulty in seeing through the other discourses she encounters: those of the romance and of domestic courtship. When Sir Frederick Fineer, a seeming baronet, courts her in the extravagant language of romance she responds, 'What a romantic jargon is here?— One would think he had been consulting all the ballads since fair Rosamond, and the children in the wood, for fine phrases to melt me into pity.'[22] However, she still gives credit to the report that Fineer is dying of love for her and is tricked into visiting him in his lodgings where he attempts to compromise her so far that she must marry him: Betsy escapes this fate, discovering that Fineer is a servant in disguise, but is so shocked by the experience that she hastily agrees to pressure from her brothers and family to marry another suitor, the outwardly respectable Mr Munden who appears to offer her domestic stability. Munden later proves to be a tyrant: 'he considered a wife no more than an upper servant, bound to study and obey, in all things, the will of him to whom she had given her hand' (p. 448).

Eliza Haywood's novel suggests that the language of domestic novelistic love is only one among many discourses that conceal the exchange function of women, rather than *the* discourse that allows them to transcend their commodification.[23] Betsy does not, like Pamela and Arabella, have to learn to find 'freedom' in the language of domestic fiction, but rather to recognise that she cannot imagine herself free in any language (romance/Fineer or novel/Munden): that both are precisely *fictions*. She does have to check her vanity and her exorbitant belief in her own power as love-object – the experience of being an unloved wife quickly disabuses her of her illusions on this – but the novel is quite clear that her eventual marriage to Trueworth (her favoured suitor who had previously abandoned his courtship persuaded of her moral weakness), after the convenient deaths of her estranged husband and Trueworth's first wife, is not necessarily an opportunity for domestic authority. Trueworth couches his proposal by letter to her as a demand that she submit to the authority of her love: 'fain would my flattering hopes persuade me, that I shall not find you a too stubborn rebel to that power, to whose authority all nature yields a willing homage' (p. 560).

Domestic authority and the power as a woman to engage, rather than find herself the circulating object, in commodity culture lies ultimately only with the female narrator who retains the organising and interpretative power over the story even as she retains her anonymity and physical distance from the action. Haywood closely imitates the stylistic and narrative techniques of Henry Fielding, but where Fielding's *Tom Jones* and *Joseph Andrews* are designed to critique the apparent 'feminisation' of culture in idealising the domestic and private virtues over acts of public heroism and benevolence, Haywood's exposes the powerlessness that this seeming feminisation inflicts on women themselves.[24] The feminine virtues of retirement, diffidence, and civility that Betsy's villainous first husband, Mr Munden, displays in his courtship of her are nothing more than an ideological trick: 'how obsequious and submissive soever he appeared when a lover, [he] had fixed his resolution, to render himself absolute master when he became a husband' (p. 448). Female mastery lies not in being the object of courtship, but in the act of representation itself, the act of narration which is foregrounded as the only place for the imitation of masculine mastery without personal cost for women.

THE BODY AS SCRIPT: THE POLITICS OF SENSIBILITY

If women's domestic fiction of the mid eighteenth century traced an inevitable trajectory in the courtship-to-marriage plot towards the silencing and commodification of women, the end of the eighteenth and beginning of the nineteenth century saw the revival of a model of feminine 'agency' in the bodily discourse of sensibility rather than the verbal 'wit' of the earlier period. Sensibility is perhaps best understood as a psychological trait induced by the encounter with human suffering. The loving and attentive detail to the ways in which that psychological trait is registered on the protagonist's physical body is the special province of the descriptive prose of the novel. John Mullan makes this comment:

In novels, the articulacy of sentiment is produced via a special kind of inward attention: a concern with feeling as articulated by the body – by its postures and gestures, its involuntary palpitations and collapses. Here sensibility is both private and public, and here, transcending the influences of speech, the novelist finds an eloquence which promises the true communication of feelings.[25]

It is perhaps unsurprising that this semi-public, non-verbal form of human interaction should come to be seen as particularly demonstrated by women. In the novel of sensibility the female body itself becomes a text to be interpreted by men and children. The original source of sensibility is more often than not the mother. Austen concludes her account of the impulsive nature of Marianne Dashwood in *Sense and Sensibility*

(1811) with the quietly ironic observation that '[t]he resemblance between her and her mother was strikingly great'.[26] Daughters, in fictions of sensibility, must learn to negotiate their way between the scylla of maternal sensibility and the charybdis of paternal severity. Despite physical and situational similarity, Frances Burney's Evelina struggles against being interpreted as a copy of her mother and falling victim to the latter's apparent fate of seduction and betrayal; Evelina pursues recognition by and reconciliation with her father, Sir John Belmont, and a suitably paternal partner in Lord Orville. Elizabeth Inchbald's Matilda in *A Simple Story* (1791) must obey her father's strict commands to avoid his presence in order not to remind him of her faithless and sensibility-suffused mother, Lady Elmwood (previously Miss Milner).[27] On his death, St Aubert of Ann Radcliffe's *Mysteries of Udolpho* (1794) charges his daughter as follows:

though I would guard you against the dangers of sensibility, I am not an advocate for apathy. At your age I should have said *that* is a vice more hateful than all the errors of sensibility, and I say so still. I call it a *vice*, because it leads to positive evil; in this, however, it does no more than an ill-governed sensibility, which, by such a rule, might also be called a vice; but the evil of the former is of more general consequence.[28]

Emily's two aunts, Madam Cheron (later Montoni) and the dead Marchioness de Villeroi offer models of the two poles which she must struggle to avoid imitating, the one allowing her passions to rule her to the point where she expires due to their excessive effect upon her, and the other silently resigning herself to being poisoned by her husband at the instigation of his mistress. These practical daughters – Elinor, Emily, Matilda, Evelina – are vulnerable to sensibility but their ability to 'govern' it properly pays off in that they are finally restored to favour, rewarded with their lovers and often also their paternal estates. Indeed, with the exception of Evelina, these daughters come to marry men who are themselves inclined to succumb to the passions. Elinor marries Edward Ferrars after he is miraculously extricated from an unfortunate early engagement to the unsuitable Lucy Steele; Emily is reunited with the weak-willed Valancourt who is imprisoned as a result of his fatal attraction to the excitements of gambling; Matilda agrees to marry her cousin, Rushbrook, out of pity for his violent feelings towards her.

As the ideology of a 'feminised' culture gains increasing purchase, the voices of women seem to be increasingly silenced. The late eighteenth-century proliferation of male authored texts that centre on the sensible *hero* (Henry Mackenzie's *Man of Feeling* (1771), Laurence Sterne's

Sentimental Journey (1768), Oliver Goldsmith's *Vicar of Wakefield* (1766) are the best known) indicate the success of the bourgeois project to refigure civil subjecthood through the analogy of gender, but in so doing the signifier 'femininity' floats free from its signified: woman. Sensibility becomes an operation that is most safely performed by men, or women who defer to patriarchal authority. 'Ill-governed', without male management, sensibility consumes its object.

Women novelists often seek to make evident their own maintenance of rule and order in the act of narration by contrast with the sensibility that so often disrupts the female body within the plot of their own fictions. It is no accident that the most influential novels of sensibility by women are rendered in the third rather than the first person, making possible some ironic reflexivity on the part of the narrator in relation to her protagonists. Narrative fiction becomes an alternative to, rather than an imitation of, the determining script of physiological sensation.

Elizabeth Inchbald's *A Simple Story is* simple in its stark exposition of sensibility as both a consequence of, and yet the only licensed response to, an untrammelled patriarchal authority. Dorriforth (later Lord Elmwood) is acknowledged early in the narrative to incline towards 'an obstinacy; such as he himself, and his friends termed firmness of mind' (pp. 33–4). He places those in his care, his ward Miss Milner and later his nephew, Harry Rushbrook, under impossible injunctions, requiring each in turn to declare their reasons for refusing the suitable marriages he has arranged for them. For Miss Milner this is impossible since her reason is her own transgressive love for Dorriforth himself; for Harry Rushbrook it is impossible because he loves his cousin, Matilda, and Lord Elmwood has expressly forbidden all those around him to mention her name. Miss Milner and Rushbrook, thus damned either by speech or silence, turn to the body to express what cannot be said in words. On the death of his elder brother, Dorriforth quits his Catholic orders to take up his title and Miss Milner entertains hopes that she may gain him as a husband. At this point, the novel spins into a series of closely scripted scenes in which the struggle to read physical signs in place of verbal utterance – and in particular to diagnose the enigmatic Lord Elmwood's feelings – becomes paramount. When Miss Milner offers to take him to the opera, he responds that he is fearful that his 'weak senses' will be unable to support such 'ravishing pleasures':

She had her eyes upon him as he spoke this, and discovered in his, which were fixed upon her, a sensibility unexpected—a kind of fascination which enticed her to look on, while her eye-lids fell involuntarily before its mighty force; and a thousand blushes crowded over her face:——He was struck with these sudden signals; hastily recalled his former countenance, and stopt the conversation. (pp. 107–8)

Despite his 'mighty force', Dorriforth/Elmwood is not an expert reader of the signs of sensibility although he falls under their spell. He takes his ward's blush as a sign of her innocence, rather than a sign of her (hitherto) illicit desire. When she blushes in response to an enquiry about her thoughtfulness, he comments, '"in the midst of your gayest follies; while you thus continue to blush, I shall reverence your internal sensations"' (p. 110). Miss Milner's lack of control over her internal sensations is conveyed through their registering upon her body while Elmwood's lack of ability to read them is conveyed through his acts of mistaken verbal interpretation. It is not until this traditionally gendered distribution of properties is reversed, establishing the male Rushbrook as the victim of sensibility and the female Matilda as the authoritarian presence, that this interpretative gridlock is overcome and a viable marital relationship posited.

The women writers of the eighteenth century often seem less experimental and more constrained than their male contemporaries such as Henry Fielding or Laurence Sterne; however, imitation of the pyrotechnics of speech, such as that of the lawyer or the raconteur, extends few opportunities for authority for the female narrator. The 'secondary' act of intelligent interpretation of narrative action is foregrounded and made primary in the quiet and unobtrusive manner which marks out the behaviour of Jane Austen's most valued heroines, Elinor Dashwood and Fanny Price. Ostensible conformism, the government of external image, and the ability to read their environment with acute judgement as well as compassion, enable these heroines to be rewarded with their most treasured secret desires (marriages to Edward Ferrars and to Edmund Bertram which have seemed at times beyond the bounds of possibility) where their bolder, more articulate counterparts are thwarted or disappointed. It is the attentive disclosure of an unspoken subjectivity, held up to critical assessment and self-conscious management of the reader's own responses through ironic narratorial intervention, which is the special characteristic of women's fiction of the eighteenth century. By the later eighteenth century 'novelistic discourse' by women has evolved a flexible yet critical narrative voice that enables the reader both to enter into and to retain a distance from action and character. The triple governance of reader response, narratorial voice, and the patriarchal plot lies firmly in the hands of an authority explicitly announced as female.

In conclusion, we consider the outburst in defence of prose fiction at the height of narrative action in Jane Austen's *Northanger Abbey*. Here, the narrator interrupts the narrative action to assert a female tradition in the novel, an authority associated with the discourse of women against that quintessentially 'civil' and 'masculine' language of the eighteenth century, the periodical (here represented by Joseph Addison's and Richard Steele's *Spectator*):

'And what are you reading, Miss—?' 'Oh! it is only a novel!' replies the young lady; while she lays down her book with affected indifference, or momentary shame.— 'It is only Cecilia, or Camilla, or Belinda;' or, in short, only some work in which the greatest powers of the mind are displayed, in which the most thorough knowledge of human nature, the happiest delineation of its varieties, the liveliest effusions of wit and humour are conveyed to the world in the best chosen language. Now, had the same young lady been engaged with a volume of the Spectator, instead of such a work, how proudly would she have produced the book, and told its name; though the chances must be against her being occupied by any part of that voluminous publication, of which either the matter or manner would not disgust a young person of taste; the substance of its papers so often consisting in the statement of improbable circumstances, unnatural characters, and topics of conversation, which no longer concern any one living; and their language, too, frequently so coarse as to give no very favourable idea of the age that could endure it.[29]

The novels listed are all by women, two by Burney and one by Edgeworth. Form expresses the argument as eloquently as content, in that the 'defence' of the novel is articulated not through the public vehicle of the spoken words of the heroine but through the concealed agency afforded by the written text. The novel's 'newness' of language is identified with an explicitly female authority, the form's hybrid status between public and private modes of discourse extending opportunities for a liberty of speech often denied elsewhere in eighteenth-century culture.

NOTES

1 Virginia Woolf, 'Modern Fiction', *The Forum*, March 1929, rpt. *Granite and Rainbow* (1958), rpt. *Collected Essays* (London: Hogarth Press, 1966), II, 145.
2 Charlotte Charke, *A Narrative of the Life of Mrs Charlotte Charke* (1755; Gainesville, FL: Scholars' Facsimiles and Reprints, 1969), p. 19.
3 Northrop Frye's *Anatomy of Criticism* (New Jersey: Princeton University Press, 1957) may be seen as the leading twentieth-century advocate of the former position, and Ian Watt's *The Rise of the Novel: Studies in Defoe, Richardson, and Fielding* (Berkeley and Los Angeles: University of California Press, 1957; rpt.

Harmondsworth: Penguin Books, 1963) of the latter. Watt's position has ultimately been the most favoured, informing the work of John J. Richetti, *Popular Fiction before Richardson: Narrative Patterns 1700–1739* (Oxford: Clarendon Press, 1969); Lennard J. Davis, *Factual Fictions: the Origins of the English Novel* (New York: Columbia University Press, 1983); and J. Paul Hunter, *Before Novels: the Cultural Contexts of Eighteenth-Century English Fiction* (New York and London: W. W. Norton & Company, 1990). See also John J. Richetti, 'The Legacy of Ian Watt's *The Rise of the Novel*' in Louis Damrosch (ed.), *The Profession of Eighteenth-Century Literature: Reflections on an Institution* (Wisconsin and London: University of Wisconsin Press, 1992), pp. 95–112.

4 Robert Mayer, *History and the Early English Novel: Matters of Fact from Bacon to Defoe* (Cambridge University Press, 1997).

5 See Margaret Anne Doody, *The True Story of the Novel* (New Brunswick, NJ: Rutgers University Press, 1996; London: HarperCollins, 1997); Ros Ballaster, *Seductive Forms: Women's Amatory Fiction from 1684 to 1740* (Oxford: Clarendon Press, 1992), ch. 2; Paul Salzman, *English Prose Fiction 1558–1700: a Critical History* (Oxford University Press, 1985).

6 Frances Burney, 'Preface', *Evelina or the History of a Young Lady's Entrance into the World*, ed. Edward and Lillian Bloom, World's Classics (Oxford University Press, 1982), pp. 8–9.

7 Michael McKeon, *The Origins of the English Novel 1600–1740* (Baltimore: Johns Hopkins University Press, 1987; London: Radius, 1988).

8 Michael McKeon, 'Historicizing Patriarchy: the Emergence of Gender Difference in England, 1660–1760', *Eighteenth-Century Studies*, 28 (1995), 295–322.

9 Nancy Armstrong, *Desire and Domestic Fiction: a Political History of the Novel* (New York and Oxford: Oxford University Press, 1987) and Michel Foucault, *The History of Sexuality, Volume I: an Introduction*, trans. Robert Hurley (New York: Pantheon, 1978; Harmondsworth: Penguin Books, 1981). On Armstrong's argument, see also ch. 1 of this volume, pp. 25–6.

10 Jane Spencer, *The Rise of the Woman Novelist: from Aphra Behn to Jane Austen* (Oxford: Basil Blackwell, 1986).

11 Janet Todd, *The Sign of Angellica: Women, Writing and Fiction, 1660–1800* (London: Virago, 1989); Catherine Gallagher, *Nobody's Story: the Vanishing Acts of Women Writers in the Marketplace 1670–1820* (Oxford: Clarendon Press, 1994).

12 Aphra Behn, *Oroonoko: or, the Royal Slave. A True History*, *The Works of Aphra Behn*, ed. Janet Todd, 7 vols. (London: William Pickering, 1992–6), *Volume III. The Fair Jilt and Other Short Stories* (1995), p. 112.

13 On this issue in the work of Aphra Behn, see my article 'Fiction Feigning Femininity: False Counts and Pageant Kings in Aphra Behn's Popish Plot Writings' in Janet Todd (ed.), *Aphra Behn Studies* (Cambridge University Press, 1996), pp. 50–65.

14 Available in Paula R. Backscheider and John J. Richetti (eds.), *Popular Fiction by Women 1660–1730* (Oxford: Clarendon Press, 1996).

15 Backscheider and Richetti, *Popular Fiction by Women*, p. 115.

16 See Carole Pateman, *The Sexual Contract* (Cambridge: Polity Press in association with Basil Blackwell, 1988). Pateman exposes the exclusion of women in the forging of models of contractual relations between subjects and their rulers in a tradition stemming from the writings of Thomas Hobbes and John Locke. For further discussion, see ch. 4, above pp. 105–6.

17 In Backscheider and Richetti, *Popular Fiction by Women*, pp. 250–320.

18 Samuel Richardson, *Pamela or, Virtue Rewarded*, ed. Peter Sabor, intro. by Margaret A. Doody (Harmondsworth: Penguin Books, 1980), p. 268. On references to *Pamela* in popular narrative forms, see Dianne Dugaw ch. 12 below, p. 276.

19 Clara Reeve, *The Progress of Romance: and the History of Charoba, Queen of Aegypt*, Facsimile Text Society Series 1: Literature and Language, vol. 4 (1930), p. 135.

20 Madeleine de Scudéry, *Clélie* (1652) was translated as *Clelia, an excellent new Romance* in 1678. Clelia leads a group of female hostages to swim across the Tiber in order to escape their potential ravishers.

21 Charlotte Lennox, *The Female Quixote*, ed. Margaret Dalziel, World's Classics (Oxford University Press, 1989), p. 377.

22 Eliza Haywood, *The History of Miss Betsy Thoughtless*, ed. Beth Fowkes Tobin, World's Classics (Oxford University Press, 1997), pp. 113, 287. On *Betsy Thoughtless* see also Gillian Skinner in ch. 4 of this volume, pp. 96–101.

23 On Richardson's *Clarissa* as an expression of this exchange function, and on the novel more generally as a unique record of changing economic and kinship structures, cf. Ruth Perry's discussion in ch. 5 of this volume.

24 On the relationship between Haywood and Fielding, see John R. Elwood, 'Henry Fielding and Eliza Haywood: a Twenty Year War', *Albion*, 5:3 (Fall, 1973), 184–92.

25 John Mullan, *Sentiment and Sociability: the Language of Feeling in the Eighteenth Century* (Oxford: Clarendon Press, 1988), p. 16. For further discussion of sensibility in the period, see 'Guide to Further Reading'.

26 Jane Austen, *Sense and Sensibility* (1811), 1, ch. i, ed. Ros Ballaster (London: Penguin Books, 1995), p. 6.

27 Elizabeth Inchbald, *A Simple Story*, ed. J. M. S. Tompkins, with a new introduction by Jane Spencer, World's Classics (Oxford University Press, 1988).

28 Ann Radcliffe, *The Mysteries of Udolpho*, ed. Bonamy Dobrée, World's Classics (Oxford University Press, 1980), p. 80.

29 Jane Austen, *Northanger Abbey* (1818, written 1798), 1, ch. v, ed. Marilyn Butler (London: Penguin Books, 1995), pp. 34–5.

CHAPTER 10

Women poets of the eighteenth century

Margaret Anne Doody

It is tempting to begin this discussion with the statement that in the eighteenth century women's poetry for the first time forms a substantial body of works in English. British women apparently were writing much more poetry in this period than they had ever done before; we notice all the volumes of poetry by individual writers, the anthologies, and the magazines (including the *Gentleman's Magazine*) in which women are represented.

We should, however, remember that we are judging from available and changeable evidence. The fact of a newly dominant print culture helps to explain what may seem the extraordinary efflorescence of women poets, and future research may modify our current impression that women's writing took a leap from near non-existence into substantial being largely within the eighteenth century. It is safe to believe that there were many women in the earlier era of manuscript culture who wrote verse. As we shall see, even in the age of print, a number of women writers left many more poems in manuscript than got printed. The existence of the print culture, however, means it is relatively easy for scholars to begin to track the women whose *printed* works were once admired, even if their names have been subsequently erased from the official 'literary history'. And an interest in the works that did emerge in print has now taught us also how to seek out the caches of manuscript.

The printing-press in peacetime offered a large challenge to the gatekeepers of high culture, by permitting all who could read and write some possibility of access to a wider 'public'. Printers would take a chance on publishing works by women, by Dissenters, by men (and sometimes women) of the lower classes, if there seemed likelihood that others would spend their money in order to read such works. If we often sigh over the 'commodification of culture', we should recognise that such commodification gave women a chance they had lacked otherwise.

Women writers who had their works printed (or found their works being printed) were addressing both a male and a female audience. They might be more certain that they could truly reach an audience of sympathetic women, and the fact of the marketplace meant that women with disposable income would buy and read volumes of works by women – including poetry – no matter what the sneers of the learned. Yet it is also the case that men and women who wrote poetry read each others' works, and were influenced by each other. The study of women's poetry has yet to be fully integrated with the study of our poetry in general.[1] There is a 'feminine tradition', from at least the seventeenth century, within English poetry of the early modern age of print, but this feminine tradition belongs also within the general British literary tradition – even if literary historians have made repeated efforts to write it out. This essay explores something of these traditions, and their interactions, in the work of a necessarily small selection from the ever-growing number of eighteenth-century women poets.

THE EARLY EIGHTEENTH CENTURY: FRIENDSHIP, POLITICS, AND CLASS

At the turn of the eighteenth century, a poem by Delarivier Manley laments the passing of the Restoration women writers Katherine Philips ('Orinda') and Aphra Behn ('Astrea'): '*Orinda*, and the Fair *Astrea* gone, / Not one was found to fill the Vacant Throne: / Aspiring Man had quite regain'd the Sway'.[2] The point of Manley's poem is to nominate a successor, the playwright Catherine Trotter, who prevents the men from taking empire over women. Women are seen as fighting for literary control over their own line, like a dynasty, their leaders keeping subjugation by 'Aspiring Man' at bay. Philips and Behn were very differently represented – Philips led what her contemporaries defined as a virtuous and chaste life, while Behn was a shady lady who went upon the stage and wrote for it – but throughout the eighteenth century these two supplied models (in Behn's case, perhaps, an increasingly negative model) for women writers in English.

The verse of Katherine Philips, known as 'the Matchless Orinda', extolled the virtue of friendship, and the desirability of a close band of friends, the sacred communion of kindred souls. The adoption within this community of names like those in contemporary prose fiction about love ('Orinda', 'Lucasia', 'Rosania') offered an abstraction of personality allowing both intimacy and intellect. The tenderest and most intimate friendships are with women, and the high calling of such friendship is expressed in poems such as 'Friendship's Mysterys, to my dearest Lucasia':

> Come, my Lucasia, since we see
> > That miracles men's faith do move
> By wonder and by Prodigy
> > To the dull, angry world let's prove
> > There's a religion in our Love.
>
> For though we were design'd t'agree,
> > That fate no liberty destroys,
> But our election is as free
> > As Angells, who with greedy choice
> > Are yet determin'd to their Joys.
>
> Our hearts are doubled by their loss,
> > Here mixture is addition grown;
> We both diffuse, and both engrosse:
> > And we, whose minds are so much one,
> > Never, yet ever, are alone.   (*Kissing the Rod*, pp. 193–4)

Orinda's poetry exhibits a sophisticated acquaintance with the Metaphysical poets. Here, for instance, we can hear echoes of Donne and references to his 'A Valediction forbidding Mourning' and 'The Good Morrow', as Philips plays off Donne's heterosexual masculinist approach to hearty physical love against the purer idealised and spiritualised friendship of love between women.

In a culture in which social status and marriage were matters to be determined outside the self, discussions of friendship provide ways of dealing with homoerotic attraction and with individual temperament and choice. Literature of friendship is also a literature of individualism. Philips is following in the train of the French women writers such as Catherine de Rambouillet, Madeline de Scudéry, and other 'précieuses' who perpetuated the ideal of 'Platonic love'. In the salons which they devised, men and women could meet and discuss literature, art, and ideas – could have a friendship not subjected to the needs of the family and state, nor limited to the ties of blood and the official bonds of kinship.

This ability to escape the marriage and kinship structure continued to be of great importance to women writers. Lacking a career, and any social and economic identity which was not merely an aspect of that of a father or husband, women in the early modern age needed to find some way of voicing themselves. An identity like 'Orinda' is an identity imaginatively separate from the filial/marital. Her poetry offered valuable models of female-to-female address, including but not limited to homoerotic statement. In the eras that follow, many poems by women are addressed to other women, emphatically written in the female voice for a female audience. Sometimes such poems (including light verse) are (like the verses of Frances Burney and Jane Austen) literally part of a private letter sent to a sister or friend.

We run the danger of categorising Orinda's poems as solely or chiefly 'private', but many of her works are about (or reflect) political issues. In 'Friendship's Mysterys', for example, Philips uses language both theological and political in her references to 'Liberty', 'free election', 'choice'. The address to other women does not preclude political statement, and her poetry has a satiric side sometimes not represented by anthologised pieces.

The stimulus provided by political controversy should not be underestimated in liberating women as writers. Like Philips, Aphra Behn was a political writer and a Royalist, very decidedly on the Tory side supporting the king. Unlike Philips, who officially disowned a printed version of her poems, Behn had no social status to lose and is one of the first female writers to have open, even blatant, recourse to publication. Behn had a varied career when careers were not supposed to apply to women: she was a spy for Charles II before she wrote for the stage as a way of making some money – and as both spy and writer used as her pseudonym her favourite *nom de guerre*, 'Astrea', from Durfé's novel *L'Astrée*. Germaine Greer has tellingly argued that Behn could not really have earned a good living by the pen and was probably a kept mistress, as well as being a dramatist.[3] Nevertheless, Behn certainly took her wares to the print market; she published her plays, her fiction, and her poems. Janet Todd's recent edition of Behn at last enables us to appreciate her versatility, and the pointedness of her wit.[4]

One of the reasons why Behn's name was so bespattered after her death is that she was on the wrong side politically: the Whig Williamite government that came in through what the victors termed the 'Glorious Revolution' in 1688–9 could have no possible interest in hearing anyone speak well of her. Women writers at the turn of the eighteenth century are often deeply influenced by political affairs. As Carol Barash has shown, many of those who become notable around this time were associated with the fallen fortunes of James II and his queen Mary of Modena, who went into exile in France after the Glorious Revolution and the joint accession of William of Orange and Mary II.[5] Delarivier Manley, who wrote in praise of Philips and Behn, would have become a

Maid of Honour to Mary of Modena had James not been deposed; she later became a leading satirist writing for the Tories against the Whigs in the age of Queen Anne. The poetry of Jane Barker, who followed the Jacobites into exile in France in 1688 or shortly after, includes some very energetic and ruthless satires against William and his party. Many of her poems remained unpublished, and are still extant only in manuscript. Barker could be unsparing in her curses. An erstwhile friend, an Anglican woman, is now hated for her treasonous words against the defeated James: 'She is the perfect emblem of her gangue / She's fit to teach the Devils to harangue.'[6] Such vitriolic political poems would have been destined to manuscript circulation only, but we may assume that they were read by some sympathetic to the cause. It would seem, for example, that Barker knew of Dryden's works, and in the last decade of the old century Dryden may have known of hers.

Following the pattern set by Orinda, Barker gives herself a romance persona, 'Fidelia', which enables her to analyse her own position, as we see in poems such as 'Fidelia arguing with herself', 'Fidelia and her friend on becoming Catholick'. In her one published volume of verse, *Poetical Recreations* (1688), there is a good deal of autobiographical content; she prints poems lamenting the death of her brother, and a statement about her own aspirations as a single woman ('Virgin Life', *Kissing the Rod*, pp. 360–1). Barker anticipates later eighteenth-century poets in her choice of unusual and often personal subject matter, and she is one of the many female poets to have left us poems in praise of the single life, and advice (explicit or implicit) against marriage. In 'On the Apothecary's Filing my Bills amongst the Doctors', for instance, the speaker admits her pride in the apothecary's treating her as a doctor. This medical ambition is also evident in her semi-autobiographical novels about her heroine Galesia, an *alter ego* who is fond of study and asks her brother to teach her Latin and medicine. In the novels, in which a number of her poems are included, Barker gives us clear glimpses of herself as a writer. In *Love Intrigues, or The Amours of Bosvil and Galesia*, she represents through Galesia what is undoubtedly her own inner struggle in relation to the image of herself as a poet. Galesia has a disturbing dream in which Apollo tells her that he and Hymen are at odds. Galesia must choose between being '*Apollo*'s darling daughter' and the wife of her on-and-off-again suitor Bosvil; it is quite evident that she believes it impossible to combine married love and the career of a poet.[7] And in *The Lining of the Patch-Work Screen* (1726), the second sequel to *Love Intrigues*, Galesia has a dream vision of Katherine Philips.

Anne Finch, née Kingsmill, later Countess of Winchilsea, is the most well known of the writing women surrounding Mary of Modena, whose Maid of Honour she became in 1683. She married Heneage Finch in 1684, and at the Revolution they lived quietly on his nephew's estate in Kent. Her connection with the political opposition may have sharpened her zest for writing and her insight into the society that surrounded her. Some of Anne's poems were in circulation in manuscript from the 1680s onward, and a few had appeared in print (including 'The Spleen') before the publication of her official volume *Miscellany Poems on Several Occasions* in 1713. In some appearances she is called 'Ardelia', in yet another reminiscence of Orinda's habit of bestowing pseudonyms on the writer and her friends. We now know that Anne Finch's manuscript volumes, collections arranged by her chiefly for herself, contain material more outspoken than what she allowed to be printed.

Finch is a witty writer who delights in paradoxes, as can be seen in her fables where she combines the sublime and the ridiculous (for example, 'The Poet and the Acorn'). Apparently calmly observant, she quietly conveys intense and often disturbed feeling. Her 'Nocturnal Reverie', for example, is a masterpiece not just of nature poetry (as Wordsworth wanted to see it) but of quiet protest – against male civilization's brutal ownership of both women and nature. Only in the twilight world away from day's definitions and imposed order can nature and women have a respite, but the time is short 'Till morning breaks, and All's confused again'. In her association of the night world with spiritual and physical fulfilment and of the day world with a disorder and confusion wrought by daylight certainties, Finch would seem to take issue with the Enlightenment's whole programme and its assurances of perfect clarity. Her poem 'The Bird and the Arras', which remained in manuscript until 1903, is a brilliant delineation of confusion and frustration. The bird, which has mistakenly ventured into a room and is anxious to get out, takes the 'Arras' or tapestry depicting foliage and the natural world for reality, and then, disillusioned, beats against the window, mistaking 'transparent Panes' for the clear air. In anxiety and frustration it flies helplessly about the room, 'Flutt'ring in endless cercles of dismay'.[8] What could be a merely neo-platonic fable about the frustrations of the soul in the world is implicitly also a description of the pain felt by the woman writer trying to get free of conventions and restrictions.

Like many women poets (and some male poets, such as Swift) Finch is often found using the four-beat line, a measure less official, more comic, more pungent, than iambic pentameter with its history of *gravitas* and public responsibility. But Finch experiments with different forms, and can use the long line to great effect. She also borrows the irregular 'ode' form developed by Abraham Cowley – as in her often reprinted and often quoted poem 'The Spleen'. Finch read widely, including works in French and Italian (some of which she translates), and might be defined as a post-neo-classical writer, aware of the boundaries and conventions established by French and (later) English theorists in the seventeenth century, but not considering herself bound by them.

Finch spends very little time in discussing religious issues, at least directly or overtly. In contrast, Elizabeth Singer Rowe, daughter of a dissenting minister, is a serious writer on religious subjects. Yet she is not at a great remove from Finch. She too took to the ode, publishing as 'the Pindarick Lady' as well as 'Philomela' (or 'nightingale', a play with the idea of her name 'Singer'). Finch's friends the Thynnes were Rowe's patrons, and her *Poems on Several Occasions* (1696) includes homage to Anne Killigrew, another female poet among the group around Mary of Modena.

Elizabeth Singer married Thomas Rowe, who died in 1715; her poem on his death is sometimes thought to have inspired Pope's 'Eloisa to Abelard'. Her later works are largely religious. Isaac Watts, a friend, supporter and posthumous editor, is very worried that she might be considered a 'mystic', which he regards as synonymous with 'heretical'. Yet many of Singer's poems do have a mystical tone. Rowe longs for the final union with the divine which will make separations and distinctions unnecessary. She dwells on the inadequacy of language:

> for human words
> Lose all their pow'r, their emphasis and force;
> And grow insipid when I talk of thee,
> The excellence supreme, the God of gods.
> Whate'er the language of those gods, those pow'rs
> In heav'nly places crown'd; however strong,
> Or musical, or clear their language be,
> Yet all falls short of thee[9]

Language is a relative, not an absolute, entity. If compared to the Divine language all human utterance falls short; there is no need to reverence the human (male) tradition overmuch. The greatest poetry can be seen trembling on the edge of the ineffable, contemplating its own dissolution. For Rowe, everything is perpetually on the brink of dissolution.

(Her most important prose work, well known in the eighteenth century, is *Friendship in Death. In Twenty Letters from the Dead to the Living* (1728).) That everything is about to die or dissolve is a source of excitement, and is connected to the joy in metamorphosis that eighteenth-century poets share.[10]

With the advent of Mary Leapor we have the first major female labouring-class poet. She was not the first labouring-class English poet of the period – that honour belongs to Stephen Duck, whose *The Thresher's Labour* (1730) had caught everyone's attention. (Duck got picked up by the Establishment, and was turned into a clergyman.) Neither was Leapor the first notable female labouring-class poet. Mary Collier had responded to Stephen Duck with *The Woman's Labour; An Epistle to Mr Stephen Duck* in 1739; the title-page advertised the fact that the author was 'a WASHER-WOMAN'.[11] (Mary Collier did not get picked up by the Establishment and turned into a clergyman; she continued to work as a washerwoman until she was sixty-three.) The fact that she had immediate predecessors among the labouring poor doubtless made it easier for young Mary Leapor to take her own ambitions seriously. A domestic servant during at least part of her life, the daughter of a gardener who lived in Brackley, Northamptonshire, Mary yet had received some education, however rudimentary. Richard Greene, her recent biographer and commentator, believes it 'likely that Mary Leapor attended the Free School in Brackley, operated by Magdalen College School'.[12] In her later life Mary Leapor owned at least a few books, including Pope's works, Dryden's fables, and some plays, but she was probably also able to borrow books from better-off neighbours and employers. At least she did not have to feel absolutely separated from the dominant literary culture – a fact which perhaps says as much about this fermenting period as it does about Leapor's undoubtedly strong intelligence and determination. When she died at the sadly early age of twenty-four, a proposal to publish her works by subscription was already mooted, and after her death such a proposal was successful. A volume of her poems was published in 1748, and a second volume (published by Samuel Richardson) in 1751. That, albeit posthumously, Leapor attracted the attention and support of Richardson, Ralph Griffiths (editor of the *Monthly Review*), and the poet Christopher Smart proves that it was not impossible for a woman to make some sort of entrée into the critical (if not the high social) world, a literary 'establishment' which was itself both varied and experimental.

Leapor's poetry reveals an intimate knowledge of Pope's works, if only to contradict him, but Swift is an equally strong influence, as can be seen in her description of a marriage in 'The Mistaken Lover':

> But I shall pass the Wedding-day,
> Nor stay to paint the Ladies gay,
> Nor Splendor of the lighted Hall,
> The Feast, the Fiddles, nor the Ball.
> A lovely Theme ! —'Tis true, but then
> We'll leave it to a softer Pen:
> Those transient Joys will fade too soon,
> We'll therefore skip the Hony-Moon.[13]

Here Leapor uses Swift's typical four-beat line, and her *occupatio* is tinged with deliberate irony; the rituals of wedding, the romanticisation of marriage, conceal its ugly truths. In the poems by Swift that Leapor is in effect answering, the ugly truth includes the woman's physical nature, but Leapor treats the *wife's* disillusionment when it becomes clear that Strephon married Celia only because she brought a dowry of 'Five thousand Pounds of Sterling clear' (p. 84). Once the husband has the money safely in his own possession, he is free to abuse his wife for her physical imperfections, thus excusing his own infidelity and carelessness. His accusations, like his excuses, are hurtful but lame: 'Besides, your Eyes are gray. – Alack! / 'Till now I always thought 'em black' (p. 88).

Leapor is particularly acute at identifying the cultural right men have asserted over the judgement of a woman by her physical charms. She is aware both of the prescriptiveness and the casual cruelty involved and of the cultural fact that a woman 'is' her face and figure, in a way that is never – or never merely – true for a man. A recurrent motif in poems by women in the eighteenth century is the idea or image of a woman's looking into the mirror. In Roger Lonsdale's invaluable anthology *Eighteenth-Century Women Poets* we find, for example, Mary Barber's 'To Mrs Frances-Arabella Kelly' ('Today, as at my glass I stood / . . . / I saw my grizzled locks with dread, / And called to mind the Gorgon's head', first published 1734); or Elizabeth Teft's 'On Viewing Herself in a Glass' ('Was Nature angry when she formed my clay?', first published 1747).[14] Terry Castle in a review of Lonsdale's anthology notes the recurrence of the mirror image and suggests that as well as some degree of self-loathing the mirror-gaze represented a desire for an alternative self, for self-communion: 'the mirror image both distilled a longing for purity and expressed a desire for escape'.[15] The anguished mirror-gaze is never more devastating than in one of the 'town eclogues' by Lady Mary Wortley Montagu. The urban mock-pastoral 'Saturday: The Small-Pox' deals with the toilet of a beauty who has succumbed to the ravages of that disease. The reader can enjoy the implicit satire on the heroine's vanity, and the emptiness of the social life that has now forsaken her. This does not, however, reduce the sense of pain so tellingly described, a pain experienced by Montagu herself.[16]

Of the many women poets who deal with personal appearance, Leapor is one of the cleverest, most uncompromising, even outrageous. In 'Corydon. Phillario. Or Mira's Picture', a mock-pastoral, she describes herself ('Mira') through the views of two condescending 'swains'.[17] Phillario is a visitor to the country, a man of society, while Corydon is the stock shepherd who can give him information upon local sights. Phillario is horrified at the uncouth figure 'With studious Brows and Night-cap Dishabille' who goes muttering by. Corydon defends Mira's dim eyes in an explanation that makes her the more odd: 'By a Rush-Candle (as her Father says) / She sits whole Ev'nings, reading wicked Plays'. Phillario thinks this awkwardly shaped creature would be better occupied in milking her cows; she is disgusting, and Phillario wishes the rains would sweep her away. The role of the inspired poet, or rural youth who goes 'Mutt'ring his wayward fancies' like the young poet in Gray's later *Elegy . . . in a Country Churchyard*, is not suited to any woman, still less to an ugly one whose very existence is an offence. Leapor seems to take a bitter pleasure in creating this self-portrait, a mocking answer to the classic injunction 'know thyself', so often interpreted as merely seeing ourselves (our social selves) as (properly socialised) others see us.

In her various exercises on the theme of appearance, Leapor seems to urge the female reader not to internalise these cultural definitions. She is a resister – and properly belongs in Donna Landry's interesting study of labouring-class women poets, *The Muses of Resistance*.[18] Clearly aware of her own poverty, Leapor refuses to be downhearted about it, and it is interesting that someone as low on the social scale as Leapor could be so alert in noticing that women in the upper classes have no control over their 'own' money, and thus suffer also from a kind of poverty. In many of her poems she delineates the possibilities of some kind of solidarity among women of different classes.

Though Leapor does not define her resistance only by her position in the labouring class, she does make that central, dealing with the realities of her own life – homely tasks of domestic service, such as making cheese, or washing dishes:

> But now her Dish-kettle began
> To boil and blubber with the foaming Bran.
> The greasy Apron round her Hips she ties,
> And to each Plate the scalding Clout applies:
> The purging Bath each glowing Dish refines,
> And once again the polish'd Pewter shines.[19]

A poet such as Leapor benefits from the eighteenth century's openness to the physicality of experience. The empiricism of Locke placed sensory experience at the root of consciousness, and thus of all knowledge and all forms of self-consciousness. Consciousness is formed through experience and through reflection on experience. If that is so, then the role of authority – already rendered politically suspect in the Revolution and the Restoration – becomes less important. A combination of political and philosophical views gave more opportunity for women and the poor to enter the literary arena, to create works that would be heard, than they ever had before. In order to understand their own society, and the world in which human beings really do live, men and women of the eighteenth century could believe it would be valuable to understand the experience of others. We can know another person, or persons, or even perhaps class, by entering imaginatively into their sensations.

Restoration poets such as Rochester and Behn had mocked the stability of genre and undercut the grand style or lyric elegance by employing these styles to accommodate a new and sceptical or critical content. Neither the Restoration nor the eighteenth century offers us the pleasures of lyric verse at its sweetest – it is not where we go for love lyric. After Milton we find not epic but mock-epic; pastorals are shot through with questions and problems about style. The early eighteenth century is an era of creative ferment, both in fiction and in poetry. Poets test the limits of 'the poetic', surprising us with the unexpected, taking a cue from the satiric and conversational poets such as Horace, and women writers participate to good effect. Leapor is writing to the taste of her age when she includes the dishes bubbling in bran. She proves herself able to capture an instant of the real world in its unexpectedness, solidity, metamorphosing activity – all of which interest eighteenth-century readers more than 'the beautiful', conventionally considered.

THE LATER EIGHTEENTH CENTURY: RETREAT AND RESISTANCE

The period of experiment and playful diversity did not last. Women's poetry began to be recategorised into its own sphere and there seems to be a growing anxiety about the suitability of topics. Samuel Richardson, the patron of Mary Leapor, in that very domesticating novel *Sir Charles Grandison* (1753–4), makes fun of an identifiably feminine kind of poetry. Miss Darlington's poem 'on the death of a favourite Linet [*sic*]' is 'a little too pathetic for the occasion; since were Miss Darlington to have lost her best and dearest friend, I imagine that she had in this piece, which is pretty long, exhausted the subject; and must borrow from it some of the images which she introduces to heighten her distress for the loss of the little songster'.[20] In the 1760s, with the extreme domesticity of women's 'place' promulgated so effectively by Rousseau in his *Emile*, it perhaps became harder for a woman to write without becoming conventional and diffident. Although it could still find an outlet in the magazines, the female poetic voice became (on the whole) somewhat less of a clubbable member in the general poetical conversation.

If a certain cultural anxiety descends again at mid century upon English women writers of verse, it would seem to affect Scottish and Northern writers less than their sisters dwelling nearer the capital. Some British women writers of the mid century seem attracted towards a kind of 'folk' writing, moving imaginatively into a peasant world of roughness, superstition, common sense, or energy that acted as a relief from the demands of civilization. Lady Anne Lindsay, daughter of the Earl of Balcarres, wrote the modern folk poem 'Auld Robin Gray', published anonymously in 1776. Susanna Blamire, daughter of a yeoman farmer living near Carlisle, writes effective and vivacious poems in dialect, such as 'The Siller Croun' (published 1790), 'Wey, Ned Man!' and 'Auld Robin Forbes' (Lonsdale, *Women Poets*, nos. 188–90). It must be admitted, however, that Blamire's dialect poetry, while it may have circulated in manuscript, did not achieve publication for the most part until 1842. A few of her songs found their way into song sheets or were reprinted in magazines. Both Lindsay and Blamire succeed primarily as song writers. Blamire's vitality and her use of the rhythm of native song and country dance can be felt in 'I've Gotten a Rock, I've Gotten a Reel' (Lonsdale, *Women Poets*, no. 186).

At an earlier date, we can trace a similar energy in the very definitely English Mary Frances Amherst. 'The Welford Wedding', written at some point in the 1740s, captures the pleasures and rhythms of the dance, as well as the fun of a ballad, in its celebration of the joys of the moment:

> Susan and Charlotte and Letty and all
> Jump and skip and caper and brawl,
> Frisk in the drawing-room, romp in the hall,
> Susan and Charlotte and Letty and all.
> Hark! the fiddle each gay spirit moves;
> See, the beaux have all drawn on their gloves.
> Mr Archer will dance,
> And Jack Hobland will prance,
> And Jack Shirley'll advance,
> If my Lady approves.
> *Chorus*: Susan and Charlotte and Letty and all &c.
> (Lonsdale, *Women Poets*, no. 122)

'The Welford Wedding' seems to me one of the era's most sophisticated and entertaining examples of manipulation of verse form in relation to sound. It is, however, the twentieth-century and not the eighteenth-century reader who can enjoy it. Amherst (later Mrs Thomas), sister of Lord Amherst the Field Marshal who took Canada in 1760, belonged to a social class too high to publish its poetry. A few of her manuscript poems did find their way into magazines, but the bulk of her verse remained unknown (save in circulation among her immediate friends); we are indebted to Lonsdale for disinterring her verses. The discovery of Frances Amherst as a 'new' eighteenth-century poet is a reminder that it is not only in Orinda's day that ladies were not expected to publish, and argues the necessity of periodically changing the gallery of writers that we thought we had arranged.

Neither Amherst nor Blamire, remaining as they did largely unknown, did much to alleviate their contemporaries' experience of poetry, in an era which was becoming (publicly, at any rate) more cautious, less energetic, and less enamoured of the direct sensuous experience. This decline of the blunt and the sensual and the shocking in verse is noticeable generally. John Sitter, in *Literary Loneliness in Mid-Eighteenth-Century England*, suggests that male writers became inturned, culturally depressed, and that a trope of isolation becomes nearly universal.[21] Sitter also diagnoses a 'Flight from History in Mid-century Poetry' (the title of his third chapter), holding that 'from the 1740s on, most of the younger poets avoid direct historical treatment of the events of their day, even of their century' (p. 83). The tone of poetry becomes conventionally melancholy, and 'retirement . . . hardened into retreat' (p. 85).

The more negative or recessive developments we trace in women's poetry may thus be related to general trends of uncertainty. Voices like Blair and Beattie are coming again from Scotland, filling a strange English silence. Scotland itself, one thinks, might rather have retreated into silence with such a devastating blow as had been wrought by the crushing of Prince Charles Edward in 1745–6, and the dismal aftermath that destroyed the clan system and dispersed the population. The poem that expresses the terrible lament, the song that gave Scotland words for her sorrow and her despair, was written by a woman, Alison Cockburn, née Rutherford: her 'The Flowers of the Forest', written to fit an old Scottish melody, was first published in 1765. This work is a sophisticated yet popular use of the folk tradition, a genuine lyric written to be sung, and a work of the public sphere (at a popular cultural level) in a situation in which merely writing in Scots dialect is an act of political as well as poetical defiance.

It may be that what John Sitter terms the 'flight from history' was in part a reaction to the crushing of Scottish resistance. Sitter notices that male poets shun contemporary history in favour of antiquity. They find voices for earlier, even pre-historic, inhabitants of these islands and turn to the Dark Ages for inspiration. Such a turn of subject matter can be read as a mode of reconciliation, even if unconsciously sought. Tribes might yet find each other by going as it were 'behind the back' of what the Enlightenment knew as 'civilization'. Such experiments in Gothic or with the 'folkish' also represent a protest against dominant and progressivist Whiggism. Whatever its causes, the phenomenon can be seen in poems like Gray's *The Bard* (1757), and in the success of Macpherson's *The Poems of Ossian* (1760–3). The personal is projected upon the figures conjured out of a deep past. Or, as Sitter notes, the personal may be projected upon feminine personifications: 'Again and again, the feminine image is used as a focus of withdrawal, a symbol of retreat from the harsh world of traditionally male history' (p. 131).

Women poets are, of course, much less happy at using feminine images as foci of withdrawal. While male poets found refuges in Dark Ages scenes and feminine personifications, women writers were often most successful when figuring their disenchantments and reactions to the socio-political state of things through non-human beings. Fairies and animals both increasingly feature in women's poetry of the later mid century. We can see, looking back, that a poet like Anne Finch early in the century also uses animals in important ways, from the bird in the arras to the old horse whose teeth chewing the grass can be heard among the night sounds of 'A Nocturnal Reverie', but the poets later in the century are more apt to identify with an animal for a sustained period. Perhaps Richardson in his mockery in *Grandison* had got wind of something not entirely new but freshly prevalent in women's poetry. Of course, it will be objected that writers like Blake also wrote about animals ('A Robin red-breast in a cage . . .'). But Blake himself is affected by women writers who had long been saying that kind of thing. In 1783 Jane Cave anticipates Blake in 'A Poem for Children. On Cruelty to the Irrational Creation':

> Were I a bird took from my nest,
> Should I not think myself oppressed,
> If tossed about in wanton play,
> Till, maimed and faint, I die away?
> . . .
> I'll not torment a dog or cat,
> A toad, a viper, or a rat:
> They're formed by an Almighty hand
> And sprang to life at his command.[22]

Cave is here more programmatic and brisk than is customary, but she does imagine the feelings of the bird. In writing about animals women writers want to give imaginative voice to this other body; they mix humour and compassion with a strong sense of the value of the immediate and physical as the speaker projects herself some or all of the time into the being of the bird, animal (or even insect) at the centre of the poem.

We find these elements in Anna Seward's poem on her cat, 'An Old Cat's Dying Soliloquy' (not published until 1792; Lonsdale, *Women Poets*, no. 212), and in Anna Laetitia Barbauld's 'The Mouse's Petition' ('Found in the trap where he had been confined all night by Doctor Priestley, for the sake of making experiments with different kinds of air', 1773). This latter may be thought a trifle too arch in its whimsicality, but in using the persona of her 'free-born mouse' Barbauld is able to protest against the assumptions at the basis of the new scientific age, the assumptions that all non-human sentient life is merely objective stuff to be used without respect or sympathy. In Barbauld's 'The Caterpillar' the sense of the value of all life extends even to the individual caterpillar on the arm of a speaker who has just been destroying the hundreds of caterpillars on her apple tree. The caterpillar's beauty ('The azure and the orange that divide / Thy velvet sides') and the reality of its presence ('the light pressure of thy hairy feet') make it impossible for her to kill the creature once she has noticed 'Thine individual existence, life, / And fellowship of sense'.[23] This sense of the unity of all life extends even to the world of insects and vermin, images of pure disgust for traditional satire. Surprisingly, pious Christian Protestant writers like Seward and Barbauld, playfully perhaps but unapologetically, adopt a system of Pythagorean metempsychosis, giving favourable play to a system of belief in which all life is one. (Perhaps contact with India was having an effect in the influence of some Indian beliefs upon the English?) So Barbauld can write

> Beware, lest in the worm you crush
> A brother's soul you find;
> And tremble lest thy luckless hand
> Dislodge a kindred mind.   ('The Mouse's Petition')

The fairies which also populate women's poems serve perhaps an even more complex set of functions. Fairies, not subject to mortal laws, to need for money, or to the prospect of illness and death, can express impulses, desires, tastes, and feelings, even drives, without such subjugation of these as 'naturally' occurs within eighteenth-century social life, where the drives and impulses of women may be held reprehensible or of no account. Part of the paradoxical appeal of fairies is that they can also hold prescribed feelings at bay: these strange beings are at liberty not to undertake the feeling-work, normally expected of women, on behalf of others or of the social order.

Fairies represent both a kind of substitute for personification, and women's escape from personification and from being personified. A good example is Frances Greville's 'A Prayer for Indifference' (1759) in which the speaker's prayer is addressed 'To *Oberon*, the fairy'. Reworking *A Midsummer Night's Dream*, Oberon is asked to find juice from a magic flower that can bestow what the speaker desires: not love, but indifference. The poem only lightly veils the inner painful subject, the feelings of a woman whose husband both neglects and ill-treats her. Oberon, the 'sweet airy sprite', capable of a limited pity but always heart-whole, could relieve the speaker by using magic to make her uncaring. In return, she would wish the fairy elf perfect happiness in his own mysterious land; he may go 'To some new region of delight / Unknown to mortal tread' (Lonsdale, *Women Poets*, no. 128). Greville's poem, which had circulated in manuscript some time before its publication in the *Edinburgh Chronicle* (and later in other miscellanies and magazines), was immensely popular, particularly with women readers, who well understood its significance. Fairies themselves are both impulse and psyche free of the pain of feeling. They can represent a part of the self which one wishes were allowed – the free, airy, floating, detached self – as well as the more painful inner self viewed with detachment. In using what we might call 'stalking fairies' rather than the animals (or stalking horses), women found they could express desires and feelings not officially appropriate or even recognised. Hester Lynch Thrale Piozzi ventured a whole fairy play, *The Two Fountains*, which remained unstaged.[24] In *The Mysteries of Udolpho*, Ann Radcliffe makes her heroine write a poem on a sea nymph, a being of the hidden green depths.[25]

The disadvantage of such embodiments is obvious: fairies may be taken as trivial, and as ultra-feminine. Women may perhaps be too safe in becoming too fantastical. Yet we should remember that in large parts of Britain, especially in the North of England and in Celtic areas, belief in fairies was certainly not quite dead, and in that context they appear somewhat less simply 'fantastical'. The fairies who frequented British landscapes were not the little harmless creatures produced for children's delectation in the past two centuries. These full-grown and powerful fairies of British lore also had their classical antecedents (naiads, dryads) who were once the objects of real belief, and not just features of neo-classical poetic decoration. The fairy writings offer an impish chance to reinterpret that aspect of the classical world picture. Such beings provided a means of saying both that the world is holy and mysterious, and that neither the flesh nor the inner world of passion and desire will be denied, however much they may be repressed.

The redoubtable Hannah More in her earlier work exhibits an interest in fays as well as folk tale. Her narrative poem 'The Bleeding Rock' (1776), a legendary tale of lost love and remorse, concludes with a fairy scene:

> To guard the rock from each malignant sprite,
> A troop of guardian angels watch by night;
> Aloft in air each takes his little stand,
> The neighb'ring hill is hence call'd Fairy Land.[26]

Fairies provide women poets with an image of a mode of consciousness not bound to prevailing rules and customs, a reflection of the hidden existence of unacknowledged creative powers in the world. It is not an anomaly that the same poet also fired one of the most outspoken statements for the abolition of slavery. More's poem 'The Slave Trade' (1790, first published 1788 as 'Slavery, A Poem') speaks of the universality of talents and creative abilities, not just of rights:

> Perish th'illiberal thought which would debase
> The native genius of the sable race!
> Perish the proud philosophy, which sought
> To rob them of the powers of equal thought!
>
> (*Works*, v, 345; Lonsdale, *Women Poets*, no. 219)

Moira Ferguson has argued that this poem made the combination of philanthropy and feeling 'part of female cultural-political terrain',[27] although a connection between public concern and female feeling might be spied in the work of writers in earlier decades such as Anna Seward. By 1788 Hannah More could know about the 'native genius' of black people because the poems of Phillis Wheatley, a female African slave living in America, had been published in England in 1773. The poems in her *Poems on Various Subjects, Religious and Moral* are largely imitative in style, and suggest that Wheatley is working under greater difficulties in finding a true voice than was the case for female labouring-class writers, partly because direct protest against slavery will be interpreted as ingratitude for the gifts of Christianity and literacy.

The success of the work of Ann Yearsley shows that interest in labouring-class women's poetry had also endured – or perhaps revived in a revolutionary period. At first Yearsley was patronised by Hannah More, but she eventually rebelled. The money raised by subscription for her *Poems on Several Occasions* (1785) had been controlled by More and her friends, with Yearsley herself and her husband treated as dependent children. The Bristol milk-woman had a sense of her own rights, a fact which alienated some of the upper-class readers of the 'Autobiographical Narrative' which Yearsley inserted in the fourth edition of her poems in 1786. Yearsley's poems treat of a variety of subjects, but consistently articulate the need to express the powers of the soul. She is one of the strongest poets of her period, possessing wit and humour as well as strong feeling and the capacity to create new expression. She freely discusses her own condition and experiences, but has no desire to sound like the untaught rustic or curio. One may find it offensive that, in a perversion of the 'Orinda' ideal, she was persuaded to sign her early works 'Lactilla' – someone's idea of a cute name for a milk-woman. Yearsley eagerly participated in the poetic and artistic heritage, picking up knowledge of Apollo and other classical figures through the print shops. She argues her right to do so in a poem 'Addressed to Ignorance. Occasioned by a Gentleman's desiring the Author never to assume a Knowledge of the Ancients'. Her retort is wittily couched in a wild Pythagorean carnival scene in which characters from the classical past are to be found in the London streets in contemporary workaday (and working-class) guise:

> Fair Julia sees Ovid, but passes him near,
> An old broom o'er her shoulder is thrown;
> Penelope bends to five lovers an ear.
> Walking on with one sleeve to her gown.[28]

Yearsley refuses to believe in the borders and barriers that separate high literature from low, great persons from the lowly – or the ancients from herself, the most unexpected of the moderns. Yearsley may eventually be deemed a truly important poet of her period; like Leapor, she far surpasses Stephen Duck in genuine poetic ability and versatility, and adds a new voice to the canon – or to the chorus, however one wishes to figure it.

With the fuller information only recently supplied to us, we can see that the eighteenth century was a period of tremendous importance for women's poetry in the English language. Women were able and willing to enter the exchange, to read each other and to publish. Women of various classes and interests participated in poetic endeavour. These women writers were, by and large, fortunate in that the philosophical and social theories dominant in the eighteenth century were in favour of exploring individual experience, and were relatively unhierarchical. One can read works by a washerwoman (Mary Collier) and by the cast-off mistress of a prince (Mary 'Perdita' Robinson) as well as by a host of middle-class educated women, some poor and some rich, some spinsters and some childbearing, all of them willing to try to find in verse ways of speaking about their version of life. Their poems exhibit a new expressiveness, a new inclusiveness. At their best, they have the vitality and unexpected force that we associate with good poetry of any kind.

NOTES

1 The groundbreaking anthology of eighteenth-century women's poetry is Roger Lonsdale's, *Eighteenth-Century Women Poets: an Oxford Anthology* (Oxford University Press, 1989). Lonsdale has chosen both poets and poems with care accompanied by research into manuscripts, variant versions, and printings in magazines. The information contained in headnotes and endnotes is of great value to all who follow him. For a very useful recent anthology which begins the process of integrating work by male and female poets, see David Fairer and Christine Gerrard (eds.), *Eighteenth-Century Poetry: an Annotated Anthology* (Oxford: Blackwell, 1999).

2 Delarivier Manley, 'To the Author of *Agnes de Castro*' in Germaine Greer, et al. (eds.), *Kissing the Rod: an Anthology of Seventeenth-Century Women's Verse* (London: Virago, 1988), p. 398.

3 See Germaine Greer, 'The Rewriting of Katherine Philips' and 'Did Aphra Behn Earn a Living by Her Pen?', chs. 5 and 6 in *Slip-shod Sibyls: Recognition, Rejection and the Woman Poet* (London: Penguin Books, 1995), pp. 147–96. Greer is taking issue with Virginia Woolf's oft-repeated praise of Behn as the first Englishwoman to make her living by her pen, a eulogy which forms part of the argument of *A Room of One's Own.*

4 See *The Works of Aphra Behn*, ed. Janet Todd, 7 vols. (London: William Pickering, 1992–6), *Volume 1. Poetry* (1992), for an admirably complete and well-presented set of texts of Behn's poems.

5 See Carol Barash's fine study, *English Women's Poetry, 1649–1714: Politics, Community and Linguistic Authority* (Oxford: Clarendon Press, 1996), esp. ch. 4, 'The Female Monarch and the Woman Poet: Mary of Modena, Anne Killigrew, and Jane Barker', pp. 149–208.

6 Magdalen College Oxford, MS 343, part 1, 3. See Carol Barash, who discusses the manuscripts themselves and their content (*English Women's Poetry*, pp. 198–208).

7 Jane Barker, *Love Intrigues; or, the History of the Amours of Bosvil and Galesia* (London: Curll, 1713), pp. 13–14. The three novels have now been republished as *The Galesia Trilogy* in *The Galesia Trilogy and Selected Manuscript Poems of Jane Barker*, ed. Carol Shiner Wilson (New York and Oxford: Oxford University Press, 1997).

8 'The Bird and the Arras' in *The Poems of Anne Countess of Winchilsea*, ed. Myra Reynolds (Chicago: University of Illinois Press, 1903), p. 51. Finch published 'A Nocturnal Reverie' in her *Miscellany Poems* (London, 1713); rpt. Lonsdale, *Women Poets*, no. 16 (modernised in spelling and incidentals); Fairer and Gerrard, *Eighteenth-Century Poetry*, pp. 33–5.

9 Elizabeth Rowe, 'Devout Soliloquies in Blank Verse: Soliloquy II' in *The Miscellaneous Works in Prose and Verse of Mrs Elizabeth Rowe*, 2 vols. (London: R. Hett; and R. Dodsley, 1739), 1, 193.

10 See my discussion in *The Daring Muse: Augustan Poetry Reconsidered* (Cambridge University Press, 1985), chs. 5 and 6, pp. 119–98.

11 Rpt. Fairer and Gerrard, *Eighteenth-Century Poetry*, pp. 257–62.

12 Richard Greene, *Mary Leapor: a Study in Eighteenth-Century Women's Poetry* (Oxford: Clarendon Press, 1993), p. 9.

13 Leapor, *Poems Upon Several Occasions* (London: J. Roberts, 1748), pp. 81–90 (p. 83). Cf. 'Strephon to Celia. A Modern Love-Letter', pp. 104–6; Lonsdale, *Women Poets*, no. 130. See also *The Works of Mary Leapor*, ed. Richard Greene and Ann Messenger (Oxford University Press, 1999).

14 Lonsdale, *Women Poets*, nos. 88, 146. Cf. also Leapor's 'Dorinda at her Glass', Fairer and Gerrard, *Eighteenth-Century Poetry*, pp. 284–7.

15 Terry Castle, 'Unruly and Unresigned', *TLS* (November, 1989), 1228.

16 'Saturday: The Small-Pox' in Montagu's *Essays and Poems and Simplicity. A*

Comedy, ed. Robert Halsband and Isobel Grundy (Oxford: Clarendon Press 1977; rpt. 1993), pp. 201–4; Lonsdale, *Women Poets*, no. 39; Fairer and Gerrard, *Eighteenth-Century Poetry*, pp. 179–81.

17 Leapor, *Poems Upon Several Occasions By the late Mrs Leapor. The second and last volume* (London: J. Roberts, 1751), pp. 295–8; Fairer and Gerrard, *Eighteenth-Century Poetry*, pp. 301–4.

18 Donna Landry, *The Muses of Resistance: Laboring-Class Women's Poetry in Britain, 1739–1796* (Cambridge University Press, 1990).

19 Leapor, 'Crumble-Hall', *Poems* (1751), p. 120; rpt. Fairer and Gerrard, *Eighteenth-Century Poetry*, pp. 297–301 (p. 301).

20 Samuel Richardson, *The History of Sir Charles Grandison*, ed. Jocelyn Harris (Oxford University Press, 1972), I, 21.

21 John Sitter, *Literary Loneliness in Mid-Eighteenth-Century England* (Ithaca and London: Cornell University Press, 1982).

22 From Jane Cave's *Poems on Various Subjects, Entertaining, Elegiac, and Religious* (Winchester: printed for the author, 1783); Lonsdale, *Women Poets*, no. 244. If the poem was meant for children primarily, it was not meant only for them, as it was published in a collection aimed at adult readers.

23 See *The Poems of Anna Letitia Barbauld*, ed. William McCarthy and Elizabeth Kraft (Athens, GA: University of Georgia Press, 1994): 'The Mouse's Petition', pp. 36–7 (also in Lonsdale, *Women Poets*, no. 196); 'The Caterpillar', p. 172. For further discussion of Barbauld, see ch. 2 in this volume; for discussion of this interest in animals in women's prose writings, see ch. 1, p. 36.

24 See *The Two Fountains A Faery Tale in Three Acts*, ed. Stuart Sherman and Margaret Anne Doody (Philadelphia, PA: The Johnsonians, 1994). Mrs Piozzi definitely intended this piece for the stage, but it never got further than its manuscript version. It is based on a fable which Samuel Johnson and Hester Thrale had written together; the story of Flora and the fairies was evidently reclaimed by Hester Lynch Thrale Piozzi as hers in many essentials, including the fairies. See my 'Critical Introduction' to *The Two Fountains*, pp. vii–xx.

25 Ann Radcliffe, *The Mysteries of Udolpho* (1794), ed. Bonamy Dobrée, World's Classics (Oxford University Press, 1980), p. 420.

26 *The Works of Hannah More*, 6 vols. (London: Cadell & Davies, 1834), V, 263.

27 Moira Ferguson, *Subject to Others: British Women Writers and Colonial Slavery, 1670–1834* (New York and London: Routledge, 1992), p. 153.

28 This poem is printed in the volume of which Yearsley herself took charge, a collection in which she could achieve more freedom. See *Poems on Various Subjects*, by Ann Yearsley, A Milk-woman of Clifton, near Bristol. Being her Second Work (London: Printed for the Author, 1787), pp. 93–9. See also my discussion in *The Daring Muse*, pp. 130–1.

CHAPTER 11

Women and the theatre

Angela J. Smallwood

EIGHTEENTH-CENTURY THEATRE, CULTURE, AND WOMEN'S WRITING

To write about eighteenth-century women playwrights is to engage with a whole barrage of issues: not just the new questions of the nature and achievement of women's writing in the early modern period, but also the traditional assumptions about the low value of eighteenth-century drama in general. While never failing to except Sheridan and Goldsmith, literary critics continue to lament that even the century's comedy, its strongest genre, declines from the brilliance of the Restoration to the dullness of later Georgian sentimentalism. Such adverse judgements are based on conventional textual criteria, such as originality of plot and psychological depth of character. But to capture the cultural meaning of drama, attention must extend beyond the words on the page to consider how the text interacts with the full complexity of the original theatrical event, the 'whole show' as it is sometimes called. Work so far on eighteenth-century women playwrights has tended to focus on women's lives and experiences as writers for the theatre, and the nature of their written texts.[1] This essay, however, argues that eighteenth-century drama's significance for feminism specifically depends on a cultural reading of the 'whole show'. Concentrating on comedy, the dominant mode of eighteenth-century drama, it focuses on the cultural developments which made the second half of the century the heyday of genteel comedy for female as well as male writers. Bringing texts and theatre together, it looks to the whole medium of stage comedy for the construction of feminist meaning.

The plays of Aphra Behn, commonly regarded as the first professional woman writer in English, inhabit a world of explicitness about both sex and sexual politics: 'a Devil on't the Woman damns the Poet', Behn protests in the preface to *The Luckey Chance* (1687), challenging unfair assessments of her work and asking for recognition of 'my Masculine Part the Poet in me'.[2] At the other end of the long eighteenth century, however, Elizabeth Inchbald, actress, playwright, novelist, translator, and friend of political radicals like Holcroft and Godwin, gained unprecedented recognition as a professional writer. She edited three major anthologies of drama including, from 1806, *The British Theatre*, for which she was commissioned (rather as Samuel Johnson had been, thirty years earlier, for *The English Poets*) to write a substantial set of critical prefaces. The contrast between Behn and Inchbald tells of progress over the century for women playwrights, but a progress that was rarely straightforward or unalloyed.

After the death of Susannah Centlivre, the last and most prolific member of 'the School of Aphra', new drama by women fell into short supply. The Stage Licensing Act of 1737, which instituted pre-production government censorship of plays, inhibited dramatic output of all kinds and turned the mid century into a lean time. This was enlivened, as far as women's writing goes, by a small number of entertainments and after-pieces written by actresses such as Catherine Clive and Susannah Cibber, often primarily as vehicles for their own talents. As in several other genres, however, the output of women in drama accelerated quite spectacularly in the second half of the century.[3] Of the 600 (known) plays written by women between 1660 and 1823, nearly 200 appeared between 1770 and 1800,[4] a period which witnessed the culmination of a number of favourable developments. Professional opportunities for women writers generally had increased markedly; the London theatre audience had broadened to accommodate more of the middling classes and a newly respectable image; acting was becoming increasingly pro-fessionalised and the star system was flourishing, notably for top female players. In this climate, from about 1760, women writers began to receive preferential treatment from the managers of the Theatres Royal of Drury Lane and Covent Garden, the only London theatres licensed to perform drama (with the addition of the Haymarket in the off-season, summer period). The managers held sole charge of theatre repertory, reviving stock plays, selecting new ones and taking it upon themselves to suggest, and sometimes make, revisions to aspiring writers' texts. The ratio of female to male playwrights active in this period was about 1:20, but the ratio of female-authored to male-authored new pieces chosen for staging was in the region of 1:5.[5] We know that David Garrick raised the profile of women playwrights during his managership of Drury Lane; and this may have been deliberate policy.[6] Part of his drive to improve the cultural standing of the theatre, the inclusion of women writers would have signalled greater propriety and refinement, and an attractive liberal-mindedness.

The reception of women's writing for the stage, however – even in these apparently favourable conditions – remained relatively ambivalent. On the one hand, in 1778 the *Gentleman's Magazine* finds praise for *Percy* by Hannah More, judging that 'on the whole, few modern tragedies have equal merit; and we cannot help congratulating our female readers on this addition to the list (already numerous and distinguished) of female writers'.[7] On the other hand, R. B. Sheridan's epilogue to More's tragedy *The Fatal Falsehood* (1779) shifts ground from conventional misogyny to supportiveness, with the self-consciousness of one ostentatiously conforming to the latest fad in political correctness. Inveighing at length against the whole notion of a woman writer ('A letter'd gossip, and a housewife wit'), the speaker suddenly checks himself and represses his 'spleen', realising that the audience's 'hearts' are 'pledg'd to her applause'.[8] George Colman, however, reviewer for the *Monthly Review* and manager of the Haymarket Theatre, was uninhibited about censuring this play; but he accepted, collaborated in, and defended *The Chapter of Accidents*, a comedy by Sophia Lee, in which the heroine's remarkable sensibility redeems the social crime she has committed in yielding her virginity to her lover. A writer in the *Gentleman's Magazine* rejoices in the opportunity which the play provides for 'a liberal mind' to feel unusually heightened pity, but then pronounces the heroine's character improper for the stage 'where inflexible virtue only ought to receive encouragement', adding 'And least of all is it proper to be introduced by a *lady*.'[9]

Despite its bid for greater respectability, the Georgian theatre was far from becoming a wholly 'proper' place. For both stage and audience, it offered public exposure, a fact exploited in the most disreputable sense by the prostitutes who traditionally occupied certain areas of the auditorium. Stage drama was thus the most problematic medium within which women writers sought to build professional reputations. Evidence about the constraints imposed on some of the plays which they produced supports the somewhat negative views of the professionalisation of eighteenth-century women's writing which were developed in the 1980s by scholars working on the novel. In prose fiction the expansion of women's writing in the period seems to have been achieved at a price: its range was limited by enforced compromises with cultural expectations of feminine propriety.[10] The pressures placed in 1786 upon *The School for Greybeards*, an adaptation of Aphra Behn's *The Luckey Chance* by Hannah

Cowley, seem to replicate this sense of deepening restriction. Cowley's preface explains that the play has required two separate revisions, one prior to and one following the opening night, to eradicate all supposed indecencies. It tells how she feels fettered, 'encompassed in chains when I write', because theatre critics deny her, as a woman, the freedom to use language which deviates from the 'line of politeness' as and when dramatic characterisation and situation demand.[11]

On another level, however, the image of greater propriety cultivated by critics and managers was a source of opportunity for women writers as well as a restriction, because it acknowledged the increasingly feminised orientation of contemporary culture. Cowley adapted plays by Centlivre as well as Behn, and her development of the stage action alone seems to signal her theatre's acceptance of an increase in female agency and female autonomy. Cowley's two-act farce, *Who's the Dupe?* (1779), expands ideas from just two scenes in the sub-plot of Centlivre's *Stolen Heiress* (1702). Centlivre very briefly brings together the heroines of her high and low plots and allows the lower-class Lavinia to propose that they both act to resist the threat of arranged marriages: 'Let the Woman work!'[12] Cowley freely develops this hint, changing the setting from Sicily to London and creating two young English women who drive the whole action of the play. Centlivre's heroines, by contrast, despite their appetite for self-assertion, control little of the plot and are regularly put down by misogynist male figures. In Behn's *Luckey Chance*, too, it is noticeable how outwardly passive a role is given even to Julia, the figure most easily read in feminist terms. Behind the scenes Julia manipulates a good deal of the action, but her control of elements of the plot has to be enacted for her by men. Her autonomy is embodied in independent thought and in speech: in the declaration to her husband of her own unorthodox code of wifely conduct ('What, because I can not simper – look demure, and justify my Honour when none questions it? Cry fie, and out upon the naughty Women, because they please themselves – and so would I?' (v.iii; Behn, *Works*, VII, 275)); and in her unexpected objection to her lover Gayman's having presumed to substitute himself for her unloved husband in her bed ('What, make me a base Prostitute, a foul Adulteress[?] Oh – be gone, be gone – dear Robber of my Quiet' (v.vi; 278)). In these plays by Behn and Centlivre, men dominate the stage space; and it is not by displaying heroines in action but by representing male tyranny and misogyny in odious terms that much of the feminist signification is released. By contrast with Julia, Seraphina, the corresponding figure in Cowley's version of *Luckey Chance*, speaks with

unabating witty energy, prosecutes her own plots, and dominates both
her husband and the stage.

It is as if, by the 1780s, it has become both practically more possible
and ideologically more acceptable to make an assertive female protagonist central to stage comedy, even to create proto-feminist figures. And
yet Seraphina is not unequivocally such. The lively heroine of Cowley's
most beleaguered play, Seraphina ultimately lacks radical impact: in plot
terms and on a deeper level too. As I shall go on to show, one explanation for this lies beyond the text of the play in the original conditions of
its performance, in the manner in which the alerted feminist awareness
which carries over from Behn to Cowley became theatrically embodied.
In other plays of the 1770s and 1780s, however, Lee's *Chapter of Accidents*
and Cowley's *Belle's Stratagem*, analyses of the 'whole show', the impact
of the whole medium of stage comedy, reveal a more positive potential
for feminist signification. 'Female plays usually build a good deal upon
the sex', James Boaden writes in his *Memoirs of . . . Kemble*, from the
vantage point of 1825, reflecting on Cowley and her generation.[13]
Opportunities in later Georgian comedy for women playwrights sprang
from the simultaneous promotion of female writers and female players,
which made possible the creation of a woman-centred version of genteel
comedy. In this context, Cowley was not alone but was perhaps foremost
in recognising how the cultural dynamism of female performance might
radicalise comedy's conformist images of women.

FEMINIST WRITING IN PERFORMANCE: DISPLACEMENT
AND RECUPERATION

The later Georgian theatre, caught up in the period's commercialisation
of leisure, has long been seen as a performers', not a writers', theatre.
Oliver Goldsmith memorably cried out in protest, as early as 1759, that
the popular attraction of spectacle in the theatre had taken over from
the pleasure of dramatic poetry: the 'celestial muse' had been sacrificed
to the 'histrionic demon', the poet to the player.[14] But in the escalation
of theatre operations in the last quarter of the century, even the actors'
interests (except for those of stars) were downgraded by the dictates of
big business, which is what the London theatres had become.[15]
Inevitably, the content of playtexts was sometimes subordinated, sometimes enhanced, in the process of production. Women's writing, Ellen
Donkin has argued, was patronised by the theatre managers (in both
senses) and limited in significant ways.[16] It is clear that, by manipulating

dramatic structure and rhetoric, women writers could sometimes set up critiques of patriarchal attitudes only to see them compromised in performance. If we look closely, however, we see a situation rather more complex and subtle than just patriarchal suppression, a situation created by the very nature of later Georgian comedy and the volatility of drama itself in a commercialised, consumer-driven theatre.

For example, *Who's the Dupe?*, the farce which Cowley built from the subplot of Centlivre's *Stolen Heiress*, provides the feminist reader with an uproarious read: a traditional, male, classical education (entrée to all professions and public office), in the person of a misogynist Oxford scholar, Gradus, is deliberately brought into unfavourable comparison with a modern English female education, represented by the attractive, articulate, and pugnacious heroine, Elizabeth. To Gradus's opening address which is heavy with classical references, Elizabeth replies: 'I believe all you have said to be very fine, Sir; but, unfortunately, I don't know the Gentlemen you mentioned. The education given to Women shuts us entirely from such refined acquaintance.'[17] Although enormously popular from the first, this farce was unlikely to be taken seriously because it was an afterpiece, a low-status play.[18] While the broadly comic figures of the pedant and Elizabeth's vulgar citizen father were criticised for being old-fashioned, the feminist remarks which pepper Elizabeth's dialogue attracted little notice, and the star part was seen as that of Thomas King, the actor who played the misogynist. King, second only to Garrick himself as a comedian and speaker of prologues at Drury Lane, was normally above playing in afterpieces.[19] The part of Gradus was 'not perfectly agreeable to himself', Cowley acknowledges in the printed text (p. 4). Unlike Sancho at the end of Centlivre's play, Cowley's pedant does not return to academe, but is won out of scholarly marginality and converted to the world of fashion, the audience's world, the world of Lord Ogleby and Sir Peter Teazle, the character parts in genteel comedies in which King regularly appeared. Part of the pleasure of the production must have arisen from watching King, surprisingly cast as the uncongenial Gradus in the first act, moving gradually back into the mode in which he was best known and loved. The feminist significance of Elizabeth, played by Mrs Brereton, no more than a middle-ranking actress,[20] would have been upstaged easily by the draw of King, and lost in the laughter and delight centring upon him.

A more substantial displacement of feminist meaning seems to have occurred in the staging of Sophia Lee's *The Chapter of Accidents*. The text constructs an extensive critique of patriarchy by presenting a sustained contrast between two fathers and their very different philosophies of education. The heroine's father, Governor Harcourt, believes in breeding women 'in retirement' to make them innocent,[21] and this repressively protective approach is exposed as self-defeating and the chief cause of her sexual fall. The Governor combines tyranny with a range of outrageous social prejudices including misogyny and xenophobia, but any critical laughter directed at him is subsumed in enjoyment of his considerable histrionic success. Actors chose this role for benefit performances, and the play was unusually popular for benefits among many members of the cast.[22]

While in *Who's the Dupe?* and *Chapter of Accidents* feminist issues of education and female virtue were displaced by the superior power of 'histrionic demons' to hold centre stage, in *School for Greybeards* Cowley's Seraphina seems sure of dominating the action. She delivers outspoken speeches about marriage, 'the quiet and sober pale . . . where we shall grow good, and stupid' (v.iii, pp. 65–6). Yet, even in the text, she challenges the conservative assumptions of genteel comedy very little. Compared with Behn's Julia, as Jane Spencer observes, Seraphina may be 'more confident' but she is also 'more conventional' in asserting her 'moral independence'.[23] But Cowley's Seraphina is not simply ultimately unchallenging; she is actually somehow disarmed. For the meaning of this figure in 1780s performances is related to the culturally powerful phenomenon of the star actress, which had become a strong feature of the London theatre prior to Garrick's retirement, and blossomed after it, commanding a range of female images which varied markedly in their significance for sexual politics.

The stage history of *The Discovery* by Frances Sheridan, as performed in 1763 and revived in the 1770s and 1780s, exemplifies vividly the cultural and theatrical evolution of a role of this type. On one level this seems yet another case of displacement of feminist meaning, but there is more to it. The plot concerns the reformation of Lord Medway, an adulterous husband and a gambler with almost overwhelming debts. He imposes his will upon each member of his family in turn and encourages another character, the young married lord, Harry Flutter, to imitate his style as a husband, 'the true art of tormenting', to secure domestic mastery.[24] The play discredits patriarchy by presenting Lord Medway's mode of life as tyrannical, immoral, and doomed, and by contrasting it with Lady Medway's, which enshrines the antithetical principle of friendship and makes redemption possible. Although Lady Medway's opposition to her husband's conduct is conscious and principled, she never questions her wifely commitment; on the contrary, she embodies a conduct-book ideal of married womanhood. Her behaviour is contrasted with the initially combative stance of the young Lady Flutter towards her husband, Sir Harry. Lady Flutter mocks Lady Medway as a 'tame' wife, and comments sarcastically on the fact that she enjoys evenings spent reading in her dressing room with her daughter (ii.i, iii.ii; pp. 67, 73). These two figures contrast a feminism reminiscent of Mary Astell's, based on inner moral independence, with a feminism which openly opposes patriarchal power by its own methods, matching aggression with aggression.[25] But Sheridan's construction of the representation gives Lady Medway's perspective priority; it positions the audience to view Lady Flutter's quarrelsome stance as immature and counterproductive. In mocking Lady Medway, she is undervaluing her mentor. While confident that the boxes and pit would relish the play, one of Sheridan's influential friends felt that, at the first performance, 'the respectable supporters of the middle gallery might require a little *leading*' and so she dressed herself in a chip hat and white linen to sit in their midst and 'point out to them *when* they should admire . . . by obstreperous thunders of applause'.[26]

The subsequent stage history of the play, however, shows that a more popular response prevailed. Among the female characters, Lady Flutter not Lady Medway captured chief attention. The first revival came in 1775–6, Garrick's retirement season, and was designed to display his comic genius in a minor character. But when the production continued to enjoy theatrical success in four seasons after that, there was one overriding reason: the triumph of Mrs Abington in the role of Lady Flutter. Indeed she did not simply dominate the play, she possessed it, taking it with her when she moved from Drury Lane to Covent Garden in November 1782, where she made her high-profile 'first appearance' as Lady Flutter. That the Lady Flutter figure should displace the Lady Medway figure is not surprising in such a strongly performance-oriented theatre: the more extrovert role is theatrically more attractive. Yet the 1780s performances of *The Discovery* could well have had less impact in terms of sexual politics than the original production in 1763, because of the 'recuperation' of Lady Flutter's outspokenness.

In Michèle Barrett's words, 'recuperation' refers to any of the ways in which 'challenges to the . . . dominant meaning of gender' are negated, defused, reabsorbed by the media to serve the interests of the status quo.[27] Endless examples could be given from the plot lines of Georgian comedies in the last quarter of the eighteenth century, in which lively

heroines are allowed a little scope within the exposition to step over the
limits of femininity or to question marriage, only to be tied down again
firmly in conventional endings. But the image of Mrs Abington gives us
something further, something applicable to more roles than Mrs
Abington herself played: the recuperation of a newly assertive feminine
identity through an identification with a type of fashionable behaviour.

At the time of her move to Covent Garden, Mrs Abington is described
as having been 'the peculiar delight of the fashionable world'.[28] Fashion
in her case extended from the sphere of women's dress, in which she was
considered unsurpassed,[29] to an assertive personal style which would
have been clearly in evidence in her playing of Lady Flutter. She was a
great speaker of epilogues and Garrick, for example, composed several
in which she entertained audiences with precocious claims for female
power.[30] At the same time, the periodicals noticed a trend towards boldness in female manners, generally. The *Monthly Review* notes in 1774 that
some of 'the ladies' have begun to react with 'an offensive and masculine hardness' to the errors of unfaithful husbands, and the *Gentleman's
Magazine* for 1781 carries a piece on the latest craze, a 'rage' among the
ladies 'for military dress'.[31] Abington's modish line in self-assertion
exceeded the mere self-assurance of the traditional coquette. Her most
famous role, Lady Teazle in R. B. Sheridan's *The School for Scandal* (1777),
opens with a typical quarrel with her husband Sir Peter, including challenges to his authority, delivered with the spirit of 'a woman of Fashion'
who is 'accountable to nobody'; but this display of independence is
entirely contained and neutralised within Sir Peter's unconcerned and
proprietorial gloss: 'with what a charming air she contradicts every thing
I say . . . I think she never appear[s] to such advantage as when she's
doing every thing in her Power to plague me' (II.ii).[32] The link with
fashion disarms female assertiveness by reducing it to style, a superficial
fashion accessory, even (as in Sir Peter's eyes) an adornment. This effect
does not depend on the manipulation of a plot line, but is more subtle:
it involves the draining of power from female roles which deliver trenchant statements, by identifying them so closely with fashion as to trivi-
alise female selfhood.

There is much the same effect when Julia's independent statements in
Behn's *Luckey Chance* are compared with the witty defiance which
Seraphina fires at her husband in Cowley's 1780s version, *The School for
Greybeards*. Seraphina's independence makes for entertaining spectacle,
even exhilaration; it is attractive where Julia's is disturbing, extrovert
where hers is reflective; it dominates the action while Julia's barely
expresses itself in action until the end when it subverts the comic

Figure 4 Joshua Reynolds, *Mrs Abington as 'The Comic Muse'* (*c.* 1768).
Reproduced by permission of the National Trust, Waddesdon Manor.

resolution; it is somehow relatively trivial (Cowley herself calls it 'innocent . . . coquetry' (p. ix)) because her striking statements on female
autonomy have been recuperated, like Lady Teazle's, within contemporary culture's image of the 'woman of Fashion'.

If the very workings of performance processes and the pressures of
ideology could, in some cases, marginalise or modify explicitly feminist
material, in what senses could the theatre and the work of women playwrights contribute positively at this time to the climate of ideas within
which the major works of late eighteenth-century feminism came to be
published? My discussion of recuperation indicates that, even if culturally neutralised in the theatre, perceptions of more active roles for some
women were current in the 1770s and 1780s and, as we shall see, when
star actresses became identified with heroines of refinement in comedy,
new possibilities opened.

THE RISE OF THE STAR ACTRESS

Cultural perceptions of actresses exerted a significant influence both
upon how eighteenth-century drama was perceived and upon Georgian
culture's assumptions about female identity.[33] The possible cultural
meanings of the actress broadened in range in the second half of the
century, sustaining the traditional degrading associations of the actress
with the prostitute but allowing certain stars to attain something close to
social acceptability among not all but certainly some people of quality
and fashion.[34] Mrs Abington's success in becoming 'the delight of the
fashionable world' is clearly part of this development, but contemporary
comments suggest that she was too flamboyant to qualify for the highest
approval, even if she had not had a history of sexual adventures.[35] One
of Mrs Abington's titled contacts was Lady Elizabeth Craven, who was
by no means universally accepted in high society herself. Horace
Walpole, although prepared to admire Lady Craven, placed limits on
Mrs Abington's claims to distinction. In his view, her performances in
genteel comedy were never convincingly of the highest class: 'Mrs
Abington can never go beyond Lady Teazle, which is a second-rate character, and that rank of women are always aping women of fashion
without arriving at the style'.[36] A few actresses in comedy did however
go further, including Elizabeth Farren, who played both Cowley's
Seraphina and Cecilia in Lee's *Chapter of Accidents* and later became
Countess of Derby, and Miss Younge, whose performance as Letitia

Hardy in Cowley's *The Belle's Stratagem* seemed to James Boaden, 'to testify that she was born to ornament a court'.[37]

While actresses had been, of course, no strangers to high social circles in Restoration times, the particular significance in the later Georgian period of their representing or consorting with people of fashion and quality was that they thereby typified, very publicly, a much wider cultural development affecting many women in, or known to, their audiences. Neil McKendrick has documented 'social imitation' in the second half of the eighteenth century, a phenomenon by which, through the expansion of leisure and consumerism (which affected women's lives especially), the middling classes consciously cultivated social activities associated with their betters, and emulated many aspects of upper-class lifestyles.[38] Rather like Walpole deliberately reinscribing a distance between the genuinely high class and an imitator such as Mrs Abington, the elite reacted by beginning to ringfence their own territory, building grandstands at racecourses, for instance, and, prior to the Old Price riots in 1809, making the boxes at the patent theatres private.[39] A related nervousness is represented in both *Who's the Dupe?* and *The Belle's Stratagem* by Cowley, where conservatively minded men express concern at the lack of social distinctions between women of different ranks which results from their united pursuit of fashion.[40] As the theatre is one of the resorts of fashion, there is an element of self-consciousness about Cowley's showing on stage, in *Belle's Stratagem*, women of different classes mixing, potentially indistinguishably, at a fashionable auction and, later, at a masquerade. The auction scene epitomises the rage for consumption (ii.ii, pp. 30–4). It opens by making the point that one of the ladies present is in fact a 'puffer', a lower-class woman paid to imitate her social superiors by dressing like a lady of quality, in order to mingle with the customers and talk up the value of the goods. When this character, Fag, complains that with insufficient allowances she cannot dress the part convincingly (p. 30), the figure of the actress inside the role is clearly visible and directly identified with female social imitation. Her presence casts the whole scene in a metatheatrical light, since the 'real' ladies are just well-dressed actresses too, although of a higher rank in theatrical terms. The audience's awareness of social difference underlying the apparent uniformity of the fashionable female images peopling this scene would, therefore, be echoed and enhanced by a sense of theatrical hierarchy.

This sort of cultural and theatrical resonance, focusing on women, is

Figure 5 Dupont, *Mrs Pope* [formerly Miss Younge] *as Monimia in 'The Orphan'*.
Garrick Club/e.t. archive.

clearly harnessed to enhance the effect of the text in the construction of both Lee's *Chapter of Accidents* and Cowley's *Belle's Stratagem*. Both writers create roles for lower-ranking actresses which include explicit enactments of social imitation, and both juxtapose them with central roles of a more refined nature played by star actresses. These contrasts act to modify the habitual association of the actress with degraded, promiscuous women and to enhance the sense of the elevation and exclusivity of the star actress in the role of the refined heroine.

In *The Chapter of Accidents*, Lee seeks to sustain the audience's endorsement of the dignity of Cecilia, a young unmarried woman of refinement and sensibility, in spite of the social disgrace of lost virginity. One device used is the contrast between Cecilia, played by Miss Farren, and her maid, Bridget, played by Mrs Wilson. Bridget cherishes a somewhat hopeless longing to go to a masquerade and, when Cecilia is out, cannot resist the temptation to dress up in some of her mistress's clothes (IV.i). She is discovered by the father and uncle of Cecilia's lover, both of whom, on the strength of her evident vulgarity, readily presume Bridget to be the kept mistress, Cecilia. The comedy of the scene lies in the men's prejudiced mistake in identifying as Cecilia a figure whose conduct is read by the audience as a hopelessly poor impersonation of genteel femininity, and who is debarred by class (signalled by slips of language) from delivering a convincing imitation of a lady of quality. The scene is a very funny satire on female social imitation but in addition Bridget's impersonation of Cecilia is metadramatic – both figures are actresses attempting to play the lady of quality. Bridget's failure in the role allows Miss Farren's Cecilia to look even more refined and enhances her gentility, an effect reinforced by the relative positions within the theatre rankings of Mrs Wilson, who played Maria in *Twelfth Night*, for instance, and Miss Farren, who played Olivia.[41]

A similar device is used by Cowley in the subplot of *Belle's Stratagem*, where a prostitute, Kitty Willis, is paid to attend the masquerade, wearing a replica of the costume chosen by virtuous Lady Frances (IV.i). Kitty's role is to decoy the lady's would-be seducer into mistaking herself for the lady of quality. The fact that the masquerade costumes are identical only intensifies the audience's sense of the social and sexual gulf between the two outwardly similar female figures: the prostitute and the innocent, well-born, chaste wife. This effect is deepened further by the part played in this scene by the heroine of the main plot, Letitia Hardy. Masquerade costume offers Letitia the freedom and anonymity with which to go out actively to win the heart of the hitherto uninterested

Doricourt.[42] When masked, Letitia changes her formerly modest demeanour for something much more extrovert; but the image which she projects, as she sings, dances, engages Doricourt in lively conversation, and conquers him, is open to damaging misinterpretation. The duplicate images of Lady Frances (lady of quality and prostitute) present a physical separation of the two identities between which Letitia, as the self-publicising incognita, hovers: the 'Woman of Family and Fortune' which, as she leaves the ball, she assures Doricourt she is; and the kept mistress which the society gossip, Flutter, is so plausibly able to suggest may be her actual status (p. 60). In this scene, the stage role of Letitia resonates with the actual cultural position of Miss Younge who played her, placed somewhere between the suspect world of the theatre and high social acceptability. James Boaden's account of the performance, however, celebrates Miss Younge's success in emerging from this ambiguous moment clearly on the side of the angels.

Miss Hardy . . . in the display of her accomplishments throws a mystery about her person. Her dance is fashioned by the graces, and her conversation realizes the eastern dreams of poetry and love. Such was the character into which Miss Younge stept, as if it had been but the *shadow* of herself, and rendered it fascinating beyond any character of the modern stage . . . Miss Younge, in Letitia Hardy, was never to be forgotten. Where was any thing to be found more graceful than her minuet? . . . [T]he superior stateliness of her figure seemed to testify that she was born to ornament a court, and to move in that measure which best represents its majesty and its grace. (Boaden, *Siddons*, 1, 203–4)

Here, the social enigma of Miss Younge, as the star actress, may well have enhanced the audience's sense of the dangerous fragility of Letitia's masquerade persona and the almost magical quality of an individual performance, in which, pitching for her own as well as Letitia's good name, Miss Younge made sheer refinement transcend the very real possibility of vulgarity.

METATHEATRICALITY AND THE CRITIQUE OF FEMININITY

The potential class mobility of the actress in the 1770s and 1780s was not simply part of the signification of female roles in comedy; it was capable, through those roles, of intensifying awareness of the class alignment of femininity as a cultural ideal and, in some cases, of questioning it. While *The Chapter of Accidents* toys with this possibility, *The Belle's Stratagem* moves much closer to embracing it.

For both Cecilia and Lady Frances the slur of sexual immorality threatens social disgrace. As Cecilia exclaims in the Larpent manuscript version of *Chapter of Accidents*, 'How low one Step in vice throw's us!'[43] But the point about Cecilia is her superiority of character and sensibility: as Captain Harcourt remarks in the published text, she is 'far above her present situation' (p. 36) and this, true to the best traditions of eighteenth-century sensibility narratives, makes her worthy of rescue. There is more than a glimpse of resistance to social convention in the attitudes of Lord Glenmore, who has chosen Miss Mortimer to marry his son Woodville (Cecilia's lover) on the basis of personal qualities, not wealth, and who is critical of Governor Harcourt's prejudices. Juxtaposing Cecilia with Miss Mortimer, the text seems poised to question the grounds on which young women are to be judged, to question the premium placed on virginity, to ask if there is any real concern about human worth or just anxiety about market value in the upper-class trade in women and estates. When Lord Glenmore comes to admire Cecilia, however, conventional assumptions about femininity and class are strongly reasserted. The plot is contrived to dispose of the marriage arranged for Woodville, and clear the way for Cecilia to marry him herself, so that she ends by regaining both her sexual integrity and her status in society. As well as 'elegance of mind and person', she exhibits exquisitely fine features, a tendency to faint, conscience, and altruism enough to internalise the patriarchal double standard and insist that her degradation should not prevent Woodville from making the marriage his father has arranged. These attributes of feminine sensibility compensate for Cecilia's loss of virginity by proving the more powerful indicators of superior class. Her fulfilment of all the visible requirements of conventional femininity qualifies her for social promotion. Key to her perfect femininity is Cecilia's shunning of publicity, her quiet, retired existence while in town, her physical passivity: her image is a denial of all vulgarity, a denial of theatricality. Cecilia was thus an attractive role for the star actress capable of expressing refinement; and the deeply conservative turn given to the play's development of the initial situation offered no critique of femininity, but rather a reaffirmation of it.

By comparison, Letitia Hardy is superficially a less controversial heroine. Whereas, regardless of all the compensations, the basic concept of Cecilia (vice rewarded) provoked objections in the press, Letitia is a figure totally at one with the romance of the companionate marriage. Her plan is to turn an arranged marriage into a love marriage and to fulfil both her own and her father's wishes by making her legally ordained husband in love with her. To achieve this, however, she has to

transgress the ordinances of femininity. Where Cecilia has every feminine quality except sexual purity, Letitia is faultless but realises that she
must shed modesty and privacy and take on self-publication through the
medium of the masquerade, an initiative which automatically calls her
class position and sexual innocence into question. As I have argued elsewhere, there is an analogy between Letitia's public wooing of Doricourt
and a woman writer's presentation of her mind, in the form of a play,
for the approval of a theatre audience.[44] In real life such a public assertion of her identity by a woman writer of middle rank required compen-
sating by strict preservation of propriety in every other respect. Lady
Craven (friend of Mrs Abington and also a playwright) showed her 'singularity' by appearing in her box at the theatre on the second night of
one of her own plays, whereas Mrs Cowley bowed to the protocol
required of upwardly-aspiring women writers by decorously staying
away from her first nights, as Frances Sheridan (though wife to an actor-
manager) had done before her.[45] For the perfect lady is passive, private,
untheatrical. But Letitia is active and self-publicising, theatrically more
daring than the figure of Cecilia – not heroine as erring lady, but heroine
as actress. Letitia's role is metatheatrical, involves the playing of multiple female roles, and sets up an environment in which there is no clear
reaffirmation of conventional femininity, as happens in the case of
Cecilia, but rather a sustained questioning of female identity.

The metatheatrical roles of Bridget in *Chapter of Accidents* and Letitia
in *Belle's Stratagem* show that, in addition to highlighting the class alignment of the feminine ideal, it was possible to suggest the performative
nature of femininity, and thus to open it to critique.[46] Given the ethos of
propriety which governed later eighteenth-century comedy, however,
the scope for questioning gender identities was very limited. Laurence
Senelick has shown how the presentation of the effeminate fop dwindled
in later eighteenth-century comedy as a direct expression of the spread
of respectability within the theatre.[47] Very few plays involve any cross-
dressing and it is significant that the only play of the 1770s and 1780s
where a woman writer proposes unconventional gender identities is in a
poetic drama not intended for the stage, Hannah More's didactic 'David
and Goliath' (1782). The youthful David personifies a spiritual courage
which is classless and genderless, his androgynous attributes crossing and
recrossing established gender boundaries: 'modest confidence', 'tem-
p'rate valour . . . chastis'd / By modesty'.[48] More herself points out that
such a figure would be inconceivable within the conventions of the contemporary stage. Her preferred audience is young readers, who are

importantly different from the spectators in commercial theatres in that they are unprejudiced, their judgements 'undebauch'd as yet with fashion's lore, / And unsophisticate, unbiass'd' (p. 5). In order to meet the conditions of the public stage in any putative alteration of this all-male drama, More reflects, she would have had to complement the figure of David by 'the introduction of Saul's daughter' (p. xxvi). Moving David out of the dramatic poem and onto a stage, to play opposite a leading actress, would have meant removing him from More's sphere of gender ambiguity and placing him instead in the theatre's polarised world of masculine and feminine, which would have destroyed the ethos of the play. In the heavily conventionalised world of stage comedy at this time, then, where issues of effeminacy and androgyny were ruled out, any material which merely questioned femininity possessed relatively radical potential.

As more than one commentator on women and ideology has pointed out, there is a gap between ideological concept and practice: no one woman lives out even the most dominant ideological image in its total-ity.[49] Eighteenth-century theatre was fond of using actresses to speak comic epilogues at the end of tragedies or other serious plays, deliber-ately opening up a gap between the actress and the high-minded role she had just finished playing. It is only with the rise in status of the star actress, however, that such an effect becomes capable of implying criti-cism of a cultural idealisation. In a cultural situation where the idea of the actress is associated with degraded status or represents some kind of taboo, the criticism is directed, tongue-in-cheek, against herself. Nell Gwynn's epilogue to Dryden's heroic tragedy *Tyrannic Love* (1670) in which she, well-known mistress of Charles II, played Catherine, saint and martyr, is perhaps the outstanding example of this.[50] The direction of the criticism cannot have been quite so clear, however, when Mrs Pritchard, whose private life was unexceptionable,[51] spoke the epilogue to Frances Sheridan's *The Discovery* in 1763, criticising the conduct-book role of Lady Medway and suggesting that all the women in the audience will agree that the character is 'out of nature – never drawn from life, / Who ever heard of such a passive wife?' (p. 102). There could be satire here, actress Pritchard dragging a morally pretentious audience down to her own level of everyday imperfection; there could also, however, be a reflection on the ideological nature of the role of Lady Medway and a suggestion that textbook wifedom, presented in the play as a fulfilling vocation, is actually somewhat remote from the experience of even the best of good wives in real life. Both of these examples, however, occur in epilogues which follow and undercut the plays, but do not interfere directly with their presentation of idealised heroines. What we have in *The Belle's Stratagem* is a refined heroine whose role calls attention to the fact of performance within the play itself. Though performative, the design of the role crucially retains contact with refined behaviour and fosters audience identification; and it is through this new closeness between role, star actress, and self-conscious audience that feminist signification becomes a possibility. The play makes a range of female identities the object of the performance, makes thematic the gap between gender identity and heroine, and opens it to critical scrutiny.

When the play begins, a marriage arrangement, made by their fathers, has existed for Letitia and Doricourt since their childhood but they have not seen each other for several years. Following a first meeting between the two at a lawyer's office, Doricourt does not fault Letitia's looks but judges her dull compared with the 'resistless charmers of Italy and France' (p. 9), finding her social demeanour as mute and static as her portrait, her official public image, which shows 'The downcast eye – the blushing cheek – timid – apprehensive – bashful' (p. 35). The starting-point of the action is thus a critique of textbook femininity in that Letitia's conscientious replication of conduct-book modesty has failed to attract Doricourt's love. At the end of the play, Letitia explains that at that initial meeting her real nature was, as it were, veiled from Doricourt's view, hidden by 'timidity' (v.v, p. 81) within an image which Saville calls 'true unaffected English beauty' (i.iii, pp. 9–10). The belle's stratagem which eventually succeeds in winning Doricourt's love involves appearing to him in two further identities: firstly, a Letitia who, having just come to town from the country, proves in conversation nothing more than an uneducated, unpolished rustic (an idea calculated to horrify the cosmopolitan Doricourt), and, secondly, the witty and fascinating masked lady at the masquerade, known to the audience but not to Doricourt, who instantly captures his heart. It is tempting to read the masquerade Letitia as somehow the 'real' Letitia, freed from social convention and able at last to project the attractiveness of her inner character to draw the attention of the man she loves. But, as Isikoff notices, the masquerade identity could be read as critiqued by the action of the play;[52] and so could Letitia's other guises, because they are all constructed either to appal or to appeal to Doricourt and, at the end of the play, Letitia does not identify herself with any of them. 'You see I *can* be any thing,' she is made to say to him; 'chuse then my character – your Taste shall fix it' (v.v, p. 81). While the action of the play highlights the artificiality of female images which are designed purely to satisfy a masculine gaze, the opportunity to reject ideological femininity is thus notably passed over in the closure of the text.

Bringing together with the text, however, the awareness of the complex cultural and theatrical signification of star actress as genteel heroine which this essay has begun to suggest, a somewhat different conclusion offers itself about the meaning of the original production. For, as we have seen, Miss Younge's appearance in the masquerade scene was a spectacular high point in performance, richly charged in cultural terms and unerasable. This image critiqued femininity by demonstrating an alternative ideal, an identity where the star actress and the woman of quality exchanged certain attributes, where the actress was credited with genuine refinement and the lady allowed a little more public scope without any necessary sense of degradation. Early in the play, an assertive young widow, Mrs Rackett, mounts a substantial and carefully nuanced defence of the modern 'Fine Lady', in reply to dismissive words from Lady Frances's repressive husband. Significantly, in spite of the merely middle-rank status of the actress who played the role, the speech was noted for its impact in the theatre (Cowley, *Plays*, 1, 228). Mrs Rackett maintains that a modern wife is of enhanced, not diminished, value compared with Sir George's wholly domesticated ideal; she is equipped by 'Education' to balance social with private life and an independent public persona with devotion to her husband; for while in her 'manner' she is 'free', in her 'morals' she is 'nice' (II.i, p. 25). In the end both Letitia and Lady Frances establish a revision of Sir George's notion of femininity, by which neither is forced back into strict privacy, modesty, and retirement. Alongside the other explicit messages of the play in its original production (nationalist and moral), there was thus a message, of a very moderate kind, about female rights; and it was no accident that this was, in a sense, endorsed by and identified with the Queen, to whom the play was dedicated and who saw it by royal command. For it must have been in the interaction between prevailing ideologies and the realities of many women in the cultural world of the production (writer, player, patron, audience) that much of its meaning for that time was made. In the 1780 stage productions of both *The Belle's Stratagem* and *The Chapter of Accidents*, then, despite their varying degrees of conservatism, a combination of cultural and theatrical dynamics came into play, within which negotiations of female identity must have been a palpable presence.

Letitia Hardy's rustic persona, to which I have made only the briefest of references, is reminiscent of – may well make reference to – the role-play of the rural barmaid performed by Kate Hardcastle in Goldsmith's long-celebrated comedy, *She Stoops to Conquer* (1773). It has often gone unobserved that, at the time of its first production, Goldsmith's play was criticised in the *Monthly Review* as old-fashioned and out of touch with the 'manners of the age'. Where the Letitia Hardy role climbs to the height of courtliness, Kate 'stoops'; and the reviewer is amused by Goldsmith's 'low mischief' but laments his failure to appreciate that the whole society is moving towards greater 'politeness'.[53] *She Stoops* has a place in the canon of English Literature, for many good reasons: the strength of the traditional comic types which the *Monthly Review* prefers to set aside, for example, and its nostalgic atmosphere, redolent of Farquhar and Fielding and Sterne. The achievement of *The Belle's Stratagem* is clearly completely different. Mrs Inchbald thought it 'the most perfect description of the modes and manners of the fashionable world' and Thomas Davies paid a very similar tribute, remarking in addition that Mrs Rackett's speech on the Fine Lady was 'worthy of Cibber or Sheridan'.[54] Studying plays by women and their contribution to the history of feminist awareness, however, we are directed beyond a criticism which pronounces upon apparent permanences, like literary wit, and into the pursuit of more immediate contemporary resonances which, for audiences and readers at the time, were just as vivid.

NOTES

I am very grateful to the British Academy for awarding me a Research Readership 1991–93 to work in the field upon which this essay draws.

1 For details of critical works on eighteenth-century theatre not referenced in this chapter, see 'Guide to Further Reading'.

2 'Preface' to *The Luckey Chance, or an Alderman's Bargain*, *The Works of Aphra Behn*, ed. Janet Todd, 7 vols. (London: William Pickering, 1992–6), *Volume 7. The Plays 1682–1696* (1996), p. 217.

3 See Judith Phillips Stanton, 'Statistical profile of women writing in English from 1660 to 1800' in Frederick M. Keener and Susan E. Lorsch (eds.), *Eighteenth-Century Women and the Arts* (New York: Greenwood Press, 1988), pp. 247–54.

4 Totals based on the directory by David D. Mann and Susan Garland Mann, with Camille Garnier, *Women Playwrights in England, Ireland, and Scotland 1660–1823* (Bloomington and Indianapolis: Indiana University Press, 1996).

5 From my analysis of *The London Stage 1660–1800* (Carbondale: Southern

Illinois University Press): *Part 4: 1747–1776*, ed. George Winchester Stone, Jr, 3 vols. (1962); *Part 5: 1776–1800*, ed. Charles Beecher Hogan, 3 vols. (1968).

6 See Ellen Donkin, 'The Paper War of Hannah Cowley and Hannah More' in Mary Anne Schofield and Cecilia Macheski (eds.), *Curtain Calls: British and American Women and the Theatre, 1660–1820* (Athens: University of Ohio Press, 1991), pp. 143–62.

7 *Gentleman's Magazine*, 48 (1778), 34.

8 [Hannah More], *The Fatal Falsehood* (London: Cadell, 1779), pp. vi–vii, in Henry W. Wells (ed.), *Three Centuries of Drama: English 1751–1800* (New York: Readex Microprint, 1961).

9 *Gentleman's Magazine*, 51 (1781), 33.

10 Jane Spencer, *The Rise of the Woman Novelist: From Aphra Behn to Jane Austen* (Oxford: Basil Blackwell, 1986); Janet Todd, *The Sign of Angellica: Women, Writing, and Fiction, 1660–1800* (London: Virago, 1989).

11 'An Address', *A School for Greybeards; or, The Mourning Bride* (London: Robinson, 1786), p. vii, *The Plays of Hannah Cowley*, ed. Frederick M. Link, 2 vols., facsimile reprint (New York and London: Garland Publishing, 1979), II.

12 Susannah Centlivre, *The Stolen Heiress: or, The Salamanca Doctor Out-Plotted*, II.i, *The Works of the Celebrated Mrs Centlivre* (1761), 3 vols., facsimile reprint (London: Pearson, 1872), I, 338.

13 James Boaden, *Memoirs of the Life of John Philip Kemble Esquire . . .*, 2 vols. (London: Longman, et al., 1825), II, 53.

14 *An Enquiry into the Present State of Polite Learning in Europe, Collected Works of Oliver Goldsmith*, ed. Arthur Friedman, 5 vols. (Oxford: Clarendon Press, 1966), I, 326.

15 Judith Millhouse, 'Company Management' in Robert D. Hume (ed.), *The London Theatre World 1660–1800* (Carbondale: Southern Illinois University Press, 1980), pp. 1–34 (p. 33).

16 Ellen Donkin, *Getting into the Act: Women Playwrights in London 1776–1829* (London and New York: Routledge, 1995).

17 Hannah Cowley, *Who's the Dupe?* (London: Dodsley, et al., 1779), I.iii, pp. 7–8, *Plays of Cowley*, I.

18 'Introduction', Richard W. Bevis (ed.), *Eighteenth-Century Drama: Afterpieces* (London: Oxford University Press, 1970), pp. vii–xvi; Leo Hughes, 'Afterpieces: Or, That's Entertainment' in George Winchester Stone, Jr (ed.), *The Stage and the Page: London's 'Whole Show' in the Eighteenth-Century Theatre* (Berkeley and Los Angeles: University of California Press, 1981), pp. 55–70. Although several women wrote afterpieces, there is no evidence that afterpieces were specially associated with women writers; indeed reviewers of drama were fond of implying the lack of affinity between femininity and the conceptualisation of all major types of drama, since tragedy required learning and loftiness of mind, comedy exuberance, and pantomime a taste for buffoonery. Only two acts long, and very diverse in nature, afterpieces

seem to have attracted novice writers of either sex, men in very much greater numbers than women.

19 Philip H. Highfill, Jr, Kalman A. Burnim, and Edward A. Langhans, *A Biographical Dictionary of Actors, Actresses, Musicians, Dancers, Managers and Other Stage Personnel in London, 1660–1800*, 16 vols. (Carbondale and Edwardsville: Southern Illinois University Press, 1973–93), IX (1984), 28.

20 Highfill, *Biographical Dictionary*, VIII (1982), 383.

21 [Sophia] Lee, *The Chapter of Accidents* (London: Cadell, 1780), 1.i, p. 5, in Wells, *Three Centuries of Drama*.

22 Part 5 of *The London Stage* lists ten benefit performances for players in seven roles between May 1781 and April 1792.

23 Jane Spencer, 'Adapting Aphra Behn: Hannah Cowley's *A School for Greybeards* and *The Lucky Chance*', *Women's Writing*, 2:3 (1995), 221–34.

24 Frances Sheridan, *The Discovery* (1763), 1.ii, *The Plays of Frances Sheridan*, ed. Robert Hogan and Jerry C. Beasley (Newark: University of Delaware Press; London and Toronto: Associated University Presses, 1984), p. 46.

25 See my discussion of a more grotesque embodiment of this second kind in *Fielding and the Woman Question: the Novels of Henry Fielding and Feminist Debate 1700–1750* (Hemel Hempstead: Harvester Wheatsheaf; New York: St Martin's Press, 1989), pp. 71–2. For further discussion of Mary Astell, see ch. 1 of this volume, pp. 31–4. On the use of the term 'feminism' and 'feminist' in the eighteenth-century context, see 'Introduction', pp. 14–15 and note 28, p. 19 above.

26 Alicia LeFanu, *Memoirs of the Life and Writings of Mrs Frances Sheridan* (London: Whittaker, 1824), pp. 224–6.

27 Michèle Barrett, 'Ideology and the Cultural Production of Gender' in Judith Newton and Deborah Rosenfelt (eds.), *Feminist Criticism and Social Change: Sex, Class and Race in Literature and Culture* (New York and London: Methuen, 1985), pp. 65–85.

28 James Boaden, *Memoirs of Mrs Siddons*, 2 vols. (London: Colburn & Bentley, 1831), I, 363.

29 James Boaden, *The Life of Mrs Jordan*, 3rd edn, 2 vols. (London: Bull, 1831), I, 17. For Clare Brant's discussion of the fashionable status of a slightly later actress and writer, Mary Robinson, see ch. 13 in this volume, pp. 290–2.

30 See Garrick's epilogues to *Zingis* and *The Maid of the Oaks*, for example, in *The Theatrical Bouquet: Containing an Alphabetical Arrangement of . . . Prologues and Epilogues* (London: Lowndes, 1778), pp. 87, 94.

31 *Monthly Review*, 50 (1774), 35; *Gentleman's Magazine*, 51 (1781), 57.

32 Cecil Price (ed.), *The Dramatic Works of Richard Brinsley Sheridan*, 2 vols. (Oxford: Clarendon Press, 1973), I, 373–6.

33 Pat Rogers, '"Towering Beyond her Sex": Stature and Sublimity in the Achievement of Sarah Siddons' in Schofield and Macheski, *Curtain Calls*, pp. 48–67; Ellen Donkin, 'Mrs Siddons looks back in Anger: Feminist Historiography for Eighteenth-Century British Theatre' in Janelle G.

Reinelt and Joseph R. Roach (eds.), *Critical Theory and Performance* (Ann Arbor: University of Michigan Press, 1992), pp. 276–90; Spencer, 'Adapting Aphra Behn'; Kristina Straub, *Sexual Suspects: Eighteenth-Century Players and Sexual Ideology* (Princeton University Press, 1992).

34 See Horace Walpole on Mrs Abington in private theatricals at Ham in November 1783 in Wilmarth S. Lewis, et al. (eds.), *The Yale Edition of Horace Walpole's Correspondence*, 48 vols. (New Haven: Yale University Press, 1937–83), XXXIII (1965), 428. For further discussion, see Kimberly Crouch, 'The Public Life of Actresses: Prostitutes or Ladies?' in Hannah Barker and Elaine Chalus (eds.), *Gender in Eighteenth-Century England: Roles, Representations and Responsibilities* (London and New York: Longman, 1997), pp. 58–78.

35 'The patronage of Mrs Abington by ladies of rank was somewhat select' (Boaden, *Siddons*, II, 96); see also *The Early Journals and Letters of Fanny Burney*, ed. Lars Troide, et al. (Oxford: Clarendon Press, 1988–), II, 94.

36 Walpole, *Correspondence*, XXXIII, 564.

37 Highfill, *Biographical Dictionary*, V (1978), 160–75; Boaden, *Siddons*, I, 204.

38 Neil McKendrick, John Brewer, and J. H. Plumb, *The Birth of a Consumer Society: the Commercialization of Eighteenth-Century England* (London: Europa, 1982), p. II.

39 J. H. Plumb, 'The Commercialization of Leisure' in McKendrick, Brewer, and Plumb, *Birth of a Consumer Society*, esp. n.71, pp. 282–3; Marc Baer, *Theatre and Disorder in Late Georgian London* (Oxford: Clarendon Press, 1992), p. 202.

40 Doiley in *Who's the Dupe?*, I.iii, p. 8, and Touchwood in Hannah Cowley, *The Belle's Stratagem* (London: Cadell, 1782), II.i, pp. 26–7, *Plays of Cowley*, I.

41 Highfill, *Biographical Dictionary*, XVI, 175–8; V, 165.

42 On cross-dressing across gender rather than class in popular cultural texts, see Dianne Dugaw on the figure of the female soldier, ch. 12, pp. 268–9, 276–9.

43 Sophia Lee, 'The Chapter of Accidents', MS 526, p. 89, in *Three Centuries of Drama: Plays submitted to the Lord Chamberlain: Huntington Library Larpent Collection*, microfiche edition (New Canaan, CT: Readex, 1991).

44 'L'Education féminine à la scène: les femmes dramaturges dans le Londres Géorgien' in Guyonne Leduc (ed.), *L'Education des femmes en Europe et en Amérique du Nord de la Renaissance à 1848: réalités et représentations* (Paris and Montreal: L'Harmattan, 1997), pp. 337–48.

45 Walpole, *Correspondence*, XXIX (1955), 43–5; 'Preface' to *The Works of Mrs Cowley: Dramas and Poems*, 3 vols. (London: Wilkie & Robinson, 1813), I, xvii; LeFanu, *Memoirs of Frances Sheridan*, pp. 224–5.

46 See Judith Butler, 'Performative Acts and Gender Constitution: an Essay in Phenomenology and Feminist Theory', in Sue-Ellen Case (ed.), *Performing Feminisms: Feminist Critical Theory and Theatre* (Baltimore and London: Johns Hopkins University Press, 1990), pp. 270–82.

47 'Mollies or Men of Mode? Sodomy and the Eighteenth-Century London Stage', *Journal of the History of Sexuality*, I (1990), 33–67.

48 Hannah More, 'David and Goliath' in *Sacred Dramas* (1782), *The Works of Hannah More*, 11 vols. (London: Cadell, 1830), 1, 76, 77. For further discussion of Hannah More, see ch.1, above pp. 40–1.

49 Lawrence E. Klein, 'Gender and the Public/Private Distinction in the Eighteenth Century: Some Questions about Evidence and Analytic Procedure', *Eighteenth-Century Studies*, 29:1 (1995), 97–109.

50 H. T. Swedenberg, Jr, and Alan Roper (gen. eds.), *The Works of John Dryden* (Berkeley, Los Angeles, and London: University of California Press, 1956–), vol. x *Plays: The Tempest; Tyrannick Love; An Evening's Love*, ed. Maximillian E. Novak (1970), 192–3.

51 Highfill, *Biographical Dictionary*, xii (1987), 183.

52 Erin Isikoff, 'Masquerade, Modesty and Comedy in Hannah Cowley's *The Belle's Stratagem*' in Gail Finney (ed.), *Look Who's Laughing: Gender and Comedy* (Langhorne, PA: Gordon & Breach, 1994), pp. 99–117.

53 *Monthly Review*, 48 (1773), 310, 311.

54 Elizabeth Inchbald, 'Preface' to *The Belle's Stratagem* in *The British Theatre*, 25 vols. (London: Longman, et al., 1808), xix, Text 4, p. 4; Thomas Davies, *Memoirs of David Garrick*, 3rd edn, 2 vols. (London: printed for the author, 1781), ii, 322.

CHAPTER 12

Women and popular culture: gender, cultural dynamics, and popular prints

Dianne Dugaw

Women contributed to the eighteenth century's widely circulating popular literature as subjects, performers, and creators of its songs and stories. At the same time, women produced, purveyed, and consumed the cheap broadside and chapbook forms in which these appeared. As consumers, then as now, women received entertainment, instruction, and a sense of life's limits or possibilities from these sources. An extensive body of printed material catered to the lower ranks of an increasingly literate society. This less-studied field of diverse texts ranges outside the boundaries of *belles lettres* and includes folk and broadside songs; short chapbook stories, plays, histories, and romances; fables and homiletic and how-to-do-it works; stage songs and dance tunes; political and religious pamphlets and satires.[1] The generic complexity of this gallimaufry of texts and images speaks to the increasingly pervasive function of printed texts for people's activities at every level, from their cooking and husbandry to their devotions and amusement. Focusing on 'literature', I am concerned here with texts that served aesthetically and instructionally as entertainment – that is, songs and stories.

Popular literature provides a key site for examining the ways that people in the eighteenth century (and, to a degree, even today) move between writing and orality. Culture at the popular level shapes how communities of people imagine events in their lives and find or assign meanings to their experiences. Typically oral forms – for example, songs, tales, jokes, and proverbs – are rooted in conventional patterns of belief and design and based on formulaic themes and narratives. Popular literature, especially in genres meant for performance such as songs and riddles, is full of recurring patterns: familiar turns of narrative, theme, and language; stock characters and images; standard metres and tunes. Convention reflects value and reiterates a community sense of rightness: the bounds of what people generally find familiar, typical, and expected. These genres value innovation less than recognisability. While workable conventionality does include accommodations for novelty, surprise, and eccentricity, conventional arts unfold with a high degree of predictability.

Linked to popular literature's conventionality and ties to orality is its anonymity, which in many circumstances stems from the commonality of cultural materials: the longstanding tale, song, proverb, and so on, passed on and reworked for generations, is not so much 'mine' as 'ours'. But anonymity results from other factors as well, foremost of which is social rank. Printed materials intended for widely popular as opposed to ruling-class consumption were not esteemed as 'art'. Created largely by people from the lower ranks, popular literature generally is both more ephemeral in its contemporary marketing, and rarely preserved by historical study. In the eighteenth century, an additional factor contributed to anonymity: the sharply satiric sensibility and the threat of retaliation that accompanied much popularly circulating literature. Authors of politically topical songs, squibs, and stories typically withheld their identities not only to protect themselves, but as part of the satirical dynamic of such works within the context of public debate. Anonymity presents a conundrum for a tradition of literary history that until recently was premised on the study of authorship.

Scholars of folksong and myth have attended to popular materials since the nineteenth century; historians and literary scholars have turned to them more recently, with different questions. Scholarship of an antiquarian bent, developing from collections of prints, drew nineteenth-century folklorists who prized anonymity and sought to uncover in such materials longstanding cultural themes, functions, and structures of thought. Looking for the cultural import of popular works, such recent scholars of broadside and chapbook literature as Leslie Shepard and Natascha Würzbach explore especially the interplay between printed forms and oral traditions.[2]

In recent decades historians have studied this literature of the lower ranks with an eye to uncovering records and facts about the publishing industry. Surveys of registries and records by such scholars as Margaret Spufford, John Barnard, and Maureen Bell sift through a wealth of data about producers, purveyors, and consumers of early modern prints, and the precise forms and functions of the latter. Joy Wiltenburg brings to this literature questions of power and rule. E. P. Thompson has also brought to analysis of nineteenth-century working-class history a consideration of customary behaviour, of popular practices and rituals, that bridges some of the gaps between the thematic orientation of folklorists and the fact- and evidence-based concerns of historians.[3]

Recent literary scholarship rethinks boundaries between (so-called) popular and polite literatures even as it re-examines previously eclipsed authors. Following the lead of John Richetti, eighteenth-century literary critics have turned to popular levels of prose fiction, especially by such women novelists as Aphra Behn and Eliza Haywood.[4] These successful and accomplished authors had over time been relegated to the fringe category 'popular' literature that marks off the ephemeral from the universal. The rediscovery of women writers has thus entailed the investigation of a whole realm of overlooked texts. Finally, work on the relation of literature to other arts by such scholars as Pat Rogers and Ronald Paulson has brought analysis of prints and texts as linked to theatre, opera, music, and visual forms.[5]

Varieties of printed texts set before us categories of class structure. Eighteenth-century prints varied in process and price, and represent gradations of economic class. Cheap woodcut broadsides with anonymous ballads or folk tales catered to a humbler audience – serving maids, shopkeepers, apprentices, farmworkers, soldiers, and so on. More expensive engraved prints with stories and songs by well-known authors and composers catered to people with both money and leisure to spend at the theatres, coffee-houses, and pleasure-gardens. By the Georgian era, however, readers of English included large numbers of people from all levels, even from the lower ranks. With the development of the Charity Schools and, by the end of the century, other moral and educational reform movements, literacy was widespread in Britain. After the Jacobite defeat in 1745, literacy increased in Scotland in the programme to replace Scots and especially Gaelic culture with English.[6] The miscellany of texts – contradictory, fragmentary, and difficult to read – gives a glimpse of the social underside to the world of *belles lettres* more cogently presented in our literary histories.

WOMEN'S INVOLVEMENT

We can only surmise the precise extent of women's involvement in many corners of a milieu in which authorial anonymity is the rule. Yet varied evidence attests to women's importance in the creation and currency of popular literature. In the middle and upper ranks, they were key participants in music-making in the home as well as in domestic literary reading and performance. At the lower ranks, women were principal keepers of oral traditions of songs and stories, as collectors from Walter Scott to our own day attest. At the least prestigious level of printing

(woodcut broadsides and chapbooks), numerous printers' wives participated in the trade and, upon widowhood, might operate the shops alone
or marry master apprentices who would then enter the management.
Women sold and performed songs at streetcorners, fairs, and theatres, as
contemporary prints of vendors repeatedly corroborate (see figure 6).
Women's textual presence as topics and addressees speaks to their
importance as consumers in the widening market of popular literature.[7]

BALLADS AND POPULAR SONGS

In the eighteenth century, popular songs at all social levels functioned
more variously and more pervasively than they do now. Today songs are
primarily entertainment or ceremonial forms, more likely lyrical than
narrative, more imaginative than documentary. For earlier Anglo-
American culture, songs had additional functions. Often integrally tied
to events, many ballads were journalistic, both informing people about
the news of the day and satirically commenting upon it. Balladry of the
early modern era might be thought to combine four separate media in
our culture: (1) popular songs intended to entertain; (2) print and broad-
cast journalism, meant to inform; (3) political cartoons that lampoon and
satirise people and happenings; and (4) stand-up comedy routines that
likewise ridicule, rail, and critique. Popular ballads will be discussed here
with a focus on two thematic types: those celebrating the woman who
dresses as a man to go to sea or to war, and those lampooning the 1720
South Sea Bubble investment scheme.

Musical traditions map cultural values and customs linked to socio-
economic rank. At the most widely popular level, broadside songs rooted
in oral traditions were sold on the streets. Songs drew on traditional
stereotypes and characters: ballads of Robin Hood; love stories with
well-known motifs such as 'Patient Griselda'; songs of seduction or of
pranksters' comic escapades. Other ballads presented (usually sensational) news items: a recent murder, the exploits of a doomed criminal,
the account of a land or sea battle. Customers bought the crudely illustrated ballad sheets to spark their own performances of the songs; for a
marginally literate public the broadsides often served more as *aides-
memoire* than as thoroughly legible texts. Many songs continued in oral
tradition long after their season of print popularity ended, passed on
from one generation to the next. Ballads likely to persist were those that
conformed most predictably to conventional forms and topics.[8]

Images of women in the popular sung and printed ballads include

ROGER TEASDELL & M.ʳˢ PARKER.

Pub.ᵈ Sep.ᵗ 16 1813. by R.S.Kirby, 11 London House Yard.

Figure 6 Portrait by M. Laroon of Mrs Parker, a well-known ballad-singer and seller of the 1680s, from a print published by R. S. Kirkby (1813). Photograph courtesy of the Harvard Theatre Collection.

fictionalised depictions of royalty, especially Queen Elizabeth I, and such recognisable 'ladies' of history as Henry VIII's third wife, Jane Seymour; Queen Eleanor, wife to Henry II; and Eleanor's nemesis Rosamund, Henry's legendary mistress. The ballads also celebrate figures of more fairytale cast such as 'Lord Bateman's Daughter' or exotically imagined princesses from romance traditions. Other ballad heroines represent social categories who would have been potential customers. Merchants' daughters figure prominently, often as the heroines of adventure and love stories or as the victims of cruel lovers or parents. Working women appear, both positively and negatively presented: wily serving girls who outwit silly tailors or rapacious squires; villainous mothers from the common ranks who betray their husbands, murder their children, give birth to monsters, or see ghostly and devilish apparitions; and milkmaids who succumb to wanted or unwanted seductions.

The female warrior, a conventionalised heroine of some 120 separate ballads that flourished as 'pop-song hits' in print and oral tradition from the Elizabethan era to the Victorian age, supplies a vigorous case study for examining the images and roles of women at the popular level. This heroine and the commercial ballads in which we find her exemplify how the ballads circulated, and demonstrate the interplay between these imaginative forms and actual people and events.[9] We may note with surprise how a seemingly subversive figure provided 'top hit' fare in a highly conventional genre for more than a century and a half.

The female warrior surfaces with some frequency in popular literature before the nineteenth century, especially in comical stories and romantic ballads. This popular heroic type ventured to sea or to war disguised as a man – usually for the sake of a lover. A two-sided heroine, she is motivated by loyal love for a soldier or a sailor. At the same time, this adventurous girl knows what she wants and sets out to get it. An example of the type is 'Jack Monroe', which in late eighteenth-century versions begins:

> In Chatham town there liv'd a worthy merchantman,
> He had an only daughter as you shall understand,
> This lady she was courted by many a noble knight,
> But there was none but Jack the Sailor could gain her hearts delight.
>   Could gain, &c.[10]

Her parents separate her from her sailor sweetheart; in defiance, the disguised heroine follows him to sea and to 'the wars of Germany', eventually revealing her identity to him on the battlefield and nursing his wounds – after she has been awarded war medals and, in some versions, 'a captain's commission'. The song ends with the happy marriage of the couple. This ballad was republished on both sides of the Atlantic well into the nineteenth century and continues to be sung by traditional singers and revived by recording artists in our own day.[11]

Ballads of this type are success stories. The protagonist is a model of beauty and pluck, deserving in romance, able in war, and rewarded in both: 'a fair and vertuous Maid', 'a virtuous damsel', 'a fearless maiden fair', and so on. She combines a romantic and heroic ideal of womanhood.

Female warrior ballads contain elements of fictional romance stories that carry from one example of the type to another. Yet, for all their conventionality, specific songs often have ties to actual people. Thus, a ballad from the mid seventeenth century sings of a 'Gallant She-Souldier',

Who for the Love that she bore to her Husband, attired her selfe in Man's Apparell and so became a Souldier, and marcht along with him through Ireland, France, and Spain, and never was known to be a Woman till at the last she being quartered neer unto Tower-hill, in London, where she brought forth a gallant Man-child, to the wonder of all her fellow-Souldiers.[12]

Beneath the ballad text, the broadside supplies information about its real-life protagonist: 'All that are desirous to see the young Souldier and his Mother, let them repair to the sign of the Black-Smith's-Armes, in East Smithfield, neere unto Towerhill, in London, and inquire fore Mr Clarke, for that was the Woman's name.' Popular ballads often had as subjects actual women of both high and low rank as well as fanciful heroines of purely imagined provenance. Fictional and factual stories were alike submitted to conventionalising paradigms. As I and others have shown, women at all levels, but especially at the lower ranks, resorted to male disguise in a range of circumstances.[13] A surprising number of reports reveal poor women passing as men in early modern armies and even in the navies of Europe and Euro-America. Generations of women familiar with songs on the subject would likely conceive of their male disguise equally through the fact of pay available to men but not to themselves, and through well-known ballads celebrating the ploy.

Anonymously created ballads like 'Jack Monroe', catering to the lower ranks, appeared on woodcut broadsides that supplied only the words; either no tune was mentioned, or the title of another tune to which the text could be sung was supplied. (The conventional metre made ballad texts amenable to a stock of well-known tunes.) On the streets or at markets, fairs, executions, and similar gatherings, the pedlar – often a woman – would sing a ballad to give prospective buyers the tune.

Alongside the thriving trade in ballads aimed at a poorer public, ephemeral and highly conventionalised popular forms were likewise sold at the middle ranks – to audiences who could afford more expensive products and whose enjoyment and use were more literate. Here, authors were somewhat less anonymous. At this 'Grub-street' level of publishing, surveyed in literary and musical works of scholarship, we encounter some recognisable literary names: Aphra Behn, Thomas D'Urfey, Ned Ward, Daniel Defoe, Eliza Haywood, Allan Ramsay, John Gay, and so on.[14] While women certainly contributed to this mid-level of print culture, the anonymity of pieces published in periodicals, short pamphlets, and single sheets makes identifiable authors the great exception. Much remains to be done to analyse the nature, function, and provenance of such works as Susannah Centlivre's chapbook poem on the South Sea Company stock scandal, 'A Woman's Case: in an Epistle to Charles Joye, Esq; Deputy-Governor of the South-Sea', or John Gay's enduringly popular ballad 'Sweet William's Farewell to Black-eyed Susan'.[15]

Such popular texts are often derivative and topical. The songs, usually sentimental or satiric, derive from theatrical dramas and afterpieces, and appear with tunes and accompaniments for home performances. Prose narratives – Eliza Haywood's serial two-part novelette *The Masqueraders* is an example – stand in the tradition of Behn's novellas and unfold with a mixture of sizzling suspense and sentimental pathos and warning as they plot the adventures of their sexually preyed-upon heroines.[16] These songs and narratives inhabit a border between two realms: on the one hand, the highly oral and traditional popular culture of the lower ranks; on the other, the so-called 'polite' culture of works sanctioned in their day and (especially) retrospectively.

Given the subsequent development of literary criticism as well as 'taste', several factors have contributed to the ephemerality of eighteenth-century popular literature at this mid-level: the anonymity and small scale of most works; their often topical nature; their function as domestic entertainment (rather than public performance); and their audience – a wide-ranging purchasing public of women as well as men at the middle ranks. The spate of texts – songs, short plays, and poems – that appeared at the time of the South Sea Bubble exemplify this level of popular culture.

The South Sea Company was founded to carry out English trade as stipulated by the Treaty of Utrecht (1713) after the War of the Spanish Succession. By 1719 the company turned to speculative stockjobbing, the buying and selling of investment stocks, in order to convert some £50 million of government debt into marketable stock shares. At the start, the company generated substantial profits by manipulating stock values and bribing key players in parliament and at court. In the early months of 1720 the British public responded with a frenzy of stock purchasing. Values rose wildly, reaching a peak in the summer of 1720. However, parliamentary moves to regulate the marketing of stocks and foreign withdrawals of investment triggered the collapse of the expanding 'bubble'. By the autumn of 1720 the first modern stockmarket crash came amidst a ministry shakeup and an official cover-up. Responding to this drama and the newly capitalising world of markets, stocks, bubbles, and crashes, people fashioned the story for themselves in popular songs, plays, and poems.[17]

During the decade of events connected with the South Sea Company, anonymous songs appeared: 'The South Sea Whim', 'The Raree Show Ballad or the English Mississippi', 'The Broken South Sea Taylor's Ditty', and so on.[18] Their composers, purveyors, and singers were from the upper- and especially middle-classes, people musically literate enough to fancy ballads accompanied by printed tunes (as a number were), and moneyed enough to pay for the engraved (rather than woodcut) broadsides that such notation required.

Buyers of South Sea Bubble ballads, hearing the songs in a theatrical or coffee-house performance, would buy the sheets so as to sing and hear the songs again, accompanied by their own viols, keyboards, and flutes. These prints served a literate endeavour: a moment of reading text and notation into performance. The linguistically and musically literate purchasers from the ruling and business classes were precisely the players who were winning and losing in a newly fashioning economic system of projected value, paper money, and speculative investment.[19]

On the engraved sheets, information as to authorship is likely to survive in some way. One of several published versions of the piece may contain an attribution, as with Thomas D'Urfey's 'Hubble Bubbles'.[20] An author may include a song that originally circulated anonymously in a compilation of works and thereby claim it, the case with Ned Ward's 'The South Sea Ballad'.[21] Or the song may be found among other autograph or attributed manuscripts, as with Ann Finch's 'Stock-jobbing

Ladies'.[22] Finch's authorship is known owing to her prominence as a literary figure from the ruling class. Authors from the middle and lower ranks rarely leave manuscripts – autographed or otherwise – that find their way into archival collections to preserve for posterity the identities of their authors. Even at this middling level, many popular works remain anonymous or, conversely, are claimed by or for more than one author. Thus, the name of the author of 'The South Sea Ballad, written by a Lady' eludes us.[23] And scholars continue to puzzle over the variously attributed pieces in the miscellanies of Swift and Pope, whose exact authorship – by these two, or by their Scriblerian colleagues such as Gay, Arbuthnot, or Parnell – may never be worked out.

Ballads on the South Sea Bubble address an audience of women as well as men, from a broad range of society's middle ranks. While the songs did not circulate on the streets on the woodcut broadsides popular among the poorest readers, they did appear in such widely accessible venues as the stage, public fairs, and book stalls. The South Sea Bubble prompted a taste for singing in a new vocabulary about 'stocks', 'ventures', 'scrips', 'shares', and 'credit'.

Anne Finch exemplifies the *literateurs* in or close to the governing or investing class who commented anonymously in the popular press upon such topical events. The Bubble especially engaged numbers of women, who, with the emergence of stock trading and individual investment opportunities, could enter an economic market of moveable value.[24] As her satirical ballad makes clear, Finch did not observe this first runaway stockmarket sanguinely. Her response resonated with the general perception, for her satirical little song quickly caught the public fancy, circulating anonymously in a range of forms and venues. In addition to the engraved broadside songsheets that conveyed text and tune together with bass and obbligato parts, the verses also appear alone on a number of prints, including the elaborate collages of texts and images published in folios by Carington Bowles near the time of the crash.[25]

Finch's 'Stock-jobbing Ladies' satirises the giddy social mixing at the height of the Bubble in 1720 (example 1). Such money-making afforded a new independence to women who here lay aside their fashionable 'ombre' and 'basset' playing-cards for the new 'games' of buying and selling stocks. Finch sees the ladies pursuing wealth by the new forms of 'gaming' in dubious company indeed. Images of games mixed with puns on financial terms (here 'divide' and 'share') are typical in ballads about the South Sea Company, especially those referring to the bubble.[26]

Example 1 Anne Finch, 'Stock-jobbing Ladies' (1720)

Ombre and Basset laid aside,
   new Games employ the Fair:
and Brokers all those Hours divide,
   which lovers us'd to share
    . . .

With Jews and Gentiles undismay'd,
   Young tender Virgins mix;
Of Whiskers nor of Beards afraid,
   Nor all their cousening Tricks.[27]

'The Stock-jobbing Ladies' foregrounds a longstanding tradition of anti-Semitism that makes its way into South Sea Bubble songs. Both reflecting and shaping popular perceptions, the ballads emphasise shifting social relations identified by culture and gender. The number of Jews – Spanish-speaking Sephardi, in particular – apparently did increase in London financial circles in the first decade of the eighteenth century. But they were never more than a small minority in South Sea Company transactions (usually 5 to 10 per cent of subscribers) – albeit a culturally conspicuous one.[28] Even more noticeable, between 1710 and 1720 women increasingly appear on the subscription lists. Finch's ballad responds to this new world of 'stock-jobbing ladies', while it takes up centuries-old gender motifs and anti-Semitic traditions.

South Sea Bubble ballads treated new financial concepts and modes in familiar terms, which included mock-heroic parodies of satirised ministers; images of longstanding ethnic rivalries and prejudices;

Example 2 Anon., 'South Sea Ballad' (1720)

conventional gender, occupational, and class caricatures; and traditional biblical tales, moral warnings, and proverbial wit. Ballads also brought key features of this newly capitalising and speculative world of value into public parlance as people responded with heady dreams and apprehensive worries. As 'A Lady' declares in her 'South Sea Ballad' (1720): 'This Gold sanded Ocean is not like the rest / But is quite of a different Nature possest' (example 2).[29] Using familiar images, songs inevitably addressed the theme of a world of changing values and conditions.

With a rather free-wheeling adaptation of biblical imagery, this 'Lady's' anonymous ballad voices the wildly alchemical hopes spurring the pyramid-scheme of investment that created the Bubble.

> All the town is so eager their fortune to try,
> That no body can the temptation deny;
> So carefully laid is the scheme of the gin,
> That some of the Parsons themselves are drawn in:
>> Which of these would choose an Archbishop to be,
>> To refuse a Directorship in the *South-Sea*.

The foreboding tone of 'The South Sea Ballad' suggests that it was written towards late summer, just as investment fortunes were about to collapse. The song ends with an ominously ironic – if slightly scrambled – biblical allusion:

> Like *Pharaoh's* lean kine that devoured the fat,
> It has knock'd down the puny contrivances flat;
> But if I mistake not, I've read that his host
> And himself in the *Red-Sea* were utterly lost:
>> He thought to get riches, and why should not we
>> Remember the *Red* when we cross the *South-Sea*.[30]

This song, like Finch's, focuses on the social mixing that the event precipitated: ''Tis a comical sight to behold the deceit / Of all ranks of men met each other to cheat.' The song follows the developments of the summer closely, if with wry detachment, sceptically commenting on the social transformations that particularly affected 'the fair':

> What numbers of upstart figures we meet,
> Set up by stock-jobbing in every street!
> They're so fond of their *Arms,* when they come to approach
> They can hardly for staring get into their coach:
>> But when we examine their true pedigree,
>> We trace their original from the *South-Sea.*

This ballad, like Finch's, takes a woman's perspective, drawing attention to the marginality of that vantage. Both songs use images drawn from biblical traditions and from popular lore and prejudice that were readily available to women of their social rank.

PROSE FORMS

As developments traced above have already suggested, the eighteenth century witnessed a cultural shift premised on increased literacy, cheaper printing, a populace with more access to currency, and the increasing substitution of orality and performance at every level by individual reading both for information and pleasure. Prose was in the ascendant. Topical events were increasingly rendered in prose accounts rather than in satiric verses and popular ballads. Fictions likewise appeared in prose and, following from Behn, such writers as Manley, Defoe, Haywood, presented readers with early examples of the modern novel. As scholars have convincingly established in recent decades, women authors writing for a female audience, especially from the middle ranks, crucially shaped this emerging form. 'Below' the level of the printed leatherbound novels of Behn, Defoe, and Haywood, we find the chapbook narratives – fictional, semi-fictional, and non-fictional – that were composed, published, and sold alongside the ballad sheets hawked on the streets of London and carried about the countryside in the packs of pedlars.

Through the eighteenth century, personal biographies became sought after at every rank. Indeed, as Johnson's *Lives of the Poets* (1779–81) and Boswell's *Life of Johnson* (1791) show at the polite level, the individual character and history took on new meaning for readers and writers.[31] In chapbook printing, picaresque rogue histories abounded alongside biblical stories and saints' lives, spiritual conversions, biographies of success and eccentricity, and didactic stories of failure and warning.[32] As with popular songs and songsheets, the printed forms of prose narratives fall into recognisable categories suggesting a range of readers, from those who could pay more for larger, leather-bound books, to those who could only pay for unbound chapbooks, some as short as eight pages.

Published 'lives' of female warriors, coexistent with broadside ballads
on the topic, exemplify materials intended for these distinct audiences.
Such tales were a commercial commonplace in eighteenth-century
popular literature, especially among publishers of chapbooks catering to
the ballad-buying public. Among the heroines are the relatively well-
known Christian Davies, Hannah Snell, Mary Anne Talbot, and Mary
Lacy, whose stories have received scholarly attention.[33] Whatever docu-
mentable 'facts' and particulars lie behind the accounts, the published
stories – along with those of a number of other cross-dressing women –
follow patterns of narrative and thematic convention, borrowing epi-
sodic structure and the roguish, trickster heroine from the picaresque,
combined with traces of the romance elements of the ballads. Certain
features of character and plot recur as standard tropes: the heroine's
independent spirit; her masked pursuit of a husband or lover; her homo-
erotically charged courting of women; proofs of her service and valour;
roguish financial ploys and disguising tricks; battle wounds to parts of
her body that suggestively point to her womanhood and threaten her disguise; and so on. The delicate sensibilities of novelistic heroines incon-
gruously weave through longer accounts aimed at higher-level buyers.
Chapbooks cut to the actions of their robust protagonists.

The best-known and variously published account celebrates the
'adventures' of Hannah Snell and began to be printed in 1750. Snell was
an historical person, a woman reportedly from Worcester, England, who
achieved notoriety in the mid-eighteenth century with narratives of her
fighting in disguise in the army and navy. Her 'adventures' show the
diverse ways that popular literature circulated among readers. The
newspaper publisher Robert Walker produced longer and shorter (more
and less expensive) versions, while *The Gentleman's Magazine* and other
periodicals ran short reports of her story. Soon broadside and chapbook
publishers in London and elsewhere began to make cheap versions of
Snell's story, some as short as eight pages.[34] Thus, Snell prospered as a
heroine alongside the ballad female warriors for several generations of
readers. Her 'life', reshaped in the writing, became an important heroic
mode in the popular imagination, along the lines of Annie Oakley's and
Amelia Earhart's in later eras. Popular literature promoted Snell's story
just as it took up such fictional heroines as Richardson's Pamela or
Defoe's Moll Flanders, whose narratives likewise circulated in pamphlet
and chapbook form.

Snell as a person was continually understood by her contemporaries
through the celebrity of her life. The diarist James Woodforde writes of

Figure 7 Portrait of Hannah Snell (*c.* 1750). Photograph courtesy of the William Andrews Clark Memorial Library, University of California, Los Angeles.

meeting Snell, then a pedlar, in the neighbourhood of his Norfolk parsonage, describing her, with considerable inflation of the accounts, as the 'famous woman in Men's Cloaths, by name Hannah Snell, who was 21 years a common soldier in the Army'. He remarks that 'Cousin Lewis has mounted guard with her abroad. She went in the Army by the name of John Gray. She has a Pension from the Crown now of 18.15.0 per annum and the liberty of wearing Men's Cloaths and also a Cockade in her Hat, which she still wears.'[35]

Complex connections and disjunctions lie between actual female warriors like Hannah Snell, their popularly circulating 'life' stories, and the conventional song motif in oral and broadside traditions we have already examined. The lived experiences of these women of the lower ranks stand in vital, but unclear, relation to what was written, printed and sold. The interesting question is not simply to what extent Snell's published 'lives' correspond in their details to what happened to her as a soldier. The literariness of virtually all such accounts presupposes that what 'facts' there are filter up through the texts only with considerable transformation. The more pertinent lines of inquiry, especially regarding stories about women of the 'lower' classes, concern representation and reception: how are we to read this account as it reveals the woman represented through (or in spite of) the representation? How are we to relate the representation to the experience of women reading?[36]

Publisher Robert Walker made no pretence that Snell recorded her account by her own hand, for *The Female Soldier* opens with pointed reference to Snell's inability to write: an affidavit as to the truthfulness of the story signed by Snell with an 'X', 'her mark'. Moreover, the affidavit notwithstanding, it is apparent from the accounts themselves that much in them is notably conventional and probably did not happen. But the definition of 'truthfulness' for a popular audience at that time includes, and perhaps even requires, such conventionality. Uniqueness is not valued over what is traditionally fitting; departures from convention would be scarcely credible – indeed, 'false'.

For the historical Hannah Snell, popular literature offered opportunities and restrictions simultaneously. Her 'life', both in the living and the telling, comprised a number of means by which she sought to make her way in a moneyed economy. She, like other women, cross-dressed for financial reasons. She would have received pay, first in the army and navy, then for Robert Walker's use of her story, adding these sums to what she mustered for herself doing military exercises as an entre'acte in the theatres. At the same time, the 'adventures' of her story on the one hand identify her as a roguish *picara*, and on the other, draw on the long conventionalised and popular female warrior heroine of ballad and chapbook narratives, whether fiction, non-fiction, or semi-fiction.

In observing that the prose stories, like the ballad narratives, unfold in highly predictable ways from one example to the next, we do not simply expose their inauthenticity. Nor, whatever the 'facts' of Snell's personal history, can we usefully reduce the obvious fictions of her narrative to evidence that she is a fake and the story some cover for lack of a story.[37] Conventional and derivative female warrior tales, whether told by a ventriloquising narrator such as that in Walker's account of Snell or by an apparently literate female warrior such as Mary Lacy represent not simply what happened, but what people wished and needed to read. Over time, the songs and stories of female warriors influenced people's lives, providing values and images, prompts and 'covers' for what stories they could imagine living out, and how they might do so. Snell herself doubtless envisioned her transvestite course of action thanks in part to songs and tales she heard as a girl and young woman.

The uneasy narrator of Robert Walker's *The Female Soldier* is at pains to enforce in the story what is socially normative, despite the fact that these 'adventures' can only adhere to and reinforce class and gender norms in a most eccentric way. Looking for precedents, the narrator places Snell in the company of celebrated amazons of *belles lettres* like 'Cleopatra' and 'Semiramis' on the one hand, and the pastoral tradition's 'Arcadian Shepherdesses' on the other. Then it is to the novel's virtuous 'Pamela' that Snell is compared: 'the real *Pamella*' whose 'Adventures and Virtues' surpass those of Richardson's 'romantick' and 'counterfeit' heroine.[38] But Snell's real predecessors come from literature's lower ranks: balladry's Pollys and Gallant She-Souldiers, and such chapbook *picaras* as Long Meg of Westminster, 'Moll Cutpurse', the female pirates Ann Bonny and Mary Read, and so on.[39]

The diverse 'adventures' of Hannah Snell illustrate the contradictions and paradoxes in the popular literature of the eighteenth century. With widespread literacy and an explosion of publishing, the period leaves us an enormous heap of cultural records for an economically and socially complex world. Popular publishing brought onto paper tradition-based literatures that represented women and men whose lives only marginally intersected with the forms and narratives to which writers of the ruling orders gave voice.

Attention to gender in popular forms disturbs our too-frequent identification of womanhood with class-based ideals of 'femininity', domesticity, and propriety. Moreover, as images and voices of women surface amidst the conventionalities of popular forms – ballads, songs, formulaic life-histories – we glimpse the profoundly social and communally shared rules, outlines, and expectations that set the boundaries for individual women and men and 'gender' their stories. Popular literature, through its ruptures and self-contradictions, opens to view the predilections and values of the culture's deeply held traditions. As it does so, it invaluably widens our frame of historical reference, notably in terms of social class. Furthermore, study of the popular sphere alerts us to those aesthetic and intellectual habits of evaluation through which our scholarship tends unwittingly to replicate systems of rank, and which narrow and distort our understanding of the past.

NOTES

1 Broadsides are single sheets, usually printed on one side only of cheap paper; chapbooks are small booklets, usually made up of single sheets folded into four or eight, and sold uncut. Both forms were sold by hawkers and pedlars.

2 Leslie Shepard, *The Broadside Ballad* (London: Herbert Jenkins, 1962; rpt. Hatboro, PA: Legacy, 1978) and *The History of Street Literature* (Newton Abbot: David & Charles, 1973); Natascha Würzbach, *The Rise of the English Street Ballad, 1550–1650*, trans. Gayna Walls (Cambridge University Press, 1990). See also: Dianne Dugaw, *Warrior Women and Popular Balladry, 1650–1850* (Cambridge University Press, 1989; rpt. University of Chicago Press, 1996), esp. chs. 1–3.

3 See, for example: Margaret Spufford, *Small Books and Pleasant Histories* (Athens: University of Georgia Press, 1981); John Barnard and Maureen Bell, 'The Early Seventeenth-Century York Book Trade and John Foster's Inventory of 1616', *Proceedings of the Leeds Philosophical and Literary Society*, 24:2 (1994); Maureen Bell, 'Mary Westwood, Quaker Publisher', *Publishing History*, 23 (1988), 46–54; Joy Wiltenburg, *Disorderly Women and Female Power in the Street Literature of Early Modern England and Germany* (Charlottesville: University Press of Virginia, 1992); E. P. Thompson, *Customs in Common* (New York: New Press, 1991; rpt. Harmondsworth: Penguin Books, 1993).

4 John J. Richetti, *Popular Fiction Before Richardson* (Oxford: Clarendon Press, 1969), and see ch. 9 of this volume.

5 Pat Rogers, *Literature and Popular Culture in Eighteenth-Century England* (Brighton: Harvester, 1985); Ronald Paulson, *Popular and Polite Art in the Age of Hogarth and Fielding* (South Bend, IN: University of Notre Dame Press, 1979).

6 Janet Sorensen, *The Grammar on Empire, the Figure of the Nation: Language and Cultural Identity in Eighteenth-Century Britain* (Cambridge University Press, forthcoming).

7 On women in the middle and upper ranks, see Richard Leppert, *Music and Image* (Cambridge University Press, 1988) and *The Sight of Sound* (Berkeley: University of California Press, 1993). Nineteenth-century ballad scholar Francis Child underscores the prominence of women in song traditions as he inquires of known early ballad sources, all of them women: 'Where is the manuscript of Mrs Brown of Falkland . . . Where are the Mrs Farquhars, the Mrs Browns, the Mrs Arnots, the Miss Rutherfords themselves, and the nurses who taught them ballads?' (review from *The Nation*, 7 (3 September 1868), 193). For women as pedlars of songs and prints, see Marcellus Laroon's images in Sean Shesgreen (ed.), *The Criers and Hawkers of London: Engravings and Drawings by Marcellus Laroon* (Stanford University Press, 1990), pp. 101, 151, 187; and William Hogarth's 'Enraged Musician' and 'Industry and Idleness (11)' in Ronald Paulson, abr. Anne Wilde, *Hogarth: His Life, Art, and Times* (New Haven: Yale University Press, 1974), pp. 185, 255. For a full discussion of women's involvement in the print trades, see ch. 6 of this volume.

8 For a sampling of ballads, see William Chappell and J. Woodfall Ebsworth (eds.), *The Roxburghe Ballads*, 9 vols. (Hertford: Printed for the Ballad Society by S. Austin & Sons, 1871–99). On the interplay of written and oral forms, see G. Malcolm Laws, *American Balladry from British Broadsides* (Philadelphia: American Folklore Society, 1957); Robert S. Thomson, 'The Development of the Broadside Ballad Trade and its Influence upon the Transmission of English Folksongs', PhD dissertation, University of Cambridge, 1974.

9 For a study of this heroine, see Dugaw, *Warrior Women*.

10 See northern broadsides at Harvard University printed by Angus (25242.85F) and Morren (25276.33, no.5).

11 For some of the hundreds of folk versions of this ballad, see Dianne Dugaw, 'The Female Warrior Heroine in Anglo-American Popular Balladry', PhD dissertation, University of California, Los Angeles, 1982, pp. 613–16.

12 *Roxburghe Ballads*, VII, 728.

13 See Dugaw, *Warrior Women*, and '"Female Sailors Bold": Transvestite Heroines and the Markers of Gender and Class' in Margaret Creighton and Lisa Norling (eds.), *Iron Men and Wooden Women: Gender and Seafaring in the Atlantic World, 1700–1920* (Baltimore and London: Johns Hopkins University Press, 1996), pp. 34–54; Julie Wheelwright, *Amazons and Military Maids* (London: Pandora Press, 1989); Rudolph Dekker and Lotte van de Pohl, *The Tradition of Female Transvestism in Early Modern Europe* (London: Macmillan, 1989); Suzanne Stark, *Female Tars* (Annapolis: Naval Institute Press, 1996). For discussion of Charlotte Charke's cross-dressing, see ch. 9 of this volume, pp. 197–8.

14 See Pat Rogers, *Grub Street: Studies in a Subculture* (London: Methuen, 1972).

15 Susanna Centlivre, *A Woman's Case: in an Epistle to Charles Joye, Esq; Deputy-Governor of the South-Sea* (London: E. Curll, 1720). Gay's ballad appeared in a 1720 collection of his poetry and on broadsides of the 1720s which set the text to several tunes. The song continued to be printed into the nineteenth

century and is still found among singers today. See Dianne Dugaw, 'The Politics of Culture: John Gay and Popular Ballads' in Tom Cheesman and Sigrid Rieuwerts (eds.), *Ballads into Books* (Berne: Peter Lang, 1997), pp. 190–2.

16 [Eliza Haywood], *The Masqueraders; or Fatal Curiosity: being the Secret History of a Late Amour*, parts I and II (London: J. Roberts, 1724, 1725). Both parts quickly appeared in various editions. They are reprinted in *Masquerade Novels of Eliza Haywood* (Delmar, New York: Scholars' Facsimiles and Reprints, 1986).

17 On the South Sea Bubble, see P. G. M. Dickson, *The Financial Revolution in England* (London: Macmillan, 1967); John Carswell, *The South Sea Bubble* (London: Cresset, 1960; rev. edn, Gloucestershire: Alan Sutton, 1993); Larry Neal, *The Rise of Financial Capitalism* (Cambridge University Press, 1990), chs. 4, 5.

18 Broadside (1711), Harvard University, Kress-Goldsmith Collection, 4721.17; Broadside with tune, British Library, H.1601 (348); Broadside with tune, British Library, H.1601 (209), 'sung by Mr Platt at Sadlers Wells'. Bart Platt was a singer who performed in the 1720s and 1730s in venues at Bartholomew Fair, Penkethman's and Norris's Great Theatrical Booth, Goodman's Fields, &c. See Ben Ross Schneider, Jr, *Index to 'The London Stage 1660–1800'* (Carbondale: Southern Illinois University Press, 1979), p. 669.

19 Because of their ties to folksong, the earlier, woodcut broadside ballads catering to a less sophisticated audience have been more extensively studied than the later songs on engraved sheets that include the ballads on the South Sea Company affair. Useful works to consult include such catalogues as Claude Simpson, *The British Broadside Ballad and Its Music* (New Brunswick, NJ: Rutgers University Press, 1966); Edyth Backus, *Catalogue of Music in the Huntington Library Printed before 1801* (San Marino, CA: Huntington Library, 1949); William C. Smith, *A Bibliography of the Musical Works published by John Walsh during the Years 1695–1720* (London: Bibliographical Society, 1948).

20 Broadside with tune, Harvard University, Kress-Goldsmith Collection, 5898.25.

21 The ballad, which appeared anonymously in various broadside versions, is also found in Ward's collection, *The Delights of the Bottle: or, The compleat vintner* (London: W. Downing, 1720), pp. 55–6.

22 Finch's ballad appeared anonymously in a number of broadside versions. The text also appears in British Library, MS Lansdowne 852, and Norman Ault attributes it to Finch in *A Treasury of Unfamiliar Lyrics* (London: Gollancz, 1938), p. 299. For discussion of other works by Finch, see ch. 10 of this volume, pp. 222–3.

23 Broadside with tune, British Library, H1601 (92) (reprinted in *Roxburghe Ballads*, VIII, 254–7).

24 See Catherine Ingrassia, 'The Pleasure of Business and the Business of Pleasure: Gender, Credit, and the South Sea Bubble', *Studies in Eighteenth-Century Culture*, 24 (1995), 191–210.

25 Broadside, Harvard University, Kress-Goldsmith Collection, 5898.11. The

'obbligato' is an independent part usually for flute, something of a counter-melody, printed at the bottom of the broadside.

26 For treatment of this theme, see Thomas Kavanagh, *Enlightenment and the Shadows of Chance* (Baltimore: Johns Hopkins University Press, 1993).

27 Broadside with tune, Harvard Kress-Goldsmith Collection, 5898.79.

28 Carswell, *The South Sea Bubble*, p. 5. Jewish creditors also had a presence because they held some of the biggest shares of stock during the early 1700s and maintained key trading connections on the continent, particularly in Amsterdam.

29 From 'The South Sea Ballad, Set by a Lady', broadside with tune, British Library, H1601 (92) (reprinted in *Roxburghe Ballads*, VIII, 254–7).

30 The stanza conflates the Pharaonic dreams that Joseph interpreted from Genesis 41 with the Egyptian pursuit of the Israelites under Moses in Exodus 14.

31 See: Patrick Coleman, Jayne Lewis, and Jill Kowalik (eds.), *Representations of the Self from the Renaissance to Romanticism* (Cambridge University Press, 2000).

32 For a sampling, see John Ashton, *Chap-Books of the Eighteenth Century* (London: Chatto & Windus, 1882; rpt. London: Skoob Books, [n.d.]).

33 See: *The Life and Adventures of Mrs Christian Davies, the British Amazon, Commonly Called Mother Ross* (London: R. Montagu, 1740); *The Female Soldier; or, the Surprising Life and Adventures of Hannah Snell* (London: R. Walker, 1750); *The Intrepid Female* (London: R. S. Kirby, 1804); [Mary Slade or Mary Lacy], *The History of the Female Shipwright* (London: M. Lewis, 1773). These 'biographies' all exist in numerous versions under diverse titles and in variant printings. Aspects of them have been discussed in Wheelwright, *Amazons*; Stark, *Female Tars*; and Dugaw, *Warrior Women* and '"Female Sailors Bold"'. These narratives are the best known of a larger body of similar accounts, most of them found in short chapbooks. For some additional titles, see Dugaw, *Warrior Women*, pp. 183–7.

34 For a summary of editions and versions of Snell's story, see Stark, *Female Tars*, pp. 187–8. Stark recommends to present-day readers a 'more readily available' nineteenth-century version in Menie Muriel Dowie (ed.), *Women Adventurers*, XV (London: Unwin Bros., 1893); however, she does not take into account Dowie's edits and cuts, which bowdlerise the original along recognisably Victorian lines. (See Dugaw, '"Female Sailors Bold"', pp. 47–8.) For a recent facsimile reprinting of the original shorter version published by Robert Walker in 1750, see *The Female Soldier; or, The Surprising Life and Adventures of Hannah Snell* (1750), Augustan Reprint Society, no. 257 (Los Angeles: William Andrews Clark Memorial Library, 1989).

35 James Woodforde, *The Diary of a Country Parson*, ed. John Beresford, 5 vols. (London: Humphrey Milford, Oxford University Press, 1924–31), I, 224–5. The entry is for 21 May 1778. Woodforde's parsonage was in Weston Longeville, Norfolk.

36 For further discussion of social class with regard to literary reshaping in accounts of Snell and others, see Dugaw, '"Female Sailors Bold"', pp. 38ff.

37 Stark's otherwise useful study is marred by reduction of the discussion to

this line of questioning. Archival materials require attention to complicated borrowings and differences among variant texts and editions, and cognisance that any records are linguistic representations both of people's experiences and of their imaginations.

38 *The Female Soldier* (1750), pp. 2, 40–1.
39 An edition of *The Life of Long Meg of Westminister* from 1635 is included in Charles Mish (ed.), *Short Fiction of the Seventeenth Century* (New York: Norton, 1968), pp. 82–113, and includes several transvestite fighting episodes. For discussion of 'Moll Cutpurse' (or Mary Frith), see Andor Gomme's introduction to Thomas Middleton and Thomas Dekker, *The Roaring Girl* (New York: Norton, 1976), pp. xiii–xix. See also, Robert R. Singleton, 'English Criminal Biography, 1651–1722', *Harvard Library Bulletin*, 18 (1970), 69, 77–8. On Ann Bonny and Mary Read, *picaras* whose accounts appear in Charles Johnson's *A General History of the Pyrates* (London: Charles Rivington, 1724), see Marcus Rediker, 'Liberty beneath the Jolly Roger: the Lives of Anne Bonny and Mary Read, Pirates' in Creighton and Norling, *Iron Men*, pp. 1–33. For a well-known seventeenth-century precursor in Spanish picaresque tradition, see Catalina de Erauso, *Lieutenant Nun: a Memoir of a Basque Transvestite in the New World*, trans. by Michele Stepto and Gabriel Stepto (Boston: Beacon Press, 1996).

CHAPTER 13

Varieties of women's writing

Clare Brant

Feminist recuperation of eighteenth-century women's writing acquired two landmarks in the 1980s: Jane Spencer's book on women novelists, and Roger Lonsdale's anthology of women poets.[1] These rehabilitations challenged the canon, but at the price of a conservative attitude to genre. Many women writers in eighteenth-century Britain were not novelists, poets, or dramatists. They were writers of letters, diaries, memoirs, essays – genres of sometimes uncertain status then and certainly liminal status now. Indeed, one of the most popular titles for women (as well as for men) in this period was *Miscellanies*; another was *Poems on Several Occasions*, in which 'several' points to diversity as well as multiplicity, to several sorts of occasions. To modern minds, writers who present themselves as miscellaneous or occasional are only half in the picture; if those writers are women, as feminist critics are well aware, they run the risk of being pushed out of the picture altogether. Miscellaneity is critically awkward, it's true: a volume which includes letters, essays, and poems is harder to discuss than a volume of poems, even though those poems can be separated into epistles, pastorals, and so on; and the generic variety within 'prose' has had less critical attention or been understood predominantly in relation to fiction. But genres supposedly marginal to print culture had some advantages – indeterminacy, informality – and should not be read simply as the consequence of patriarchal disempowerment. This is not to overlook the fact that many women were prevented from becoming published authors, but so-called 'private' genres like letters are often highly social, and engage with public-sphere subjects like travel and politics in ways which go beyond the formation of a gendered subject.

I want to show the rewards of using genre to uncover some of the diversity of eighteenth-century women's writing, whilst recognising its limits. Genre has three drawbacks. Firstly, genres are not always distinct. For example, Sylviana Sola's 1752 volume entitled *Various Essays* consists of themed letters, dialogues, an allegory, verses, and a series of reflections headed 'Various Thoughts'. The templates of several genres can fit the same text. Secondly, genre has an ambivalent relationship with biography. If writings are generically diverse, the figure of the author can stabilise them. Thus Lady Mary Wortley Montagu's letters, essays, poems, and romance writings, or Hannah More's poems, tracts, dialogues, letters, and educational and political writings, are brought together. Biography remembers the sex of a writer, and a female author can be connected to other sorts of women. The figure of an author also supplies a literary cohesion which can then be 'discovered' in other works. Thus once Samuel Johnson is understood to be an author, any work by him can be read as Johnsonian. But there is a slippage between 'writing' and 'author' which makes it harder for women to attain the status of being authors. The third problem is that author figures can erase the significance of genre even when critics are particular about it: so a letter, a satire, or a poem by Swift have virtually equal potential to disclose that Swiftian irony beloved by an older generation of male eighteenth-century scholars. It is harder to find paradigms which relate, say, the poems of Laetitia Pilkington to the memoirs in which she published them in 1748–54. It is tempting for feminist critics to make gender itself such a paradigm: hence displays of wit or expressions of desire can be read in terms of orthodoxies and transgressions within norms of femininity. This makes women writers inescapably *women* writers, even with attention to class or race as equally powerful constituents of identity.[2] Without advocating androgyny, genre-based criticism can relate women's writing to a variety of literary discourses.

A stress on the diversity of women's writing raises questions of canonicity particular to the study of eighteenth-century literature. Though new canons usually begin with single works – Behn's *Oroonoko*, or Wollstonecraft's *Vindication of the Rights of Woman*, for example – canonicity can serve diversity, as 'complete works' appear and show an author to be various in herself. Conversely, it can mean more of a writer's works reductively marketed as classics: hence Jane Austen stays commercially evergreen. The debate about what to claim in the absence of canonicity should also consider impersonation, ventriloquism and transvestism as varieties of women's writing, since male authors of fiction in particular invented heroines who became patterns, and rivals, for writing women. As Kathryn Shevelow has shown, many letters which purported to come from women were probably male-authored.[3] The tragic Portuguese Nun, supposed author of the popular *Lettres Portugaises* (first translated 1678), and Rousseau's Julie, heroine of *La Nouvelle Héloïse* (1761), became patterns of feminine desire, and Richardson's *Pamela* was a landmark for working-class texts. So the editor of Hannah Snell's life-story declared that Snell's determination to preserve her chastity was greater than Pamela's, and her story more sensational.[4] This competition between working-class woman and fictional heroine has been explained by Dianne Dugaw as the intrusion of middle-class discourses into the world of rumbustious ballads about cross-dressing; the polite colonises the popular.[5] A reverse disjunction of high life and middle-class fictions can be seen in the claims of some memoirists that they did not read novels. However unlikely this seems, it was as strategic for them to claim ignorance of fictional models of seduction as it was for Snell's editor to assume his readers' familiarity with them. The complex relations between fiction, male-authored or otherwise, and non-fictional women's writing, add to the difficulties of classification.

Anyone trying to comprehend the variety of women's writing has to re-consider anonymity, pseudonymity, and (un)originality. The commonplace book, for instance, used by many readers to make copies of favourite texts or extracts, could involve more than functional transcription. In 1705, Frances Lady Norton published two devotional works composed mostly of other people's words, but, unusually, signed by herself. Her daughter also took up the genre, if one can call it that, as something more authored than we usually understand.[6] To cite an authority made writing culturally deferential to men, but more authorised for women. As Lady Mary Walker put it, 'you must not call me a plagiarist, for sometimes having recourse to my common place-book'.[7] Again, Hester Thrale's marginalia, usually paragraph-length reflections containing criticism, witticisms, or anecdotes, blur the dividing line between primary and secondary texts, making annotation almost a form of dialogue.

There were three kinds of eighteenth-century misconceptions about women's writing. The first was, predictably, that what women wrote was not in fact written by women. So Sarah Chapone reported that on a visit to Oxford, her brother '"heard a whole room full of [men] deny that a thing was or could be written by a woman"'.[8] Conversely, the second misconception assumed female authorship on the basis of stereotypical feminine discourse. So the Bishop of Rochester wrote to Pope that he thought the Arabian Tales were wild and absurd: worse, 'observing how full they are in the descriptions of Dress, Furniture &c. I cannot help thinking them the product of some Woman's imagination'.[9] That

attention to daily life which made travel-writing by women such as Lady
Mary Wortley Montagu authentic and authoritative was grossly material
to a hostile male reader. If good books could not be written by women,
and bad books must be written by women, a third and most peculiar
view of women's writing reduced its variety to a single corrupting effect.
The following comment is by Oliver Goldsmith, and I quote it at length
because Goldsmith is himself a writer whose variety has not hampered
his canonical status, and because his paranoid fusion of different genres
into a single negative category shows how the concept of 'women's
writing' expels literary particularity.

The female miss, it must be owned, has of late been tolerably fruitful. Novels
written by ladies, poems, morality, essays and letters, all written by ladies, show
that this beautiful sex are resolved to be, one way or another, the joyful mothers
of children. Happy it is that the same conveyance which brings an heir to the
family shall at the same time produce a book to mend his manners, or teach him
to make love, when ripe for the occasion. Yet, let not the ladies carry off all the
glories of the late production ascribed to them; it is plain by the style, and a
nameless somewhat in the manner, that pretty fellows, coffee-critics, and dirty
shirted dunces have sometimes a share in the achievement. We have detected
so many of these imposters already, that in future we shall look on every publication that shall be ascribed to a lady as the work of one of this amphibious fraternity.[10]

Collapsing procreation into literary creativity, Goldsmith is resentful
that women should correct men or instruct them even as he concedes
the part women's writing plays in upholding conservative family values.
Women, no more than bodies, are simultaneously denounced and
erased. The feminine is a semiotic blank, 'a nameless something in the
manner' which turns male authors into pseudo-men, adulterous
'imposters'. Just as their role mushrooms from 'sometimes' to 'every' literary occasion, so the diversity of women's writing is read as uniformly
corrupting and doubly false, neither genuinely by a woman, nor by a
genuine man. It's true that literary competition between men generated
abuse of Grub Street rivals as effeminate, ephemeral, and abject. But so
long as men denounced men's writing through a discourse abusive of
femininity, women's writing was likely to be seen as a bodily mass.

  If this chapter was about varieties of men's writing, it would look
slightly different. It would cover more historiography, political and doc-
trinal literature, more protest writing, more things we classify under the
umbrella of the pamphlet. It would address, as this will, letters, essays,
life-writings, and dialogues, but it would cover more of the sorts of texts

entitled An Enquiry into, An Account of, Remarks on, A Defence of – genres in which authorship is anchored by a seemingly confident place in discourse. It is these genres in which women writers are fewer. But they may be found discussing the same subjects in an unexpected place. So political economy turns up not just in tracts but in novels and poems.[11] The texts discussed below are no more than a small sample of the variety of women's writings in the eighteenth century.

MEMOIRS

Eighteenth-century women had three recurrent motives for writing memoirs: to raise money; to defend their reputations; to promote themselves as writers. The examples discussed here show women negotiating the meanings of their own transgressions. Fictional plots of courtship and conduct-book models of marital fidelity provided analogues from which the tales of their lives were sorry departures, but of which they were also critiques. Their stories foregrounded capitalism's commodification of their sexuality, and their struggles not to be treated as their husband's property. An ideologically charged mix of penitence and defiance produced counter-readings of patriarchy in which men's hypocrisy licensed women's cynicism. With the sharpness of hindsight they were elegiac, tender of their younger selves as ignorant, neglected, misunderstood or maltreated by an array of parents and step-parents of both sexes. Hence they fought the sexual double standard as adolescents as well as adults. For mid-century women, satire was a better means than melodrama to expose the family romance as dysfunctional; for later eighteenth-century women, pity was secured more by self-pity than a quickwittedness allowed no outlet.

Catherine Jemmat's *Memoirs* (1762) detailed her adventures growing up in Plymouth where sexual escapades were part of the culture of a naval town. Openly critical of her hot-tempered father, she married Jemmat to escape, but found him to be impossibly jealous, profligate, and sexually abusive. But these brutish men were bookends to her story, which is more about adventures she organised – a romance, a tryst, a jape, and so on. As in Laetitia Pilkington's *Memoirs*, a desire and ability to write is unquestioned; it is part of an identity which her husband can't touch, literally or figuratively. The narrative ends with men telling stories about her cheerfulness even as an abused wife, and her liveliness as a child, instanced in the events of an afternoon on board a ship carrying wild horses to the Queen of Hungary. She insisted on mounting one; she also fired a cannon, won a flirting match and was accounted by all the men (except her father) to be exceptionally charming. A Mr C. concluded 'SHE was a girl of the most extraordinary turn of disposition I ever met with, and for the sake of her I never married and nor never will; and her father was the whole cause of her ruin.'[12] The giddy girl, then, was also the romantic icon and the wronged woman, and giddiness itself was something dazzling. Likewise, the poems to and from lovers show her openly interested in men and encouraging their adulation. This drive is never repudiated, although the outcome is lamented: the sexually active woman and the witty poet were impelled by the same vivacity.

Another writer who used memoirs to convert licentiousness into literariness was Mary Robinson. Her text fitted 1790s sentimentalism, stressing her maternal tenderness and generosity to fellow-unfortunates. Robinson became famous as a beautiful young actress when the Prince of Wales saw her playing Perdita and fell for her. He ended the affair abruptly and without explanation, and she struggled with ill-health and debt to establish herself as a poet. On her deathbed, Robinson made her daughter promise to publish her *Memoirs*. Was it to put the record straight at last about the prince (though she avoids personal reproach), or to confirm her as a writer with a book-length epitaph? The ambiguity may be the point. On the one hand, the *Memoirs* (1801) restored her to the public as a speaking subject after years of being stared at and talked about: 'Whenever I appeared in public, I was overwhelmed by the gazing of the multitude. I was frequently obliged to quit Ranelagh, owing to the crowd which staring curiosity had assembled round my box.' Yet Robinson was complicit with this celebrity through fashion: 'I was consulted as the very oracle of fashions; I was gazed at and examined with the most inquisitive curiosity.'[13] But fashion to be fashion must be changeable, and the gaze, unable to pin down what it gazes at, can only move on. Women memoirists struggled not only against infamy, but also against being famous for being famous.

The diversity of memoirists, however, should not be homogenised. Some varied their own story, like Elizabeth Gooch who published two versions: the first, in 1788, a vindicatory appeal to the public; the second, in 1792, a more complex three-volume saga. Her downfall was occasioned by a note from her music teacher which her husband (perhaps not mistakenly) took as an assignation note. He banished her to France: their families prevented a reconciliation, she claimed, and financial entanglements inevitably led to amorous ones. Gooch conceded her behaviour

had been 'blameable and improper', but pointed out that the consequences had fallen primarily on her, echoing stage melodrama or sentimental fiction: 'I have been continually the dupe of treacherous lovers,
false friends, and worthless acquaintance; those who have appeared
most zealous to serve me, have been almost constantly the first to
deceive, and to betray!'[14] Like Jemmat, the plot is as much parental as
marital: in this case, alienation of her mother is 'the deepest of my
wounds'. It is a sort of victim feminism.

In the 1792 *Memoirs*, Gooch still blamed her relations but, like
Mary Robinson, she anchored her defence in an elegiac sensibility.
Anticipating Wordsworth pocketing a souvenir at the Bastille, Gooch
picked up a stone at Fountains Abbey – 'no inspired nun ever kissed a
relic with more devotion'— neatly turning her notoriety for kissing into
a chaste passion for history.[15] Although still histrionic, claiming 'I was
born to a life of woe' (1, 81), the *Memoirs* offered more than amorous confessions and filial laments. Writing up her travels in Switzerland in 1790,
for instance, Gooch cited the ambience of *La Nouvelle Héloïse*. But it is 'the
divine Rousseau' who inspires her rather than Julie or the writing
woman, as if, at the same time that Rousseau was writing his *Confessions*,
women were simultaneously working on a discourse in which their transgressions might put lust to the service of Romantic wanderlust.

One of the most remarkable *Memoirs* to expose the economy of vice
featured Sophia Baddeley, in fact written by her friend Elizabeth Steele.
Her conquests ran to six volumes, though Steele, herself an unusual,
forceful, and cross-dressing character, dispatched bills and lovers with
equal adroitness. Baddeley's charisma was such that tradesmen initially
let her off debts and dukes queued at her door, though her extravagance
and indiscretions eventually left her poor and almost abandoned. As
Steele put it with understatement, 'she had a natural turn for spending
of money profusely'.[16] Baddeley was given to sprees: 'she was determined, she said, to go a *shopping*' (1, 126) and though her regular lover
Lord Melbourne used to leave banknotes for several hundred pounds on
her table, it was rarely enough. On one outing to Covent Garden she
spent £700, mostly on jewellery, giving a new meaning to the moralists'
phrase 'an ornament to her sex'. Like other memoirists (and the heroine
of *Fanny Hill*), Baddeley was sentimental about her first lover; she also
liked to have a handsome lover in tow to whom she gave her favours for
free. In all the transactions of 'presents' and 'favours', Baddeley and
Steele considered themselves wise to men's ploys. In this they echoed
conduct books, but with a class edge – as Steele's business agent

complained that 'breach of faith in a tradesman would be counted highly dishonourable, but, that Noblemen seemed to pride themselves on their want of integrity' (v, 120). Class struggle is imaged not through the wickedness of lordly libertines from fiction, but openly through money.

If Steele anticipated the 'sex and shopping' genre by two hundred years, Baddeley transgressed by making a success of prostitution. She was threatening because she conferred sexual status on men: 'the notice of Mrs Baddeley was at that day sufficient to give credit and eclat to a man of the ton' (i, 71). She also upset the class structure by living like an aristocrat: her clothes and furnishings were so elegant and costly that 'she lived, and made an appearance equal to a woman of the first rank' (ii, 161). But although she enjoyed masquerades, Baddeley was not living one; like Mary Robinson, she was a fashion victim – 'one might as well be dead as not in the fashion' (iv, 16). Fashion attracted envy and involved ruinous expense, but it is not straightforwardly a story of conspicuous consumption. When Robinson first went to Ranelagh, her simplicity was sensational – no ruffles, no powder, no ornaments. At the Pantheon, in pink satin trimmed with sable, Robinson was stared at by men of fashion, and, like Baddeley, complained that this was no way to treat a lady: 'I was not accustomed to the gaze of impertinent high breeding.'[17] Fashion proved women had taste which then extended beyond questions of dress. To be looked at was to attract men whose conduct was then open to scrutiny. Even as a woman became a sex object, she could become a subject, with the help of print to undo the gaze and project it back onto men.

LIFE-WRITINGS: DIARIES, JOURNALS, AND ANECDOTES

The term 'autobiography' is an anachronism for eighteenth-century writing,[18] and though 'life-writings' seems a little awkward, it does connect first- and third-person records in a common sociability. In both, writers could be subjectively present but not necessarily autobiographical subjects. Like Mr Spectator in Addison and Steele's periodical, they observed and commented, though they may do so in secluded or encoded contexts, so we (mis)take them as private. From innumerable examples, the texts discussed here show a variety of generic conventions and historical moments at work.

Elizabeth Freke's diary ran from 1671 to 1714. One copy she bound herself; the other, with additions, she inscribed in a large folio bound in white vellum given to her by her husband in 1684. It was subtitled 'some few remembrances of my misfortuns which have atended me in my unhappy Life since I were marryed: wch was November the i4: i67i'.[19] Most of the entries were monthly; they varied in length. Freke married a cousin who proved prodigal; after some years shuttling between England and Ireland, she settled alone in Norfolk. She registers some complaints, for example, over her husband's harsh parting words, that he hoped never to see her face again: 'This struck deep in my stomack' (p. 30). She comments that she tells no one, but of course she is confiding in the diary; writing a secret is different from telling it. Her husband reappeared to appropriate her money, but, surprisingly, they were reconciled, and she mourned his death sincerely even as she logged in detail the cost of his illness, burial, and legacies.

Accountancy was always compatible with passion for Freke, but her diary did change from a utilitarian record to a more imaginative miscellany. She recorded dreams, illnesses, exceptional weather, charitable donations, violent accidents, occasional state news, wrangles with fellow-villagers over rents, quarrels with her erratically dutiful son, and a dispute with the Bishop of Norwich. There are exhaustive inventories of her house, including a catalogue of her books, and numerous prescriptions for herbal remedies (her mother was a member of the Culpeper family). There are copies of letters, and dialogues. Some topics represent disruptions to everyday life; others, its even tenor. Finance was a creative register of emotion; efficiency a sign of self-worth and care. So Freke calculated, in elaborate sums, that over the course of her marriage she had brought her husband £21,950. Like those collections of letters of Love and Business popular at the end of the seventeenth century, she saw a parallel between estates and passions: both were to be managed and made profitable.

Although Freke's diary is obviously interesting as social history, it is literary too. Like her sister Lady Norton she wrote occasional verse, and her dialogues drew on the psalms and emblems (a copy of Quarles's *Emblems* was listed among her books). Strikingly, her herbal expertise supplied a discourse for spiritual complaint and remedy. So in 'A Diologue [*sic*] betwen the Soule & Jesus', Jesus diagnoses the sick soul and prescribes a cordial. In rhyming prose, Freke pondered the Christian paradox: 'Canst thou be sick, & such A Doctter By? Thou canst not Live unless thy doctter dye. Strang kind of Griefe, that finds no Medicyne Good to swage her pains Butt the physition's Bloude' (p. 90).

Freke's folio accommodated more various materials after 1700. This may have less to do with a whiggish teleology of journals becoming more reflective than with personal factors of having settled business interests or grown-up children, and with manifesting self-expression through a range of interests rather than depth of subjectivity.[20] To separate those interests into the province of the social historian, the literary critic, and the historian of medicine is to disregard their contingency for Freke. This is not to make a prescription for a cough commensurate with a religious exclamation, but to recognise that the power of literacy as it becomes the power of literature may have historical significances which elude us.

At the other end of the century, Frances Burney's correspondence flows like fiction for twenty volumes. One journal-letter Burney called 'a Babiana', a history of the doings of her young son Alexander, sent to her favourite sister Susan in 1797.[21] Burney focuses on her child's entry into language, which has interest for feminist theorists. She observes his (mis)pronunciation, his (mis)classification of objects, and his cultural lexicon. Burney encourages the child to adopt normative associations, but his deviance catches her attention. So, because a dog was the first quadruped he identified, when he saw a horse or cow, he called out '*A Bow wow, Mamma!*' (p. 323). Anecdotes like this dramatise the child as an educational subject familiar to mothers through Locke; they also enact the dialogic pull between reason and imagination in romantic writings for children, where didacticism needs perversity to work upon. The issue of control is present: is it rude or a democratic liberty (and what does that mean in the 1790s?) to let the child say to every man he meets, '*At's a Man*'? This matriarchal control can be read as an analogue to those patriarchal decorums which govern women's conduct. But there is seduction for Burney, pleasure in an oedipal plot of infantile desire for the mother: 'As soon as I enter the Room, after any absence, however short, he flies to me, crying, "*Don't do eay* [go away], *mamma, aden* [again]!"' (p. 325). Burney is a female spectator watching masculine entry into language through demands and commands. It seems more than coincidence that the child wants to identify men, to say to 'every *person of that sort . . . At's a Man –*' (p. 324), and that he will only respond to his parents if they call him not by his Christian name but by 'Boy'. Moreover, what mothers notice may reflect their own unconscious drives. 'I told him, one Day, to say I want Milk & Water – he looked very thoughtful, and then said "*I*, Boy – *I*, Mamma, – *I*, papa – *I*, Buff –" as if reflecting upon the general use of *I*, & finding it too indefinite for his comprehension unaided. *Buff* he says for *Puss*, which he cannot yet pronounce' (p. 324). Burney's choice of this anecdote may manifest unconscious recognition of, or pleasure in, an uncertain subject position.

One of the better known 'ana' or collections of anecdotes is that compiled by Hester Thrale: between 1775 and 1809 she kept anecdotes, verses, and witticisms in a book her husband entitled 'Thraliana' (which she thought pompous). An associated volume, *Anecdotes of the Late Samuel Johnson*, was a best-seller when published in 1786. Here the writer is an auditor, though as Thrale remarked, the distractions of child-care would 'soon drive out of a female Parent's head a Conversation concerning Wit, Science or Sentiment'.[22] But she increased the literary value of the anecdote so that the Romantic genre of table-talk was possible (even if taken over by men like Hazlitt). As a contemporary put it, 'it is not every Man that can relate a Bon Mot' (p. 89). Where Johnson's *Lives of the Poets* used personal history to partner literary analysis, Thrale juxtaposed formal reputation with informal performance – her own included, since the anecdote above all genres treats throw-away wit as precious.

Thrale was an inspiring example of a woman writer sharing rational conversation and literary games with a male intellectual. Being a good listener involved something more stimulating than tea and sympathy. So Johnson told Thrale the story of how he became a Christian, which he had hitherto told to only his wife and one cleric: aged ten, he threw by a religious book and felt so guilty he vowed to be pious ever after. 'I cannot imagine says he on a sudden what makes me talk of myself to you so, unless it is that Confidence begets Confidence' (p. 6). Thrale showed the anecdote was more than verbal ephemera: it kept conversation more broadly based than male clubs, helped sociability and polite curiosity to be cross-gendered virtues, and made public-private distinctions irrelevant for women who had company at home.

LETTERS

Letters were especially important for women in personal correspondence, published and unpublished, and epistolary fiction. Few female novelists did not write a novel in letters.[23] But there were many non-fictional uses of letters: in travel, by writers as diverse as Lady Mary Wortley Montagu, Anna Maria Falconbridge, Jemima Kindersley, and Anne Grant; in political and social commentary, by Helen Maria Williams and Hannah More; in history, by Catharine Macaulay; in scientific work, by the astronomer Caroline Herschel and many others;[24]

and it was a staple of the literature of conduct, advice, morality, and religion. There was significance for women writers in the letter's openness and flexibility, and in its indeterminate position between public and private spheres, it suited the diffident. But although a paradigm of correspondence presumed an exchange of views which tempered assertion, letters, like dialogues, enabled women to argue.

Many eighteenth-century letter collections dissolved the apparent distinctions between epistolary fiction and personal correspondence. Both could count as 'familiar letters', as the following example shows. Mary Masters's *Familiar Letters and Poems on Several Occasions* (1755) sandwiched two lots of prose letters around poems (which included epistles). In the first group of a dozen or so letters, 'Evadne' and 'Maria' discuss love and friendship. Some of the letters have dates, suggesting the existence of originals from which these have been adapted. The thematic focus suggests at least one coat of polish, though the differences between correspondents could lie in real lives. So Maria's father has obstructed her education, and Evadne's encouraged hers. Evadne has an 'enchanting Man' in tow but yearns for a more affect-laden friendship with a real friend of her own sex, 'what I may more properly call an *abstracted Lover*'.[25] Maria thinks women can be better friends to each other than men, but is wary of erotic implications, and converts Evadne from chimerical Platonic notions by redirecting profane passion to Christian piety. There follows a sequence of letters concerning visits to friends, country rambles, poetic fancies, and feminist sentiments, occasionally in verse: 'Souls have no Sex, nor Male nor Female there, / A manly Mind informs the well-taught Fair' (p. 77). The topics and turns of thought of these letters are typical of personal correspondence, and there are one or two references to identifiable real people. Finally, following the poems, are six letters, mostly on the capacities of women. Maria here answers an anonymous Miss who thinks women can't write well, invoking Astell, Rowe, and Cockburn as evidence that they can. Yet her feminism is held in check by whiggish beliefs: 'I . . . must still insist that a *Woman is equal to a Man* . . . Yet I allow every Husband to be superior to his Wife, . . . *not as a Man*, but as a *Husband*, being made so by the Nature of the Contract' (p. 323). The letters in this volume share discourses of reason, humour, and enquiry and have a common protagonist, Maria, but they unfold questions of how women desire, how women are, and how women are judged, through epistolary fiction, personal correspondence, and epistolary argument.

One kind of letter widely taken up by women writers was the moral or religious letter. Some of these are pretty tedious to modern tastes, but their appeal to an eighteenth-century readership should be understood. Twentieth-century critics have read women's letters in terms of subjectivity or sexuality, with a trope either of voice or of signature to register the disembodiments of epistolary writings. Both tropes are convincing, but can block out a third: the soul. Many eighteenth-century women writers insisted that 'The Soul, and its Faculties, are not of any Sex.'[26] This located epistolary writing in a discursive realm both androgynous and 'higher'.

The letters of Elizabeth Rowe illustrate this. Her collections *Friendship in Death, or Letters from the Dead to the Living* (1728), an epistolary version of dialogues of the dead, and *Letters Moral and Entertaining* (1728–32) circulated in many editions long after Rowe's own death in 1737. Distinctions between prose and fiction break down in Rowe's personal correspondence, which reads like letters from the dead to the living: 'I . . . had much rather talk of the next world than this', she declared.[27] Since her chamber was 'silent as a sepulchre' (II, 203), letters inscribed neither voice nor body, both of which she wished to shed beyond what she needed, temporarily, to articulate the contrast between this world and the next:

I am still below the stars, confin'd to these dusty regions, breathing the gross element of air, and drinking tea instead of nectar, and encumber'd with a body of clay, instead of sparkling in a vehicle of light. I am still no better than a wretched mortal, and am forc'd to content myself with walks of turf or gravel, however ambitious you think me of setting my feet on the spangled pavement, and tracing the milky way. (II, 211)

Paradoxically, the first person in Rowe's letters struggled not to be: 'I' yearns to be transformed into something not-I. This melancholy drive gave her letters a peculiar emptiness which is like, but also different from, the deferral characteristic of more secular drives.

ESSAYS

'O what Pleasures, what transporting Joys do rational instructive Thoughts afford!'[28] The essay was a genre attractive to women as both writers and readers engaged in contemplative thoughts of which the writer's words were the means rather than ends. Writing 'deeply imprints the Truths I've learn'd' as Chudleigh put it, but they started from 'hints' which might occur to any woman, and the argument did not stop with the writer's last word.

Exactly what was an essay? 'No other genre ever raised so many theoretical problems concerning the origin and definition of its Form.'[29] The moral essay was a self-contained piece, usually a few pages in length, which considered a particular topic and which indicated explicitly through title conventions or implicitly through seriousness that it was an essay. Definition is not clear-cut. When Mary Deverell published her *Sermons* she acknowledged that sermons were 'a sacred province', which meant off-limits to women writers: 'I would both readily and gladly have altered the title of *Sermons*, to that of *Essays*, *Reflections*, or any other which might have been deemed more proper, as less assuming, than the present.'[30] The pieces meditated on sacred texts: the most interesting, on mercy, concerns the woman taken in adultery, and leads into a remarkable critique of the sexual double standard in both biblical and current times.

Both moral and periodical essays were vehicles of argument, and both inclined towards satire in so far as they criticised behaviours which deviated from rational and Christian models. Essays by women often moderated that satire as it projected female faults, in the consciousness that men were piling it on elsewhere. As the editorial persona of the *Female Tatler* (1709–10) put it, 'Tho' most women are fond of ridiculing one another, it was always my temper to extenuate, rather than aggravate, the frailties of my own sex, when at the same time, I have blush'd for other womens infirmities, as much as if they had been my own.'[31] Though this paper goes on to ridicule women in the name of impartiality, the claim of sorrow rather than anger at women's faults was common.

The periodical essay usually required a persona to make it cohere.[32] Women tended to disclaim the essay's authority to address men, claiming a female readership as more appropriate to the author's modest abilities. But ironically this made the essay more radical as women writers considered the condition of women. If the essay's aim was to improve women's minds, logically essayists had to believe women's minds could be improved. Hence some of the most trenchant or polemical pieces of eighteenth-century feminism were essays: Lady Mary Wortley Montagu's sixth number of *The Nonsense of Common-Sense*, in which she exposes misogyny as self-interested, or Catherine Jemmat's *Essay in Vindication of the Female Sex*, in which she defends prostitutes.[33]

One solution to the unstable gender-bias of the essay was to neutralise gender through class. For example, pride could be condemned through images of upper-class vanity. Although essays certainly serviced bourgeois ideology, part of that ideology's success was in projecting itself as human nature. An essayist's modesty was then awareness of her human flaws; her frailties were no longer feminine. But the power to discuss those frailties as human was, perversely, masculine. Certainly in the first half of the eighteenth century, most female essayists aspired to be a rational *being* rather than a rational woman, and to make their readers so too. As Mary Lady Chudleigh expressed it,

What can afford a higher, a more masculine Pleasure, a purer, more transporting Delight, than to retire into our selves, and there curiously and attentively inspect the serious Operations of our Souls, compare Idea's, consult our Reason, and view all the Beauties of our Intellect, the inimitable Stroaks of Divine Wisdom, which are visible in our Faculties, and those Participations of infinite Power, which are discoverable in our Wills?[34]

Chudleigh includes women as part of that community which has intellect, faculties, and wills – all prefixed as 'our' – but engaging with them through the medium of the essay remained a masculine pleasure. Hence nobody noticed any difference in anonymous but female-authored essays by women slipped into periodicals by men.[35] No matter how rambling, how idle, how adventurous male essayists seemed, ultimately masculine authority could not be sacrificed. The essay, one might say, looks like a good bet for *écriture masculine*.

DIALOGUES

The versatility of dialogues is even less recognised than that of letters. Published examples include Mary, Lady Chudleigh's *The Ladies Defence* (1701) in verse, Elizabeth Carter's poem *A Dialogue* (between the Body and Mind, 1741), and Elizabeth Montagu's three contributions to Lyttleton's *Dialogues of the Dead* (1760).[36] There were many more: moral dialogues by Elizabeth Rowe and Catherine Talbot; dialogues for children by Dorothy Kilner and Eleanor Fenn, in which earnest but kindly mammas teach inquisitive daughters; philosophical dialogues by Hester Thrale; playful dialogues by Anna Laetitia Barbauld; political dialogues by Hannah More. The three examples I propose to discuss give a sample of the dialogue's variety, and also its kinship with drama, the letter, and the essay.

In 1752 Sylviana Sola published *Various Essays*, which included a collection of dialogues. The first dozen were dialogues of the dead, in which worthies of the past challenge each other's preconceptions. Part of the pleasure was in unlikely pairings; another, in whether opposed world views could be reconciled, either through one party surrendering or both finding common ground. Sola follows this model but with the unusual scenario of having women converse with men in a majority of the dialogues. The relative merits of ancient legislators and Christian moralists are debated by Pythagoras and Theodora (who wins, no surprise). Virgil discusses his epics with Moderna, who proves an able critic. Most inventively, Queen Elizabeth and Tiberius discuss being heads of state. When he supposes her kingdom was tricky to govern because she was female, and timid, she flashes back, 'It is true, I had Fears, but they were not at all in respect to Men; I only fear'd I should offend my Maker . . . whose Deputy I was.'[37] The dialogue subordinates temporal power to spiritual self-government; a queen who rules men and is obedient to God both cancels and upholds patriarchy.

Sola's second section features dialogues of the living, again with a high proportion of female figures. Questions of gender are explicitly addressed in the fifth dialogue, between Philogynia and her old but not to be underrated opponent Misogynia, and in the sixth dialogue, between two women who discuss pastoral, one of whom pleads for fantasy. The question of what women are is thus followed by one about what women want. Like many essayists this dialogist recommends conquering one's passions, but in dialogues victory is often pyrrhic as reason can be on passion's side too.

Dialogues were hospitable to fantasy in numerous ways. For example, Hester Thrale indulged in a sort of revenge fantasy in 'Three Dialogues on the Death of Hester Thrale'.[38] These should be as well-known as Swift's 'Verses on the Death of Dr Swift', their predecessor in a specialist genre one might call 'post-mortems'. Described by Thrale's biographers as 'brilliant and cutting parody', 'her cleverest piece of creative writing', and as rivalling Burney and Montagu in lightness and wit,[39] the role of gender in these dialogues is missed by all three commentators. The first dialogue, set at Mrs Vesey's assembly, has Johnson, Burke, a bumbling Mr Pepys, and Elizabeth Montagu discuss Hester Thrale's death in ways which reveal the subtle jockeyings and slights amongst what critics liked to call the Johnson circle. In the second dialogue, two men who had retired to enjoy their money discuss Hester Thrale's domestic economy with Baretti (no friend to the author though he tutored her daughter). They have no idea of her influence or lack of it over her husband's money (in fact she cleared his debts by her shrewd handling of his brewing business), but their discussion implies that if she spent money, she was an extravagant wife; if she was economical, she must have been stinting her husband. She is damned either way. When the one woman in the room falls asleep (a nice touch), the talk turns faintly bawdy as the old men fantasise about wives: 'Woman is a Drug now – a mere Drug', says one (p. 104). The men don't remember Thrale as a real woman at all; instead, they close up the discursive space left by her supposed death with misogynist misrepresentations. It is a remarkable piece of writing. In the third dialogue a doctor friendly to Thrale, and his friend, visit a hypochondriac, whom they try to interest in something other than himself. The company reassembles at Lady Lade's, where she is sneering about women with wit. These dialogues do need footnotes, but a second reading reveals how very unsparing they are. The characterisation and dialogue are indeed sharp, but only half the point; the other half is Thrale's feminism, her exposure of men's thoughts about women as casually utilitarian or misogynist. When the hypochondriac says 'why Women are like Bitters to be sure, they do give a Stimulus, but then Marriage is Chamomile Tea, a mere Emetick' (p. 108), his metaphor implies women make him sick. This outdoes Swift's description of callousness imaged through women unable to regret his passing. For Thrale, men's failure to mourn her death is shockingly connected to their failure to value her sex when alive.

The power of dialogues to play with ideas is demonstrated by Anna Laetitia Barbauld's 'Dialogue between Madame Cosmogunia and a Philosophical Inquirer of the Eighteenth Century'.[40] This jokes about time, history, and that story of progress assumed now to be a staple narrative of the Enlightenment. The whimsical Madame Cosmogunia can't remember exactly how old she is, since in her youth she kept no almanac: historiography is comically troped as an old lady's memoranda-book. Her early memories include being turned out of a garden of fruit: Barbauld puts the story of Eve which gave women writers so much trouble barely in conscious range. Medieval scholasticism is also treated with insouciant bathos:

E[nquirer]. Pray what did you do when you were in middle age? – that is usually esteemed the most valuable part of life.
C[osmogunia]. I somehow got shut up in a dark cell, where I took a long nap.
E. And after you waked –
C. I fell a-disputing with all my might. (p. 282)

The Enquirer's principal query is about progress: as one opinion has it 'as you increase in years, you grow wiser and better'; others 'pretend you are almost in your dotage . . . you are become suspicious, selfish,

interested, fond of nothing but indulging your own appetites and continually setting your children together by the ears for straws' (pp. 278–9).
Madame Cosmogunia sweeps away conduct-book complaints with a
common-sense reply: 'I do not remember the time when I have not
heard exactly the same contradictory assertions.' Culture and its institutions – the church, government, art, science – are all treated with light
scepticism.

For all that Barbauld described a piece like this as a *'jeu d'esprit'*, it
showed a woman writer commanding powers of argument and play.
Like Hannah More, whose *Cheap Repository Tracts* included dialogic
material and whose *Village Politics* (1792) argued against republican ideas
for the labouring class, Barbauld and other women writers used the dialogue to take a place in the public sphere. Since dialogues had a respectable literary history going back to Plato, they claimed classical standing
but without any burden of learning. Lacking a clear authorial voice, the
dialogue accommodated women's anxieties about authorship, but its
double-sided argument simultaneously asserted women's powers of reasoning. The form also dramatised that adversarial aspect of eighteenth-
century argument which was connected to attacks on women. In
Chudleigh's *Ladies Defence*, Melissa has to contend with a brute, a libertine, and a parson. With less aggressive antagonists, like the ungendered
Enquirer, the dialogue released a discourse of playfulness which made it
a creative form of communicative action, even as it turned orthodox
ideas of learning on their head.

The relative invisibility of dialogues, letters, essays, and life-writings, and
other genres not discussed here, has made it easier to sideline them. The
heterogeneity of women's writing cannot be understood without revis-
ing orthodoxies of literary history with which feminist criticism has been
(strategically) complicit. Revision leads to something messier, undoubtedly, and less marketable, but also something which strengthens feminism's commitment to difference by articulating the politics of being
miscellaneous.

NOTES

1 Jane Spencer, *The Rise of the Woman Novelist: From Aphra Behn to Jane Austen*
 (Oxford: Basil Blackwell, 1986); Roger Lonsdale (ed.), *Eighteenth-Century
 Women Poets: an Oxford Anthology* (Oxford and New York: Oxford University
 Press, 1990).
2 See Donna Landry, *The Muses of Resistance: Laboring-Class Women's Poetry in*

Britain, 1739–1796 (Cambridge University Press, 1990) and Paula R. Feldman and Theresa M. Kelley (eds.), *Romantic Women Writers: Voices and Countervoices* (Hanover and London: University Press of New England, 1995).

3 Kathryn Shevelow, *Women and Print Culture: the Construction of Femininity in the Early Periodical* (London and New York: Routledge, 1989).

4 *The Female Soldier; Or, The Surprising Life and Adventures of Hannah Snell* (1750), Augustan Reprint Society, no. 257 (Los Angeles: William Andrews Clark Memorial Library, 1989).

5 *The Female Soldier*, pp. vii–ix, and for further discussion by Dugaw of versions of the Hannah Snell story, see ch. 12 of this volume, pp. 276–9.

6 Lady Grace Gethin, *Misery's Virtues Whet-stone. Reliquae Gethinianae* (London: D. Edwards for the author, 1699).

7 Lady Mary Walker, *Letters from the Duchess de Crui and Others*, 2nd edn, 5 vols. (London: Robson; Walter; and Robinson, 1777), 1, 3.

8 Margaret J. Ezell, *Writing Women's Literary History* (Baltimore: Johns Hopkins University Press, 1993), p. 82.

9 Alexander Pope, *Mr Pope's Literary Correspondence*, 5 vols. (London: E. Curll, 1735), v, 89.

10 *Critical Review*, August 1759; quoted by Alison Adburgham, *Women in Print: Writing Women and Women's Magazines From the Restoration to the Accession of Victoria* (London: George Allen & Unwin, 1972), pp. 114–15.

11 See Isobel Armstrong's brilliant reading of a poem by Barbauld in relation to Burke, Malthus, Adam Smith, and Hume, 'The Gush of the Feminine: How Can We Read Women's Poetry of the Romantic Period?' in Feldman and Kelley, *Romantic Women Writers*, pp. 13–32.

12 Catherine Jemmat, *The Memoirs of Mrs Catherine Jemmat, Daughter of the late Admiral Yeo of Portsmouth*, 2nd edn, 2 vols. (London: printed by subscription, 1762), ii, 91.

13 M. J. Levy (ed.), *Perdita: the Memoirs of Mary Robinson* (London and Chester Springs: Peter Owen, 1994), pp. 113, 94. See Judith Pascoe's valuable discussion of Robinson in *Romantic Theatricality: Gender, Poetry and Spectatorship* (Ithaca and London: Cornell University Press, 1997), ch. 6; see also Angela J. Smallwood's discussion of actresses and the world of fashion in ch. 11 of this volume, pp. 246–9.

14 Elizabeth Gooch, *An Appeal to the Public on the Conduct of Mrs Gooch, The Wife of William Gooch, Esq.* (London: G. Kearsley, 1788), p. 61.

15 Elizabeth Gooch, *The Life of Mrs Gooch*, 3 vols. (London: C. & G. Kearsley, 1792), i, 30. Cf. Wordsworth, *The Prelude* (1805), book ix, lines 63–7.

16 Elizabeth Steele, *Memoirs of Miss Sophia Baddeley, Late of Drury Lane Theatre*, 6 vols. (London: printed for the author, 1787), i, 83. The *Dictionary of National Biography* attributes the *Memoirs* to Alexander Blicknell rather than Elizabeth Steele.

17 Levy, *Perdita*, p. 53. Robinson implied that troubles with her in-laws arose partly because they envied her dress sense.

18 See Felicity A. Nussbaum, *The Autobiographical Subject: Gender and Ideology in*

Eighteenth-Century England (Baltimore and London: Johns Hopkins University Press, 1989), pp. 1–2.

19 Mary Carbery (ed.), *Mrs Elizabeth Freke her Diary 1671–1714* (Cork: Guy & Company Ltd., 1913), p. 20. In size and quality, the volumes resembled account ledgers.

20 Compare the modern curriculum vitae, in which personal history is presented impersonally.

21 *The Journals and Letters of Fanny Burney*, ed. Joyce Hemlow, et al., 12 vols. (Oxford: Clarendon Press, 1972–84), III (1973), 322–8.

22 Richard Ingrams (ed.), *Dr Johnson by Mrs Thrale* (London: Chatto & Windus, 1984), p. 3.

23 See Ruth Perry, *Women, Letters and the Novel* (New York: AMS Press, 1980); Ros Ballaster, *Seductive Forms: Women's Amatory Fiction from 1684 to 1740* (Oxford: Clarendon Press, 1992); Linda Kauffman, *Discourses of Desire: Gender, Genre and Epistolary Fictions* (Ithaca and London: Cornell University Press, 1986); Nicola J. Watson, *Revolution and the Form of the British Novel, 1790–1825: Intercepted Letters, Interrupted Seductions* (Oxford: Clarendon Press, 1994); Mary Favret, *Romantic Correspondence: Women, Politics and the Fiction of Letters* (Cambridge University Press, 1993).

24 See Ann B. Shteir's valuable study, *Cultivating Women, Cultivating Science: Flora's Daughters and Botany in England 1760–1860* (Baltimore: Johns Hopkins University Press, 1996).

25 Mary Masters, *Familiar Letters and Poems on Several Occasions* (London: printed for the author, 1755), p. 2.

26 Sylviana Sola, *Various Essays* (London: printed for the author, 1752), p. 115.

27 *The Miscellaneous Works in Prose and Verse of Mrs Elizabeth Rowe*, 2 vols. (London: R. Hett; and R. Dodsley, 1739), II, 100. See also Margaret Anne Doody's discussion of this aspect of Rowe's writing in ch. 10 of this volume, pp. 223–4.

28 *The Poems and Prose of Mary, Lady Chudleigh*, ed. Margaret J. Ezell (New York and Oxford: Oxford University Press, 1993), p. 246. *Essays Upon Several Subjects* was first published in 1710.

29 Reda Bensmaia, *The Barthes Effect: the Essay as Reflective Text*, trans. by Pat Fedkiew (Minneapolis: University of Minnesota Press, 1987), p. 96. My thanks to Wendy Gan for this reference, and for concentrating my thoughts on essays.

30 Mary Deverell, *Sermons on Various Subjects*, 2nd edn (London: Dodsley; Lewis; Robson; et al., 1776), pp. xi–xii.

31 Fidelis Morgan (ed.), *The Female Tatler*, Everyman's Library (London: J. M. Dent & Sons Ltd.; Rutland, VT: Charles E. Tuttle Co., 1992), p. 9.

32 On the periodical essay, see Ros Ballaster, Margaret Beetham, Elizabeth Frazer and Sandra Hebron (eds.), *Women's Worlds: Ideology, Femininity and the Woman's Magazine* (London: Macmillan, 1990), pp. 43–74, and, with a useful list, Adburgham, *Women in Print*.

33 *The Nonsense of Common-Sense*, Tuesday, 24 January 1738, in Lady Mary Wortley Montagu, *Essays and Poems and Simplicity, a Comedy*, ed. Robert

Halsband and Isobel Grundy (Oxford: Clarendon Press, 1977; rpt. 1993), pp. 130–4; Catherine Jemmat, *Miscellanies in Prose and Verse* (London: printed for the author, 1766), pp. 101–15. Roger Lonsdale notes that 'twenty-three of the subscribers to her *Memoirs* sheltered in the unusual anonymity of asterisks', which he attributes to the radicalism of this essay (Lonsdale, *Eighteenth-Century Women Poets*, p. 235).

34 Chudleigh, *Poems and Prose*, p. 386.

35 E.g. Wortley Montagu's *Spectator* (no. 573, a sardonic discussion of husbands); Elizabeth Carter's *Ramblers* (no. 44, an allegorical dream, and no. 100, a Christian critique of modish diversions).

36 In, respectively: Chudleigh, *Poems and Prose*, pp. 15–40; Lonsdale, *Eighteenth-Century Women Poets*, no. 111; and Frederick M. Keener, *English Dialogues of the Dead: a Critical History, An Anthology, and a Check List* (New York and London: Columbia University Press, 1973), pp. 227–39.

37 Sola, *Various Essays*, p. 101.

38 This seems to be the accepted critical title, although M. Zamick, their editor, preferred a simpler title: 'Three Dialogues by Hester Lynch Thrale', *Bulletin of the John Rylands Library*, 16 (1932), 77–113.

39 William McCarthy, *Hester Thrale Piozzi: Portrait of a Literary Woman* (Chapel Hill and London: University of North Carolina Press, 1985), p. 32; James L. Clifford, *Hester Lynch Piozzi (Mrs Thrale)*, 2nd edn (Oxford: Clarendon Press, 1952; rpt. 1968), p. 179; Zamick, 'Three Dialogues', 77.

40 Written on New Year's Day, 1793; in *The Works of Anna Laetitia Barbauld with a Memoir by Lucy Aikin*, 2 vols. (London: Longman, et al., 1825), II, 277–87.

Guide to further reading

This 'Guide' is intended to supplement the many primary and critical works which are cited in the preceding chapters, references to which can be found in the notes to individual chapters. Discussions of individual writers and texts, and of particular topics can also be located by using the index.

REFERENCE WORKS

Blain, Virginia, Patricia Clements, and Isobel Grundy, eds. *The Feminist Companion to Literature in English: Women Writers from the Middle Ages to the Present.* London: Batsford, 1990.

Sage, Lorna, ed. *The Cambridge Guide to Women's Writing.* Cambridge University Press, 1999.

Todd, Janet, ed. *A Dictionary of British and American Women Writers 1660–1800.* London: Methuen, 1984.

ANTHOLOGIES

Ferguson, Moira, ed. *First Feminists: British Women Writers 1578–1799.* Bloomington: Indiana University Press; New York: Feminist Press, 1985.

Hill, Bridget. *Eighteenth-Century Women: an Anthology.* London: Allen & Unwin, 1984.

Mahl, Mary and Helene Koon, eds. *The Female Spectator: English Women Writers Before 1800.* Bloomington: Indiana University Press, 1977.

McCormick, Ian, ed. *Secret Sexualities: a Sourcebook of 17th and 18th Century Writing.* London and New York: Routledge, 1997.

Rogers, Katharine M., ed. *The Meridian Anthology of Restoration and Eighteenth-Century Plays by Women.* New York: Penguin Books USA, 1994.

GENERAL

Armstrong, Nancy and Leonard Tennenhouse, eds. *The Ideology of Conduct: Essays on Literature and the History of Sexuality.* London: Methuen, 1987.

Barker, Hannah and Elaine Chalus, eds. *Gender in Eighteenth-Century England: Roles, Representations, and Responsibilities.* London: Longman, 1997.

Ezell, Margaret. *Writing Women's Literary History*. Baltimore: Johns Hopkins University Press, 1993.

Grundy, Isobel and Susan Wiseman, eds. *Women, Writing, History, 1640–1740*. London: Batsford, 1992.

Hufton, Olwen. *The Prospect Before Her: a History of Women in Western Europe, Volume I 1500–1800*. London: HarperCollins, 1995.

Laurence, Anne. *Women in England 1500–1760: a Social History*. London: Macmillan, 1994.

MacCurtain, Margaret and Mary O'Dowd, eds. *Women in Early Modern Ireland*. Edinburgh University Press, 1991.

Tobin, Beth Fowkes, ed. *History, Gender and Eighteenth-Century Literature*. Athens, GA: University of Georgia Press, 1994.

PUBLIC AND PRIVATE

Eger, Elizabeth, Charlotte Grant, Cliona O'Gallchoir, and Penny Warburton, eds. *Women and the Public Sphere: Writing and Representation, 1700–1830*. Cambridge University Press, 2000.

Fraser, Nancy. 'Rethinking the Public Sphere: a Contribution to the Critique of Actually Existing Democracy'. In Craig Calhoun (ed.), *Habermas and the Public Sphere*. Cambridge, MA and London: MIT Press, 1992.

Landes, Joan. *Women and the Public Sphere in the Age of the French Revolution*. Ithaca: Cornell University Press, 1988.

Meehan, Johanna, ed. *Feminists Read Habermas: Gendering the Subject of Discourse*. New York and London: Routledge, 1995.

Shoemaker, Robert B. *Gender in English Society, 1650–1850: the Emergence of Separate Spheres?* London and New York: Longman, 1998.

Vickery, Amanda. 'Golden Age to Separate Spheres: a Review of the Categories and Chronology of English Women's History'. *Historical Journal*, 36:2 (1993), 383–414.

ENLIGHTENMENT, EDUCATION, AND 'FEMINISMS'

Hulme, Peter and Ludmilla Jordanova. *The Enlightenment and its Shadows*. London: Routledge, 1990.

Leranbaum, Miriam. '"Mistresses of Orthodoxy": Education in the Lives and Writings of Late Eighteenth-Century Women Writers'. *Proceedings of the American Philosophical Society*, 121:4 (1977), 281–301.

Miller, P. J. 'Women's Education: "Self-Improvement" and Social Mobility – a Late Eighteenth-Century Debate'. *British Journal of Educational Studies*, 20 (1972), 302–14.

Rendall, Jane. *The Origins of Modern Feminism: Women in Britain, France and the United States, 1780–1860*. Basingstoke: Macmillan, 1985.

Smith, Hilda L. *Reason's Disciples: Seventeenth-Century English Feminists*. Urbana and London: University of Illinois Press, 1982.

Tomaselli, Sylvana. 'The Enlightenment Debate on Women'. *History Workshop Journal*, 19 (1985), 101–24.
Women in the Enlightenment. Special issue of *Women and History*, 9 (1984).

WOMEN, WORK, AND PRINT CULTURE

Barker, Hannah. 'Women, Work and the Industrial Revolution: Female Involvement in the English Printing Trades, *c.* 1700–1840'. In Hannah Barker and Elaine Chalus (eds.) *Gender in Eighteenth-Century England: Roles, Representations, and Responsibilities.* London: Longman, 1997, pp. 81–100.
Bell, Maureen. 'A Dictionary of Women in the London Book Trade, 1540–1730'. Masters of Library Studies dissertation, Loughborough University, 1983.
Berg, Maxine. 'What Difference did Women's Work Make to the Industrial Revolution?' *History Workshop Journal*, 35 (1993), 22–44.
Charles, Lindsey and Lorna Duffin, eds. *Women and Work in Pre-Industrial England.* London: Croom Helm, 1985.
Hill, Bridget. *Women, Work and Sexual Politics in Eighteenth-Century England.* Oxford: Basil Blackwell, 1989.
Hunt, Margaret R. 'Hawkers, Bawlers, and Mercuries: Women and the London Press in the Early Enlightenment'. *Women and History*, 9 (1984), 41–68.
Hunt, Tamara. 'Women's Participation in the Eighteenth-Century English Publishing Trades'. *Leipziger Jahrbuch zur Buchgeschichte*, 6 (1996), 47–65.
McDowell, Paula. *The Women of Grub Street: Press, Politics and Gender in the London Literary Marketplace 1678–1730.* Oxford: Clarendon Press, 1998.
Sharpe, Pamela. *Adapting to Capitalism: Working Women in the English Economy, 1700–1850.* Basingstoke: Macmillan, 1996.

LAW AND THE FAMILY

Bowers, Toni. *The Politics of Motherhood: British Writing and Culture, 1680–1760.* Cambridge University Press, 1996.
Okin, Susan Moller. 'Patriarchy and Married Women's Property in England: Questions on Some Current Views'. *Eighteenth-Century Studies*, 17 (1983–4), 121–38.
Perry, Ruth. 'Colonizing the Breast: Sexuality and Maternity in Eighteenth-Century England'. *Journal of the History of Sexuality*, 2:2 (1991), 204–34.
Perry, Ruth. 'De-Familiarizing the Family: or, Writing Family History from Literary Sources'. *Modern Language Quarterly*, 55:4 (1994), 415–27.
Staves, Susan. 'British Seduced Maidens'. *Eighteenth-Century Studies*, 14 (1980–81), 109–34.
Staves, Susan. 'Where is History but in Texts? Reading the History of Marriage'. In John M. Wallace (ed.), *The Golden and the Brazen World: Papers in Literature and History, 1650–1800.* Berkeley: University of California Press, 1985, pp. 129–43.

Stone, Lawrence and Jeanne Stone. *An Open Elite? England 1540–1880*. Oxford: Clarendon Press, 1984.

CONSUMPTION AND POPULAR CULTURE

Brewer, John and Roy Porter, eds. *Consumption and the World of Goods*. London and New York: Routledge, 1993.

Brewer, John and Susan Staves, eds. *Early Modern Conceptions of Property*. London and New York: Routledge, 1994.

Castle, Terry. *Masquerade and Civilization: the Carnivalesque in Eighteenth-Century English Culture and Fiction*. London: Methuen, 1986.

Eighteenth-Century Studies, 31:1 (1997). Special issue.

Kowaleski-Wallace, Elizabeth. *Consuming Subjects: Women, Shopping, and Business in the Eighteenth Century*. New York: Columbia University Press, 1997.

Lemire, Beverly. *Fashion's Favourite: the Cotton Trade and the Consumer in Britain*. Oxford University Press, 1991.

Sekora, John. *Luxury: The Concept in Western Thought, Eden to Smollett*. Baltimore: Johns Hopkins University Press, 1977.

SEXUALITIES

Donoghue, Emma. *Passions Between Women: British Lesbian Culture 1668–1801*. London: Scarlet Press, 1993.

Friedli, Lynne. ' "Passing Women": a Study of Gender Boundaries in the Eighteenth Century'. In G. S. Rousseau and Roy Porter (eds.), *Sexual Underworlds of the Enlightenment*. Manchester University Press, 1987, pp. 234–60.

Hitchcock, Tim. *English Sexualities, 1700–1800*. London: Macmillan; New York: St Martin's Press, 1997.

Spacks, Patricia Meyer. ' "Ev'ry Woman is at Heart a Rake" '. *Eighteenth-Century Studies*, 8 (1974), 27–46.

Trumbach, Randolph. 'London's Sapphists: from Three Sexes to Four Genders in the Making of Modern Culture'. In Julia Epstein and Kristina Straub (eds.), *Body Guards: the Cultural Politics of Gender Ambiguity*. New York and London: Routledge, 1991, pp. 112–41.

SENSIBILITY

Conger, Syndy McMillen, ed. *Sensibility in Transformation: Creative Resistance to Sentiment from the Augustans to the Romantics*. Rutherford: Fairleigh Dickinson University Press; London: Associated University Presses, 1990.

Hagstrum, Jean H. *Sex and Sensibility: Ideal and Erotic Love from Milton to Mozart*. Chicago and London: University of Chicago Press, 1980.

Jones, Chris. *Radical Sensibility: Literature and Ideas in the 1790s*. London: Routledge, 1993.

Todd, Janet. *Sensibility: an Introduction*. London: Methuen, 1986.

Van Sant, Ann Jessie. *Eighteenth-Century Sensibility and the Novel: the Senses in Social Context*. Cambridge University Press, 1993.

GENDER, 'RACE', AND CLASS

Brown, Laura. *Ends of Empire: Women and Ideology in Early Eighteenth-Century English Literature*. Ithaca: Cornell University Press, 1993.
Clark, Anna. *The Struggle for the Breeches: Gender and the Making of the British Working Class*. Berkeley and Los Angeles: University of California Press, 1995.
Earle, Peter. *The Making of the English Middle Class: Business, Society and Family Life in London, 1660–1730*. London: Methuen, 1989.
Hendricks, Margo and Patricia Parker, eds. *Women, 'Race', and Writing in the Early Modern Period*. London: Routledge, 1994.

WRITING WOMEN

Armstrong, Isobel and Virginia Blain, eds. *Women's Poetry in the Enlightenment: the Making of a Canon 1730–1820*. Basingstoke: Macmillan, 1998.
Backscheider, Paula. *Spectacular Politics: Theatrical Power and Mass Culture in Early Modern England*. Baltimore: Johns Hopkins University Press, 1993.
Canfield, J. Douglas and Deborah C. Payne, eds. *Cultural Readings of Restoration and Eighteenth-Century Theatre*. Athens, GA and London: University of Georgia Press, 1995.
Cotton, Nancy. *Women Playwrights in England ca. 1363–1750*. Lewisburg, PA: Bucknell University Press, 1980.
Ferguson, Moira. *Eighteenth-Century Women Poets: Nation, Class, and Gender*. State University of New York Press, 1995.
Gonda, Caroline. *Reading Daughters' Fictions 1709–1834: from Delarivier Manley to Maria Edgeworth*. Cambridge University Press, 1996.
Pearson, Jacqueline. *The Prostituted Muse: Images of Women and Women Dramatists 1642–1737*. London and New York: Harvester Wheatsheaf, 1988.
Richetti, John. *The English Novel in History 1700–1780*. London and New York: Routledge, 1999.
Schofield, Mary Anne and Cecilia Macheski, eds. *Fetter'd or Free? British Women Novelists, 1670–1815*. Ohio and London: Ohio University Press, 1986.
Spencer, Jane. 'Women Writers and the Eighteenth-Century Novel'. In John Richetti (ed.), *The Cambridge Companion to the Eighteenth-Century Novel*. Cambridge University Press, 1996, pp. 212–35.

Index